Praise For Gourmet Cooking For Dummies

"Charlie Trotter and Chicago go together like gourmet food and fine wine. No one knows great food better than Charlie Trotter — and this book will help bring some of the world's delicious meals to your home."

— Richard M. Daley, Mayor of Chicago

"Cooking a gourmet dinner doesn't have to be a frightening experience — Charlie Trotter's *Gourmet Cooking For Dummies* will dispel all your fears and help you turn out wonderful dishes."

— Ferdinand E. Metz, President, Culinary Institute of America

"Look to Charlie Trotter for great wine choices for gourmets — dummies or not! Educational, instructive, and delicious."

— Robert Mondavi, Robert Mondavi Winery

"Just when I thought I was out of the kitchen... Charlie pulled me back in. *Gourmet Cooking For Dummies* rules!"

— Steven E. Greystone, Food and Wine Connoisseur

"Look. If you were to desire to understand the mysteries of space, you'd probably appreciate the concise brilliance of Carl Sagan's works.

"If unveiling the mysteries of a lover's heart is in need, read Colette.

"If peering past the face of the cosmic clock's face makes your heart take flight, you might try Stephen Hawking or Lao Tzu.

"Why not then unravel the secrets of 'the grand cuisine' (and have a helluva good series of meals in the process) with one of our gustatory geniuses — one *Charlie Trotter*?"

— Norman Van Aken, Norman's, Miami

"Charlie Trotter has become famous for his unique and detailed approach to food. This book is no different, and entertaining as a bonus."

— Keith Keogh, Chief Executive Chef and President, California Culinary Academy

More Praise For Gourmet Cooking For Dummies

Charlie Trotter's approach is not only amazingly forward-looking, creative, flavorful, and healthful; it is laid out so as to make sure that the home cook can succeed using the methods and recipes of this very modern master chef. A graceful achievement, indeed."

> — Sara Moulton, Executive Chef of *Gourmet* Magazine and Host of *Cooking Live,* Television Food Network

"No American chef is closer to the cutting edge of today's cuisine than Charlie Trotter. This book is a sharply honed primer for anyone who aspires to be a modern gourmet cook."

> — William Rice, Food and Wine Columnist, *Chicago Tribune*

"Anyone's first stab at gourmet cooking could be an intimidating mess. I lift my toque to Charlie Trotter for providing a veritable A to Z of essentials and insights that make it the wonderful and simple pleasure it should be."

> — Daniel Boulud, Chef and Owner of Restaurant Daniel

™

BUSINESS AND GENERAL REFERENCE BOOK SERIES FROM IDG

References for the Rest of Us!™

Do you find that traditional reference books are overloaded with technical details and advice you'll never use? Do you postpone important life decisions because you just don't want to deal with them? Then our *...For Dummies*™ business and general reference book series is for you.

...For Dummies business and general reference books are written for those frustrated and hard-working souls who know they aren't dumb, but find that the myriad of personal and business issues and the accompanying horror stories make them feel helpless. *...For Dummies* books use a lighthearted approach, a down-to-earth style, and even cartoons and humorous icons to diffuse fears and build confidence. Lighthearted but not lightweight, these books are perfect survival guides to solve your everyday personal and business problems.

> *"More than a publishing phenomenon, 'Dummies' is a sign of the times."*
> — *The New York Times*

> *"...you won't go wrong buying them."*
> — *Walter Mossberg, Wall Street Journal, on IDG's ...For Dummies*™ *books*

> *"A world of detailed and authoritative information is packed into them..."*
> — *U.S. News and World Report*

Already, millions of satisfied readers agree. They have made *...For Dummies* **the #1 introductory level computer book series and a best-selling business book series. They have written asking for more. So, if you're looking for the best and easiest way to learn about business and other general reference topics, look to** *...For Dummies* **to give you a helping hand.**

GOURMET COOKING FOR DUMMIES™

by Charlie Trotter
with Judi Carle and
Sari Zernich

Photography by Tim Turner
Foreword by Emeril Lagasse

IDG Books Worldwide, Inc.
An International Data Group Company

Foster City, CA ♦ Chicago, IL ♦ Indianapolis, IN ♦ Southlake, TX

Gourmet Cooking for Dummies ™

Published by
IDG Books Worldwide, Inc.
An International Data Group Company
919 E. Hillsdale Blvd.
Suite 400
Foster City, CA 94404
www.idgbooks.com (IDG Books Worldwide Web site)
www.dummies.com (Dummies Press Web site)

Library of Congress Catalog Card No.: 97-80117

ISBN: 0-7645-5029-2

Printed in the United States of America

10 9 8 7 6 5 4 3 2

1O/RR/QY/ZX/IN

Distributed in the United States by IDG Books Worldwide, Inc.

Distributed by Macmillan Canada for Canada; by Transworld Publishers Limited in the United Kingdom; by IDG Norge Books for Norway; by IDG Sweden Books for Sweden; by Woodslane Pty. Ltd. for Australia; by Woodslane Enterprises Ltd. for New Zealand; by Longman Singapore Publishers Ltd. for Singapore, Malaysia, Thailand, and Indonesia; by Simron Pty. Ltd. for South Africa; by Toppan Company Ltd. for Japan; by Distribuidora Cuspide for Argentina; by Livraria Cultura for Brazil; by Ediciencia S.A. for Ecuador; by Addison-Wesley Publishing Company for Korea; by Ediciones ZETA S.C.R. Ltda. for Peru; by WS Computer Publishing Corporation, Inc., for the Philippines; by Unalis Corporation for Taiwan; by Contemporanea de Ediciones for Venezuela; by Computer Book & Magazine Store for Puerto Rico; by Express Computer Distributors for the Caribbean and West Indies. Authorized Sales Agent: Anthony Rudkin Associates for the Middle East and North Africa.

For general information on IDG Books Worldwide's books in the U.S., please call our Consumer Customer Service department at 800-762-2974. For reseller information, including discounts and premium sales, please call our Reseller Customer Service department at 800-434-3422.

For information on where to purchase IDG Books Worldwide's books outside the U.S., please contact our International Sales department at 415-655-3200 or fax 415-655-3295.

For information on foreign language translations, please contact our Foreign & Subsidiary Rights department at 415-655-3021 or fax 415-655-3281.

For sales inquiries and special prices for bulk quantities, please contact our Sales department at 415-655-3200 or write to the address above.

For information on using IDG Books Worldwide's books in the classroom or for ordering examination copies, please contact our Educational Sales department at 800-434-2086 or fax 817-251-8174.

For press review copies, author interviews, or other publicity information, please contact our Public Relations department at 415-655-3000 or fax 415-655-3299.

For authorization to photocopy items for corporate, personal, or educational use, please contact Copyright Clearance Center, 222 Rosewood Drive, Danvers, MA 01923, or fax 508-750-4470.

is a trademark under exclusive license to IDG Books Worldwide, Inc., from International Data Group, Inc.

About the Author and His Staff

Charlie Trotter is the chef/owner of Charlie Trotter's restaurant, located in Chicago, Illinois. Charlie Trotter's has emerged as one of the country's finest restaurants, having been awarded five diamonds from AAA, a five-star rating from Mobil Travel Guide, and member status in the prestigious Relais & Chateaux. Charlie has been named America's Best Chef (Midwest) by the James Beard Foundation, and has also won their Award for Outstanding Wine Service. The restaurant has received the Grand Award from *Wine Spectator,* which also named Charlie the Best Chef Currently Working in the United States. Charlie Trotter is the author of three other cookbooks: *Charlie Trotter's, Charlie Trotter's Vegetables,* and *Charlie Trotter's Seafood.*

Judi Carle is the Controller for Charlie Trotter's. In addition to overseeing the financials, she worked as the project coordinator and general editor of this book and assisted with the book's overall development. She has worked as the project coordinator and general editor on all of Charlie's cookbooks.

Sari Zernich is a graduate of The University of Illinois and The Culinary Institute of America. She was responsible for the recipe development and testing, in addition to the book's research and development. She also worked closely with Charlie on his other cookbooks.

Tim Turner resides in Chicago, where he is a food and tabletop photographer and a commercial director. He has done the photography for all of Charlie Trotter's cookbooks, as well as *The Inn at Little Washington Cookbook* and *Norman's New World Cuisine.* Tim's photographs have appeared in several other cookbooks, as well as in advertising campaigns.

ABOUT IDG BOOKS WORLDWIDE

Welcome to the world of IDG Books Worldwide.

IDG Books Worldwide, Inc., is a subsidiary of International Data Group, the world's largest publisher of computer-related information and the leading global provider of information services on information technology. IDG was founded more than 25 years ago and now employs more than 8,500 people worldwide. IDG publishes more than 275 computer publications in over 75 countries (see listing below). More than 60 million people read one or more IDG publications each month.

Launched in 1990, IDG Books Worldwide is today the #1 publisher of best-selling computer books in the United States. We are proud to have received eight awards from the Computer Press Association in recognition of editorial excellence and three from *Computer Currents'* First Annual Readers' Choice Awards. Our best-selling ...For Dummies® series has more than 30 million copies in print with translations in 30 languages. IDG Books Worldwide, through a joint venture with IDG's Hi-Tech Beijing, became the first U.S. publisher to publish a computer book in the People's Republic of China. In record time, IDG Books Worldwide has become the first choice for millions of readers around the world who want to learn how to better manage their businesses.

Our mission is simple: Every one of our books is designed to bring extra value and skill-building instructions to the reader. Our books are written by experts who understand and care about our readers. The knowledge base of our editorial staff comes from years of experience in publishing, education, and journalism — experience we use to produce books for the '90s. In short, we care about books, so we attract the best people. We devote special attention to details such as audience, interior design, use of icons, and illustrations. And because we use an efficient process of authoring, editing, and desktop publishing our books electronically, we can spend more time ensuring superior content and spend less time on the technicalities of making books.

You can count on our commitment to deliver high-quality books at competitive prices on topics you want to read about. At IDG Books Worldwide, we continue in the IDG tradition of delivering quality for more than 25 years. You'll find no better book on a subject than one from IDG Books Worldwide.

John Kilcullen
CEO
IDG Books Worldwide, Inc.

Steven Berkowitz
President and Publisher
IDG Books Worldwide, Inc.

VIII WINNER

Eighth Annual Computer Press Awards 1992

IX WINNER

Ninth Annual Computer Press Awards 1993

X WINNER

Tenth Annual Computer Press Awards 1994

XI WINNER

Eleventh Annual Computer Press Awards 1995

IDG Books Worldwide, Inc., is a subsidiary of International Data Group, the world's largest publisher of computer-related information and the leading global provider of information services on information technology. International Data Group publishes over 275 computer publications in over 75 countries. Sixty million people read one or more International Data Group publications each month. International Data Group's publications include: **ARGENTINA:** Buyer's Guide, Computerworld Argentina, PC World Argentina; **AUSTRALIA:** Australian Macworld, Australian PC World, Australian Reseller News, Computerworld, IT Casebook, Network World, Publish, Webmaster; **AUSTRIA:** Computerwelt Osterreich, Networks Austria, PC Tip Austria; **BANGLADESH:** PC World Bangladesh; **BELARUS:** PC World Belarus; **BELGIUM:** Data News; **BRAZIL:** Annuário de Informática, Computerworld, Connections, Macworld, PC Player, PC World, Publish, Reseller News, Supergamepower; **BULGARIA:** Computerworld Bulgaria, Network World Bulgaria, PC & MacWorld Bulgaria; **CANADA:** CIO Canada, Client/Server World, ComputerWorld Canada, InfoWorld Canada, NetworkWorld Canada, WebWorld; **CHILE:** Computerworld Chile, PC World Chile; **COLOMBIA:** Computerworld Colombia, PC World Colombia; **COSTA RICA:** PC World Centro America; **THE CZECH AND SLOVAK REPUBLICS:** Computerworld Czechoslovakia, Macworld Czech Republic, PC World Czechoslovakia; **DENMARK:** Communications World Danmark, Computerworld Danmark, Macworld Danmark, PC World Danmark, Techworld Denmark; **DOMINICAN REPUBLIC:** PC World Republica Dominicana; **ECUADOR:** PC World Ecuador; **EGYPT:** Computerworld Middle East, PC World Middle East; **EL SALVADOR:** PC World Centro America; **FINLAND:** MikroPC, Tietoverkko, Tietoviikko; **FRANCE:** Distributique, Hebdo, Info PC, Le Monde Informatique, Macworld, Reseaux & Telecoms, WebMaster France; **GERMANY:** Computer Partner, Computerwoche, Computerwoche Extra, Computerwoche FOCUS, Global Online, Macweb, PC Welt; **GREECE:** Amiga Computing, GamePro Greece, Multimedia World; **GUATEMALA:** PC World Centro America; **HONDURAS:** PC World Centro America; **HONG KONG:** Computerworld Hong Kong, PC World Hong Kong, Publish in Asia; **HUNGARY:** ABCD CD-ROM, Computerworld Szamitastechnika, Internetto online Magazine, PC World Hungary, PC-X Magazin Hungary; **ICELAND:** Tolvuheimur PC World Island; **INDIA:** Information Communications World, Information Systems Computerworld, PC World India, Publish in Asia; **INDONESIA:** InfoKomputer PC World, Komputek Computerworld, Publish in Asia; **IRELAND:** ComputerScope, PC Live!, Publish; **ISRAEL:** Macworld Israel, People & Computers/Computerworld; **ITALY:** Computerworld Italia, Macworld Italia, Networking Italia, PC World Italia; **JAPAN:** DTP World, Macworld Japan, Nikkei Personal Computing, OS/2 World Japan, SunWorld Japan, Windows NT World, Windows World Japan; **KENYA:** PC World East African; **KOREA:** Hi-Tech Information, Macworld Korea, PC World Korea; **MACEDONIA:** PC World Macedonia; **MALAYSIA:** Computerworld Malaysia, PC World Malaysia, Publish in Asia; **MALTA:** PC World Malta; **MEXICO:** Computerworld Mexico, PC World Mexico; **MYANMAR:** PC World Myanmar; **NETHERLANDS:** Computer! Totaal, LAN Internetworking Magazine, LAN World Buyers Guide, Macworld Netherlands, Net, WebWereld; **NEW ZEALAND:** Absolute Beginners Guide and Plain & Simple Series, Computer Buyer, Computer Industry Directory, Computerworld New Zealand, MTB, Network World, PC World New Zealand; **NICARAGUA:** PC World Centro America; **NORWAY:** Computerworld Norge, CW Rapport, Datamagasinet, Financial Rapport, Kursguide Norge, Macworld Norge, Multimediaworld Norge, PC World Ekspress Norge, PC World Nettverk, PC World Norge, PC World ProduktGuide Norge; **PAKISTAN:** Computerworld Pakistan; **PANAMA:** PC World Panama; **PEOPLE'S REPUBLIC OF CHINA:** China Computer Users, China Computerworld, China InfoWorld, China Telecom World Weekly, Computer & Communication, Electronic Design China, Electronics Today, Electronics Weekly, Game Software, PC World China, Popular Computer Week, Software Weekly, Software World, Telecom World; **PERU:** Computerworld Peru, PC World Profesional Peru, PC World SoHo Peru; **PHILIPPINES:** Click!, Computerworld Philippines, Publish in Asia; **POLAND:** Computerworld Poland, Computerworld Special Report Poland, Cyber, Macworld Poland, Networld Poland, PC World Komputer; **PORTUGAL:** Cerebro/PC World, Computerworld/Correio Informático, Dealer World Portugal, Mac*In/PC*In Portugal, Multimedia World; **PUERTO RICO:** PC World Puerto Rico; **ROMANIA:** Computerworld Romania, PC World Romania, Telecom Romania; **RUSSIA:** Computerworld Russia, Mir PK, Publish, Seti; **SINGAPORE:** Computerworld Singapore, PC World Singapore, Publish in Asia; **SLOVENIA:** Monitor; **SOUTH AFRICA:** Computing SA, Network World SA, Software World SA; **SPAIN:** Communicaciones World España, Computerworld España, Dealer World España, Macworld España, PC World España; **SRI LANKA:** Infolink PC World; **SWEDEN:** CAP&Design, Computer Sweden, Corporate Computing Sweden, Internetworld Sweden, it.branschen, Macworld Sweden, MaxiData Sweden, MikroDatorn, Nätverk & Kommunikation, PC World Sweden, PCaktiv, Windows World Sweden; **SWITZERLAND:** Computerworld Schweiz, Macworld Schweiz, PCtip; **TAIWAN:** Computerworld Taiwan, Macworld Taiwan, NEW ViSiON/Publish, PC World Taiwan, Windows World Taiwan; **THAILAND:** Publish in Asia, Thai Computerworld; **TURKEY:** Computerworld Turkiye, Macworld Turkiye, Network World Turkiye, PC World Turkiye; **UKRAINE:** Computerworld Kiev, Multimedia World Ukraine, PC World Ukraine; **UNITED KINGDOM:** Acorn User UK, Amiga Action UK, Amiga Computing UK, Apple Talk UK, Computing, Macworld, Parents and Computers UK, PC Advisor, PC Home, PSX Pro, The WEB; **UNITED STATES:** Cable in the Classroom, CIO Magazine, Computerworld, DOS World, Federal Computer Week, GamePro Magazine, InfoWorld, I-Way, Macworld, Network World, PC Games, PC World, Publish, Video Event, THE WEB Magazine, and WebMaster; online webzines: JavaWorld, NetscapeWorld, and SunWorld Online; **URUGUAY:** InfoWorld Uruguay; **VENEZUELA:** Computerworld Venezuela, PC World Venezuela; and **VIETNAM:** PC World Vietnam.
3/24/97

Author's Acknowledgments

I would like to give special thanks to Judi Carle, whose red pen never left her side, and to Sari Zernich, whose sharp knives were in constant motion. Without their invaluable help, this book would not have been possible. I would also like to thank Brian Cronin for the great food and wine pairing information.

Thanks also go to Pam Mourouzis, whose incredible (and sometimes irritating) attention to detail kept the book on track. And to Joe Jansen, whose corny sense of humor made the editing process much less painful.

The following companies or associations provided us with invaluable information: Tom Cornille, Geo. Cornille & Sons Produce; Rod Mitchell, Browne Trading Company; Tim Doyle, Wild Game, Inc.; the National Cherry Foundation; the Oregon-Washington-California Pear Bureau; the California Melon Research Board; the International Apple Institute; the National Live Stock & Meat Board; and the Mushroom Council.

Publisher's Acknowledgments

We're proud of this book; please send us your comments about it by using the IDG Books Worldwide Registration Card at the back of the book or by e-mailing us at feedback/dummies @idgbooks.com. Some of the people who helped bring this book to market include the following:

Acquisitions, Development, and Editorial

Senior Project Editor: Pamela Mourouzis

Acquisitions Editor: Sarah Kennedy, Executive Editor

Senior Copy Editor: Joe Jansen

General Reviewer: Charlie Lilly

Editorial Manager: Leah P. Cameron

Editorial Assistant: Darren Meiss

Production

Project Coordinator: Sherry Gomoll

Layout and Graphics: Lou Boudreau, Elizabeth Cardenas-Nelson, Pamela Emanoil, Angela F. Hunckler, Jane E. Martin, Mark Owens, and Brent Savage

Special Art: Elizabeth Kurtzman, illustrations; Tim Turner, photography

Proofreaders: Mildred Rosenzweig, Nancy Reinhardt, Kelli Botta, Joel Draper, Nancy Price, and Rob Springer

Indexer: Sharon Hilgenberg

Special Help

Diana R. Conover, Associate Editor/Online

General and Administrative

IDG Books Worldwide, Inc.: John Kilcullen, CEO; Steven Berkowitz, President and Publisher

IDG Books Technology Publishing: Brenda McLaughlin, Senior Vice President and Group Publisher

Dummies Technology Press and Dummies Editorial: Diane Graves Steele, Vice President and Associate Publisher; Judith A. Taylor, Product Marketing Manager; Kristin A. Cocks, Editorial Director; Mary Bednarek, Product Development Director

Dummies Trade Press: Kathleen A. Welton, Vice President and Publisher

IDG Books Production for Dummies Press: Beth Jenkins, Production Director; Cindy L. Phipps, Manager of Project Coordination, Production Proofreading, and Indexing; Kathie S. Schutte, Supervisor of Page Layout; Shelley Lea, Supervisor of Graphics and Design; Debbie J. Gates, Production Systems Specialist; Robert Springer, Supervisor of Proofreading; Debbie Stailey, Special Projects Coordinator; Tony Augsburger, Supervisor of Reprints and Bluelines; Leslie Popplewell, Media Archive Coordinator

Dummies Packaging and Book Design: Patti Sandez, Packaging Specialist; Lance Kayser, Packaging Assistant; Kavish + Kavish, Cover Design

◆

The publisher would like to give special thanks to Patrick J. McGovern, without whom this book would not have been possible.

◆

Contents at a Glance

Recipes at a Glance

Meats

Architectural Elements and Dishes

Luxury Foods

Desserts and Dessert Sauces

Table of Contents

Foreword

As Webster says:

Gourmet: A connoisseur of food and drink

Cooking: Suitable for or used in cooking

Dummy: Could not find Master Chef Charlie Trotter

When looking at a manuscript, one tries to figure out what knowledge, what secrets, what plots, if any, are included in this book. This book of art. It's obvious that this is a subject near and dear to my heart. Gourmet cooking by one of the masters of the subject with so many interesting facts, tips, history, and recipes by this great man. I can tell you he is no dummy.

Ever since I met Charlie and had the pleasure of eating his food and dining in his restaurant, but also becoming dear friends and certainly great cooking buds, I have been amazed by Charlie's passion, his commitment to the profession, and his excellence with his staff. To watch and learn and see him in action is clearly a pleasure.

For one to have gourmet food, one must find what one likes. One must want to expand one's knowledge and importantly one's passion for food and wine. In this manuscript there are over 20 solid chapters, each containing facts, glossaries, history, recipes, and tips. There are also user and cooking friendly stories and facts that will guide you and help you to love cooking and to plan, whether you're cooking for two or cooking for that special dinner party. This very condensed offering is on a subject of love and passion from a man who makes it simple for all of us. This book is for all of us. Cook, eat, drink. Enjoy!

— *Emeril Lagasse, Chef/Owner of Emeril's, Nola, and Emeril's New Orleans Fish House, and Host of TV's* The Essence of Emeril.

Introduction

*W*elcome to *Gourmet Cooking For Dummies* — and congratulations on your interest in taking everyday cooking to the next level of excellence. Although gourmet cooking can seem intimidating, this book makes the techniques and terminology of the gourmet's kitchen accessible and easy to understand.

I think of food not only as sustenance, but as art. And through my art, I have been able to express my own food philosophy: that creating elegant gourmet cuisine involves more than just using sophisticated cooking techniques. To me, the essence of preparing outstanding gourmet dishes is to use the freshest, finest ingredients available. My approach is then to join these first-rate foods together in ways that surprise and delight the palate.

In this book, I show you how to select the most vibrant fruits and vegetables, the most succulent seafood, and the freshest meats, herbs, and other gourmet food basics. I then show you how to use these ingredients to prepare some of my favorite dishes, which include unique and surprising combinations of flavors and textures.

In *Gourmet Cooking For Dummies,* I create a very personal cuisine with you, and I take you through the process of actually preparing it. But more important, I give you tips and guidelines to help you improvise for yourself and personalize these recipes to your own taste. In no time at all, you'll be developing your own personal repertoire of gourmet cuisine.

About This Book

I don't expect you to read this book straight through, from cover to cover. You can use *Gourmet Cooking For Dummies* as your reference book to the world of epicurean creativity. This book covers everything from buying kitchen equipment to throwing fabulous gourmet dinner parties.

I've written each chapter to stand on its own. Depending on your cooking skills, you can either start right at the beginning or jump ahead to the chapters that interest you. For example, if you are a beginning gourmet cook and you need to stock your kitchen with the best pots, pans, utensils, and food staples, check out the early chapters. If you already have a little epicurean expertise under your belt, you can flip ahead to later chapters, where you'll discover how to take your gourmet cooking skills to the next level.

I also include a section containing color photos of many of the dishes. You can use these photos to see how to arrange and serve the recipes in this book. You can also use these beautiful photos to spark your imagination on ways to present your own unique creations.

Foolish Assumptions

If you picked up this book, I assume that you probably have a few cookbooks in your kitchen and have some experience handling recipes. You're probably familiar with basic cooking terms and techniques like *blanch and shock, render,* and *deglaze.* You may have some sense of which foods work well together, but you're intimidated by the whole mystique that surrounds the term *gourmet cooking.*

Maybe you read *Cooking For Dummies* (also published by IDG Books Worldwide, Inc.), and now you want to get serious in the kitchen. Whatever the reason, I assume that you're interested in crossing the bridge from "normal cooking" to "gourmet cooking." Don't be afraid!

Some terms are basic to cooking, and I assume that, having cooked before, you've already run across them. I use these terms repeatedly throughout the book, usually without stopping to explain what they mean. If you're unfamiliar with any of the following terms, see Chapter 3 for their definitions:

- ✔ Blanch and shock
- ✔ Caramelize
- ✔ Deglaze
- ✔ Infuse
- ✔ Render
- ✔ Sear
- ✔ Sweat

Conventions Used in This Book

For each recipe in this book, I include preparation and cooking times so that you have an idea of how much time you can expect to spend creating the dish. I also list the specialty tools (if any are required) that you need on hand to prepare the recipe.

In general, you should follow these conventions when using the recipes in the following chapters:

✔ Read through the recipe beforehand to see what utensils and implements you need to gather. Determine what foods you have on hand and what foods you need to go a-hunting for. If you see an unfamiliar food item or term in the recipe, check one of the chapters in Part I for an explanation.

✔ Many recipes use ingredients that you prepare as recipes in other chapters. For example, when my recipe for Yukon Gold Potato Soup calls for "Chicken Stock," I give you a cross-reference to the chapter where you can find my Chicken Stock recipe.

✔ Some recipes include secondary recipes that accompany the main dish. For other recipes, I give a basic recipe and then a couple variations — different and interesting ways to prepare and present the dish.

✔ At my restaurant, I serve _multicourse degustation_ (or tasting menus) consisting of 8 to 12 small courses. I present many of the recipes in this book in the same manner — smaller preparations that usually yield four to six small servings. Although this format is great for an elegant dinner party, it's not very practical for everyday dining (especially if you're cooking for the family). You can easily increase the recipes to accommodate additional servings or larger portions. Look at each recipe before you prepare it, determine the portion size, and increase it as necessary (the easiest way is just to double the recipe).

✔ Usually, I tell you to season _each individual component_ of a dish as you prepare it — if each part is seasoned to your tastes, the final dish will be to your liking as well. Any salt and pepper that you use to season the recipes I leave to your own individual taste.

✔ All temperatures in the recipes are shown in degrees Fahrenheit. If you're used to temperatures in Celsius, I include a conversion chart on the Cheat Sheet at the front of the book.

Also, each recipe in this book assumes certain conventions about the ingredients themselves. When you see the following ingredients or instructions listed in my recipes, keep in mind that I mean the following:

✔ All milk is _whole milk._

✔ All cream is _heavy_ (or whipping cream).

✔ All butter is _unsalted._

✔ All eggs are _large._

✔ All pepper is _freshly ground._

✔ All salt is _kosher._

✔ All flour is _all-purpose._

✔ All olive oil is _extra-virgin._

✔ The oven or grill is always _preheated._

How This Book Is Organized

This book is organized to take you from the basic tasks all the way through putting together an extravagant dinner party. Each part contains chapters that guide you through the specifics of dealing with different foods and cooking techniques. This section explains how the parts are broken down and what you can expect to find in each part.

Part I: Building Your Way to a Well-Stocked Kitchen

This part contains all the basic information you need to know before you can journey into the world of gourmet cooking. In Part I, you can find out about the necessary kitchen equipment — and also discover some fun gadgets that come in handy. This part covers food staples and what every gourmet kitchen should always have on hand. Part I also contains a comprehensive listing of different fruits and vegetables, when they are available, and what to look for when you want only the freshest, ripest items on the market.

Part II: So You Know How to Boil Water and Fry an Egg

Part II shows you how to prepare vegetable, seafood, poultry, and meat dishes. This part talks about which cooking techniques work best for each type of food and includes step-by-step instructions for each recipe to guide you through the different techniques. Part II helps you expand your repertoire of rice and grains by using some of the less-common varieties that are now available. You'll also discover different sauces and condiments that you can use to dress up ordinary meals. But most important, throughout this part, I talk about flavors and textures and how to combine and contrast them to create your own amazing dishes.

Part III: Bumping It Up a Notch and Taking It to the Next Level

This part shows you different ways to present and serve a gourmet recipe, which can change a dish from a simple meal to a stunning creation that will wow your friends and family. Part III covers the ways in which you can create impressive *architectural cuisine:* layered dishes that rise above the plate with dimension and height. This part also gives you information on how to purchase and prepare the most luxurious and extravagant foods used by gourmet chefs, such as truffles, caviar, and foie gras.

Part IV: Ooh, You Sweet Thing!

This is the part everyone loves: dessert. In Part IV, you can find out every-thing from the basic building blocks, such as doughs and ice creams, to putting it all together for a stunning dessert. These chapters show you how to turn your old favorites into something even more special by changing a few ingredients or adding a new flavor. And best of all, Part IV includes a chapter devoted *entirely* to chocolate. What could be better than that?

Part V: The Home Stretch: Taking It to Your Dinner Table

Part V is where you put it all together. This part includes helpful hints for creating a dinner party menu; in fact, this part includes over a dozen different menus using recipes from throughout the book. Each menu in-cludes preparation notes that show you how far in advance you can prepare each item. The menus also include wine recommendations for each course to help guide you through that sometimes-confusing process of pairing wines with foods.

Part VI: The Part of Tens

Part VI contains a wide variety of information, including classic food and wine pairings and some of my favorite cookbooks (which are worth keeping close at hand in the kitchen). This part also gives you a list of sources for those hard-to-find ingredients that gourmet chefs love to use. And for those occasions when cooking it yourself just won't do, you can find information about some of my favorite gourmet restaurants around the world. Call it research!

Icons Used in This Book

To make this book easier to navigate, I include icons in the margins to mark important and noteworthy information. Here's a guide to what those icons mean:

I use this icon when I give you substitutions or easier methods of prepara-tion that I may not approve of personally, but which home gourmets may want to take advantage of in a pinch.

These tidbits of my philosophy give you insights into the way I view different foods, preparations, flavors, and textures.

This icon marks extraneous (but fun) information about gourmet foods. Reading these fun facts isn't critical, but they're great for impressing friends with your amazing food knowledge.

When I show you shortcuts, easier ways to do things, or ways to handle unusual ingredients, I mark these helpful hints with this icon.

I use this icon to mark recipes and foods that are low in fat or to tell you about substitutions that you can make to lower the fat or calories in a recipe.

This icon warns you about potentially hazardous foods, food handling techniques, or kitchen equipment. The sections marked with this icon give you ways to deal with food and kitchen implements safely.

When a piece of information is particularly worth remembering, I stick this icon in the margin.

Where to Go from Here

Creating gourmet meals can be fun (after you get over the nervous hives). This book arms you with the knowledge that you need to create the dishes in this book and to design wonderful dishes on your own. Don't let the _G_ word intimidate you; it's still just food. So get out your chef's hat and get cooking!

Part I
Building Your Way to a Well-Stocked Kitchen

The 5th Wave   By Rich Tennant

"Oooo, what's in here? Is that sun-dried eye of newt? How *gourmet*!"

In this part . . .

*I*f you have some experience with cooking, you may know your way around a typical kitchen already. But some of the elements that go into a *gourmet* kitchen may be new to you. This part talks about the equipment that you need to prepare gourmet dishes, explains some of the techniques and terms that you need to master, and walks you through the produce market, identifying all those strange-looking fruits and vegetables that are so important in gourmet cuisine.

Chapter 1

What Makes It Gourmet?

For some reason, the word *gourmet* often sends tremors of terror through even the most avid home cooks. But gourmet food doesn't have to be intimidating. To me, gourmet cooking simply means taking the extra time to find the freshest products, taking a little more care in the preparation, and taking the time to put the food on the plate in an appealing manner.

That doesn't sound so scary, does it?

Buying the Freshest Ingredients

Finding the finest, freshest products available may take some time initially, but once you have found good, reliable sources for ingredients, it can be as easy as placing a phone call. Getting the best ingredients doesn't mean that you need to take out a second mortgage on your house. I like to go to farmers' markets: They're the best sources for great fresh produce, and they're usually inexpensive because you cut out the middleman.

Also, don't be afraid to try your hand at growing a few things on your own. Even if you live in a tiny apartment, you can grow a few herbs on your windowsill. They look nice and are guaranteed to be fresh.

Combining Flavors and Textures

Gourmet food is also about flavors and textures — combinations and contrasts. When I think about a new dish, I first determine what I want for an end result. Then I think about what basic ingredients it should contain. From there, I think about how to blend the ingredients with a complementing sauce, create textural contrasts, or give the dish a little extra zip.

You have to be careful not to have too many textures or flavors going on in the same dish; but some contrasts are necessary, or you may as well just eat pureed baby food.

Taking Extra Care in Preparing Dishes

Taking more care in gourmet cuisine preparation really involves only time:

- ✔ Time to cut vegetables into even, precise cuts
- ✔ Time to cook foods separately before tossing them together
- ✔ Time to shock blanched vegetables in ice water to stop the cooking process and keep them from getting too soft
- ✔ Time to make crispy garnishes or tuiles

Putting a little extra time and effort into preparing your gourmet foods makes an enormous difference in the final look and taste of a dish.

Plating Foods in Attractive Ways

You can take all the time in the world buying food and cooking a wonderful dish, but if you just toss it all on a plate, you may as well be serving last night's leftovers. The way that you present a dish (what chefs call *plating* a dish) is almost as important as the flavor of the dish itself.

When you put food onto a plate, try to think of interesting, appealing ways to present it. Can you stack a couple of the ingredients? Can you fan one of the foods around another? Can you garnish the plate with some fresh herbs or a contrasting-colored oil? Can you serve the food on interesting plates or bowls? These kinds of creative elements can turn ordinary food into gourmet cuisine.

For some great ideas on appealing and attractive ways to plate your gourmet cuisine, take a look at the color photos that appear later in this book. These photos show some of the exciting ways that we present cuisine at the restaurant. Notice that all the food is on white plates — you don't *need* to serve gourmet food on fancy china; the cuisine itself provides the visual appeal. Of course, if you're having a special dinner party, you can go ahead and use your best china, but it's nice to know that you don't have to.

Learning the Lingo of Gourmet Cuisine

Part of the mystique of gourmet cooking is in the lingo. Because gourmet cooking has its roots in French cooking, many of the terms that are used today come from the French. It may be called "the language of love," but French is also "the language of food." Often, these words are used because no good translation for them exists (at least without going into a complete dissertation).

But the rest of the time, I think that chefs use these fancy terms just to sound impressive — and it works! For example, your guests would certainly be more impressed if you served them crème brûlée than if you told them that it was vanilla custard, even though these are two names for basically the same dish.

A fair number of English words are part of the gourmet cooking lingo, too. But English cooking terms usually describe a whole *procedure*. For example, *caramelize the onion* means to cook the onion over medium-high heat in some type of oil or butter until golden-brown. These types of technique words are used repeatedly in gourmet talk because they describe both the procedure *and* the result at the same time. All this may sound very confusing, but trust me; once you learn the lingo, you'll be using it right along with the rest of us gourmands.

CHARLIE SAYS

The beginner's guide to gourmet patois

You don't need to be intimidated by all the daunting lingo used in gourmet cooking. When I first got interested in cooking (when I was in college studying political science), I didn't know much about gourmet cooking or all that fancy terminology that chefs used. Although I started out with simple survival cooking, I soon realized how much fun I was having and decided to pursue cooking further.

So I went out and bought several cookbooks and started to try many different types of dishes. Some were great; but others were, well. . . . Okay, so maybe I used a whole *bulb* of garlic in the veal scaloppine instead of a *clove* (good thing I like garlic). And it probably would have been better if I had figured out before the fire department arrived that *blackened* fish meant to blacken the *spices,* not the ceiling in

my kitchen (don't worry, my insurance covered the smoke damage). And I did spend quite a bit of time puzzling over how I was supposed to layer food in a *tureen* (a large soup bowl), before I figured out that they meant a *terrine* (a small food mold).

Be patient — gourmet cooking lingo just takes a little getting used to. Use this book as a resource (in fact, most cookbooks have a section that explains unusual terms or cooking techniques). If there's a term or technique that you just can't decipher, ask the chef at your favorite restaurant, the staff in a gourmet food shop, or even the folks at the supermarket, all of whom are usually more than happy to share their knowledge about cooking. It worked for me, and it can work for you, too!

Being Flexible with Ingredients and Tools

They say that "necessity is the mother of invention," and this maxim is never more true than in gourmet cooking. You have to be flexible when planning and cooking a gourmet meal. Don't let one unobtainable ingredient send your whole menu plan down the drain — improvise! Determine what place the food had in the dish. Did the ingredient add a certain flavor? Did it add a different texture? Did it have an interesting shape or color? It could be one, two, or all three of those things, but just try to match those characteristics (as best you can) with another food.

For example, most recipes that call for baby carrots can just as easily use large carrots cut into smaller pieces; spinach can be substituted for Swiss chard in most cases; and zucchini can be substituted for yellow squash. You can make an endless number of substitutions in cooking, and very seldom will you find a substitution that doesn't work — as long as you're thinking about the overall result of the dish.

The second part of the improvise theory relates to your kitchen equipment. Most professional chefs have a plethora of different utensils and tools available to them. Unfortunately, home cooks sometimes have trouble finding (or storing) all the kitchen tools that they would like to have. Don't let the lack of some specific piece of equipment stop you from trying a recipe. Again, improvise!

For example, what if you don't have a terrine mold? Instead, try using a loaf pan, filling half of the width with raw potatoes, and lining the pan with plastic wrap to create a smaller mold. Can't find a timbale mold? Try using a shot glass instead. Just as with food, think about the end result and decide what you can use that will give you similar results.

Taking Risks with Your Recipes

Very few absolutes exist in gourmet cooking. You can use the recipes in this book as a starting point, but feel free to experiment by adding foods or flavors that you like (though I'd do this first when cooking for family or very close friends).

The worst that can happen is that you'll come up with a dish that even the dog won't eat (yes, we've all had a few) — but at least you can discover what *not* to do. By trying different flavor and texture combinations, you'll soon come up with your own repertoire of dishes.

Chapter 2

Stocking Your Kitchen for the New Millennium

In This Chapter

▶ Choosing the best cookware for the job

▶ Selecting good-quality knives

▶ Spending your lottery winnings on kitchen gadgets

▶ Stocking your pantry

*E*very time you turn on your television, you're assaulted with ads for revolutionary new products, guaranteed to be the be-all, end-all kitchen gadgets that you can't live without. Some of these products are very good, and others are useless. Unfortunately, you usually don't know whether a new kitchen tool is useful until you've already spent your money. Most of us have one or two (okay, maybe four or five) of these doodads buried some- where in the deep recesses of our kitchens, collecting dust. The truth is, you don't need a huge kitchen supplied with every gadget in order to create great cuisine. In fact, the very best gadgets you have at your disposal are your own hands!

No matter what the size of your kitchen, you can make the most of it by utilizing your space effectively, being organized, and cleaning as you go. Cleaning as you go is especially important if you don't have a heavily stocked kitchen. Not only does this practice make it easier to clean up at the end of a meal, but your utensils will always be clean and ready for the next use.

To help you figure out which equipment you *really* need, I have divided the first part of the chapter into two sections:

✔ The basics that you need to function in the kitchen

✔ What I call the *lotto list*

The basics are just that: basics — pots, pans, knives, and so on. The "lotto list" includes all the other gadgets and appliances that are not required, but that can make cooking a lot easier. So if you win the lottery or come into a large inheritance, by all means, go out and buy everything on the list. But if you're like most people, you can add these items to your holiday wish list or pick them up one at a time as you need them. Remember, no matter how large or small, new or old, high-tech or simple your kitchen is, as long as you have some basic equipment, you can create marvelous food.

Along with the basic equipment, you need a supply of basic, or *staple,* ingredients on hand. Everyone's idea of what's considered a staple varies, but many items are included on everyone's list. For example, no kitchen can be without some form of flour, sugar, salt, pepper, butter, or eggs. Beyond those basics, though, the list can go in many different directions, according to your preferences. Some people keep a large supply of fresh fruit in the kitchen; others can't live without dried beans. Personally, I can't imagine cooking without onions, garlic, and a lot of fresh herbs. This chapter gives you tips for stocking your own pantry.

Choosing Basic Equipment

Outfitting your kitchen can be a daunting task. But don't feel bad; you aren't alone. Even professional chefs are constantly trying new equipment in hopes of finding the perfect item. You can use the following information to get an idea of the features you want to look for in your kitchen equipment, but then you need to spend a little time in the housewares section of a department store. Pick up the pots, pans, and knives and see how they feel. Does the weight feel good to you? Do the handles feel comfortable in your hand? Only you can answer these questions.

Pots and pans

Every kitchen should have some basic pots and pans: a stockpot, a sauce pot, a saucepan, a sauté pan, a sautoir, and a nonstick sauté pan, as shown in Figure 2-1. (Other pots and pans are covered later in this chapter in "Other kitchen necessities.")

- **Stockpot:** A large pot, anywhere from $2^1/_2$ gallons to as large as 20 gallons. A 5 gallon stockpot is a good size to have on hand. Stockpots have two handles and sometimes have a spigot to facilitate draining.

- **Sauce pot:** A pot with two handles and straight sides. Sauce pots are smaller than stockpots and come in various sizes, ranging from 1 gallon to 3 gallons.

- **Saucepan:** A pan with one long handle. Saucepans are generally smaller than stockpots and come in sizes as small as 2 cups and as large as 2 gallons.

Figure 2-1:
The
essential
pots and
pans.

saute pan

sautoir

stockpot

sauce pot

saucepan

> ✔ **Sautoir:** A sauté pan with straight sides; normal people call it a *frying pan,* but a gourmand calls it a *sautoir.* This pan has a long handle and sometimes with larger-sized pans, has a small handle opposite the long one for easier lifting.

> ✔ **Sauté pan:** Also known as a *sauteuse.* A sauté pan is a shallow skillet with sloping sides and a single long handle.

Each of these types of pans can be purchased with a nonstick coating. I recommend buying at least one or two different sizes of nonstick sauté pans, plus saucepans and sauce pots that are *not* nonstick. Beyond that, it's purely personal preference.

Picking the right pans

Selecting the proper cookware is important. There seems to be no perfect material for constructing pots and pans. Copper is heavy and needs to be recoated with tin often; stainless steel is expensive and is a poor conductor of heat, so it heats slowly and unevenly; aluminum stains certain sauces; and the list of disadvantages goes on. The best (and most expensive) pots and pans have a combination of these materials layered in the bottom to make the optimum use of each type. All-Clad, Calphalon, Faberware, and Revere Ware all make good-quality pans.

Whatever brand or material you choose, the most important consideration in selecting pots and pans is that they have thick, heavy bottoms. If not, they heat unevenly, and the bottoms may burn or scald, and possibly warp. Having at least one saucepan and one sauté pan with metal handles also comes in handy so that the pan can go from the stove, straight into the oven.

Copper

Copper is an excellent conductor of heat and has long been the material of choice for professional cookware. Every kitchen should have at least one copper-lined or copper-bottomed stainless-steel saucepan for making sauces that contain eggs, such as hollandaise, or for whipping egg whites.

When made of heavy-gauge copper, saucepans and sauté pans distribute heat evenly, decreasing the risk of burning your pan drippings or scalding your sauces. Because it conducts heat evenly, a copper pan is also less likely to warp.

However, copper pots and pans are expensive, and they must be recoated with tin on a regular basis so that the copper does not come directly in contact with foods. Using pots with exposed copper is dangerous — sauces can absorb toxic doses of copper if allowed to sit in an untinned copper pan.

When you purchase copper cookware, be sure to select pots and pans with iron rather than brass handles. Because iron is a poor conductor of heat, the handles don't get hot as quickly.

Copper also needs to be cleaned with copper polish each time you wash it in order to maintain its appearance.

Aluminum

Aluminum has become popular as cookware primarily because it is inexpensive. Good-quality, heavy-gauge aluminum conducts heat fairly well, so it can be used for roasting pans, sauté pans, and, to a limited degree, saucepans. Aluminum is especially practical for large stockpots, which would be prohibitively expensive if made of copper or stainless steel. The problem with aluminum is that large aluminum sauté pans and roasting pans tend to warp because the center expands before the outside does. You can avoid this warping by choosing the heaviest gauge aluminum possible.

Aluminum saucepans can discolor white sauces — especially sauces containing egg yolks. But Calphalon uses a special treatment that renders the aluminum inert, preventing it from reacting with foods.

Stainless steel

Stainless steel cookware is almost completely inert; it doesn't rust, tarnish, or react with foods. Unfortunately, stainless steel is a relatively poor conductor of heat and is expensive. The best stainless steel pots and pans have a thick disk of copper in the base of the pan, which helps to conduct heat and prevent scalding.

Enameled cast iron

Enameled cast iron is impractical for saucepans and sauté pans for several reasons: It rusts easily, it may discolor some foods, and it's very heavy. Enameled cast iron is excellent for braising because it is extremely thick and conducts heat slowly and evenly.

Nonstick

Nonstick pans are great for lowfat cooking because you don't need to add butter or oils to keep foods from sticking. They also make perfect pancakes and omelets. But nonstick pans don't work well for making sauces that involve deglazing, which simply means dissolving the caramelized drippings from the bottom of the pan with some type of liquid. These drippings are loaded with flavor, but they will not form on nonstick surfaces. Imagine your Grandma's gravy without the pan drippings — sounds like wallpaper paste to me!

Knives

Good-quality knives are a must. They are expensive, but if you take care of them, they last forever. When selecting knives, make sure that they feel comfortable in your hand.

Knives that you use frequently should have a full *tang* — a continuation of the blade that extends into the knife's handle. A full tang extends the entire length of the handle, making the knife much stronger. Although blades with partial tangs are not as durable as those with full tangs, partial-tang blades are acceptable for less-often-used knives. Many different brands are available to choose from, but I prefer Forstner, Global, Henkel, or Wustoff.

You can get away with having only three basic knives (see Figure 2-2), although most people find that having a couple of different sizes of paring knives comes in handy.

Figure 2-2:
The essential knives.

- **Chef's knife or French knife:** This is an all-purpose knife that you use for chopping, slicing, and mincing. The blade is normally 8 to 14 inches long.

- **Paring knife:** You use this short knife for paring and trimming vegetables and fruits. The blade is usually 2 to 4 inches long.

- **Slicer:** You can use this knife for slicing cooked meat or smoked fish. A slicer has a long blade with a round or pointed tip. The blade may be taper-ground, which is smooth, or have a serrated edge like a bread knife.

Other good knives to have on hand include the following (see Figure 2-3):

Figure 2-3:
Four other useful knives.

- **Boning knife:** You use a boning knife to separate raw meat from the bone. The blade, which is thinner and shorter than the blade of a chef's knife, is about 6 inches long and is usually rigid.

- **Cleaver:** A cleaver is a heavy blade used for chopping. It is often heavy enough to cut through bones. Cleavers have a rectangular blade and vary in size according to their use.

- **Filleting knife:** You use this knife for filleting fish. A fillet knife is similar in size and shape to a boning knife, but it has a flexible blade.

- **Utility knife:** You use this smaller, lighter chef's knife for lighter chopping chores. The blade is generally 5 to 7 inches long.

Picking the right metal

Carbon steel blades *take an edge,* or sharpen, better than either regular or high-carbon stainless steel, but they tend to lose their sharpness quickly. Also, carbon steel blades discolor when they come in contact with high-acid foods, such as tomatoes or onions. Carbon steel blades must be treated carefully to avoid discoloring, rusting, and pitting. You should wash carbon steel blades by hand only, and thoroughly dry them between uses and before storing them.

Stainless steel is much stronger than carbon steel and doesn't discolor or rust. Getting a good edge on stainless steel blades is very difficult, although after an edge is established, it tends to last longer than the edge on a carbon steel blade.

High-carbon stainless steel combines the advantages of carbon and stainless steel. The higher percentage of carbon allows the blade to take and keep a keener edge. Because these blades are stainless steel, they don't discolor or rust.

Caring for your knives

After you select your knives, no matter what brand, make sure that you keep them sharp! More people get cut from dull knives than from sharp ones, and your work is much easier with a sharp tool. You give knife blades an edge on a sharpening stone and maintain that edge between sharpenings by honing the blades with a tool called a *steel*.

- ✔ **Sharpening stone:** Several types of sharpening stones are available, but the most common are *Arkansas stones* and *diamond-impregnated stones*. Arkansas stones are naturally made stones that are available in several grades of fineness. Some consist of three stones of varying degrees of fineness, mounted on a wheel. Although diamond-impregnated stones are expensive, some people prefer them because they feel that these stones give a sharper edge.

- ✔ **Steel:** A *steel* is a long, thin, pointed, round rod that is also known as a *butcher's steel.* A steel should be used immediately after sharpening the blade with a stone and also between sharpenings to straighten any little nicks in the blade. Hard steel is the traditional material for steels, but you can also find them in glass, ceramic, and diamond-impregnated surfaces. See Figure 2-4 for instructions for using a steel.

How to Use a Sharpening Steel

Figure 2-4:
Keeping your knives sharp is important.

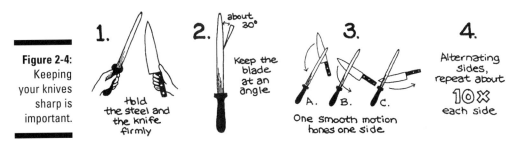

Other kitchen necessities

Baking pans: A couple 9-x-13-inch baking pans are a must. You can use them for roasting meats, vegetables, or, most important, for baking brownies. Baking pans are made from many different types of materials, all of which seem equally good.

Blender: A blender is great for thoroughly mixing vinaigrettes and for making purees, herb oils, or anything that needs to be pureed, blended, ground, or chopped.

Cover the blender with a towel whenever you blend hot ingredients. The hot ingredients can expand and blow the cover off the blender, causing the ingredients to fly all over your kitchen.

Cheesecloth: Cheesecloth works well to drain foods. You can turn a colander into a fine-mesh sieve simply by lining it with several layers of cheesecloth. Before using, you should rinse cheesecloth first in hot water and then in cold water to remove any loose fibers in the cloth.

Cutting board: I could go round and round on whether you should use wood or plastic cutting boards, but I won't. Whatever type of cutting board you use, make sure that you wash it thoroughly between uses — and when dealing with raw meat, chicken, or fish. Disinfect your cutting boards regularly with a solution of bleach and water.

Colander: A colander (or sieve) is a bowl-shaped object with many holes for draining the liquid from foods like pasta or blanched vegetables. Colanders are hard to live without. (See Figure 2-5.)

Grater: A grater (also shown in Figure 2-5) usually has four sides from which you can select different degrees of fineness. Try to find one that also has a slicing side so it can do double-duty by slicing fruits, vegetables, or even cheese.

Figure 2-5:
Two essential kitchen tools: a colander and a grater.

colander   grater

Half sheet pans (or cookie sheets): Half sheet pans are commonly known as *cookie sheets,* but no self-respecting chef would ever call them cookie sheets. It's best to invest in a few heavy-bottomed sheet pans with $3^1/_2$-inch-high sides, which can make a world of difference in even cooking and durability. Don't fall prey to the air-cushioned cookie sheets that have two thin layers of metal with an "air cushion" in between. These pans can't go in the dishwasher and don't conduct heat very well.

Measuring cups (liquid and dry): I don't need to explain measuring cups, except that you must use liquid measuring cups for liquids and dry measuring cups for dry ingredients. You cannot get an accurate liquid measurement in a dry measuring cup.

Measuring spoons: Every kitchen should already have a set of measuring spoons, which are a necessity in baking.

Mixer: A professional mixer that is self-standing and operates without being held is a great time-saver. KitchenAid makes a great one (check out their Web site at www.KitchenAid.com/). You can be whipping something while assembling the other components of a recipe, or while you answer the phone. These professional mixers come with a dough hook, a whip, and a paddle attachment. You can also purchase grinding and various other attachments. If you don't have a self-standing mixer, a hand-held mixer with a strong motor can also do a good job.

Mixing bowls: A graduated set of glass or stainless steel bowls is a good investment. They can range in size from $^1/_4$ cup to several gallons.

Spatulas: Rubber spatulas are a *must* for any kitchen. Spatulas are cheap, and they're the best way to scrape a bowl, except when making cookie dough — then hide the spatulas and use your fingers. Metal spatulas are good to use when grilling or for turning items over in sauté pans.

Timer: Unless you have a mental clock that never fails, use a timer so that you don't burn dinner — or, more important, dessert.

Tongs: Not only do tongs serve their purpose on the barbecue grill, but they are very useful inside the kitchen as well. You can use tongs to turn large pieces of meat in a braising pan, to move bones around in a roasting pan, or just about anytime you deal with hot food.

Vegetable peeler: Vegetable peelers come in a wide range of prices. Whether you decide to purchase one for 39 cents or $15, vegetable peelers generally serve the same purpose — some just look fancier than others. Beware, though: The cheaper peelers can rust.

Whisks: I suggest keeping two sizes of whisks on hand. A smaller whisk works great for small pan sauces or simply smaller quantities of food. A large whisk has numerous uses: For example, you can use it to whip eggs or frosting, or to blend larger quantities of sauces.

Wooden spoons: Wooden spoons are great to have around — they don't scrape the bottom of your nonstick pans, the handles don't get hot, and they don't react with high-acid foods like tomato sauce the way metal spoons do.

Lining Up Your Lotto List

This section lists all the gadgets that make cooking easier. These items are not required; in fact, you probably don't need all the tools in this section. (For example, an oyster shucker isn't of much use to you if you don't eat oysters.) Simply look through the list and pick out the things that you can use — although, if you have won the lottery, you may want to go out and get everything on the list. You never know when Robin Leach may stop by your villa to borrow an oyster shucker!

Apple wedger: This gadget is great for coring and wedging an apple at the same time. You can then peel the wedges in one motion and slice them for pies or tarts. (See Figure 2-6.)

Figure 2-6:
An apple wedger can save you a lot of time.

Braising/roasting pan: This large, thick pan does double duty as a braiser and a roaster, conducting heat slowly and evenly. Some have a tight cover, which enables you to cook meats or vegetables very slowly with a minimum of liquid. If you make a lot of stocks, you need to have one of these pans around for roasting bones and vegetables. You can also use this pan to roast a turkey or pot roast. (See Figure 2-7.)

Cake pans: Cake pans come in many different sizes and shapes, but a 9-inch round cake pan is the most common size. Wilton makes great cake pans that hold up well.

Figure 2-7:
A braising/
roasting pan
is a handy
pan to have
for slow-
cooking
foods.

Cheese slicer: A cheese slicer is a Y-shaped tool with a thin wire running across the top of the Y. This gadget is particularly effective on softer cheeses, which can stick to a knife when you slice them. This tool allows for clean, even cuts of cheese.

Chinois: *Chinois* is French for "Chinaman's hat." But a chinois (see Figure 2-8) is really a fine-mesh sieve that has three layers of fine mesh. Nothing but liquid can pass through this fine mesh, not even a raspberry seed. A chinois works wonderfully for straining soups, sauces, oils, and so on. They are expensive, but once you get your hands on a chinois, it will never leave your side.

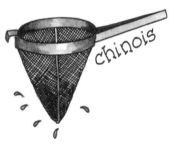

Figure 2-8:
You use a
chinois to
strain
liquids.

Coffee grinder: A coffee grinder is great for grinding fresh coffee beans, but it also does double-duty as a spice grinder. Spices ground at the last minute are fresher and have more flavor. Just make sure that you clean out the spice or coffee grounds between uses so that your coffee doesn't taste like cumin, and vice versa.

For more flavor, roast whole spices in the oven for a few minutes before grinding them. This trick releases the essential oils.

Fish spatula: This handy, flexible, slotted spatula delicately turns fish without applying much pressure to the delicate flesh. It has a beveled edge that slides under the edge of the fish, and has enough flexibility to flip the fish over in one shot so you avoid overhandling it. (See Figure 2-9.)

Figure 2-9:
A fish
spatula is
handy for
turning
delicate
fish.

Food processor: A food processor has more uses than your average blender, such as dough-making, grinding, grating, slicing, shredding, chopping, blending, pureeing, julienning, and so on.

Hand blender: This tool is great to have around; it is economical and has many uses. You can use a hand blender to make emulsion sauces, such as mayonnaise, or you can puree soups and sauces right in the pot. A hand blender can also work overtime as a mini-bar blender. (See Figure 2-10.)

Figure 2-10:
You can
use a hand
blender to
make
sauces,
puree
soups, and
blend
drinks.

Juicer: With all the hype about power juice drinks, vegetable-juice sauces, and vegetable broths, having a juicer at home saves on the expense of purchasing pre-juiced products. Better yet, when you juice it yourself, the freshness is guaranteed.

Ladle (2 ounce): A small ladle works great with a chinois. It helps pass liquids or purees through the chinois without damaging the fine mesh.

Loaf pans: Loaf pans are a must for baking breads, pound cake, and brioche.

Mandoline: This tool can help make your life easier, or it can put you in stitches, depending on how careful you are. You can use a mandoline (shown in Figure 2-11) as a mini hand-held food processor to quickly julienne vegetables, slice them paper-thin, or slice up to $1/4$ inch thick, in precise cuts.

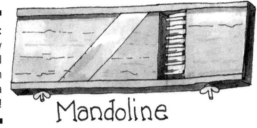

Figure 2-11: Be very careful when using a mandoline!

You need to be very careful when using a mandoline — people have been known to slice off the tips of their fingers with this razor-sharp slicing machine.

Mushroom brush: This small, soft brush is great for cleaning mushrooms. It brushes away any impurities without damaging the delicate mushrooms.

Oyster shucker: An oyster shucker, as shown in Figure 2-12, is a small knife with a beveled tip, designed specifically for opening oyster shells.

Parchment paper: Basically, parchment paper is a fancy wax paper that can bake in the oven without falling apart. Using parchment paper saves on cleanup — and it cuts out the need to grease pans, so you can eliminate some fat.

Figure 2-12: If you love oysters, you need an oyster shucker.

Pasta machine: Not a necessity, but if you want to impress your friends with homemade fresh pasta, these little machines are a must. Pasta machines come in small hand-crank versions (see Figure 2-13) and large electric versions. The small hand-crank ones work just fine in a home kitchen, as long as you're not making pasta for 30 hungry Italians.

Figure 2-13:
A pasta machine in action.

Pastry brush: A pastry brush is very helpful for brushing liquids, such as butter or egg, onto dough. You can also use a pastry brush to brush excess flour from doughs.

Pizza cutter: A pizza cutter is a sharp wheel on a handle, used for cutting pizza, doughs, or pasta sheets.

Reamer: A reamer is a handy tool for extracting the juice from lemons, limes, or oranges. (See Figure 2-14.)

Ricer: A ricer, also shown in Figure 2-14, resembles a large garlic press and is most commonly used to prepare cooked potatoes or turnips. You place the cooked potato or turnip in the container and push a lever-operated plunger down into the food, forcing it out through numerous tiny holes in the bottom of the container. The result is food that vaguely resembles grains of rice. A ricer works great for mashed potatoes to ensure no lumps.

Figure 2-14:
A reamer and a ricer.

Ring molds: Ring molds (shown in Figure 2-15) come in a variety of sizes, but generally the 2$\frac{1}{2}$- to 3-inch size is used most frequently. Ring molds are a necessity for making individual cakes, soufflés, or other desserts. They are also great for layering foods neatly for a restaurant presentation at home. Because the food is often cooked or held in the ring molds until just before serving, make sure to buy enough to complete the entire recipe (at least four to six ring molds, depending on the number of servings that you're preparing).

Figure 2-15:
Create individual desserts by using a ring mold.

ring mold

Rolling pin: You use a rolling pin for rolling doughs, puff pastry, or pasta. You can also use a rolling pin in a pounding fashion to tenderize meat or to threaten anyone who criticizes your cooking.

Round cutters: Cutters come in a variety of graduated sizes, from as small as $\frac{1}{2}$ inch to as large as 5 inches. (See Figure 2-16.) The small cutters are great for preparing bite-sized hors d'oeuvres — the larger ones to cut dough for individual tarts and pastries. You can purchase them individually, but I think it's better to buy a set that comes in a closed container — they're easier to keep track of that way.

cutters

Figure 2-16:
A variety of cutters.

Scissors: Kitchen scissors are great for cutting through poultry bones or for snipping herbs.

Silpat: A silpat is a rubbery sheet that fits perfectly onto a sheet pan; it is the ultimate nonstick surface. You could burn sugar on a silpat and peel it off easily with little effort. Silpats are great for drying fruit or making tuiles (those delicate, thin wafers), but you can use them for anything for which you would use a nonstick sheet pan. Silpats are hard to come by, so when you do find them, buy a couple; take care of them and you'll have them forever.

Small saucepans: A kitchen can never have enough small saucepans. They're great for making sauces, cooking small quantities of vegetables or beans, or heating up foods.

Slotted spoons: You use slotted spoons for removing solid foods from liquids. They're great for removing blanched herbs or cooked vegetables from the cooking water.

Springform pan: This pan, shown in Figure 2-17, is very handy to have for making tarts, cheesecakes, and cakes. It has a detachable bottom and a spring release so that you can remove the side piece easily without damaging the cake.

Figure 2-17:
You need a springform pan for making tarts and cheesecakes.

springform pan

Tart rings (small): Tart rings (see Figure 2-18) are a great way to jazz up your regular desserts. You can make mini apple pies or tarts with the same recipe that you use to make a large one. People are always impressed with individual desserts; the only trick is to make them smaller. I like the $^1/_2$-inch-high-x-3-inches-in-diameter size.

Figure 2-18:
Small tart rings are great for making mini tarts and pies.

tart ring

Terrine mold: These molds come in a variety of sizes and shapes, although they are most commonly found in rectangular shapes. (See Figure 2-19.) Traditionally, terrine molds are used for shaping mousse or pâté, but I like to use them to layer different foods, such as asparagus and goat cheese. After the food sets, you can remove the mold and slice the food for an interesting presentation.

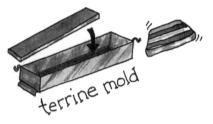

Figure 2-19: A terrine mold has many uses in gourmet cooking.

Thermometers: You can find two types of thermometers: meat thermometers (which usually go up to about 220 degrees), and candy thermometers (which go as high as 400 degrees). Meat thermometers are handy to determine the exact doneness of meat and poultry, but candy thermometers are a necessity for most candy-making. When making candy (which is a much more exact science), a temperature variation of as little as 5 degrees can mean the difference between chewy caramels and ones that crack your teeth.

Timbale: A timbale (shown in Figure 2-20) is a small, drum-shaped mold, about the size of an espresso cup. You can fill timbales with custards to create wonderful, individual desserts.

Zester: This tool is great for quickly removing the *zest* (the colored part of the skin) from citrus fruits. A zester (see Figure 2-21) cuts off only the zest, leaving the bitter white pith on the fruit.

Figure 2-20: Beat your dessert drum with a timbale.

Figure 2-21: You use a zester to remove the outer skin of citrus fruit.

Stocking Up with Staple Ingredients

Keeping your pantry stocked with frequently used ingredients makes it easier to be spontaneous in your cooking. Nothing is worse than getting an urge to try something new, only to find that you're missing a key ingredient. Most kitchens have some basic items, like eggs, milk, and butter. But the items I talk about in this section enable you to take the next step in cooking.

Pantry items

Everyone has their own version of staple pantry items. This list covers the basic items, but you can also add foods that you find yourself reaching for over and over.

- ✔ **Chocolate:** Cocoa powder, unsweetened chocolate, and semisweet chocolate are good to have on hand to use in desserts.

- ✔ **Dried beans:** Dried beans are very nutritious, and you can prepare them in a variety of ways. See Chapter 8 for more information.

- ✔ **Grains:** Grains (such as barley and quinoa) store well, are nutritious, and cook fairly quickly for last-minute meals. See Chapter 8 for more information.

- ✔ **Kosher salt:** Kosher salt is additive-free and coarse-grained. It leaves liquids clear, whereas table salt often causes liquids to become cloudy.

- ✔ **Oils:** Always have olive oil on hand. You should also have a neutral-flavored oil, like canola, grapeseed, or sunflower oil, for cooking and for making your own herb oils.

- ✔ **Onions:** It's always good to have a selection of red, yellow, and white onions for making stock and for general cooking.

- ✔ **Potatoes:** I generally keep several varieties of potatoes on hand: white baking potatoes, small red potatoes or *new* potatoes (known as A or B potatoes, depending on their size), and specialty potatoes, such as white rose, purple Peruvian, or fingerlings.

- ✔ **Shallots:** Shallots cost more than other onions, but they have a wonderful, sweet flavor that can make a world of difference in your cooking.

- ✔ **Sugar:** Keep a stock of confectioners' sugar and brown sugar on hand, as well as granulated sugar.

- ✔ **Vanilla beans:** Vanilla beans are essential for many desserts. There's no comparison between these fresh, intensely flavored beans and the extract.

- ✔ **Vinegars:** Balsamic vinegar, rice wine vinegar, and flavored vinegars can help accent sauces, create interesting vinaigrettes, or even decorate a plate. See Chapter 13 for more information on aged balsamic vinegar.

- ✔ **Wine:** A bottle or two of white, red, and port wines are nice to have for use in stocks and sauces.

Refrigerator and freezer items

You also need to have a good supply of fresh and frozen items. Unfortunately, fresh items usually have a short shelf life, so purchase only what you can use within a few days.

- ✔ **Carrots:** Carrots are too versatile not to have around. You can juice them, puree them, use them to flavor stocks, or just eat them raw.

- ✔ **Celery:** Celery is a staple ingredient for stock-making, and it's great to eat raw.

- ✔ **Cheese:** It's nice to have a selection of cheese for use in sauces and pasta or just for eating. See Chapter 17 for more information about different types of cheese.

- ✔ **Citrus fruits:** Citrus fruits are extremely versatile. You can use them on seafood, in salads, or in vinaigrettes. Citrus fruits are also used in desserts and in many different types of drinks. But best of all, they are available year-round and keep well in the refrigerator.

- ✔ **Garlic:** Fresh garlic goes with almost anything. Keep a supply of garlic around and cook with it often.

- ✔ **Hot sauce:** Hot sauce is great to have around to add flavor and spice to a dish. I usually have several bottles in my refrigerator. Inner Beauty makes a great line of sauces ranging from fairly spicy to knock-your-socks-off hot.

- ✔ **Lettuce:** I always keep *mesclun greens* (a mixture of various leafy greens) in my refrigerator. These greens are great to have handy to toss together a quick salad.

- ✔ **Seasonal fruits and vegetables:** No matter what the season, you should always have a selection of fresh fruits and vegetables available at home. Having plenty of fruits and vegetables around helps to make your cooking spontaneous and healthy. (See Chapter 4 for more about produce.)

- ✔ **Stocks and sauces:** Having a variety of stocks and sauces in your freezer is handy. Chicken, beef, and vegetable stock; beef reduction; and tomato sauce are good to keep on hand. See Chapter 5 for information about making your own stocks and sauces.

Making your own stocks and sauces is definitely worth your time. The canned versions are less flavorful and loaded with salt, so if you reduce a canned stock to thicken it, the end result can be as salty as soy sauce.

CHARLIE SAYS

Herbs

Herbs, the leafy part of aromatic plants, are an important part of gourmet cuisine. They add so much flavor and texture that I can't imagine cooking without them. But forget about the dried version and remember fresh, fresh, fresh. I can't emphasize enough the difference between fresh and dried herbs — there's just no comparison. For information about fresh herbs, see Chapter 5.

If you absolutely can't find fresh herbs, use the dried variety, but keep in mind that dried herbs are three times as strong as fresh. Adjust your amounts accordingly. Also, make sure that you use dried herbs within a couple months after opening them. After that, you may as well be using old grass clippings.

Spices

Spices come from the bark, fruit, seeds, or roots of aromatic plants. You should purchase spices in small quantities because they lose flavor over time. If spices are tightly sealed and stored away from excessive heat, they last about six months. Buy whole spices whenever possible and grind them yourself for the freshest flavor. You may want to keep the following spices in your spice rack:

- **Allspice:** This pea-sized berry has the flavor of cinnamon, nutmeg, and cloves.

- **Anise:** This small, annual plant is a member of the parsley family. Both the leaves and the seed have a distinctive, sweet licorice flavor.

- **Caraway:** These aromatic seeds come from an herb in the parsley family. Caraway seeds have a nutty, delicate anise flavor and are widely used in German, Austrian, and Hungarian cuisine.

- **Cardamom:** A member of the ginger family, this aromatic spice is native to India and grows in many other tropical areas, including Asia, South America, and the Pacific Islands. Cardamom has a pungent aroma and a warm, spicy-sweet flavor.

- **Cayenne:** A hot, pungent powder made from several of various tropical chili peppers that originated in French Guyana.

- **Celery seed:** The seed of a wild celery called *lovage* ("LUHV-age"), most of which comes from India. Celery seed has a strong flavor and should be used sparingly.

- **Chili powder:** Chili powder is one of the wonders that Christopher Columbus brought back from the New World. More than 200 varieties of chili peppers exist, over 100 of which are indigenous to Mexico. Their spiciness varies from mildly warm to mouth-blistering hot.

- **Cinnamon:** Cinnamon is the inner bark of a tropical evergreen tree. The bark is harvested during the rainy season, when it's more pliable. When dried, cinnamon curls into long quills, which are either cut into lengths and sold as cinnamon sticks, or ground into powder.

- **Cloves:** Considered one of the world's most versatile spices, cloves are the dried, unopened flower bud of the tropical evergreen clove tree.

- **Coriander:** Coriander (also known as *cilantro*) is related to the parsley family. Coriander is known for both its seeds and for its dark-green, lacy leaves. The flavors of the seeds and leaves bear absolutely no resemblance to each other. The seeds are mildly fragrant and have an aromatic flavor akin to a combination of lemon, sage, and caraway. The leaves have an extremely pungent odor and a flavor that lends itself well to highly seasoned food.

- **Cumin:** Shaped like a caraway seed, cumin is the dried fruit of a plant in the parsley family. Its aromatic, nutty-flavored seeds come in three colors: amber, white, and black. The amber and white seeds are very similar in flavor and can be used interchangeably, but the black is extremely pungent in flavor.

- **Curry powder:** A blend of spices containing turmeric, cinnamon, cardamom, cloves, nutmeg, mace, chilies, red and black pepper, and sesame seeds.

- **Dill seeds:** These tan, flat seeds are actually the dried fruits of the dill herb.

- **Fennel seeds:** The seeds come from common fennel. Fennel seeds are available whole and ground and are used in both sweet and savory foods.

- **Ginger:** The flavor of ginger is peppery and slightly sweet, while the aroma is pungent and spicy. This extremely versatile root has long been a mainstay in Asian and Indian cooking. Fresh ginger is available in two forms: young and mature. I use young ginger — it is very tender and has a milder flavor.

- **Juniper berries:** These astringent blue-black berries are native to both Europe and America. Juniper berries are too bitter to eat raw, so they are sold dried and are usually crushed before using, in order to release their flavor.

- **Mace:** This spice tastes and smells like a pungent version of nutmeg. Mace is the bright-red membrane that covers the nutmeg seed. After the membrane is removed and dried, it becomes yellow-orange in color.

Is it coriander, or is it cilantro?

Coriander or cilantro, that is the question. Unfortunately, no simple answer exists. The plant called *coriander* produces both leaves and seeds: The leaves are usually called *cilantro* and the seeds are called *coriander seeds*. Oftentimes, the leaves are referred to as *coriander* as well. And to make matters worse, some people call the seeds *cilantro*. The thing to remember here is that they are still just leaves and seeds, no matter what they're called. So look at the recipe, decide whether you want leaves or seeds, and purchase whatever the store calls them.

- **Mustard seed:** White and brown species of this spice are available. White mustard seeds are much larger than the brown variety, but a lot less pungent. White and brown seeds are blended to make English mustard, whereas brown mustard seeds are used for pickling.

- **Nutmeg:** This seed comes from the nutmeg tree, a tropical evergreen. The flavor and aroma are delicately warm, spicy, and sweet.

- **Paprika:** Paprika is a powder made by grinding certain sweet red pepper pods. The pods are quite tough, so several grindings are necessary to produce the proper texture. The flavor of paprika ranges from mild to pungent and hot. The color ranges from orange-red to deep blood-red.

- **Saffron:** Saffron is the yellow-orange stigma from a small purple crocus. It is the world's most expensive spice. Look for whole threads ($3/4$ inch) that are either bright red or yellow. (See Chapter 13 for more about saffron and to find out where to order saffron through the Internet.)

- **Star anise:** Star anise is a star-shaped, dark-brown pod that contains a pea-sized seed in each of its eight segments. Star anise comes from a small evergreen tree and has a pronounced licorice flavor that is slightly more bitter than that of regular anise seed.

- **Turmeric:** This spice is the root of a tropical plant related to ginger. It has a bitter, pungent flavor and an intense yellow-orange color. Turmeric is mainly used to add color to foods.

Grinding and crushing spices

You can break down spices in several ways:

- Grind them in a coffee grinder (but make sure to clean it out before and after you use it).

- Crush them with a mortar and pestle.

- Crush them with the flat side of a chef's knife.

Chapter 3

Getting Your Cooking Permit

· ·

In This Chapter

▶ Understanding cooking techniques

▶ Finding out about formal knife cuts

▶ Deciphering gourmet cooking terms

· ·

*U*nderstanding the terms used in gourmet cooking makes the difference between simply browsing a gourmet cookbook and actually being able to prepare a recipe you find in there. Cryptic instructions like "sauté the red onion until caramelized; chiffonade the basil; toss with the tomato concassé, brunoise of red pepper, and julienned daikon; and then place in a timbale," can send a novice running for the take-out menu faster than you can say *al dente.* Yet all these instructions really say is to "cook the onions until they are golden-brown; cut the basil into $^1/_{16}$-inch strips; toss with the peeled, seeded, and diced tomato; cut the red pepper into $^1/_8$-inch cubes; cut the daikon into $^1/_{16}$-inch-x-2-inch strips; then place them all in a small, drum-shaped mold."

Although some of the instructions in gourmet recipes may seem picky, they really are used for a reason. After you're familiar with the terms commonly used in gourmet cooking, using these terms is easier than specifically describing the techniques. For example, it's easier to say "blanch and shock the herbs" than it is to say "briefly plunge the herbs into boiling, salted water, and then immediately place the herbs in ice water."

Gourmet recipes are usually very specific about different sizes of cuts that you use on the ingredients because the recipes are trying to achieve a certain look and texture. Although these cuts generally don't affect the flavor, they do affect the appearance, texture, and cooking time of your recipe. For this reason, most recipes list the cooking time and the *desired result.* For example, a recipe may say, "Sauté the onion over medium heat for 3 to 4 minutes or *until translucent.*" The desired result (for example, a translucent onion) is always more important than the actual cooking time (because cut sizes and cooking temperatures may vary).

In this chapter, I describe the terms and techniques in detail to help you understand and tackle even the most complicated recipes with confidence.

Cooking Techniques

Understanding different cooking techniques is important for two reasons. First of all, it's hard to successfully complete a recipe for poached salmon if you have no idea what *poaching* means. But beyond that very basic reason, there is a relationship between cooking techniques, the expected result, and the best types of food to use. That probably sounds confusing, but all it means is that if you understand how a cooking technique works, you can choose the best foods to use with that method.

For example, if you are preparing salmon, you want to use a technique that enhances the delicate fish, such as grilling, broiling, or even smoking. But you *wouldn't* want to braise it or stew it because the salmon would disintegrate. Understanding these basic techniques is your first step on the way to becoming a gourmet cook.

Dry heat cooking methods

Dry heat cooking simply means that no liquid is added to either the food or the pan. Any fats or oils that you add during cooking are meant to add flavor and do not act as a cooking medium. The end result of the following cooking techniques is a highly flavored exterior and a moist interior.

- ✔ **Baking:** *Baking* cooks foods by surrounding them with hot, dry air. This technique is basically the same as roasting, except that you don't generally baste the food as you do when roasting.

- ✔ **Broiling:** You *broil* foods by using a heat source located above the food item. Broiling is a quick technique that is generally used for smaller pieces of meat or fish. You can broil almost any food, but delicate items (lean whitefish, for example) should be brushed with butter or a marinade to help keep them moist and to facilitate browning.

- ✔ **Grilling:** You *grill* foods by using a heat source located below the food. Grilled foods have a smoky, slightly charred flavor, resulting from the flaring of the juices and fats that render out as the item cooks. The drippings that would otherwise collect or reduce if you cooked in a sauté pan actually reduce directly on the grilled food's surface.

    You can use special woods such as grapevines, mesquite, hickory, or apple to introduce a specific flavor to your grilled foods. You can achieve similar results whether you use an inexpensive Smoky Joe or a high-tech barbecue pit. Also, keep your grill clean and brush the grilling rack with oil to help prevent foods from sticking.

- ✔ **Roasting:** *Roasting* is a technique that cooks foods by surrounding them with hot, dry air. Roasted foods are often basted during cooking. Meat should always be *seared* (or browned) first over direct heat or in a very

hot oven, and then elevated on a rack so that the hot air can reach all sides. Allow roasted items to *rest* (sit out on the counter for 15 to 20 minutes) before serving, in order to redistribute the juices evenly throughout the food.

Don't forget that the food continues to cook while it rests, so remove it from the oven just slightly underdone.

The juices from a roasting pan are very flavorful and make great gravy — just add a splash of water or wine to the pan to loosen the drippings (what gourmets call *deglazing*). See Chapter 5 for more information about gravies and sauces.

- **Smoking:** *Smoking* foods is easy and adds a lot of flavor. You can smoke foods on a grill, in a smoker, or even in a pan on your stovetop. You can use two different methods to smoke foods:

    - **Hot smoking:** Some of the wood chips have a red glow to them, which conducts heat and helps cook the item being smoked.

    - **Cold smoking:** Only smoke is present — no heat. You should be able to hold your hand above the wood chips and feel only slight warmth. This method does not completely cook the food — it only infuses it with a smoky flavor.

If you frequently smoke foods, you may want to purchase a small smoker or a grill with a smoking compartment so that you can grill and smoke at the same time.

Smokin' up the backyard

Converting a common backyard grill into a smoker is easy — just replace the coals with dry wood chips and light the chips. Then cover the dry chips with wet wood chips and close the lid. Use the wet chips to control the heat — fewer wet chips for a hot smoke, more wet chips for a cold smoke.

You can also smoke items right on your stovetop by placing the wood chips in the bottom of a deep pan, lighting them, putting the food on a rack above the chips, and covering with a tight lid.

Whether you use a grill or a pan on your stove, you need to check the smoker frequently to make sure that the smoke hasn't died out. Also, make sure that you have proper ventilation if you do this inside the house, or you'll have your smoke detectors blaring.

Dry heat cooking methods using fats and oils

The following cooking techniques are still considered *dry heat* methods even though they use fats or oils. Although oil pours freely at room temperature, it functions differently than liquids such as stock, milk, and water, and therefore it is not considered a liquid for cooking purposes. I know that's about as clear as mud, but thinking of the end result helps. Dry heat methods of cooking seal the outside of the food, locking in most of the juices, while moist heat methods keep the outside of the food tender and allow moisture to be retained in the food. The following dry heat methods use high heat, cook foods quickly, and are best when used with smaller, tender pieces of meat, poultry, or fish:

- **Sautéing:** *Sautéing* is a rapid method of cooking over high heat using a small amount of oil or other cooking medium. The key to successful sautéing is to heat the pan before adding the oil. This technique ensures a caramelizing effect, which sears the outside of the food. Sautéing is probably the most commonly used cooking method.

- **Stir-frying:** *Stir-frying* is similar to sautéing, except that the food is cut into small pieces and kept in constant motion during cooking. In a stir-fried dish, you fry all the ingredients quickly in the same hot pan, adding the various items at different times. You generally make the sauce in the same pan, also.

- **Pan-frying:** *Pan-frying* is similar to sautéing, except that you add a substantial amount of oil or clarified butter to the pan. Pan-fried foods are usually breaded or batter-coated. In pan-frying, the hot oil seals the food's coated surface and locks the natural juices inside instead of releasing the flavors.

You should allow pan-fried foods to brown completely on one side before you turn them — excessive turning causes the breading or batter to fall off.

- **Deep-frying:** When *deep-frying,* you cook the food by completely submerging it in hot fat. Deep-fried foods are often coated with flour, batter, or breading, which acts as a barrier between the fat and the food. The coating also adds flavor and a crunchy texture to the food.

Make sure that your oil is clean, or your food can pick up unwanted flavors from the oil. And before serving fried foods, always blot them on a paper towel to remove the excess oil.

Moist heat cooking methods

Moist heat cooking produces flavorful foods by cooking them in a liquid bath. Unlike dry heat methods, moist heat cooking doesn't form a seal on the food as it cooks, so some of the flavor can be lost into the liquid. For that reason, the cooking liquids that remain in the following methods are also often used as the base for a sauce to accompany the main item:

- **Braising:** In *braising,* you first sear the food in hot oil and then slowly cook it in a liquid (such as stock) that covers the food about one-half to three-quarters of the way. This technique is good for meats that are not extremely tender, such as pot roast, because slow-cooking in the liquid helps to tenderize the meat. The meat is done when it is *fork tender* or falls off the bone.

  During cooking, the meat releases its flavor into the cooking liquid, which you can then reduce to make a sauce. See Chapter 5 for more information on making reduction sauces.

- **Poaching:** *Poaching* is a technique that calls for a food to be completely submerged in a liquid and simmered (not boiled) at a constant, moderate temperature. Stocks, broths, and court bouillon work well as poaching mediums and add nice flavors. You can also infuse poaching liquids with herbs to flavor the food.

  You can easily turn poaching liquids into flavorful broths by reducing them to concentrate the flavor.

- **Steaming:** *Steaming* cooks the food by surrounding it with hot steam. The steam circulating around the food provides an even, moist environment that allows the food to retain most of its flavor and natural juices. You can add herbs, stock, beer, or wine to the liquid to add flavor during cooking.

- **Stewing:** *Stewing* is similar to braising, except that you cut the food into bite-sized pieces. In stewing, you first brown the meat and vegetables separately, and then you mix them together and cook them in the liquid.

Formal Knife Cuts

Formal knife cuts have very specific dimensions and shapes. Using these cuts is a simple but key way to upgrade an ordinary dish to a gourmet dish. A large part of gourmet cooking is visual, and using these precise cuts can make your dish look more interesting and appealing. (See Figure 3-1 for an illustration of these cuts.)

Figure 3-1:
Formal knife
cuts, shown
actual size.

✓ **Allumette:** $^1/_8$ x $^1/_8$ x 1 to 2 inches. An allumette is a "matchstick"-sized cut that gets its name from the French word for *match.*

✓ **Bâton (bâtonnet):** $^1/_4$ x $^1/_4$ x 2 to $2^1/_2$ inches. A bâton, from the French word meaning *small stick,* is a cut somewhat larger than an allumette.

✓ **Brunoise:** $^1/_8$ x $^1/_8$ x $^1/_8$ inch. A brunoise is a very precise, fine dice that is used primarily for vegetables.

- **Chiffonade:** Fine strips, about $1/16$ inch wide. Chiffonade comes from the French phrase meaning "made of rags." It is typically used in reference to leafy vegetables, such as lettuce or herbs, which are rolled up and finely sliced for use as a garnish.

- **Small dice:** $1/4$-inch cubes.

- **Medium dice:** $1/3$-inch cubes.

- **Large dice:** $3/4$-inch cubes.

- **Julienne:** $1/16$ x $1/16$ x 1 to 2 inches. This long, slender, rectangular cut is most often used to prepare foods as a garnish.

- **Paysanne:** $1/2$ x $1/2$ x $1/8$ inch. These thin squares resemble the tiles used in Scrabble. This cut is most often used on vegetables that garnish stews and soups.

- **Tourné:** 2 inches x 7 sides. Literally translated, this French word means *turning*. A tourné requires a series of cuts that trim and shape the vegetable into a long, thin, football-like shape.

Gourmet Cooking Terms

Understanding and using the terms in this section will take you to the next level in cooking. They are all commonly used in the food world, and they'll help you show off your expertise. So the next time you go out for dinner, you can tell the chef that his emulsion sauce broke and his ganache was grainy (and then run for it).

Al dente (pronounced "AHL DEN-tay") is an Italian phrase meaning "to the tooth." Food cooked al dente is soft, but not overcooked, and offers a slight resistance when you bite into it. It is most commonly used in reference to pasta, but vegetables can also be referred to as al dente.

Blanch and shock means to briefly plunge a food into boiling salted water and then immediately place the food in ice water to stop the cooking process, as shown in Figure 3-2. You can use this technique to loosen the skin of fruits such as peaches or tomatoes, or to heighten and set the color and flavor of herbs and greens.

A *bouquet garni* (pronounced "boo-KAY gar-NEE") is a combination of fresh herbs that are tied together and used to flavor soups, stews, or broths. Traditionally, a bouquet garni contains parsley, bay leaf, and thyme, but almost any herbs work well.

In cooking lingo, *break* means that a sauce separates. For example, when hollandaise breaks, it takes on a curdled appearance. A sauce usually breaks when it is exposed to too much heat.

Figure 3-2:
Blanching
and
shocking
can
heighten
the color of
herbs or
loosen the
skins of
vegetables.

To *brown* foods, quickly cook them over high heat until the surface of the food turns golden-brown. This technique gives your food (particularly meats) a nice brown color and a richer flavor.

Usually, *caramelizing* involves heating a food until its natural sugars liquefy and become a golden-brown syrup. Caramelizing also enhances vegetables by bringing out their natural sugars and adding a rich flavor. To caramelize vegetables, heat a sauté pan until it is very hot and add enough oil to coat the bottom of the pan. Place the vegetables in the pan, reduce to medium heat, and continue to cook, stirring occasionally, until the vegetables are golden-brown.

Chopping is a rough cut, as opposed to the formal cuts listed in the preceding section. You chop food into pieces when the appearance doesn't matter. Chopping is quick and works fine when the foods are used for their flavor and then discarded (or when the foods are to be mashed or pureed).

Clarified butter, or *drawn butter,* is unsalted butter with the water and milk solids removed. You prepare clarified butter by slowly melting the butter so that the water evaporates and the mild solids fall to the bottom of the pan. The clarified butter is then either spooned out of the pan or carefully poured out, leaving the milk solids behind. Because the milk solids are removed, clarified butter has a much higher *smoke point,* meaning that you can use it to cook at high temperatures without the butter burning or smoking.

Compound butter is a mixture of butter and flavoring ingredients. Compound butters are commonly made in sweet flavors (like honey butter or strawberry butter) and served with scones or biscuits. But I like to use them in savory dishes. An easy version that goes well with almost any dish is chopped herbs, shallots, and a little lemon juice combined with the butter. It is a very simple way to add richness and flavor to almost any dish.

Consommé is a clarified stock or broth. Traditionally, the stock or broth was clarified by using a combination of egg whites, protein (like ground meat or fish), and acid (such as tomatoes) that form a raft to trap the impurities. But it can also be clarified with just the egg white for a lighter-flavored consommé.

Court bouillon is a combination of water, seasonings, herbs, and usually an acid such as wine or vinegar. This bouillon is used as a poaching liquid for fish. The flavorings in the bouillon are absorbed into the fish as it cooks, resulting in a moist piece of fish with subtle herb flavors.

True *crème fraîche* (pronounced "krem fresh") is an unpasteurized, 30-percent cream that has been allowed to ferment and thicken naturally. It has a nutty, faintly sour flavor and a velvety rich texture. In the United States (where all commercial dairy products are pasteurized), crème fraîche is made with whipping cream and buttermilk.

Store-bought crème fraîche can be expensive, so make it at home by combining 1/2 cup of whipping cream with 1 tablespoon of buttermilk. Cover and let it sit out at room temperature for 8 to 24 hours or until it is very thick. Then stir it well, cover, and keep it in the refrigerator for up to 10 days. Crème fraîche is a classic combination with smoked salmon and caviar, but it goes equally well with fresh fruit or warm fruit desserts.

Curing is the process of preserving meat or fish. Curing originated before the advent of refrigeration, and was used to hold meat for longer periods of time. These days, curing is more often done for the flavors it provides. Foods can be *smoke-cured,* as with ham; *pickled,* as with herring; or *salt-cured,* as with salt cod.

Decant means to carefully ladle off the liquid substance from a container without disturbing the solids that have fallen to the bottom (which are then discarded). This term is commonly used in reference to wine, but it also applies when making flavored oils and vinegars.

Deglazing is the process of using a liquid such as wine, water, or stock to dissolve food particles and caramelized drippings left in a pan after roasting or sautéing. The food particles stuck to the bottom of the pan are loaded with flavor, and deglazing releases all that flavor into the liquid. The liquid is then used to make a gravy or sauce.

Devein means to remove the vein from foie gras or from the back of a shrimp. Shrimp are usually deveined for cosmetic reasons, but for foie gras, deveining is necessary because the veins can be very tough.

Dredging is the process of lightly coating foods with flour, bread crumbs, or corn meal. You dredge foods prior to frying to help give them a crispy texture and an even, golden-brown color.

A *duxelle* (pronounced "duck-SELL") is a mixture of finely chopped mushrooms, shallots, and herbs that are slowly cooked in butter until they form a thick paste. A duxelle can be used to flavor soups and sauces, or as a garnish.

An *emulsion* is a sauce that is formed when one substance is suspended in another. For example, in hollandaise sauce, melted butter is suspended in partially cooked egg yolks. Emulsions are particularly fragile because they are not a true mixture — if not handled properly, they can separate, or *break*.

The *fond* is the drippings and caramelized food particles from the bottom of a pan, used for color and flavor. These drippings are deglazed and used to make sauces and gravies. If you really want to impress your friends, just tell them that dinner will be ready as soon as you deglaze and reduce the fond (translation: make the gravy).

Ganache (pronounced "ga-NAHSH") is a combination of chocolate and whipping cream, which can be poured over cakes or tortes. The same mixture can be whipped and refrigerated and then used as a filling for cakes or scooped into balls to make truffles. Technically, after the mixture has been whipped, it is called *ganache soufflé,* but it is usually just called *ganache.*

Génoise (pronounced "jen-WAHS") is a rich, light cake with a texture that resembles a moist sponge cake. It is usually prepared in a very thin layer and then used in dessert preparations such as petit fours or cake rolls.

A *glace* (pronounced "glahss") is a stock or rémoulade that has been reduced to a syrup consistency that will coat the back of a spoon. A glace is typically used to add flavor and color to sauces.

Infuse means to add flavor to a liquid through steeping, as you do when you make tea. The item used to infuse the flavor (usually herbs or spices) doesn't actually stay in the liquid; it just gets left in long enough to impart the flavor and is then removed. Infusing herbs into a hot liquid, such as a sauce, is a very quick process, sometimes taking only a few seconds, whereas infusing a flavor into a cold liquid, such as vinegar, can take several weeks.

Juicing is the process of extracting the juice from fruits or vegetables. Hand juicers are fine for citrus fruits, but an electric kitchen juicer is most effective for other fruits and vegetables, such as apples, celery, or bell peppers.

Larding is inserting long thin strips of fat or other ingredients into a piece of fish or meat. This cooking technique is performed with a *larding needle,* which has a sharp tip and a long, hollow body into which you insert the strips of fat or other items. The needle is then pulled through the meat, leaving the strips inside. This technique was originally used as a way to add fat to a drier cut of meat, but it can also be used to combine two foods in an unusual way, such as tuna larded with anchovies.

Marinating is the process of allowing food to sit in a seasoned liquid. It is sometimes done to tenderize a tough cut of meat, but most often it's done to add flavor. Foods that are marinating need to be turned frequently to ensure an even distribution of flavors.

Resealable bags work great for marinating foods. Just put the food and the marinade right in the bag and seal it tight. When it's time to turn the food, you can just flip over the whole bag. And better yet, no cleanup — when you are finished marinating, you can just throw the bag away.

Mincing is another rough cut, meaning that it has no formal size require-ments. Mincing means to chop into very fine pieces.

Mirepoix (pronounced "meer-PWAH") is a mixture of chopped carrots, onion, and celery: 25 percent carrots, 50 percent onions, and 25 percent celery. Mirepoix is used for flavoring soups, sauces, or roasted meats. This mixture is usually discarded after cooking.

Pavé is the French word for "paving stone," or "cobblestone." In cooking, this term describes any layered preparation cut into a square or rectangle.

Pectin is a substance that's present in various ripe fruits and vegetables. You can use pectin to thicken jams, jellies, and preserves. Pectin works properly only when mixed with the correct balance of sugar and acid. It's available in two forms: liquid (usually made from apples) and dry (made from citrus fruits).

A traditional *quenelle* (pronounced "kay-NELL") is a three-sided, oval-shaped dumpling made of *forcemeats* (very finely ground meats). In modern cooking, a quenelle is thought of as a shape, not as the ingredient. It's often made with ice cream, sorbet, or other semi-soft foods and can be formed easily with two spoons. (See Figure 3-3.)

Preparing Quenelles

Figure 3-3:
A quenelle in the making.

fini!

A *raft* is a combination of egg whites, protein (ground meat or fish), and acid (tomatoes) that is used to clarify consommé. The ingredients rise to the surface, creating a semi-solid floating mass that traps the impurities. The raft is discarded after the consommé is clarified. A raft can also be made with just the egg white for a lighter-flavored consommé.

Reduce means to cook a liquid, such as a stock or broth, until the volume reduces due to evaporation. This process thickens the liquid and intensifies its flavors.

Rémoulade (pronounced "ray-moo-LAHD") is a sauce made by combining mayonnaise with various seasonings and herbs, such as mustard, anchovies, and chives. It is usually served chilled to accompany cold meats or shellfish.

Rendering is the process of melting animal fat over low heat so that it separates from any pieces of tissue. The fat is then strained through cheesecloth to remove any dark particles. The clear fat is used in sautéing or pan-frying.

Ribbon is a stage in mixing — when the whisk or beater is lifted out of the mixture, the mixture falls slowly back onto the surface, forming a ribbonlike pattern. Another way to test for the proper consistency is to draw a line in the mixture with your finger — if the line stays for a few seconds, you are at the ribbon stage. (See Figure 3-4.)

Roux (pronounced "roo") is a cooked combination of equal parts flour and fat, used to thicken liquids. See Chapter 5 for more information about roux.

A *sachet* is a combination of herbs and spices wrapped in cheesecloth and tied with string. Sachets can be added to soups or sauces to infuse flavors (and then are easily discarded).

Scoring is the technique of making shallow cuts in the surface of certain foods, such as meat or fish, which allows them to cook evenly.

Searing is the method of quickly cooking the exterior of meat or fish over high heat, which gives it color and adds richness to the flavor.

Ribbon Stage

Figure 3-4:
Ribbons mean it's ready.

when you lift the beater out of the mixture it forms a ribbonlike pattern!

or

Draw a line in the middle of the mixture with your finger. If it stays, you're at ribbon stage!

Skimming means to remove the fat and/or impurities from the top of a liquid. Skimming can be very important, particularly in making stocks and sauces, because the impurities can cloud the sauce.

Sweat means to cook a food slowly in an uncovered pan, over medium or low heat with very little fat, until the food is soft or translucent. This term also refers to your physical state 30 minutes before your dinner party starts.

Tempering is the process of slowly adding a hot liquid to a cold substance, while constantly whisking until the cold liquid is warm. This method is often used in preparing ice cream and custard; tempering prevents the egg yolks from curdling.

The word *terrine* is used to describe both a terrine mold and the food that has been prepared in the mold. To make things easier, I call the food a *terrine* and the mold a *terrine mold*. Terrine molds come in many shapes, but they are most commonly rectangular with removable sides (so that the food can be taken out of the mold without damaging the shape of the food). Terrines were traditionally made with pâté or mousses. In modern cooking, however, terrines are usually a combination of layered ingredients.

Tomato concassé is just the French way to say "peeled, seeded, and diced tomato." You can use tomato concassé in sauces or as a garnish. See Figure 3-5 for directions for making tomato concassé.

How to Peel, Seed, and Dice Tomatoes

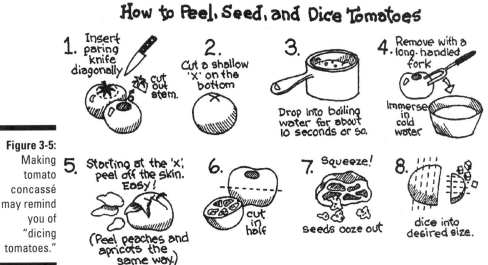

Figure 3-5:
Making tomato concassé may remind you of "dicing tomatoes."

A *tuile* (pronounced "tweel") is a thin, crispy wafer. Tuiles are often molded around a curved surface immediately after they come out of the oven, which gives them a shape resembling a curved tile. They can also be prepared as flat disks and used for layering foods.

A *water bath* is the method of placing one container into another water-filled container. A water bath can be used to quickly cool a food, such as a stock or sauce, by placing the smaller container into ice water held in the larger container. This technique allows the food to cool without directly touching the water. You can also use a water bath to ensure even heat distribution when preparing custards and baked puddings — simply bake the custard pan in a larger pan that contains about 1 inch of water.

The *zest* (no, I don't mean the soap) is the outer peel of a citrus fruit (minus the bitter white pith), which is grated or julienned.

Chapter 4

Surviving Your First Trip to the Produce Market

. . . .

In This Chapter

▶ Discovering different varieties of fruits and vegetables

▶ Selecting the freshest fruits and vegetables

▶ When you're hot, you're hot! A guide to hot peppers

. . . .

*U*sing fresh ingredients at the peak of their season is one of the keys to successful gourmet cooking. With the advances that have been made in the agricultural and transportation industries, many fruits and vegetables are now available year-round. But beware! Just because a fruit or vegetable is available doesn't mean that it's worth buying.

Some produce just doesn't seem to have the same flavor when you buy it out of season. Fruits are the best example of this, particularly berries and stone fruits. Have you ever bought peaches in the middle of the winter, only to find that they were dry and flavorless? With some produce, it's better to wait for it to come back in season. Plus, the anticipation seems to make that first bite of a ripe, juicy peach taste even better.

Shopping for fresh produce can be overwhelming the first few times you do it, but you can master the art in a very short time. You can use the following information to determine what types of produce are best for each purpose and when it's best to buy them.

Fruits

Fruits are great for eating as a snack or for making different desserts, but don't get stuck within those traditional boundaries: Expand your horizons and incorporate fruits into your main dishes as well. Fruit can go with almost any meat or seafood; try using a tropical fruit salsa on grilled shrimp, for example. Or how about apple-fennel relish over roast pork? Or fig, raisin, and thyme chutney with lamb chops?

The recipes for all those fruit accompaniments are in Chapter 6. They can give you a good start, but don't stop there. Use the information in this section to help you pick out the freshest fruits and then let your imagination go wild. You will soon be able to come up with some amazing combinations of your own.

Apples

The first American orchard was planted on Beacon Hill, overlooking Boston Harbor, in the early 1600s. Ever since, apples have become, well, "as American as apple pie." The scent of apples, whether it be in the form of baked apple pie, apple spice fragrance, or a mug of mulled cider, has been known to relax people.

After being picked, apples are stored in sealed rooms filled with nitrogen and kept at a temperature of 32 to 34 degrees. This storage method slows the natural ripening process, enabling many apples to be shipped at peak condition throughout the year. The best apples are firm and bright in color, with no bruises or dark spots.

Following are ten common varieties of apples:

- **Fuji:** Yellow-green to orange, mildly sweet, with crisp flesh. Fujis are great for eating but are available only in October.
- **Gala:** These apples are yellow with red highlights, sweet, juicy, and excellent for eating. They are available during the month of August.
- **Golden Delicious:** Sweet, semi-firm, with crisp, white flesh, they are great for cooking and eating. Golden Delicious apples are speckled yellow-green and are available year-round.
- **Granny Smith:** These apples are bright green, tart, and very juicy. They cook and bake well and are available year-round.
- **Jonathan:** Bright red, with sweet flesh and chewy skin. They are good for eating and baking and are available from September through July.
- **McIntosh:** Can be purchased in shades of red or green. McIntosh apples are juicy and tend to bruise easily. They make great applesauce but are available only in September and October.
- **Red Delicious:** Mildly sweet and crunchy; great for eating. They are bright red and easily identified by the five knobs at the blossom end. They are available year-round and are America's favorite eating apple.
- **Rome Beauty:** These dark-red, pungent apples have mealy flesh. They are good for baking and are available from September through July.

- **Stayman:** Bright red, aromatic, and crisp, with a rich flavor. They are good for cooking and are available in October.
- **Winesap:** Dark red, fragrant, juicy apples with a lot of flavor. They make great cider and are available from August through October.

Apricots

Apricots were found in China as early as 2500 B.C. They were brought to Europe through the Far East and the Mediterranean, which is probably why they are used heavily in Moroccan and Persian cuisine. Apricots were among the first fruits planted in Southern California in the 18th century, and California is now one of the major producers of apricots. Fresh apricots have a flavor that is entirely different from that of the dried fruit. They should be golden-yellow in color and feel firm and plump. Avoid buying apricots that are soft or shriveled. Apricots are available from May to August.

Avocados

Avocados vary widely in weight, texture, color, shape, and skin thickness. Whatever type you buy, look for fruit that yields to light pressure from your palm. Avoid avocados that have dark, soft, sunken spots on their skin or appear bruised. You can ripen underripe avocados in a paper bag at room temperature.

After cutting open an avocado, coat the exposed flesh with lemon or lime juice to retain its gold-green color.

The two most common types of avocados are

- **Fuerte:** Smooth, slightly mottled, thin green skin and creamy flesh. Fuerte avocados are available from October to March.
- **Hass:** Pear-sized, with rough, pebbly skin that turns from green to black when ripe. This is the most popular type because of its creamy flesh. Hass avocados are available year-round.

Avocados are one of the only fruits that contain more than a trace amount of fat. They can have up to 25 percent monosaturated fats (the "good" kind) when they are mature.

Bananas

Bananas are the least expensive and most popular fruit on the market. Every year, Americans eat more than 25 pounds of bananas per capita. Bananas are one of only two fruits that are better ripened off the tree. They are shipped green and ripen domestically before arriving at your store. Ripe bananas are bright yellow in color; the more yellow the skin, the sweeter the fruit. You can purchase bananas while they are still green and let them ripen at home. Bananas can be stored in the refrigerator to delay ripening; the skin turns brown, but the flesh remains firm.

Berries

Fresh berries are a great treat during the spring and summer months. They are juicy and delicious and can be used in many ways. You can use them for fresh fruit desserts, in salads, or in juice drinks; bake them into cobblers or tarts; or make them into jelly or jam — the possibilities are endless. But no matter what you plan on doing with them, make sure to buy extra because it's hard to resist popping the little beauties right into your mouth.

Look for berries that are firm, plump, and full-colored. Strawberries are the only berry that should have a hull attached; every other berry should be free of hulls when ripe. Whatever variety you buy, plan to use your berries quickly, because they have a very short shelf life.

Berries last longer when you keep them refrigerated in a single layer. Stacking them causes the fruit to become soft and mushy.

Many berries are available year-round. When bought out of season, however, they may look ripe, but they taste about as good as last week's movie popcorn.

- **Blackberries:** Large, long, dark reddish-black berries that are available from mid-May to July.
- **Black currants:** Firm, thick-skinned black berries that are good for cooking. Black currants are available from June to August.
- **Blueberries:** Small, round blue berries that are available from May through August.
- **Boysenberries:** Large, long, dark reddish-black berries that are slightly acidic. Boysenberries are available from June to August.
- **Cranberries:** Firm, round, plump red berries with a tart flavor. They are available from September to January.

✔ **Elderberries:** Very small black berries, generally used in cooking and wine-making. Elderberries are available in June and July.

✔ **Gooseberries:** Small, light-amber-colored berries. They are available from May to August.

✔ **Loganberries:** Large, long dark red berries that are high in acid and flavor. They are available in June and July.

✔ **Raspberries:** Come in red, black, golden, and apricot-colored varieties. They are available year-round but are best from June to September.

✔ **Red currants:** Firm, thin-skinned red berries. They are available from June to August.

✔ **Strawberries:** Small to large red berries. They are available year-round but are best from mid-April to mid-July.

Carambolas (star fruit)

When cut crosswise, this fruit has a star shape. It is a waxy, yellow, five-sided fruit with edible skin. Carambolas (see Figure 4-1) favor tropical climates and range from 3 to 5 inches in length. When ripe, the carambola is exceedingly juicy and fragrant. Its flavor can range from exotically sweet to refreshingly tart. In general, the broader set the ribs, the sweeter the fruit. They are available from summer's end to mid-winter. Choose firm fruit that have a bright, even color and leave them at room temperature until you can smell their floral-fruity perfume. Carambolas are great in fruit or vegetable salads because they don't discolor when exposed to the air.

Figure 4-1: Carambolas are also known as star fruit.

carambola

Cherimoyas (custard apples)

Cherimoyas originated in the highlands of South America. They are thought to be the earliest recorded New World fruit. This large, tropical fruit tastes like a delicate combination of pineapple, mango, and strawberry. Cherimoyas are heart-shaped with gray-green skin, indented all over, as shown in

Figure 4-2. The flesh is creamy white with shiny black seeds. Cherimoyas are available from November through May. Purchase fruit that is heavy for its size and without blemishes; avoid those with brown splotches. Store at room temperature until ripe and then refrigerate. You can cut cherimoyas in half and eat them right out of the shell; for something different, try pureeing them and adding them to a custard.

Figure 4-2: Cherimoyas taste like a combination of pineapple, mango, and strawberry.

Cherries

Two kinds of cherries exist: the sweet varieties that people love to eat by the handful, such as Bing cherries, and the tart, sour cherries that are great for jams and pies. Whether sweet or tart, cherries ripen fast and their season is short, so take advantage when they are in season. Look for cherries that are firm with no bruising.

Michigan is the leading producer of tart cherries, with 75 percent of the nation's crop coming from the five-county area around Traverse City. The region yields up to 80 million pounds of fruit annually.

Sweet cherries

The most common sweet cherry varieties are

- ✔ **Bing:** Large, firm, juicy, and sweet; almost black when fully ripe. Bing cherries are the leading commercial variety and are available from mid-June to mid-August.

- ✔ **Lambert:** Dark red, heart-shaped, slightly smaller than Bing, with a firm texture and rich flavor. Lamberts are available from late June to mid-August.

- ✔ **Rainier (Royal Anne):** These beauties are large and golden yellow-colored with a thin skin. Their plump, juicy sweetness makes them the cream of the crop, but they are in short supply because they are very fragile. They are available from late June to early August.

- ✔ **Van:** A lot like Bing, red to dark red, with a sweet, juicy flavor. Van cherries are available from mid-June to mid-August.

Tart cherries

These are the most common tart cherry varieties:

- ✔ **Early Richmond:** Dark red, round, medium to large, juicy, and considered good for canning or baking only. They mature in early June.
- ✔ **English Morello:** Dark red, medium to large, juicy, and considered good for canning or baking only. They are harvested in mid-July.
- ✔ **Montmorency:** Light to dark red, medium to large, and very juicy. The Montmorency is the most popular sour cherry variety because it can also be eaten fresh. This cherry is available in July.

Citrons

This semi-tropical citrus fruit looks like a huge 6- to 9-inch-long yellow-green lumpy lemon. (See Figure 4-3.) Citron pulp is very sour and is not suitable for eating raw. This fruit is grown instead for its very thick peel, which is candied and used for baking.

Figure 4-3:
Citrons are
used for
their peel.

citron

Coconuts

Coconuts are often called the king of tropical fruits because of their versatility. According to an old South Seas saying, "He who plants a coconut tree plants vessels and clothing, food and drink, a habitation for himself, and a heritage for his children." Although most Americans don't wear coconut clothing or live under coco palms, we do enjoy many of the uses of coconuts. Coconut is used in savory foods, sauces, puddings, desserts, and even oil.

Look for coconuts that are heavy for their size and have milk sloshing around inside. Nuts that have moldy or wet "eyes" or no sloshing sound are probably spoiled.

To open a fresh coconut, pierce the three soft spots with a sharp object and drain the juice, and then tap all over with a hammer until the hard shell falls off.

Dates

Dates have thin, papery skin and very sweet, sticky flesh. Fresh dates are yellow, golden brown, or black; but dates are more commonly sold semi-dried, which are brown. Dried and semi-dried dates are available year-round.

Date palm trees can take up to 5 or 6 years to produce fruit, but once they start, they can produce up to 150 pounds of fruit per year for up to 80 years.

Figs

Figs were one of the first fruits; they were growing before recorded history. Many different types of figs exist, but the following four main varieties are sold in the United States:

- ✔ **Black Mission:** Medium to large, with skin that is almost black when fully ripe. They are available from July to September.
- ✔ **Brown Turkey:** Medium to large and pear-shaped, with brownish-purple skin and red flesh. They are available from mid-May to December.
- ✔ **Calimyrna:** Large, with greenish-yellow skin and a very sweet, some-what nutty flavor. They are available from June to September.
- ✔ **Kadota:** Large and pear-shaped, with green or yellow-green skin and juicy, violet-tinted flesh. They are available from June to September.

Fresh figs are good for salads, cooking, and just eating out of hand. Look for fruits that have even coloring, are soft to the touch, and have a sweet aroma. You can detect overripe figs by their sour odor, caused by the fermentation of the juice.

Grapefruit

Grapefruit is a tropical citrus fruit that grows in great abundance in Arizona, California, Florida, and Texas. Its name comes from the fact that the fruit grows in grapelike clusters. Two main categories of grapefruit exist: seeded and seedless. Fresh grapefruit is available year-round.

Choose grapefruit that have thin, fine-textured, brightly colored skin. They should be firm yet springy when held in the palm and pressed. The heavier they are for their size, the juicer they are. Do not store grapefruit at room temperature for more than a day or two. Grapefruit keeps in the refrigerator for up to two weeks when wrapped in a plastic bag and placed in the crisper.

- ✔ **Pink:** Similar to a Ruby Red, but with lighter-colored skin and flesh
- ✔ **Ruby Red:** Large, smooth yellow-pink skin with pink or red flesh that is juicy and sweet
- ✔ **White:** Large, usually seedless, with smooth, yellow skin and white to light-yellow flesh that is tart and sweet

Grapes

Grapes are one of the oldest known plants. In fact, grapes are known to have been around for 2 million years. They have been a popular fruit throughout the centuries and are grown in large quantities in the United States. They are divided into four major groups: table, raisin, wine, and juice. Table grapes come in three different varieties: red, white, and Concord. Red and white grapes are generally seedless and are used for eating fresh and for salads. Concord grapes are generally used for cooking and jams. Look for bunches that are well-formed and have even coloring. Fully ripened grapes are soft to the touch. White and red grapes are available year-round, but Concords are available only in early fall.

Guavas

Many varieties of guavas exist (see Figure 4-4). Guavas can range in size from that of a small egg to that of a medium apple. Typically, the fruit is oval in shape and 2 inches in diameter. The flesh can range from pale yellow to bright red. Some guavas taste of pineapple, and others of strawberry, but they all should have a full, fruity, perfumey aroma when ripe. Choose guavas that give to gentle pressure but have not yet begun to show spots. You can ripen guavas at room temperature, but refrigerate them after they are ripe. Guavas can be eaten out of hand, added to custards or ice cream, or used as a sauce for poultry or pork.

Guava's strong aroma is not surprising, considering its family tree. It is a member of the myrtle family, which is full of aromatic plants such as clove, allspice, eucalyptus, and the bay rum tree.

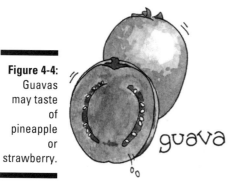

Figure 4-4:
Guavas
may taste
of
pineapple
or
strawberry.

Kiwi fruit

Kiwis have gained a tremendous following in recent years. They are great for salads, compotes, or eating fresh. Kiwis have more vitamin C than oranges, as much potassium as bananas, more vitamin E than avocados, and more dietary fiber than most cereals — yet they contain only about 45 calories per kiwi.

For the best eating, look for fruit that is soft to palm pressure. You can ripen kiwis at room temperature and then refrigerate them for a longer life. Kiwis are available year-round.

Kumquats

The name *kumquat* comes from the Cantonese word for "golden orange," which perfectly describes this fruit's color. Kumquats look like tiny, oval oranges (see Figure 4-5) and have an edible rind that is sweet, while the pulp is very sour. Look for firm fruit with good color and no blemishes. Kumquats are available from November to March. You can use kumquats as a flavoring in sauces, in relishes and salsas, or even candied.

Figure 4-5:
Kumquats
look like
very tiny,
oval-shaped
oranges.

Lemons

Throughout the years, lemons have been used for a multitude of nonculinary purposes, such as for toothpaste, for invisible ink, and as a bleaching agent. Lemons can range in size from that of a large egg to that of a small grapefruit. Some lemons have thin skins, and others have thicker skins; they are all equally good.

Lemons are available year-round, with a peak season during the summer months. Choose fruits with smooth, brightly colored skin with no tinge of green (which signals underripeness). Lemons should be firm, plump, and heavy for their size. You can refrigerate them in a plastic bag for up to ten days. Two main types are available:

- **Lisbon:** Has a pointy knob opposite the stem side. Lisbons are seedless, with shiny yellow skin and very acidic juice.
- **Meyer:** Large, with golden thin skin and sweet juice. A Meyer is a cross between a tangerine and a lemon.

Limes

Limes originated in tropical Asia and continue to grow in tropical and subtropical climates. Look for brightly colored, smooth-skinned limes that are heavy for their size. Small brown areas known as *scald* on the skin don't affect flavor or succulence, but hard or shriveled skin does. Limes are available year-round. They come in two main varieties:

- **Key:** Small and round, with lighter-green skin and slightly sweet flesh
- **Persian:** Small, with dark green skin and highly acidic juice

Lychees

The lychee has been one of China's cherished fruits for over 2,000 years. Lychees have a rough, bright-red shell and smooth, aromatic, juicy, white flesh inside. (See Figure 4-6.) Their flavor is sort of a combination of sweet grapes and roses. Lychees are available from June to about mid-July. Choose those with brightly colored skins, free of blemishes. You can store them in the refrigerator in a plastic bag for up to a week. Lychees are great eaten right out of the shell, but they can also be added to sauces or salads for an interesting flavor twist.

Mangoes

The mango tree is considered sacred in India, the land of the fruit's origin. The mango's skin is tough and green and turns to yellow and red as it ripens. The flesh is golden-yellow and very juicy. Because the seed is so oversized, the larger the fruit, the higher the fruit-to-seed ratio. Look for full, firmish fruit with taut skin and a slight perfumey aroma at the stem end. Allow mangoes to completely ripen at room temperature before eating, or they can be so stringy you can floss your teeth with them. Mangoes are in season from May to September.

Melons

Melons grow on vines and need warm weather and plenty of water. Two main kinds of melons exist: muskmelons and watermelons.

A ripe watermelon responds with an echo when thumped with a thumb. For all the rest, look for melons that have the correct color and skin characteristics for the variety you are buying. They should have a rich aroma and be slightly soft at the blossom end. A slight rattling of seeds when you shake the melon is a sign of maturity, but if the seeds feel loose and watery, the melon is on its way out. Unripe melons ripen at room temperature, but after a melon is ripe or you cut into it, you should refrigerate it.

Melons can be grown inside molds; people form them into pyramids, squares, and other intriguing shapes. Following are some common types:

- ✔ **Cantaloupe:** Golden or light greenish-gray skin with yellow netting, and juicy, golden-orange flesh. Available year-round.

- ✔ **Casaba:** Large and oval-shaped, with pale yellow, slightly ridged skin and creamy white, moderately sweet flesh. Available from July to September.

- ✔ **Crenshaw:** Very large, with light or golden-yellow rind and golden to peachy-pink, spicy-sweet flesh. Available from July to September.

- ✔ **Honeydew:** Very large with smooth, cream-colored skin and pale green flesh. Available year-round.

- ✔ **Persian:** Gray-green, finely netted skin and firm, deep-orange flesh. Available from July to September.

- ✔ **Watermelon:** Very large, with a thick rind and pale, dark, or mixed green-hued skin and deep-red or yellow flesh. Available year-round.

Nectarines

Nectarines are one of the oldest known fruits; in fact, the word *nectarine* comes from the Greek *nektar,* which in mythology is the "drink of the gods." They come from the same family (rosaceae) as peaches, plums, cherries, apricots, and almonds. In recent years, nectarines have been cross-bred with peaches to increase their size and firmness, which is probably why people think of them as fuzzless peaches.

Because most newer varieties of nectarines have a full, red color before they are mature, color is not a good indication of ripeness. Look for round, shiny, plump fruit that is firm to palm pressure. Avoid hard, dull, or slightly shriveled fruit because it was probably immature when picked. Nectarines are available from mid-spring to late September.

Oranges

Fresh oranges are available year-round. Oranges can be stored at cool room temperature for a day or so, but they should then be refrigerated, where they can be kept for up to two weeks. Oranges are an excellent source of vitamin C.

After an orange is cut or squeezed, the vitamin C quickly begins to dissipate. After only 8 hours at room temperature (or 24 hours in the refrigerator), oranges lose 20 percent of their vitamin C.

The weight of a citrus fruit is indicative of its juice content, so choose fruit that is firm and heavy for its size, with no mold or spongy spots. Unfortunately, because oranges are sometimes dyed with food coloring, a bright color isn't necessarily an indicator of quality. Regreening sometimes occurs in fully ripe oranges, particularly with Valencias. Rough, brownish spots on the skin don't affect flavor or quality, either. Common orange varieties are

- ✔ **Blood:** Medium-sized with few seeds, orange-red skin, and dark red flesh that is tangy and juicy. They are available from December to April.

- ✔ **Navel:** Large, seedless, with bright orange, thick skin that is easy to peel. They are available year-round.

> ✔ **Valencia:** Medium-large, usually seedless, with yellow-orange, often green-tinged thin skin. They are known for their juice and are available year-round.

Contrary to popular belief, oranges were not named for their color; they were named for their fragrance — which leads to the question: How did they know that it smelled like an orange?

Papayas

Papayas range in size from 1 to 20 pounds and are available year-round. When ripe, they have vivid golden-yellow skin. Their sweet flesh can be yellow or strawberry-orange. The center of the papaya is filled with shiny, grayish-black seeds. Though the peppery seeds are edible, they are generally discarded. Slightly green papayas can be ripened at room temperature in a paper bag. They should be refrigerated once they are ripe, and you should use them quickly. Ripe papayas start to lose their fragile flavor in only a day or two.

Passion fruit

Passion fruits are small and round, about 2 inches in diameter. (See Figure 4-7.) When ripe, they have dimpled, deep-purple skin and soft, golden flesh, generously punctuated with tiny, edible black seeds. The flavor is an intense, sweet-tart combination of jasmine, honey, and lemon, and the fragrance is tropical and perfumey. Passion fruit is available from March through September. Choose large, heavy, firm fruit with a deep amber color. Because it has such a strong perfume and so little pulp, passion fruit works best as a flavoring agent. It can be used to flavor custards, mousses, or even sorbet.

Figure 4-7:
Passion fruit has an intense, sweet-tart flavor.

Peaches

Peaches are one of Americans' most-loved fruits. Literally hundreds of different varieties are available, and new and better varieties are being introduced every year. Peaches come in two different types:

- **Clingstone:** These peaches have a pit that clings to the flesh. Clingstones have slightly firmer flesh and are generally used for canning (thus the cans of *cling* peaches you find at the store).

- **Freestone:** These peaches have a pit that separates easily from the flesh. Freestones are typically eaten out of hand.

Chances are that the peaches at your local market are freestones, but it doesn't really matter. Both types are fine for eating and cooking. More often than not, stores label peaches by where they come from, such as Georgia peaches, rather than by type or variety. The only truly important thing is — is it ripe? Look for very fragrant fruit that yields to palm pressure. Avoid peaches that have soft spots or greening. Peaches are available year-round, but are usually best during the summer months.

Pears

Pears are usually picked before they are fully ripe. But you can't depend on color to tell you when a pear is ripe. Bartletts turn from green to yellow. Some red varieties turn from dark red to bright red, but others remain dark red. Winter pears such as Anjou, Bosc, or Comice change very little or not at all. So how do you tell whether a pear is ripe? Gently apply pressure with your thumb near the base of the stem. If it yields slightly, it's ripe. After your pear is ripe, eat it the same day or store it in the refrigerator.

You can ripen a pear by placing it in a paper bag and letting it stand at room temperature.

Here are the most widely available types of pears:

- **Anjou:** Egg-shaped, with mild, spicy-flavored flesh that is very juicy. Available from October to June.

- **Asian:** Round, with pale-yellow skin and crisp, white flesh. Available from November to April.

- **Bartlett:** Bell-shaped, yellow when ripe, with white, juicy, full-flavored flesh. Available from August to December.

- **Bosc:** Long, tapered neck with slightly rough, golden-brown skin and creamy flesh. Available from October to June.

- ✔ **Comice:** Short-necked with yellow-green skin, sometimes with a pink blush, and very sweet flesh. Available from October to June.

- ✔ **Forelle:** Small and bell-shaped, with crimson-speckled, yellow skin and sweet, juicy flesh. Available from February to September.

- ✔ **Nelis:** Small, light-green skin with brown russeting and sweet, flavorful flesh. Available from October to June.

- ✔ **Red Bartlett:** Bell-shaped, with crimson skin and white, juicy, full-flavored flesh. Available from August to December.

- ✔ **Seckel:** Small, with skin that has a blush of dark red and sweet flesh. Available from August to January.

Pears were nicknamed *butter fruit* in the early 1700s due to their soft, melting flesh.

Pears should be fully ripe when used in salads or when eaten raw. However, when cooking pears, choose fruit that is firm and slightly underripe.

Persimmons

When ripe, the persimmon (see Figure 4-8) has smooth, red-orange skin and flesh. The flesh has a creamy texture and a tangy, sweet flavor that is sort of a cross between a plum and a pumpkin. You should eat persimmons only when they are fully ripe: plump and soft, but not mushy (they ripen at room temperature). Unripened, this fruit tastes like bad leather and leaves a tingly, acidic feel in your mouth. Persimmons don't handle cooking well — they tend to get tough and tasteless, so eat them out of hand or in salads. Or you can puree them as a sauce for cakes or puddings. They are available in late fall and early winter.

Figure 4-8: Persimmons are available in late fall and early winter. Eat them only when they're fully ripe.

persimmon

Pineapples

Pineapples were named for their pinecone shape and appearance. They are universally popular for desserts, salads, and eating fresh. Choose fruit that is plump, fresh-looking, and as large as possible. Fresh, deep-green crown leaves are a good sign, but contrary to popular belief, the ease with which you can pull out these leaves is not necessarily a sign of quality. Pineapples are available year-round.

Raw pineapple contains the enzyme *bromelin*, which breaks down protein. Because protein is found in gelatin, don't use pineapple in gelatin-based dishes — the gelatin will not set.

Plantains

Plantains are a relative of bananas, although they are longer and wider than bananas, with thicker skin. These fruits are starchy and less sweet than their relatives and are generally used only for cooking. Look for plantains that are brown or almost black to get them at their ripest and sweetest. They are available year-round. Try plantains thinly sliced and fried like potato chips or cut in chunks and added to soups or stews.

Plums

Hundreds of plum varieties are cultivated throughout the world. They all grow in clusters and have smooth, deeply colored skin and a center pit. Plums can range in shape from oval to round, and in size from 1 to 3 inches in diameter. Plum varieties, like peaches, are either *clingstone* or *freestone,* depending on the ease with which you can pull the flesh away from the stone. Choose firm plums that give slightly to palm pressure. Avoid those plums with skin blemishes, such as cracks, soft spots, or brown discoloration (which indicates sunburn). A very firm plum may be stored at room temperature until slightly soft.

Following are the plum varieties you may see at your store:

- **Damson:** Purple-skinned, with purple flesh and a tart flavor; good for cooking. Available from mid-July to September.

- **El Dorado:** A deep-red-skinned clingstone with sweet, red flesh. Available from late June to early September.

- **Elephant Heart:** A blackish-red-skinned clingstone with sweet, red flesh. Available from mid-July to September.

- **Friar:** A blackish-red-skinned clingstone with sweet, yellow flesh. Available from late July to late September.

- **Italian prune:** A purple-skinned freestone with sweet, amber-green flesh. Available from late July to September.
- **Kelsey:** A green-golden-skinned clingstone with sweet, yellow flesh. Available from mid-July to late September.
- **Santa Rosa:** Red-skinned clingstones with sweet, yellow flesh. Available from early June to late August.

Pomegranates

Pomegranates are about the size of a large orange and have thin, leathery skin that can range in color from red to pink-blushed yellow. Inside are hundreds of seeds packed in compartments that are separated by bitter, cream-colored membranes. The red pulp that surrounds each edible seed has a sparkling, sweet-tart flavor. This fruit is available in October and November. Choose pomegranates that are heavy for their size and have a bright, fresh color and blemish-free skin. They can be refrigerated for up to three months.

Pomegranates are one labor-intensive fruit, and certainly are not a fruit for the impatient. Removing the pulp-encased seeds from the bitter membrane is a very laborious process. But once they are cleaned, pomegranates are great for eating out of hand or as a garnish for salads.

Pomelos

These giant citrus fruits, shown in Figure 4-9, are native to Malaysia. They range from cantaloupe-size to as large as 25 pounds. Pomelos have a very thick, soft rind that varies in color from yellow to pale yellowish-brown to pink. The light-yellow to coral-pink flesh varies from juicy to slightly dry and from seductively spicy-sweet to tangy and tart. Choose fruit that is heavy for its size, blemish-free, and sweetly fragrant. You can use pomelos in the same ways you use grapefruit.

Figure 4-9:
Pomelos
are huge
fruits that
you use in
the same
ways
you use
grapefruit.

Prickly pears (cactus pears)

This barrel-shaped fruit, shown in Figure 4-10, is about the size of a large egg with prickly skin that can range in color from green to purplish-red. The soft flesh is scattered with black seeds and can range from light yellow-green to garnet red. They have a melon-like aroma and are rather mild in flavor. Choose fruit that gives slightly to palm pressure and has a deep, even color. Prickly pears are available from fall through spring and can be used in salads with other soft fruits or pureed for a sauce or sorbet.

Figure 4-10:
Prickly
pears are
rather mild
in flavor.

Quinces

This yellow-skinned fruit looks and tastes like a cross between an apple and a pear. The hard, yellowish-white flesh is quite dry and has a tart flavor. Quinces taste better cooked than raw. Because they are high in pectin, they are often added to jams or jellies to help them set. Quinces are available from October to December. Select fruits that are large, firm, and yellow with no sign of green.

Tamarillos

This egg-shaped fruit (see Figure 4-11) is also known as the *tree tomato.* It has a very tough, bitter skin that comes in various shades of yellow and red. The tart, but very flavorful, golden-pink flesh is tinged with purple around the seeds. Tamarillos taste somewhat like sweet tomatoes. They are available from May through October. When ripe, they should be fragrant and should yield slightly to palm pressure. Tamarillos are best when cooked. They can be sliced and baked with poultry or meat or cooked with some sugar and added to fruit chutneys or salsas.

Figure 4-11: Tamarillos (or tree tomatoes) are tart but highly flavorful.

Tangerines and mandarins

Tangerines and mandarins are the same variety of fruit, but they are generally called *mandarins* if they are grown outside the United States and *tangerines* if they are grown in the United States. This loose-skinned orange category includes several varieties, the three most common of which are listed below. They can be sweet or tart, seedless or not, and can range in size from as small as an egg to as large as a medium grapefruit. They all have skins that slip off the fruit easily.

- ✔ **Clementine:** Small and seedless, with shiny, bright-orange skin and very flavorful flesh. Available from November to January.
- ✔ **Dancy:** Also known as a *Christmas tangerine,* it is medium-sized and seedy with shiny orange skin. Available from November to May.
- ✔ **Kinnow:** Medium-sized, with some seeds, smooth, light-orange skin, and a mild, sweet flavor. Available from January to May.

Tangelos

Tangelos are juicy, sweetly tart citrus fruit with few seeds. This fruit takes its name from the fact that it's a cross between a tangerine and a pomelo. You can find many hybrids of this loose-skinned fruit, ranging in size from that of a tiny orange to that of a small grapefruit. Two of the most common varieties are

✔ **Minneola:** Medium-large, almost seedless, with fairly thin, pebbly skin. Very juicy. Available from December to April.

✔ **Orlando:** Small and round, with tangy flesh. Available from November to April.

Ugli fruit

Ugli fruit, as shown in Figure 4-12, got their name as part of a marketing plan, but they really aren't that ugly. Their size ranges from as small as an orange to as large as a grapefruit. They have a sort of puffy, thick, semi-loose skin that can be slightly bumpy. Their acid-sweet flavor suggests grapefruit with hints of mandarin. This fruit's large, juicy, yellow-orange pulp sections have an unusually soft succulence for citrus. Ugli fruit is available from winter to spring. Choose fruit that is heavy for its size and gives slightly to palm pressure. Store at room temperature and use within five days, or refrigerate for up to three weeks. You can use ugli fruit in the same ways you use grapefruit.

Figure 4-12:
Ugli fruit really aren't all that ugly.

White sapotes

This fruit has a very thin green to yellow skin with pale, sweet, creamy flesh that has hints of peach, citrus, or vanilla. (See Figure 4-13.) Choose fruit that is soft to the touch. If not ripe, leave at room temperature for a few days. White sapotes are available from May through August. They are great served cold in salads, salsas, compotes, or even sorbets and ice creams.

Vegetables

I think that vegetables are the most interesting part of cuisine. Unlike meat or seafood, vegetables are multidimensional. They can be served raw or just al dente. They can be pureed into a sauce or soup. They can be roasted, grilled, braised, sautéed, blanched, steamed, or stir-fried.

So it's time to widen your vegetable repertoire. Forget about the same old steamed broccoli or carrots — try roasting some parsnips or experimenting with Swiss chard. Many vegetables are now also available in *baby* sizes that are fun to try. The following sections can give you some ideas to get you started.

Artichokes

Artichokes are the large, unopened flower buds of a thistle-like plant. The "choke" in the center is actually an immature flower encased in leaf scales. Look for artichokes with compact, heavy, plump globes that yield slightly to pressure and large, tightly clinging, fleshy leaf scales of a good green color. Artichokes are available year-round. See Figure 4-14 for instructions for cleaning and trimming an artichoke.

Asparagus

White asparagus grows beneath mounds of earth that are watched closely for the first hint of cracking — an indication that the stalks are about to push through the dirt. Harvesters rush to the asparagus fields in the predawn to snip the asparagus before the tip pushes through the earth. After the sun touches the tender tips, they turn light purple, losing their grade-A status.

Cleaning an Artichoke

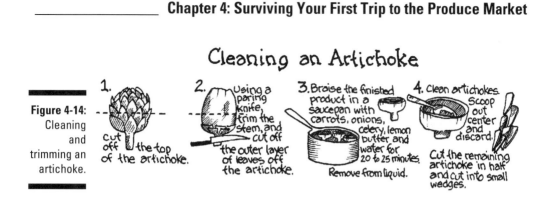

Figure 4-14:
Cleaning and trimming an artichoke.

The more popular green asparagus has spears that become dark green in sunlight. Asparagus is one of the most perishable vegetables sold commercially. To maintain the sweet flavor, store asparagus below 41 degrees and keep the cut end damp.

Contrary to popular belief, thin asparagus spears aren't any more tender than fat ones. Tenderness is related to color — the greener (or whiter) the better. Look for stalks that are straight with compact, pointed tips and a fresh appearance. Asparagus is available from April to June.

Beans (fresh)

Green or waxy yellow, round or flat, all are equally good. Look for beans with long, straight pods, crisp enough to snap easily between your fingers. Don't be tempted to buy them if they are even the least bit soft; they will have no flavor at all. Beans are best between June and August. (See Chapter 8 for information about dried beans and legumes.)

Green and yellow beans are native to North America. They weren't introduced to Europe until Columbus brought them back from his journeys.

Beets

Beets are sometimes called the *bossy vegetable* because their color can take over the whole kitchen. But even though they can be messy to work with, their subtle sweet flavor and beautiful rich color make them worth it. Fresh, prime-quality beets should have a good globular shape with smooth, firm flesh and a rich, deep-red color. (Yellow, white, and candystripe varieties are available, too, but they are more difficult to find.) Small to medium-sized beets are less likely to be tough. They are available year-round but are at their best in the fall.

Don't throw away those beet tops. The spinach-like beet greens are delicious when cooked, and they are loaded with vitamin A.

Bok choy (Chinese white cabbage)

Bok choy, shown in Figure 4-15, has recently become a regular in most produce markets in the U.S. It is great for use in stir-fry and in soups. It can have green or white stalks that range in width from 2 inches to 4 inches. They are thick toward the base and thinner toward the dark-green leafy tops. What type you buy doesn't matter; they are all equally good. For an interesting side dish, try the very small baby bok choy, cut in half and steamed, sautéed, or braised with a little chicken stock for extra flavor.

Figure 4-15:
Bok choy is great in stir-fries and soups.

Broccoli

When you buy broccoli, look for plenty of green color in the heads as well as the stems. The size of the heads may vary, but size has no bearing on quality. Stalks should be tender and firm with compact, dark-green or purplish green buds in the head. Avoid broccoli with yellow flowers visible; it is tough. Broccoli is available year-round.

When steaming broccoli, lift the lid two or three times to allow the steam to escape, which keeps the color bright green.

Brussels sprouts

Brussels sprouts get their name from the Belgian city of Brussels, where they were first grown in the 1700s. Good sprouts are firm, compact, fresh, of bright appearance, and have a good green color with no traces of yellow. Brussels sprouts should be cooked uncovered in plenty of water to retain their bright green color. They are available from October to January.

Cabbage

Cabbage has gotten a bum rap because so many of us remember it as that overcooked stuff that stank up the house when our grandmothers made it. Try it cut in wedges, cooked lightly (about five minutes in boiling water), and tossed with butter and chopped parsley — I think you may change your mind. Whether red or green, well-trimmed, reasonably solid cabbage heads that are heavy for their size and show no discolored veins are your best buy. Cabbage is available year-round.

You can decrease cabbage cooking odors considerably by dropping a whole walnut, in the shell, into the water during cooking.

Carrots

Cooking without carrots is unthinkable. They are a staple for stocks, broths, soups, and stews. They are great roasted along with meat and poultry. You can even make wonderful desserts with carrots. When selecting carrots, look for firm, well-formed, smooth orange to orange-red carrots with well-trimmed tops. Avoid wilted, soft, or shriveled carrots or carrots with large green areas (sunburn) at the top. Carrots are available year-round.

Cooked carrots are even better for you than raw ones — cooking the carrots partially dissolves the cellulose-stiffened cell walls, making the nutrients easier to absorb.

Cauliflower

Mark Twain once described this vegetable as "cabbage with a college education." I'm not sure if he said that because he thought it was an elevated form of cabbage or if he just thought it looked like brains. I vote for the former.

Although cauliflower is a member of the cabbage family, it has a much more subtle and delicate flavor. The size of a cauliflower head is no indication of quality. Look for cauliflower that is white or creamy-white, very firm, and compact. Loose, open flower clusters indicate overmaturity. Spotted, speckled, or bruised florets should be avoided unless they can be trimmed off with little waste. Cauliflower is available year-round.

Celery

Like carrots, celery can be used for almost anything, but most people don't think of it as a vegetable in its own right. Lightly cooked and tossed with butter and herbs, it makes a great addition to any meal with its wonderful, delicate flavor. Celery should have a tight heart formation (the center of the bunch) with stalks that are of medium length and thickness. The stalks should be brittle enough to snap easily, and the leaves should be fresh or only slightly wilted. Celery is available year-round.

Chiles

Chiles have been used for centuries in different cultures around the world, but only in the last couple decades have they gained more mainstream popularity in the U.S. Chiles are now available fresh, frozen, dried, canned, and powdered. Generally, the smaller the chile, the hotter it is — most of the heat is contained in the seeds and the ribs, and a smaller chile has a much higher ratio of seeds and ribs than a larger chile. Over 100 varieties of chiles are available (see Figure 4-16), but most are not produced commercially. Table 4-1 shows you some of the more popular chiles, in order from mildest to hottest.

Figure 4-16:
Chiles come in over 100 varieties (not all pictured here, of course!).

Table 4-1	Chiles
Kind	*Description*
Anaheim greens	Pale to medium green; slightly sweet; great for stuffing, sauces, and stews
Anaheim reds	Bright red; pronounced sweet flavor; good for stuffing, sauces, stews, and pickling
Poblanos	Dark green; earthy flavor; good for roasting and stuffing
Anchos	Dried poblanos; aromatic; sweet flavor
Jalapeños	Medium to dark green; hot, green vegetable flavor; good for salsas, stews, or breads
Chipotles	Dried, smoked jalapeños; smoky, sweet flavor; good for sauces, soups, and salsas
Serranos	Dark-green to red when ripe; hotter but more flavorful than jalapeños; used in salsas, pickled, or roasted
Thai chiles	Bright-green to red when ripe; lingering, fiery heat; used in Southeast Asian cooking
Habañeros	Dark-green to orange to red when fully ripe; very hot (30 to 50 times as hot as a jalapeño); used fresh in salsas and chutneys

Soaking fresh chiles in cold water for an hour will take away some of the heat.

Corn

Nothing tastes better than the first ultra-sweet corn of the season. No matter what color the corn — yellow, white, or bicolored — look for husks that are a fresh green color and kernels that are tender, milky, and large enough to leave no spaces between the rows. Corn is available most of the year, but it is best from May to September.

Cucumbers

Cucumbers have mild-flavored flesh and a very high water content, which makes them one of the most refreshing summer vegetables. Whether they are seeded or seedless (the seedless variety usually still have a few seeds), they taste the same. Look for cucumbers that are firm with a good green color and no soft spots. The shade of green is important because older cucumbers tend to be dull green or even yellowish. Cucumbers are available year-round.

Daikons

A daikon is a Japanese radish that is large, white, tapered, and 8 to 10 inches long (it looks like a large, smooth, white carrot — see Figure 4-17). Daikon has a flavor similar to that of a radish, but it's a little hotter. It's great added to salads, or anytime you want to add a little zip to a dish. Look for daikons that are firm and fairly smooth. They are available year-round.

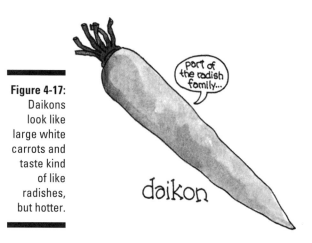

Figure 4-17: Daikons look like large white carrots and taste kind of like radishes, but hotter.

Eggplant

Eggplant can be white, purple, or red, depending on the variety. They all have a very similar flavor and can be used interchangeably. Whatever the color, the entire surface of the skin should be clear and glossy. Heaviness and firmness of flesh are also important. Buy eggplants that are pear-shaped and 3 to 6 inches in diameter. Eggplants are available year-round.

Fava beans

Fava beans are a long, round, velvety-podded variety of bean. (See Figure 4-18.) They resemble lima beans, except they're rounder, with thick, somewhat larger pods. Favas require a little patience to remove them from the pods, but they have a great fresh taste and hold up well when cooked. (Hannibal Lechter liked these with a nice Chianti.) They are available during the spring and summer.

Figure 4-18:
Fava beans
look like
lima beans
and have a
great fresh
taste.

fava beans

Fennel

I love fennel! The delicate licorice/anise flavor goes with almost anything.
It's great raw in salads and relishes, or cooked and accompanied by pork,
lamb, or fish. Fennel has a pale-green color with celery-like stems and
feathery tops that are used as an herb. Fennel is available most of the year,
but is most prevalent in the winter months. Although it looks like celery, it
doesn't keep as well. It is best if used within three or four days.

Fiddleheads

Fiddleheads, shown in Figure 4-19, are the young shoots from the ostrich
fern. They get their name from their shape, which resembles the scrolled
head of a violin. They have a flavor that is similar to green beans with a hint
of asparagus. Because they look exotic and are relatively new to produce
markets, fiddleheads are great for impressing your friends. Try boiling these
delicate shoots lightly and tossing them with butter to give your next dinner
guests a delectable treat. Look for crisp, tightly rolled shoots with a good
green color. They are available from April through July.

Figure 4-19:
Fiddleheads
are great
vegetables
for
impressing
your
friends.

fiddleheads

Jicama

Jicama (pronounced "HICK-a-ma") is a root tuber that is used in Mexico as often as a potato is used in the United States. It looks like a turnip (see Figure 4-20) but has a bland flavor similar to that of a water chestnut. Choose jicama as you would potatoes, but stick to the smaller ones, as the larger ones can be woody. Jicama is available year-round.

Figure 4-20:
You can use jicama in the same way you use a potato.

Lettuce

Hundreds of varieties of lettuce are grown throughout the world, and because they peak at different times of the year, there's always an abundance. When shopping for lettuces, choose those that are crisp and free from blemishes. Quite often, produce markets will carry something called *mesclun mix,* a mixture of several tender baby lettuces and herbs. Mesclun mix is a great way to buy lettuces because you can get a mixture of several types without having to get too much of any one type. As with all greens, you should wash lettuce and dry it to remove any excess moisture.

Following are some handy types of lettuce (see Figure 4-21 for an illustration of each type):

- **Arugula:** Peppery mustard flavor; very perishable
- **Belgian Endive:** White and yellow leaves in a tightly packed cone shape; crisp and slightly bittersweet
- **Bibb:** Delicate light-green leaves; small, loose head; mild and elusive flavor
- **Chicory:** Crisp, curly green leaves; quite bitter flavor
- **Endive:** Crisp, curly green leaves; whiter heart than chicory; quite bitter flavor
- **Escarole:** An endive with broad green leaves shading to white in the center; mild taste

✔ **Frisee:** Frilly, light-green leaves with firm white ribs; the least bitter of the chicory family

✔ **Lollo Rossa:** Red-tipped, crinkly leaves that are loosely bound at the root

✔ **Mache:** Small, deep-green leaves; buttery flavor

✔ **Oak Leaf:** Soft, dark-green leaves that resemble oak leaves; the red oak variety is shaded from brown to crimson

✔ **Radicchio:** Cupped, deep crimson leaves with white ribs; peppery flavor

✔ **Romaine:** Long, flat, flavorful leaves that are very crunchy; red romaine has red-tipped leaves and is milder in flavor

✔ **Watercress:** Peppery mustard flavor; very perishable

Figure 4-21:
There's more to salad than plain old iceberg lettuce!

Mushrooms

Literally thousands of mushroom varieties exist. Sizes and shapes vary widely, and colors range from white to orange to black and even pink and yellow. (See Figure 4-22 for illustrations of various types, and Table 4-2 for descriptions of those types.) The cap's texture can be smooth, pitted, honeycombed, or ruffled. Flavor can range from bland to rich, nutty, and earthy. Look for mushrooms that are firm and evenly colored, with tightly closed caps. Avoid specimens that are broken or damaged or that have soft spots or a dark-tinged surface. If you are cooking your mushrooms whole, select mushrooms of equal size so that they cook evenly.

Store mushrooms in the refrigerator laid out in a single layer so that air can circulate, and cover with a damp paper towel. Before use, mushrooms should be wiped with a damp paper towel or a mushroom brush. Mushrooms should never be soaked because they absorb water and become mushy.

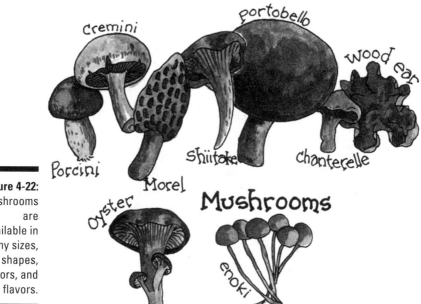

Figure 4-22: Mushrooms are available in many sizes, shapes, colors, and flavors.

Table 4-2	Various Types of Wild Mushrooms
Mushroom	*Description*
Chanterelle	Mild and meaty, sometimes with a nutty flavor; frilly, yellow, trumpet-shaped head
Cremini	Firm, brown, nice earthy flavor; closely related to button mushrooms (the domestic variety that you always find in grocery stores)
Enoki	Fragile, long-stemmed, pin-headed; very mild flavor
Morel	Dark-brown, spongy head and a thick stem; strong, heady flavor
Oyster	Delicate flavor; silken texture much like an oyster
Porcini	Rich and meaty flavored, with a thick stalk and a flat cap; usually sold dried (also known as *cepes*)
Portobello	Impressive in size, with a meaty flavor and texture; has dark-brown gills that you can remove if desired
Shiitake	Dark-brown, meaty caps; earthy flavor holds up well in cooking
Wood ear	Musty and mild flavored with a thin, chewy texture; named after its appearance; can be spread out to resemble a small elephant's ear

There are 38,000 different varieties of mushrooms, some edible, some not. So unless you're a skilled mushroom hunter, you may be best off searching for wild mushrooms in the supermarket. If you must hunt for them, make sure that you know what you're looking for, or it may be your last hunt!

Napa cabbage

Napa cabbage, also known as *Chinese cabbage,* has characteristics of both romaine lettuce and cabbage. I like to use the large leaves to *wrap a package* (for example, take a piece of fish topped with chopped mushrooms and wrap it in the cabbage leaves). Napa cabbage should have bright-green leaves and a long, oval-shaped head that is firm and fresh. (See Figure 4-23.) It is available year-round.

Okra

Okra may be green or white in color, with pods that are either long and thin or short and chunky. Look for pods that snap easily or puncture with slight pressure. Okra is available year-round.

To avoid the pastiness that can occur in okra, cook it whole. If you must cut the okra, cook it very rapidly.

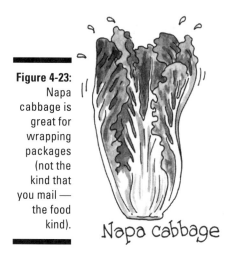

Figure 4-23:
Napa cabbage is great for wrapping packages (not the kind that you mail — the food kind).

Napa cabbage

Onions

Onions are one of the most versatile foods around. They add flavor to everything they touch. They can be used raw for a sharp, pungent flavor or cooked for a luscious, sweet flavor. Onions are broken down into two classifications: green onions and dry onions. The green onion category contains just that — green onions, or *scallions* as they're called in gourmet circles. The dry onion category contains all the rest. Personally, I think that the most logical way to categorize onions is by their flavor. Look for onions that are firm with no gray coloring or soft spots.

Mild onions can be used along with stronger onions for an added dimension. Scallions and shallots can be used raw or cooked, whereas leeks and pearl onions should be cooked slightly.

- **Scallions:** Also known as *green onions*. These onions are picked before the globe has a chance to form and are sold with the edible greens attached. They are great for eating raw, in salads or as a garnish.
- **Leeks:** Look like giant scallions. They are great in soups or braised alongside meats.
- **Pearl onions:** Tiny white onions that are perfect for stews or ragouts because they hold their shape during cooking.
- **Shallots:** Small onions with a light-purple color. Raw, they have a mild flavor that is great in salads or delicate dishes. Cooked, they have a wonderful sweet flavor that goes with delicate fish preparations, salsas, or almost anything.

Strong onions are great for making stocks and soups and for caramelizing. They hold on to most of their pungent flavor even with extended cooking times.

- ✔ **Rustic white onions** have a great pungent flavor that is great for cooking. They can be used in soups, stews, or almost any preparation.

- ✔ **Yellow onions** are probably the most commonly found member of the onion family. These versatile onions can be roasted whole, used with roasting meats, or tossed into almost any dish.

Sweet onions can be eaten raw or cooked. Vidalia and Maui onions are so sweet that you can bite into them like an apple if you're a big onion fan.

- ✔ **Maui onions** come from, you guessed it, Maui. They range in color from white to light yellow and are shaped like a slightly flattened circle. They have a mild, sweet flavor that is great for eating raw or cooked.

- ✔ **Red onions** are another commonly found onion. Their reddish-purple color makes them a nice addition to sandwiches or salads.

- ✔ **Spanish onions** are large with yellowish skins. They have a mild, sweet flavor that is good for using raw, but they are even sweeter when cooked.

- ✔ **Vidalia onions** are grown in the sandy soil around Vidalia, Georgia. These famous sweet onions are usually available only in the late spring and early summer. They don't keep well at room temperature, but if you wrap them individually in foil and put them in the cold part of your refrigerator, you can enjoy them for a couple months.

Onions contain sulfuric compounds that cause you to cry when you cut them. You can lessen the effect by cutting the top off first and peeling down toward the bottom, leaving the bottom intact for as long as possible.

Parsnips

Parsnips require a long, cool growing season and are best when planted in early spring, grown during a mild summer, and harvested late in the fall after the first frost. Small to medium-sized parsnips are generally of the best quality, as long as they are firm and well-shaped. Larger parsnips tend to have a woody core. They are available most of the year but are best in early winter.

Peas

There is no comparison between canned peas and fresh peas straight from the shell. When buying fresh peas, select fairly large, bright-green, angular pods that are full and snap readily. Avoid pods that are yellowish; they are on their way out. Peas store best when they are kept cold and moist in the pod.

Potatoes

Many different varieties of potatoes exist, most of which are available year-round. Potatoes of any kind or size should be firm, relatively smooth, clean, and reasonably well-shaped. Avoid potatoes that are cut, bruised, wilted, soft, or sprouted. Size doesn't affect quality; it is simply a matter of choice for the particular use.

Potatoes can be broken down into four basic categories:

- **Russet or Idaho:** Good for baking or frying.
- **Long whites:** Good for boiling.
- **Round whites:** Good for boiling, mashing, and frying; mealier varieties can also be baked.
- **Round reds:** Good for boiling. Young versions of this type are called *new potatoes;* they are best boiled in their tender skins.

You can find many types of specialty or *boutique* potatoes on the market today, such as purple Peruvian or fingerling potatoes. They are grown in much smaller quantities and can be difficult to find in some markets. But if you come across them, buy some: They can be a fun change from everyday potatoes.

Radishes

Radishes come in red, white, and black varieties. Red radishes are the most popular for eating fresh, but the black and white varieties are also very good and can be used in a variety of ways. Look for smooth, crisp, firm roots with no blemishes or cuts on the skin. Radishes are available year-round.

Rhubarb

Rhubarb was used only for medicinal purposes until the 18th century (the roots have purgative qualities). It's surprising that it took people that long to find out how delicious rhubarb can be. Field-grown rhubarb is a rich dark red color, with coarse green foliage and a very tart flavor, and it's good for pies and sauces. Choose stalks that are fairly thick, firm, and crisp, with fresh-looking foliage. Rhubarb is available from February to June.

Don't eat the leaves of the rhubarb plant. They contain serious quantities of oxalic acid, which is poisonous in large amounts.

Rutabagas

The roots of good-quality rutabagas should be smooth-skinned, firm, and heavy for their size, although size is not a quality factor. Rutabagas are often dipped in edible wax to help them keep better, but this coating doesn't affect the flavor at all. Rutabagas are available from February to June.

Snow peas

Snow peas are flat Chinese pea pods that are 2 to 4 inches long. They are used heavily in Asian cooking, but they are also a great addition to salads. Snow peas are available year-round but are best from May to September. Look for crisp, flat pods with a bright color and no brown spots.

Spinach

Both the curly and flat-leaf types of spinach are good for cooking, but choose the small, tender leaves for eating raw. Look for fresh, crisp leaves of a good green color. Avoid leaves that are wilted or are starting to turn yellow. Spinach is available year-round but can be woody or tough during the hottest summer months.

Squash

Summer squash (see Figure 4-24) have thin, edible skins and soft seeds. The tender flesh has a high water content and a mild flavor and doesn't require long cooking. Summer squash is best from early through late summer, although some varieties are available year-round. Select the smaller specimens with bright-colored skin that's free of spots and bruises. Store squash in the refrigerator in a plastic bag.

- ✔ **Chayote:** Also called *mirliton*. About the size of an avocado, with dark-green skin and mild-flavored flesh.

- ✔ **Crookneck:** Long, curved neck that is slightly more slender that the bulbous base.

- ✔ **Pattypan:** Very small; green, dark green, or golden; identified by their scalloped edges. The different colors may be used interchangeably.

- ✔ **Yellow straightneck:** Zucchini-shaped, with smooth, yellow skin.

- ✔ **Zucchini:** Long, thin, and dark-green skinned. Look for smaller zucchini; they are less fibrous than the larger ones.

Figure 4-24:
Varieties of
summer
squash.

Winter squash (see Figure 4-25) have hard, thick skins and hard seeds. The deep-yellow to orange flesh is firmer than that of the summer squash and requires longer cooking. Choose squash that is heavy for its size and has a hard, deep-colored rind that's free of blemishes or moldy spots. The hard skin protects the flesh and allows it to be stored longer than summer squash. Winter squash does not require refrigeration and can be kept in a cool, dark place for a month or more.

Figure 4-25:
Varieties of
winter
squash.

- **Acorn:** Round with ribbed, dark-green skin and orange flesh.
- **Butternut:** Pear-shaped; light-brown skin and yellow flesh.
- **Delicata:** Shaped like a grooved watermelon, with creamy yellow mottling and dark-green stripes.
- **Golden Nugget:** Shaped like a small pumpkin with a pumpkin flavor.
- **Hubbard:** Knobby green skin with bright-orange flesh.
- **Spaghetti:** Large and oblong; creamy skin with yellowish flesh that separates into translucent strands resembling pasta.
- **Sweet Dumpling:** Small and pumpkin-shaped; creamy skin that has dark-green striations.

Sweet peppers

Sweet peppers are available year-round in green, yellow, orange, purple, red, and even white varieties. The flavors vary slightly from one color to another, but not enough to make a difference in how you use them. Look for peppers that are well-shaped, thick-walled, and firm, with a uniform glossy color. Pale color is a sign of immaturity, and blister-like spots on the surface indicate that decay may set in soon.

Have you ever wondered why green peppers are so much less expensive than the other colors? Green peppers are picked as soon as they are large enough to send to market. All the other peppers are left on the vine to ripen and develop their color. For the growers, the extra time on the vine translates into extra cost.

Sweet potatoes

Several different types of sweet potatoes are available. Some are creamier, some are starchier, some are sweeter, but all are equally good; the type you choose is just a matter of taste. Look for sweet potatoes that are thick, chunky, and medium-sized and that taper toward the ends. Avoid those with blemishes or any signs of decay. Sweet potatoes come in red and white varieties and are available year-round.

Swiss chard

Swiss chard is a type of beet that doesn't develop a fleshy root. It has large leaves with thick center ribs. You can use it in the same ways you use spinach. Like all salad greens, it is important that the leaves are fresh, crisp, and have a good green color. Swiss chard is available year-round.

Tomatoes

Yes, I know, tomatoes aren't technically a vegetable, but because they are used more like vegetables than fruits, I include them here. When tomatoes are in season, they are ripe, juicy, and wonderfully sweet — but get them out of season and they can be mealy, dry, and very disappointing. If you have to buy tomatoes when they are not at their prime, try Roma or plum tomatoes; these varieties seem to handle hot-house conditions better than other types. Commercially produced tomatoes are available in green, yellow, red, and sometimes (though rarely) orange. Good tomatoes are firm, have good color, are free from blemishes, and are heavy for their size. Tomatoes are best in August and September.

If you can get your hands on *heirloom tomatoes,* they're worth every penny. These tomato types had been abandoned for years because they were not suitable for large-scale production. Now, heirloom tomatoes are being grown in specialty markets because of their interesting colors and unusual sweetness. They can be found in almost every color of the rainbow: red, yellow, orange, purple, green, white, and even striped!

Turnips

Turnips are a much-underappreciated vegetable. They have a natural sweetness and a peppery flavor that is delicious with roasted meats or in stews. The roots of good-quality turnips should be smooth-skinned, firm, and heavy for their size, although size is not a quality factor. Turnips are available in May and June and again in the fall.

Water chestnuts

There's no substitute for fresh water chestnuts. Canned water chestnuts completely lose their flavor, whereas the frozen variety lose their texture. If you can't get fresh water chestnuts, don't use them at all.

Fresh water chestnuts have crisp, apple-like flesh that is both sweet and starchy, with a flavor similar to that of coconut. When selecting fresh water chestnuts, press the water chestnut all over to check for soft spots, which usually mean bruising and decay. Fresh water chestnuts should be rock hard and should not appear shriveled. They are available irregularly year-round.

Part II

So You Know How to Boil Water and Fry an Egg

The 5th Wave   By Rich Tennant

"Here's a recipe for Chinese Thousand Year Old Eggs. Thank goodness for microwave ovens."

In this part . . .

This begins the recipe-heavy part of the book. From sauces to soufflés, from poached swordfish to potato-Parmesan pavé, this part provides recipes for a wealth of tantalizing treats. It also explains a little about each category of cuisine and defines the techniques that you use to cook each particular type of food.

Chapter 5

Getting Sauced

"In the symphony of the kitchen, it is the saucier who is the soloist."

— Fernand Point, *Ma Gastronomie*

Sauce-making is perceived as an art, and the *saucier* (the guy who makes sauces, not the guy who looks saucy) is the master of that art. Sauces are not just an afterthought in gourmet cooking; they serve a major function in the composition of a dish. Not only do sauces complement the flavor of a dish, but they also add succulence, visual interest, and texture. They give a dish its character. After all, it's the "special sauce" that makes the Big Mac the star of all burgers.

Oftentimes, amateur chefs associate the word *sauce* only with the *grand,* or *mother sauces:* velouté, béchamel, tomato, demi-glace, and hollandaise. These sauces can be intimidating because they are temperamental — if you've ever overcooked a hollandaise until it was more like a lemon quiche, you know what I mean. The good news is that sauce-making doesn't have to be an intimidating process. A sauce can be as simple as a vegetable puree or as elaborate as an herb-infused red wine reduction.

Don't be afraid to start with the basic sauces listed in this chapter; you have to learn to walk before you can run (or should I say puree before you infuse?). From there, you can move on to the more involved and complex sauces that accompany other recipes throughout this book. With little effort on your part, the art of sauce-making can be demystified, and you can get on your way to becoming an accredited sauce-maker.

The Mother Sauce Name Game

The *mother sauces* (or *grand sauces*) are the cornerstone of traditional French cuisine, and I mention them in this chapter because I think it's important for you to know about them. The mother sauces are a large part of the history of gourmet cooking, and they can help you understand the roots of modern gourmet cuisine. But as modern cuisine moves toward cleaner, purer flavors, the use of these heavier sauces is diminishing. Instead of cream-based sauces or sauces thickened with a roux, for example, you can use sauces that are more brothlike.

The mother sauces are

- **Velouté sauce:** Chicken or white stock thickened with a blond roux
- **Béchamel sauce:** Chopped onions and milk thickened with a white roux
- **Tomato sauce:** Tomatoes, stock, and pork bones thickened with a roux
- **Demi-glace:** Brown veal stock and tomato puree thickened with a brown roux
- **Hollandaise sauce:** Vinegar, butter, and lemon juice thickened with egg yolks

Each of these sauces has many variations, which come from adding different flavorings to the basic sauce. For example:

- Adding chopped tarragon to hollandaise sauce makes béarnaise sauce.
- Adding heavy cream to velouté sauce makes suprême sauce.

You may have noticed that the French have specific names for all their sauces. Don't worry about learning all the names; the basic idea is that adding herbs, wine, or spices to any of these sauces creates a new sauce with a different flavor, no matter what it's called.

Creating Savory Stocks

A *stock* is a flavorful liquid made by gently simmering bones or vegetables in a liquid to extract their flavor, aroma, color, body, and nutrients. The first stocks were simple broths that were the by-products of poached meat and fish dishes. Before the method of preparing stocks was refined, cooks often braised or roasted meat with a thick slice of ham or veal to give the sauce extra body.

Stocks are the beginning of many sauces. You can make one basic stock, divide it into two or three portions, and flavor each portion with different herbs or vegetables to make three stocks or sauces with their own identity.

Because stocks are often more intensely flavored than the foods they accompany, you must prepare them with the best available ingredients.

Traditional recipes for stocks are divided into white and brown. White stocks are prepared by blanching meat and bones in water, whereas brown stocks are prepared by first browning the meat or bones in the oven, which results in a deep amber color and a richer flavor. Brown stock can be used as the base for reduction sauces and stews. You can use white stocks in many savory recipes that call for water, or as a base for soups or sauces.

The do's and don'ts of stock-making

Making stocks isn't difficult if you remember these few basic guidelines:

- ✔ **Always start a stock with a cold liquid.** If you add hot water to meat, it causes the meat to release soluble proteins (albumin) quickly into the surrounding liquid. These proteins immediately coagulate into very fine particles and cloud the stock. When you use cold liquid and heat it slowly, the proteins in the meat or fish coagulate in larger clumps and float to the top, where you can easily skim them. When adding liquid to an already simmering stock to compensate for evaporation, make sure that the liquid is cold.

- ✔ **Never allow a stock to boil.** As meat and bones cook, they release proteins and fats into the surrounding liquid. If the stock is kept at a slow simmer, these components appear as scum on top of the stock and can be skimmed. If the stock is boiling, these substances are churned back into the stock and become emulsified. The resulting stock is cloudy and has a dull, muddy, greasy flavor, which only worsens if you reduce the stock for a sauce. When the stock comes to a simmer, skim it every 5 to 10 minutes for the first hour to prevent fat and scum from working their way back into the stock. After the first hour, you need to skim the stock only every 30 minutes to an hour.

  For the same reasons, a stock should be slowly heated to a simmer. Rapid heating causes the meat to release albumin too quickly into the surrounding liquid.

- ✔ **Don't use too much liquid.** The higher the proportion of solid ingredients to liquid, the more flavorful the stock is. Many beginning cooks completely cover the solid ingredients with liquid at the beginning of cooking. Because the solid ingredients in a stock settle during cooking, cooks often find that they have added more liquid than necessary, and the resulting stock is unnecessarily thin. When adding water, add only enough liquid or stock to come three-quarters of the way to the top of the ingredients. The only exceptions to this rule are stocks with extremely long cooking times, where excess liquid evaporates anyway.

✔ **Don't move the contents of the stock during cooking and straining.** As the stock cooks, albumin and other solids settle along the bottom and sides of the pot. If the stock is disturbed, these solids break up and cloud the stock. When straining the finished stock, do not press on the ingredients in the strainer; allow enough time for the liquid to drain naturally.

✔ **Don't add the thickener until you thoroughly degrease the stock.** Traditional recipes often suggest adding thickener, such as roux, cornstarch, or arrowroot, to stock to thicken it lightly and give it texture. If you're using these thickeners (I sincerely hope that you aren't!), you should not add them to the stock until you carefully skim all the fat and scum. After you add starch to a stock, any fat emulsified in the liquid is held in solution by the starch and is difficult to skim.

✔ **Store stocks carefully.** Warm stock is a perfect medium for bacteria (beef stock was originally used to line petri dishes in laboratories). Avoid keeping stocks at temperatures that most favor bacteria (between 40 degrees and 140 degrees) for long periods. The danger of spoilage increases in hot weather and when you're preparing larger amounts of stock. Cool stocks in an ice bath, stirring every 5 minutes.

Making your own stocks

Stock-making takes some time, but if you can set aside one or two Sunday afternoons, you can make large batches and store them in the freezer for use months down the line. After you have a few stocks in your freezer, you'll be surprised at how easy it is to create delicious sauces.

You can freeze stocks and reduction sauces in ice cube trays, pop them out, and store them in plastic bags in the freezer. This makes it easy to use any amount you need.

Beef Stock

Beef stock has many uses. You can use it to poach beef, use it as a braising liquid, reduce it down for a sauce, or clarify it for a consommé. You can also use this basic recipe for beef stock to create different kinds of stocks, such as veal or venison stock. By simply substituting different types of bones, you can create a stock with its own unique flavor.

(continued)

Preparation time: *10 minutes*

Cooking time: *7 to 9 hours*

Yield: *2 quarts*

6 pounds beef bones, cut into 2-inch-long pieces (ask your butcher to do this)

2 cups chopped carrots

2 cups chopped celery

4 cups chopped onions

3 cloves garlic, peeled

2 tablespoons canola oil

1/2 cup chopped tomato

2 cups red wine

1 bay leaf

1 tablespoon whole black peppercorns

1 Place the bones in a large roasting pan and bake at 450° for 1 hour or until they are golden-brown. Turn the bones after 30 minutes to ensure even browning.

2 In a large stockpot, sauté the carrots, celery, onion, and garlic in the canola oil over high heat for 7 minutes or until caramelized.

3 Add the tomato and continue cooking for 2 minutes. Deglaze with the red wine and continue to cook until most of the wine is cooked out.

4 Add the browned bones, bay leaf, and peppercorns.

5 Drain the grease from the roasting pan, scrape the bottom of the pan, and add the scrapings to the stockpot. Cover with cold water, bring to a boil, reduce the heat to low, and slowly simmer for 6 to 8 hours, or until reduced to 2 quarts, periodically skimming away the impurities that rise to the surface.

6 Strain the stock through a fine-mesh sieve.

Chicken Stock

Chicken stock is very versatile and great to have on hand. You can use it as the base for chicken soup or as the liquid for cooking dried beans. It works great for poaching chicken, making velouté, or clarifying into chicken consommé. Chicken stock can be added to vinaigrettes in place of some of the oil. You can also use it in many recipes that call for water or vegetable stock.

Preparation time: *10 minutes*

Cooking time: *4 hours and 45 minutes*

Yield: *2 quarts*

(continued)

6 pounds chicken bones

3 cups chopped onions

2 cups chopped carrots

2 cups chopped celery

1 cup chopped leeks

1 tablespoon whole white peppercorns

1 bay leaf

1 Place all the ingredients in a large stockpot and cover three-fourths of the way with cold water (about 2 gallons).

2 Bring to a boil, reduce the heat to low, and slowly simmer for 4 hours, skimming every 30 minutes to remove the impurities that rise to the surface.

3 Strain and continue to cook over medium heat for 30 to 45 minutes or until reduced down to about 2 quarts.

Vegetable Stock

You can easily modify this vegetable stock recipe to create any flavor you want, depending on which vegetables you use. You can make a stock with roasted vegetables for a darker, richer stock. Or you can use vegetables that are basically white in color (such as parsnips, turnips, onion, and celery root) to create a stock with a pale color and a lighter flavor. You can caramelize vegetables to create a stock with a deep amber color, or you can use specific vegetables such as fennel or corn to create a stock intensely flavored with one specific vegetable. The possibilities with vegetable stock are endless — you can use it for soups, sauces, or even as a poaching liquid.

Preparation time: *15 minutes*

Cooking time: *1 hour and 45 minutes*

Yield: *2 quarts*

1 cup chopped Spanish onion

1 cup chopped carrot

1 cup chopped celery

1 cup chopped fennel

1 red bell pepper, seeded and chopped

3 cloves garlic

$^1/_2$ cup chopped parsnip

1 tablespoon black peppercorns

1 bay leaf

(continued)

1 Place all the ingredients in a large stockpot and cover with about 4 quarts of cold water.

2 Bring to a boil. Reduce the heat to low and continue to slowly simmer for 1 hour.

3 Strain, return the liquid to the stockpot, and continue to cook over medium heat for 30 to 45 minutes or until reduced to about 2 quarts.

Shellfish Stock

Shellfish stock is often used as the base for various bisques and shellfish consommés. Whenever you cook shrimp, crab, or lobster at home, reserve the shells and store them in plastic bags in the freezer. After you collect a few pounds, you can make a shellfish stock. You can use all types of shells together or a specific type of shell to create an individual stock.

Preparation time: *15 minutes*

Cooking time: *4 hours and 15 minutes*

Yield: *2 quarts*

5 pounds fresh lobster shells	*2 tablespoons canola oil*
¹/₂ cup chopped carrots	*2 tablespoons tomato paste*
¹/₂ cup chopped celery	*1 cup red wine*
1 cup chopped leeks	

1 Roast the lobster shells in the oven at 400° for 40 minutes or until bright red and slightly golden-brown.

2 Sauté the vegetables in the canola oil over medium-high heat for 10 minutes or until caramelized. Add the tomato paste and continue cooking for 2 to 3 minutes. Deglaze with the red wine and continue cooking for 3 minutes or until most of the wine is absorbed.

3 Add the lobster shells and cover three-fourths of the way with cold water. Simmer over medium-low heat for 3 hours.

4 Strain through a fine-mesh sieve and return the liquid to the pan. Continue to cook for 15 to 20 minutes or until reduced to about 2 quarts.

Fish Stock

Fish stock is a wonderful cooking medium for poaching fish. It is the base for *court bouillon,* which is a broth infused with vegetables, herbs, and white wine that is used for poaching fish. Fish stock is used to make fish velouté, or it can be used to deglaze a pan when making a pan sauce. You can use almost any type of fish bones to make a fish stock. If the heads of the fish are available, they are great for making a more flavorful stock.

Preparation time: *10 minutes*

Cooking time: *1¹/₂ hours*

Yield: *2 quarts*

5 pounds fish bones	*¹/₂ cup chopped leeks*
1 cup chopped celery	*¹/₂ cup white wine*
1 cup chopped carrots	*1 tablespoon white peppercorns*
1 cup chopped Spanish onion	

1 Place all the ingredients in a large stockpot and cover three-fourths of the way with cold water. Bring to a boil, reduce the heat to medium-low, and simmer for 40 minutes.

2 Strain though a fine-mesh sieve, return the liquid to the stockpot, and continue cooking 30 to 40 minutes or until the liquid has reduced to about 2 quarts.

Various ways to thicken stocks and sauces

You can choose from several different methods to thicken stocks or sauces. Traditional French cooks almost always use *roux* for thickening. Asian cooks have been using *slurries* to thicken sauces for generations. Modern cuisine calls for reductions and vegetable purees to do the job.

Most of the more traditional methods still have a place in modern gourmet cuisine. Although I prefer the clean, pure flavors of reductions and vegetable puree-thickened sauces, sometimes the more traditional methods are appropriate. Gumbo, for example, needs brown roux to give it a dark brown color and rich flavor, and slurries are still used by Asian cooks to thicken sauces quickly.

I list the following methods in my order of preference. Whenever possible, take the time to reduce your stocks, broths, or juices because the intensely flavored sauce that results is well worth the extra time.

✔ **Reduce the stock slowly.** The further you reduce a stock, the more intense the flavors become. Just be careful not to reduce it too much. The flavors can become so concentrated that they become overwhelming.

✔ **Add various vegetable purees.** Vegetable and fruit purees can thicken a stock simply by adding a large bulk of fine, solid particles. I like to take a little bit of mushroom and blend it into a stock to give it a nice mushroom flavor and smooth texture. Chicken stock and roasted shiitake mushrooms pureed together create a sauce that has body and flavor but isn't too rich.

✔ **Add egg yolks.** Egg yolks provide the base for emulsified sauces, such as mayonnaise and hollandaise, and are used in conjunction with cream to turn the cooking liquid of poached meats and fish into sauces. Egg yolks not only form emulsions of fat and liquids, but also combine with air, so they can be used for light, airy sauces. They are also used to give richness and texture to crème anglaise.

Sauces containing egg yolks should not be allowed to boil unless they contain flour, which stabilizes them. When combining egg yolks with hot liquids, be sure to *temper* the yolks. You do so by slowly adding a small amount of the hot liquid to the egg yolks and whisking them together until the yolks are hot to the touch. You then can add this mixture to the remaining hot liquid without causing it to curdle.

✔ **Use a slurry.** A *slurry* is cornstarch, arrowroot, or potato starch mixed with a touch of water, added to a stock, brought to a boil, and simmered for 10 minutes or until the desired thickness is achieved. A good slurry should have the consistency of heavy cream.

The use of slurries in modern gourmet cuisine is about the same as putting ketchup on filet mignon. After spending hours making a beautiful pure stock, the thought of masking the flavor with a slurry gives me chills, but in certain Asian preparations it is appropriate.

• **Arrowroot:** Arrowroot is the best of the purified starches for thickening sauces because it remains stable even after prolonged exposure to heat. You use it in the same way you use cornstarch.

• **Cornstarch:** Cornstarch should be used only as a last-minute thickener for sauces and cooking liquids that are being served immediately. When it is cooked for long periods, cornstarch begins to break down and loses its thickening power. Cornstarch can leave your sauce somewhat cloudy.

- **Potato starch:** Although potato starch was one of the first starches to be used in French cooking, it has never been popular as a sauce thickener in the United States. You use it the same way you use cornstarch and arrowroot, but, like cornstarch, it tends to break down after prolonged exposure to heat.

✔ **Use a roux.** A *roux* is a combination of 50 percent flour and 50 percent fat (butter, oil, duck fat, or bacon fat), which is cooked until it creates a paste that thickens the sauce while simmering. Three types of roux exist:

  - **Brown roux** is used for brown sauces.

  - **Blond roux** is used for velouté.

  - **White roux** is used for béchamel.

The only difference among these three types is the amount of time you cook the roux: The longer you cook it, the darker it becomes. Roux is not used as often as it used to be because it adds extra fat to the sauce, and the flour can block the flavor of the stock. Use it only as a last resort.

Intensifying Flavors with Reductions

Reduction sauces can be appealing on a variety of levels. They are lighter than sauces made with thickeners and can be used in many ways. They're great when infused with different herbs at the last moment to give them another dimension. Infusing herbs into a stock is like making tea; simply add the herbs to the hot stock and let them steep. Steeping a larger quantity of herbs for a short time is better than allowing the herbs to steep for a long time, because the herbs become bitter once they break down. A good rule is never to allow an herb to steep for more than 10 minutes.

Beef Stock Reduction

You can make this recipe with lamb, venison, veal, or any other type of meat stock — they are fairly interchangeable. Seasoning a meat reduction sauce is not necessary; it has enough natural salt that gets concentrated during the reduction process.

Preparation time: 10 minutes

Cooking time: 2 hours

Yield: 1¹/₂ cups

(continued)

2 cups chopped Spanish onions

1 cup chopped carrots

1 cup chopped celery

2 tablespoons canola oil

1 cup red wine

1¹/₂ quarts Beef Stock (see recipe earlier in this chapter)

4 sprigs thyme

1 In a medium saucepan, caramelize the vegetables over high heat in the canola oil for 10 minutes or until golden-brown.

2 Add the red wine to deglaze the pan and continue cooking until most of the red wine has cooked away.

3 Add the beef stock and simmer over medium heat for 1 hour.

4 Strain, return to the saucepan with the thyme and simmer for 5 minutes, and then remove the herbs. Continue to simmer for about 30 minutes in a medium saucepan until you have about 1¹/₂ cups of beef stock reduction. Strain through a fine-mesh sieve.

You make red wine reductions by slowly reducing red wine with *mirepoix* (chopped celery, carrots, and onions), chopped apple, and oranges. You can make wine reductions with Zinfandel, Burgundy, or Pinot Noir, but hold on to your hat: It takes three bottles of red wine to yield about 1 cup of reduction sauce. The end result is an intensely flavored, syruplike reduction that's great simply spooned over a piece of meat or fish.

Don't break the bank making red wine reductions; a moderately priced cooking wine works just as well as an expensive wine. Save your money for a good bottle to go with dinner.

Red Wine Reduction

This sauce is a great way to move fish dishes away from the traditional white wine pairing. By adding a red wine reduction (or a combination of red wine and meat reductions), you can easily pair fish with red wine. ***Tip:*** For an easy match, make the red wine reduction with the same type of wine that you plan to serve with the meal.

(continued)

Preparation time: *10 minutes*

Cooking time: *2 hours*

Yield: *1 cup*

1¹/₂ cups chopped onions	*1 Granny Smith apple, chopped*
1 cup chopped carrots	*1 orange, peeled and chopped*
1 cup chopped celery	*6 cups Burgundy wine*
2 tablespoons canola oil	*3 cups port*

1 In a medium saucepan, cook the onions, carrots, and celery over high heat in the canola oil for about 10 minutes or until caramelized.

2 Add the remaining ingredients and simmer over medium heat for 1 hour.

3 Strain through a fine-mesh sieve and return to the saucepan. Continue to simmer for 30 to 45 minutes or until the sauce is reduced to 1 cup.

Vegetable Broths

More and more, I find myself using broths as a flavoring agent. They are easy to prepare, are not as time-consuming as reduction sauces, and are very versatile. You can steep broths with herbs or spices for any flavor combination you desire, or you can add noodles, rice, vegetables, and meat for a one-pot meal. They store well in the freezer, but don't keep broths for more than a few days in the refrigerator — they can turn sour.

You can really stretch your imagination in making vegetable juice broths. Start with your choice of vegetables; carrots, celery, bell pepper, beets, and fennel all work well. Simply juice the vegetable with an electric juicer, slowly simmer the juice to bring the impurities to the surface, strain the juice through cheesecloth, and continue to simmer until the desired concentration is reached.

Vegetable broths can be served flavored with various herbs or spices. You can thicken them with butter or vegetable purees or by reducing them further. They can be used as either a sauce or a broth, depending on the consistency.

Curried Carrot Broth

A piece of grilled fish served with some vegetables and this light, sweet curried carrot broth is easy to make and delightful to eat.

Preparation time: *10 minutes*

Cooking time: *30 minutes*

Yield: *2 cups*

3 cups fresh carrot juice

3 tablespoons butter, softened

2 teaspoons curry powder

1 teaspoon paprika

Salt and pepper

1 Place the carrot juice in a medium saucepan and simmer for 15 minutes over medium heat.

2 Strain through a fine-mesh sieve lined with cheesecloth. Return to the saucepan and reduce over medium heat for 15 minutes or until you have about 2 cups. Strain again if necessary.

3 In a small bowl, stir the curry power and paprika into the soft butter.

4 Whisk the butter mixture into the hot carrot juice and season with salt and pepper.

Types of consommé

Consommé is an intensely flavored and very elegant dish. You can garnish it with small diced pieces of meat, chicken, or fish and a brunoise of vegetables for a beautiful presentation. Following are the common types of consommé:

✓ **Beef consommé:** Made with beef stock or broth and ground beef and clarified

✓ **Chicken consommé:** Made with chicken broth or stock and ground chicken and clarified

✓ **Fish consommé:** Made with fish stock and raw fish and clarified

✓ **Shellfish consommé:** Made with shellfish stock and raw shellfish meat and clarified

Consommés

Consommés are crystal clear and intense in flavor. They are usually enriched by the addition of lean chopped or ground meat, mirepoix, and egg whites. All consommés are prepared in the same manner and can be made from either stocks or broths.

Chicken Consommé

This wonderfully rich broth can be served alone as an early course for a dinner party. Or you can add diced vegetables or rice noodles for a heartier soup.

Preparation time: 15 minutes

Cooking time: 1 hour

Yield: About 1¹/₂ quarts

6 egg whites	*1 pound ground chicken*
¹/₂ cup small diced onion	*2 quarts cold Chicken Stock (see recipe earlier in this chapter)*
¹/₃ cup small diced carrot	*Salt and pepper*
¹/₃ cup small diced celery	
¹/₄ cup small diced tomato	

1 In a medium bowl, whisk together the egg whites, onion, carrot, celery, and tomato until slightly frothy. Whisk in the ground chicken.

2 Place the chicken stock in a medium saucepan and whisk the egg white mixture into the stock. Bring to a slow simmer while constantly stirring in one direction with a wooden spoon. Stir for about 15 minutes or until a *raft* begins to form (see the following FYI icon). Reduce to a slow slowly simmer and stop stirring.

3 After the raft forms, break a small hole in the raft to allow the consommé to break through. Continue to simmer for 45 minutes or until the liquid appears crystal-clear.

4 Strain through a fine-mesh sieve lined with cheesecloth, being careful not to break the raft. Discard the raft and season the consommé with salt and pepper.

The *raft* forms through a coagulation of proteins in the egg whites and meat. These products are rich in albumin, a protein that is insoluble in water. When heated, these proteins solidify, rise to the surface, and collect the tiny particles that cloud the stock, leaving it perfectly clear. Acids such as those in tomatoes and white wine help the raft solidify.

Do not season your consommé until you strain it, because salt can weaken the raft. Don't allow a consommé to boil, either. Boiling causes agitation, which may break up the raft, causing the consommé to become cloudy. A large amount of gelatin may also cloud the consommé. For this reason, making a consommé with veal stock is not recommended.

Infused Oils

Infused oils are made by actually pureeing the herb (or other flavoring agent) with the oil. The oil is allowed to sit until the solids have dropped to the bottom. The solids are then strained out, leaving a brightly colored, intensely flavored oil. Infused oils have a stronger flavor than scented or flavored oils.

Scented or flavored oils are often found in markets; they are decorative, but you basically pay an arm and a leg for a bottle of average olive oil garnished with a few herbs. You can use store-bought oils in a pinch, but I recommend making your own whenever possible. Scented or flavored oils are made by simply placing some of the herb, or other flavoring agent, into the oil and allowing it to steep.

Understanding the label on a bottle of olive oil

What is *extra-virgin* olive oil, anyway? *Extra-virgin* simply means "the oil from the first pressing." It has perfect flavor, color, and aroma, and no more than 1 percent acidity. *Virgin* or *pure* oil comes from the second pressing of the olives; its flavor is not as intense as the first pressing of the olives.

If a label says *cold-pressed,* it is just trying to impress the consumer, because all olive oils are cold-pressed. Cold-pressing is done by spinning a paste of ground-up olives in a centrifuge and filtering the oil that separates from the residue.

Light olive oil is a product that was created for the American market. The adjective refers to the milder taste of the oil, not a lower fat or lower calorie oil. It has the same calorie count as any oil — 120 calories and 14 grams of fat per tablespoon.

You can drizzle infused oils on a plate with a piece of meat or fish or whisk them together with some vinegar to make a vinaigrette for topping vegetables or greens. The result is something very flavorful, yet light and delicate.

Because infused oils actually have particles of herbs or spices suspended in the oil, they can spoil. Keep infused oils in the refrigerator and use them within a month or so, just to be safe. Nothing ruins a dinner party worse than giving your guests food poisoning!

Making infused oils

Infused oils are surprisingly easy to make and are far superior to those purchased in markets because they are more intensely flavored — and you are able to use the oil at its freshest. At the restaurant, we use neutral-flavored oils like grapeseed, canola, or cottonseed oil (you can even use salad oil). You can make infused oils with any type of fresh herb, such as basil, dill, fennel tops, chive, sage, or tarragon.

If you're scenting an oil with whole garlic cloves, you must blanch the garlic clove in boiling water first; otherwise, a bacteria present in the garlic grows after it is covered by the olive oil, and you can get very sick.

Herb Oil

You can prepare this basic recipe as a single herb oil, such as *parsley oil;* or you can make this oil with any combinations of herbs that you like. The bright color and wonderful flavor of this herb oil make a nice addition to almost any plate.

Preparation time: *5 minutes, plus overnight refrigeration*

Yield: *¹/₂ cup*

1 cup chives	*1 cup watercress*
1 cup Italian parsley	*1 cup canola oil*

1 Blanch the chives, parsley, and watercress in boiling salted water for 20 seconds to release the essential oils. Immediately shock the herbs in ice water to stop the cooking process and then drain off the ice water. Squeeze out any excess liquid and then coarsely chop the herbs.

2 Puree the herbs in a blender with the canola oil for 3 to 4 minutes or until the mixture appears bright green.

3 Pour into a container and refrigerate overnight.

(continued)

4 Strain through a fine-mesh sieve and discard the solids. Refrigerate for 24 hours and decant the oil (remove just the clear oil and discard the impurities that have settled on the bottom).

5 Store in the refrigerator for up to a month. Remove the amount needed from the top, being careful not to disturb the impurities that have settled to the bottom. (See Figure 5-1.)

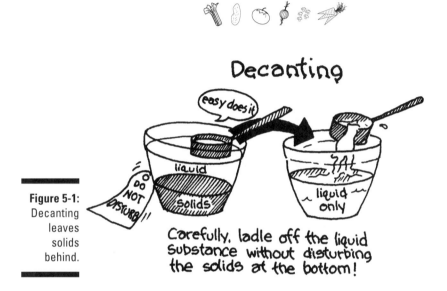

Figure 5-1:
Decanting
leaves
solids
behind.

Making spice oil is quite easy, and spice oils can add very interesting flavors to a dish. You simply sauté spices with a little bit of oil to help release their flavors, and then blend them with oil and allow them to steep. You can make infused spice oils with almost any spice, but cumin, saffron, mustard, chili pepper, turmeric, paprika, and fennel seed work especially well. Curry makes a nice infused oil, too, as in the following recipe.

Curry Oil

You can drizzle Curry Oil over salads, use it to add complexity to coconut broth (see Chapter 9), or brush it on bread the same way you might use olive oil.

Preparation time: *3 minutes, plus 1 day and 3 hours refrigeration*

Yield: *¹/₂ cup*

(continued)

¹/₂ cup chopped onion   *2 tablespoons curry powder*

³/₄ cup canola oil

1 Over medium heat, sauté the onion in 2 tablespoons of the canola oil until translucent.

2 Add the curry power and simmer for 3 minutes over medium-low heat.

3 Puree in a blender with the remaining oil for 3 minutes or until combined. Pour into a container and cover.

4 Refrigerate for 1 day and then strain through a fine-mesh sieve. Let stand for 3 hours in the refrigerator and then carefully decant the oil.

Vinegars

The word *vinegar* is derived from the French *vin,* which means "wine," and *aigre,* meaning "sour," indicating that it first occurred naturally from the spoilage of wine. As early as 5000 B.C., the Babylonians were making vinegar as an end-product of wine from the date palm. Vinegar was the strongest acid known to the ancient world.

In modern times, vinegar has moved into the spotlight. Today, vinegar is used as a condiment, a food preservative, a primitive antibiotic, and even as a household cleaning agent.

I like to use rice wine vinegar for pickling, making infused vinegars, or adding to sauces — it is neutrally flavored and not too acidic. But when it comes to dressing up vegetables or foie gras, balsamic vinegar is the perfect answer. This vinegar is so smooth and sweet that you can even use it on ice cream.

Making infused vinegars

You can make *flavored vinegars* simply by pouring vinegar over berries, hot peppers, spices, or fruit, covering them tightly, and letting them stand to infuse the flavors. There's no need to strain the vinegar; all you need to do is spoon off the desired amount as needed. The berries, peppers, spices, and fruit look great in the bottle, and they last as long as the vinegar.

If you prefer a stronger-flavored vinegar, you can make *infused vinegar* by pureeing the fruit with the vinegar and letting it stand in the refrigerator for three days, which infuses the fruit flavor into the vinegar. After three days, strain the vinegar through a fine-mesh sieve, and it's ready to use.

Aged balsamic vinegars and what makes them so darn smooth!

Whatever you do, don't confuse the balsamic vinegar that you can purchase for five bucks at the local market for the sensational, traditional, aged balsamic vinegar of Reggio Emilia in Modena, Italy. This stuff *rules!* This balsamic vinegar is made from pressed grapes that are cultivated in the traditional manner in the province of Reggio Emilia. It is then cooked over an open flame, cooled, and aged in a rotation of wood casks for a minimum of 12 years. As the vinegar ages, it evaporates and condenses.

Then the annual tasting begins, where a committee rates the vinegar and, on the basis of the score, if deemed acceptable, it qualifies with a red, silver, or gold tag in increasing order of quality. The bottle is then properly sealed with sealing wax.

Numerous testimonials to the quality of balsamic vinegar can be found in the dowry lists of noble Reggio Emilia families in the 1800s. In that era, in fact, it was considered proper for noblewomen who were to be wedded to enrich their dowries with bottles of prized balsamic vinegar.

You can purchase aged balsamic vinegar with these qualities that has been aged as little as 12 years or as many as 100 years. The older it is, the smoother and more syruplike it is. All aged balsamic vinegars should have a dark brown color that is clear and shiny. Its bouquet should be fragrant with pleasant acidity, and the flavor should be well-blended, sweet, and sharp. You can find younger balsamic (12 to 20 years old) at the supermarket. For the older versions, you will probably need to go to a gourmet food shop or even a gourmet mail order catalog, such as Dean and Deluca or Williams-Sonoma (see Chapter 20 for more information about these catalogs, or Chapter 13 for online sources of balsamic vinegar).

You can display your infused oils and vinegars in decorative bottles and even give them as gifts. Infused vinegars keep their color and flavor longer if stored in the refrigerator, but they keep for quite some time out on your countertop. Infused vinegars can be used to make interesting-flavored vinaigrettes or to add a bit of flavor to sauces.

Spicy Vinegar

This flavored vinegar is great to use anytime you need to add a little heat to a sauce, vinaigrette, or soup.

Preparation time: *5 minutes, plus 2 weeks refrigeration*

Yield: *2 cups*

(continued)

2 cups assorted whole chile peppers
(such as jalapeño, red chile, or
habañero)

4 sprigs thyme

4 baby carrots, cut in half lengthwise

$^1/_4$ cup sliced onion

2 cups rice wine vinegar

2 tablespoons olive oil

1 Place the chile peppers, thyme, baby carrots, onion, and vinegar in a 1-quart container with a lid. Top off with the olive oil and close the lid tightly.

2 Let stand for 2 weeks in the refrigerator before opening. Doing so allows a very spicy vinegar to develop.

3 Store in the refrigerator and spoon off the desired amount as needed.

Blackberry Vinegar

Not only do fruit vinegars look great on your countertop, but they also add flavor and body to vinaigrettes and marinades.

Preparation time: *5 minutes, plus 3 days refrigeration*

Yield: *3 cups*

2 cups rice wine vinegar

2 cups blackberries, cleaned

1 Puree the ingredients in a blender for about 1 minute or until smooth. Pour into a container and let stand in the refrigerator for 3 days.

2 Strain through a fine-mesh sieve and discard the solids. Store the vinegar in the refrigerator.

Vinaigrettes

I like to use vinaigrettes because they're easy to make and also very flavorful. A classic vinaigrette is usually two or three parts oil to one part acid (such as vinegar), which are then whisked together. You can use flavored oils or flavored vinegars, or you can use other types of balancing agents, like lemon juice or orange juice, instead of vinegar. I like to work other elements, such as chicken stock or vegetable juice, into a vinaigrette for a more complex flavor.

Vinaigrettes don't necessarily have to be whisked together. You can arrange some asparagus tossed with olive oil in the center of a plate and drizzle some balsamic vinegar along with some herb oil around it to create an asparagus vinaigrette.

You can whisk chicken stock into a vinaigrette in place of some of the oil. Using stock still gives the vinaigrette a nice body and a complex flavor, but it reduces the fat and calorie content.

Lemon-Thyme Vinaigrette

Don't get stuck on the idea that vinaigrettes are only for salads. This vinaigrette is great with a fresh green salad, but you can also warm it and spoon it over a piece of poached fish.

Preparation time: *10 minutes*

Yield: *1 cup*

¹/₄ cup lemon juice	*5 tablespoons canola oil*
1 tablespoon Champagne vinegar	*1¹/₂ tablespoons chopped thyme*
5 tablespoons olive oil	*Salt and pepper*

Place the lemon juice and vinegar in a small bowl. Slowly whisk in the olive and canola oils. Whisk in the thyme and season to taste with salt and pepper.

Waters

Who would have thought that such intense flavors could result from vegetable or fruit waters! You can make tomato, cucumber, or watermelon waters simply by pureeing the product with a little salt (which helps leech out the water) and allowing it to slowly drain through a sieve lined with cheesecloth. The result is a beautifully clear, intensely flavored water.

With other vegetables or fruits that have less liquid (such as celery or apples), you may have to try a different approach to get a water. You have to juice them first, bring the juice barely to a boil, turn off the heat immediately, skim away the solid that separates from the water, and strain the resulting liquid through cheesecloth. This process results in a pure, clean water or essence of that vegetable or fruit.

You can use tomato water chilled in gazpacho, or warmed as a broth with a piece of fish. You can serve fruit waters chilled with a scoop of ice cream or sorbet for a light summer dessert. Fruit and vegetable waters make a great base for cold soups or for refreshing summer drinks. They can be poured over ice or blended, or you can even spice them up with a shot of liquor. Try sweetening fruit waters with a touch of sugar or the pulp from a fresh vanilla bean.

Watermelon Splash

This refreshing drink would be a nice addition to a summer luncheon, a barbecue, or just to surprise your kids. Add a shot of vodka to each glass and you'll surprise the adults, too!

Preparation time: *5 minutes, plus 1 hour refrigeration*

Yield: *4 8-ounce glasses*

8 cups sweet watermelon chunks, seeded

Pinch of salt

4 twists of lemon or lime

1 Puree the watermelon and salt in a food processor for 3 minutes or until no chunks remain.

2 Pour into a strainer lined with cheesecloth and place in a container to catch the liquid. Let stand in the refrigerator for 1 hour until most of the liquid passes through. Discard the pulp.

3 Pour into chilled glasses over ice and top with a twist of lemon or lime.

Chapter 6

Saucing Up a Plate in Nontraditional Ways: Salsas, Relishes, and Chutneys

In This Chapter

▶ Understanding the differences among salsas, relishes, and chutneys

▶ Making salsas, relishes, and chutneys

▶ Using these condiments to add zip to meals

Salsas, chutneys, and relishes are fun, flavorful ways to jazz up a plate. These condiments provide excitement and flavor in a healthy, natural way. They are very easy to make and go with almost every type of cuisine. The popularity of salsas, chutneys, and relishes has been increasing in the last decade as Americans adapt more and more ethnic cuisine into their everyday cooking.

Salsas, relishes, and chutneys are all accompaniments to an appetizer or a main dish. Their only real differences stem from the countries where they originate, and the use of fruits and vegetables that are indigenous to those areas.

✔ **Salsas** come from Mexican cuisine; in fact, salsa is the Mexican word for sauce. Traditionally, they are made with vegetables, fruits, or beans and some type of heat, such as chile peppers.

✔ **Relishes** were an indispensable part of the 19th-century menu in the United States. They were made with different fruits or vegetables that were usually pickled with vinegar and canned for use year-round.

✔ **Chutneys** originated in Indian cooking, where they are considered an essential accompaniment to curry dishes. Traditional Indian chutneys are made with tropical fruits, such as mango, coconut, or dates, or with herbs, such as cilantro or mint.

In true "melting pot" fashion, the words *salsa, relish,* and *chutney* are often used interchangeably today. But no matter what they're called, these sauces are simple and delicious, and they're certainly worth exploring.

Doing the Salsa

The use of salsa as a condiment has boomed in the past several years. Thanks to the explosion of Mexican and Southwestern cuisines across the United States, almost everyone has tried tomato, onion, and chile salsa. Although this type of salsa may be the most common, it's certainly not the only version.

You can toss together any combination of fruits and vegetables to make a salsa. You generally combine these ingredients with some sort of acid, such as lime or lemon, along with some chile peppers and herbs. You can use salsas to top a dish, or in a larger portion as a side dish. Salsas are very versatile — they're great with grilled shrimp or chicken, fajitas, or even in omelets.

Some of the best salsas are the simplest ones, like those containing tomato, cucumber, lime, jalapeño, and cilantro. The cilantro and jalapeño act as spice elements, and the tomato and cucumber refresh your palate and cleanse away some of the heat. You can also add some papaya or mango for a sweeter salsa. In a good salsa, each component retains its own taste, texture, and personality, and each spoonful should contain a little of all the flavors.

Vegetable and fruit salsas should be made at least 30 minutes ahead of time to allow their flavors to blend. But don't make them too far in advance! When salsas are kept overnight, they begin to break down, become watery, and lose some of their texture.

When making salsas, you should always use the freshest and ripest ingredients available. In doing so, you ensure that your salsa has the freshest and purest flavors.

Tomato Salsa

This is the basic salsa that's usually served with tortilla chips. You can easily jazz up the flavor by adding tomatillos or poblano chiles.

Preparation time: *15 minutes, plus 1 hour refrigeration*

Yield: *About 5 cups*

4 cups diced ripe Roma tomatoes (about 8)

1 cup diced red onion (about 1 medium)

2 jalapeños, seeded and minced

3 tablespoons lime juice

3 tablespoons chopped cilantro

Salt and pepper

Tabasco (optional)

1 Place the tomatoes, onion, jalapeños, lime juice, and cilantro in a medium bowl and toss together.

2 Season to taste with salt and pepper, and add Tabasco if you want additional heat.

3 To blend the flavors, let sit in the refrigerator for 1 hour before serving.

Tropical Fruit Salsa

Fruit salsas are great with grilled seafood. You can spoon the salsa on a plate and place the fish or shrimp on top, or you can just spoon the salsa right over the fish. Fruit salsas are also great straight from a spoon to your mouth.

Preparation time: *15 minutes, plus 1 hour refrigeration*

Yield: *About 3 cups*

1 cup diced mango

$^1/_2$ cup diced strawberry papaya

$^1/_2$ cup diced avocado

$^1/_2$ cup diced jicama

$^1/_2$ cup diced red onion

3 tablespoons lime juice

3 tablespoons chopped cilantro

1 Toss together all the ingredients in a medium bowl.

2 To blend the flavors, let sit for 1 hour in the refrigerator before serving.

Sweet Corn and Black Bean Salsa

This corn and bean salsa can really dress up a grilled chicken breast. It also works great as a side dish. You can even fold this salsa into pancake batter and cook up individual corn and bean pancakes, which make a great snack.

Preparation time: *15 minutes, plus 1 hour refrigeration*

Yield: *About 5 cups*

3 cups cooked sweet corn kernels	*¹/₂ cup chopped scallions*
1¹/₂ cups cooked black beans	*3 tablespoons lime juice*
¹/₄ cup chopped chives	*Salt and pepper*

1 Combine all the ingredients in a medium bowl. Season to taste with salt and pepper.

2 To blend the flavors, let sit for 1 hour in the refrigerator before serving. Serve hot or cold.

Red Chile Pepper, Chipotle, and Yellow Tomato Salsa

This chipotle and yellow tomato salsa gets its nice smoky flavor from the chipotle peppers. It's a great addition to enchiladas or grilled chicken. Because this salsa has a kick to it, you may want to cool yourself down with a margarita.

Preparation time: *15 minutes, plus 1 hour refrigeration*

Yield: *About 4 cups*

2¹/₂ cups diced yellow tomatoes	*1 tablespoon lemon juice*
1 cup chopped scallions	*2 tablespoons lime juice*
2 tablespoons diced red chile peppers	*Salt and pepper*
3 tablespoons finely chopped dried chipotle peppers	

1 Toss together all the ingredients in a medium bowl. Season to taste with salt and pepper.

2 To blend the flavors, let sit in the refrigerator for 1 hour before serving.

Grilled Swordfish with Red Chile Pepper, Chipotle, and Yellow Tomato Salsa

Swordfish has a strong enough flavor to be matched up with the flavorful peppers in this dish and not be overpowered. This Southwestern dish is terrific for a barbecue.

Preparation time: *2 minutes*

Cooking time: *8 minutes*

Yield: *4 servings*

4 4-ounce pieces of swordfish

2 tablespoons olive oil

Salt and pepper

Red Chile Pepper, Chipotle, and Yellow Tomato Salsa (see preceding recipe)

1 Rub the swordfish with the olive oil and season both sides with salt and pepper.

2 Grill over medium heat for 3 to 4 minutes on each side or until done.

3 Place a piece of the grilled swordfish on each plate and spoon the salsa over the fish.

Relishing Your Dishes

Believe it or not, there's more to relishes than that neon green stuff you put on hot dogs. Relishes are similar to salsas, although relishes often have more of a fruit and berry influence, usually have pickled or brined elements, and are not as spicy as salsas. The ingredients for relishes can be grated, chopped, or julienned.

Relishes stand up well to heavier items such as swordfish, halibut, pork, and chicken. Vegetable relishes taste even better when they are made a couple days in advance so that the flavors have a chance to marry. (Talk about a short engagement!)

Ginger, Orange, and Cranberry Relish

You can jazz up a turkey or Cornish hen with a tart and tangy fruit relish, especially one with a touch of ginger or lemongrass. This is a great holiday recipe, but I'm tempted to use it whenever I cook poultry.

Preparation time: 10 minutes

Cooking time: 30 minutes

Yield: About 3 cups

3 tablespoons chopped ginger

1 tablespoon olive oil

2 cups orange segments, skin and seeds removed

2 cups dried cranberries

3 tablespoons minced shallots

¹/₂ cup rice wine vinegar

¹/₄ cup brown sugar

4 tablespoons chopped basil

1 teaspoon allspice

1 Place all the ingredients in a medium saucepan. Cook over medium heat, stirring occasionally, for 20 to 30 minutes or until the cranberries are soft and most of the liquid has cooked out.

2 If you prefer a smooth relish, you can puree it in the blender; otherwise, leave it chunky.

Papaya and Pickled Red Onion Relish

Pickled tropical fruit relishes are interesting and quite refreshing. This papaya and pickled red onion relish complements swordfish, tuna, lobster, or even shrimp. You can toss the papaya with some of the pickling juice for extra pickled flavor.

Preparation time: 15 minutes

Cooking time: 5 minutes

Yield: About 4 cups

(continued)

2 teaspoons pink peppercorns, crushed

$^{1}/_{2}$ cup water

$^{1}/_{4}$ cup Champagne vinegar

2 tablespoons sugar

1 tablespoon salt

1 whole clove

1 cup julienned red onion

2 cups diced papaya

3 tablespoons chopped chives

1 tablespoon olive oil

1 To make the pickling liquid, place the pink peppercorns, water, vinegar, sugar, salt, and clove in a small saucepan. Add the red onion and simmer over medium heat for 5 minutes or until the onion is bright pink.

2 Set aside until the liquid is cool; then discard the clove, strain off and discard the liquid, and reserve the onions. (You can save the cooking liquid for other uses and store it in the refrigerator for a few days if you like.)

3 Toss together the papaya and onions in a small bowl. Fold in the chopped chives and olive oil.

Apple-Fennel Relish

In this recipe, apple and fennel meet to create a crisp and flavorful combination. This relish goes great over pork tenderloin or grilled catfish. The anise flavor from the fennel in this relish is enhanced by the addition of the fennel tops. People generally toss fennel tops away without realizing that they're packed with flavor and make a wonderful garnish.

Preparation time: *10 minutes, plus 1 hour marinating*

Cooking time: *2 minutes*

Yield: *About 4 cups*

$^{1}/_{4}$ cup rice wine vinegar

$^{1}/_{2}$ teaspoon fennel seed

$^{1}/_{4}$ teaspoon nutmeg

3 tablespoons brown sugar

2 cups diced fennel

2 cups diced Granny Smith apples

$^{1}/_{2}$ cup golden raisins

3 tablespoons lemon juice

$^{1}/_{4}$ cup chopped fennel tops

Salt and pepper

(continued)

1 Place the vinegar, fennel seed, nutmeg, and brown sugar in a small saucepan and cook over medium heat for 2 minutes.

2 Add the fennel, apples, and raisins and then remove from the heat. Fold in the lemon juice and fennel tops and season to taste with salt and pepper.

3 Allow the mixture to marinate for at least 1 hour before using. (You can make this relish a day ahead.)

Hot and Spicy Zucchini, Napa Cabbage, and Mustard Relish

This spicy zucchini relish is great with grilled pork chops, or as a side dish in place of cole slaw. If you make it a day ahead and let it stand in the refrigerator, this relish has a chance to marinate and explodes with even more flavor.

Preparation time: *15 minutes, plus overnight refrigeration*

Yield: *About 3 cups*

4 cups julienned zucchini

2 cups grated Napa cabbage

3 tablespoons coarse (or whole-grain) brown mustard

2 tablespoons minced jalapeño

3 tablespoons rice wine vinegar

$^1/_4$ cup olive oil

2 teaspoons sugar

Salt and pepper

1 Toss together all the ingredients in a medium bowl. Season to taste with salt and pepper.

2 Let stand in the refrigerator overnight to blend the flavors.

Grilled Brats on Sourdough Buns with Hot and Spicy Zucchini, Napa Cabbage, and Mustard Relish

Here's a fun way to zip up ordinary bratwurst. This spicy relish is an easy way to show off your new gourmet skills to your neighbors and friends.

Preparation time: *2 minutes*

Cooking time: *20 minutes*

Yield: *4 servings*

4 turkey bratwurst

Salt and pepper

4 sourdough hot dog buns, halved and toasted

Hot and Spicy Zucchini, Napa Cabbage, and Mustard Relish (see preceding recipe)

1 Season the turkey bratwurst with salt and pepper.

2 Grill the bratwurst over medium heat for 8 to 10 minutes on each side or until done.

3 Place a cooked bratwurst in each bun and spoon some of the relish over the bratwurst.

Charming Your Cuisine with Chutney

Chutneys are an important part of Indian cuisine. They emphasize different flavors and textures, with hot, sour, sweet, and spicy all melded into one. Chutneys can be coarse, with chunks of fruits and vegetables, or they can be cooked down to a paste or a fine puree. They are usually a sweet and sour relish containing sugar and fruit, and are generally cooked anywhere from 20 to 60 minutes.

You can make chutneys in advance and keep them in the refrigerator for several days.

Chutneys go great with hearty meats, such as lamb or pork, and are a delicious accompaniment to curried dishes. Sweet chutneys make interesting spreads for bread and are also a perfect partner to cheese.

Caramelized Onion and Tomato Chutney

This caramelized onion and tomato chutney is a great filling for a tart or a topping for fresh sourdough bread. It makes a nice sauce alongside a piece of baked chicken; you can even add it to tomato sauce to make a flavorful marinara sauce.

Preparation time: *10 minutes*

Cooking time: *30 to 40 minutes*

Yield: *About 2 cups*

2 cups julienned Spanish onions

2 tablespoons canola oil

3 cups diced red tomato

1 tablespoon brown sugar

$^1/_2$ cup chopped basil

1 tablespoon balsamic vinegar

Salt and pepper

1 In a medium sauté pan over medium-high heat, cook the onion in the canola oil for 8 to 10 minutes or until caramelized and golden-brown.

2 Add the tomato and brown sugar and then reduce the heat to medium. Continue to cook, stirring occasionally, for 20 to 25 minutes or until most of the liquid has been cooked out.

3 Remove from the heat, add the basil and balsamic vinegar, and season to taste with salt and pepper.

Fig, Raisin, and Thyme Chutney

Whether you use black or green figs for this chutney, you get marvelous results — as long as the figs are ripe. The onion nicely cuts through the sweet, dense figs. This sweet fig chutney is a must for pork or lamb.

Preparation time: *10 minutes*

Cooking time: *20 minutes*

Yield: *About 2 cups*

(continued)

^{1}/$_2$ cup chopped shallots

^{1}/$_2$ cup golden raisins

1 cup chopped Spanish onion

1 tablespoon chopped thyme

2 tablespoons canola oil

1^1/$_2$ teaspoons rice wine vinegar

3 cups ripe purple figs, chopped

Salt and pepper

1 In a medium sauté pan, cook the shallots and onion in the canola oil over medium-high heat for 3 minutes or until slightly golden-brown.

2 Add the figs and raisins, reduce the heat to medium, and continue to cook for 10 minutes, stirring occasionally.

3 Add the thyme and rice wine vinegar and continue to cook for 5 more minutes, or until the figs have broken down but are still slightly chunky.

4 Season to taste with salt and pepper.

Sautéed Pork Chops with Fig, Raisin, and Thyme Chutney

Fig, raisin, and thyme chutney goes wonderfully with pork. It adds sweetness and a smooth texture that perfectly complements the meat.

Preparation time: *2 minutes*

Cooking time: *10 minutes*

Yield: *4 servings*

4 6-ounce pork chops

Fig, Raisin, and Thyme Chutney (see preceding recipe)

Salt and pepper

2 tablespoons canola oil

1 Season the pork chops with salt and pepper and place the pork chops in a hot sauté pan containing the canola oil. Cook for 5 minutes on each side or until just cooked.

2 Warm the chutney in a small saucepan over medium heat for 3 minutes or until hot.

3 Place a pork chop on each plate and spoon some of the chutney over each pork chop.

Hot and Sour Mango Chutney

Hot and sour is a great combination for grilled beef tenderloin, especially when paired with sweet, tropical mango. This chutney is also great with spice-rubbed meats (see Chapter 11).

Preparation time: *10 minutes*

Cooking time: *15 to 20 minutes*

Yield: *2 cups*

1 cup chopped Spanish onion

2 tablespoons canola oil

2 jalapeños, seeded and minced

¹/₂ cup brown sugar

¹/₂ cup rice wine vinegar

3 cups chopped mango

1 In a medium sauté pan, cook the onion in the canola oil for 5 to 7 minutes or until caramelized.

2 Add the jalapeños, brown sugar, and rice wine vinegar and continue to cook for 5 minutes.

3 Add the mango and cook for 10 more minutes. Serve warm or cold.

Chapter 7

Where's the Beef? Vegetable Cuisine

In This Chapter

▶ Making vegetable preparations

▶ Cooking with fresh herbs

▶ Cooking with mushrooms

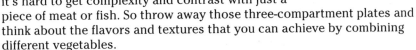
*V*egetable cuisine isn't necessarily vegetarian, and it doesn't contain just vegetables. Vegetable cuisine encompasses vegetables, grains, rice, legumes, and sometimes even a sauce made with meat stock. It simply *focuses* on vegetables because they are one of the most interesting aspects of cuisine. Whether you're eating them for philosophical reasons, for health reasons, or just because you like them, vegetables provide complexity, texture, and depth and come in an incredible range of flavors and colors.

Vegetables have been relegated to the side-dish category for too long. It's time to start thinking about how you can incorporate them into the meal as a whole. Don't think of a meal as separate servings of meat, starch, and vegetables. Think about how you can integrate each of those components into a dish. Remember, gourmet cooking is about complex flavors, textures, and contrasts — it's hard to get complexity and contrast with just a piece of meat or fish. So throw away those three-compartment plates and think about the flavors and textures that you can achieve by combining different vegetables.

CHARLIE SAYS

Most meats, seafoods, and grains are available year-round. But most vegetables have specific seasons and should be used during the height of their season in order to get the fullest flavor. In an ideal world, everyone would have the time to shop each day for produce, and freshness would be guaranteed. But with life's busy schedules, you often have to purchase produce several days in advance, so selecting produce that is ripe, fresh, and in season is essential. (Chapter 4 describes different vegetables, tells when they're in season, and explains how to tell whether they're ripe.) After you choose the dishes you want to make, you can check the availability of the produce in those dishes and refresh your shopping skills.

The demand for fresh vegetables has risen drastically, causing supermarkets to stock many more types of fresh and organic vegetables than they did ten years ago. Farmers' markets are also a great place to get fresh produce. They usually carry the basics as well as many types of specialty vegetables.

Use organic produce whenever possible because it is cultivated and processed without pesticides, fertilizers, or insecticides and has no artificial coloring, flavoring, or additives. Organically grown vegetables may cost a bit more, but they have a naturally purer flavor, and you can be assured that you are eating environmentally safe food.

After you select an assortment of vegetables, designing a meal is easy. I often just lay all the vegetables on the counter, see what grains, rice, or pasta I have in the cupboard, and let my imagination run wild. I might braise one vegetable, juice another for a sauce or broth, puree another, and sauté the remaining vegetables, resulting in a dish with many different textures and flavors.

If you don't feel confident enough yet to "wing it," try one of the following recipes for great flavor and texture combinations.

Caramelized Onion Tart with Sweet Curry Crust

Onions and curry are a natural flavor combination. The sweet caramelized onions and the spicy-sweet curry meld with the buttery crust. You can make this tart in smaller tart shells for individual servings, or you can make it in an 8-inch-square pan and cut it into small squares, triangles, or rounds as an appetizer.

Specialty tools: *8-inch tart pan*

Preparation time: *20 minutes, plus 30 minutes refrigeration*

Cooking time: *1 hour*

Yield: *6 servings*

(continued)

2 cups flour

1 teaspoon salt

1 tablespoon sweet curry powder

1 cup plus 2 tablespoons cold butter, cubed

²/₃ cup cold water

3 large Spanish onions, julienned

1 egg yolk

¹/₂ cup heavy cream

Salt and pepper

1 Place the flour, salt, sweet curry powder, and 1 cup of the butter in a mixing bowl. Using the paddle attachment of an electric mixer (or by hand, using a dough cutter), mix on low until all the ingredients are combined and the texture is coarse. Add the water all at once and mix on low until the dough just starts to come together.

2 Remove the dough from the mixing bowl and work into a ball on a floured surface. Wrap the dough in plastic and place in the refrigerator for 30 minutes or until you're ready to use it.

3 Sauté the onions in a large sauté pan with the remaining 2 tablespoons of butter, stirring occasionally, for 15 to 20 minutes or until the onions are golden-brown and caramelized. Season with salt and pepper. Cool the onions to room temperature.

4 Roll out the dough on a lightly floured surface until it's about ¹/₄ inch thick. Lay the dough in the tart pan, smooth it out, and cut away the excess dough.

5 In a small bowl, whisk together the egg yolk and heavy cream. Place the cooled onions on top of the dough, pour in the cream mixture, and top with freshly ground black pepper.

6 Bake at 375° for 40 to 45 minutes or until just firm to the touch and slightly golden-brown. Cool slightly before cutting and serving.

Yukon Gold Potato Soup with Braised Leeks

Creamy Yukon Gold potatoes create a velvety smooth soup. The braised leeks provide flavor and texture to the soup as they melt away in your mouth.

Preparation time: *15 minutes*

Cooking time: *35 minutes*

Yield: *4 servings*

(continued)

1 large leek	*3 cups Vegetable Stock (see Chapter 5)*
2 cups Chicken Stock (see Chapter 5)	*2 tablespoons butter*
2 sprigs fresh rosemary	*1 cup milk*
2 pounds Yukon Gold potatoes, peeled and diced	*Salt and pepper*

1 Cut off the root end and most of the green tip of the leek, leaving 2 inches of green. Cut in half lengthwise and rinse with cold water, removing any dirt and sand.

2 Place the leek in a large, shallow pan wide enough to hold it. Add the chicken stock and one sprig of the rosemary. Simmer over medium-low heat, covered, for 25 minutes or until the leek is tender. Remove the leek from the liquid and chop it into bite-sized pieces.

3 While the leek is cooking, cook the potatoes in boiling salted water for 20 to 25 minutes or until done. Drain and set aside.

4 Place the vegetable stock and remaining rosemary in a small saucepan and simmer for 10 minutes over medium heat. Discard the rosemary.

5 Puree the potatoes, vegetable stock, 2 tablespoons butter, and milk until smooth. Season with salt and pepper. Reheat prior to serving if necessary.

6 Fold the chopped leek into the hot potato soup. Pour into warm bowls and serve while hot.

Tomato, Red Onion, and Roasted Yellow Bell Pepper Flat Bread with Fresh Mozzarella Cheese

Flat bread is a crunchy alternative to focaccia. You can serve it hot or at room temperature, and the flavor combinations for the toppings are endless. Think of it as gourmet pizza and let your imagination run wild.

Preparation time: *30 minutes, plus 45 minutes rising time*

Cooking time: *30 minutes*

Yield: *4 servings*

(continued)

For the Flat Bread:

7 tablespoons warm water

¹/₄ ounce active dry yeast

Pinch of sugar

2 tablespoons butter, melted and cooled

¹/₄ teaspoon salt

1¹/₄ to 1¹/₂ cups flour

1 tablespoon fennel seeds, toasted at 350° for 10 minutes and then coarsely ground

1 egg white mixed with 2 tablespoons water

Salt

1 Combine the warm water, yeast, and sugar in a small mixing bowl. Let sit for 3 minutes; then add the melted butter and salt.

2 Using an electric mixer fitted with a dough hook (or mixing by hand), add the flour and fennel seeds and mix until fully incorporated. The dough should be smooth but not sticky.

3 Form the dough into a ball, place in a lightly oiled bowl, and cover with a damp cloth. Let rise in a warm place for about 45 minutes, or until it triples in volume.

4 Divide the dough into 4 equal portions. On a lightly floured surface, roll each piece of dough into a thin, round disc about 8 to 10 inches in diameter. Place on a lightly oiled sheet pan and score with the tines of a fork. Brush with the egg white mixture and lightly sprinkle with salt. Bake at 375° for 8 to 10 minutes or until golden-brown. Remove from the pan and let cool.

For the Assembly:

1¹/₂ cups julienned red onion

1 tablespoon butter

2 small tomatoes, thinly sliced

1¹/₂ tablespoons balsamic vinegar

Salt and pepper

¹/₄ cup Basil Oil (see Chapter 5)

1 Roasted Yellow Bell Pepper, cleaned and julienned (see following recipe)

¹/₄ cup basil, cut into a fine chiffonade

8 ounces fresh mozzarella, broken into small pieces

1 In a small sauté pan, caramelize the red onion with the butter over medium-high heat for 7 to 10 minutes or until golden-brown.

2 Toss the tomato slices with the balsamic vinegar and season with salt and pepper. Using a pastry brush, brush the flat bread with the basil oil.

3 Arrange some of the red onion, roasted yellow bell pepper, tomato slices, basil, and fresh mozzarella pieces on top of each flat bread.

4 Bake at 375° for 7 to 10 minutes or until the cheese is melted and golden-brown.

Roasted Yellow Bell Peppers

Roasted peppers are juicy, tender, and full of flavor. You can roast any type of bell pepper, such as red, green, or yellow. You can use this same technique to roast poblano chile peppers, as well. The sweet roasted peppers can be simply chopped up and used in a salad, or you can puree them to make a sauce or vinaigrette.

Preparation time: *1 minute*

Cooking time: *13 minutes*

Yield: *1 pepper*

1 yellow bell pepper   *1 teaspoon canola oil*

1 Rub the outside of the pepper with the oil until it is completely covered.

2 Place the pepper on a grill, under the broiler, or on an open flame of the stovetop. Cook on each side for 2 to 3 minutes or until the skin has turned black and bubbly.

3 Place the pepper in a small bowl and cover tightly with plastic wrap. Let stand for 10 minutes to steam.

4 To clean the pepper, remove the black outer skin and rinse gently under cold water to remove any tiny black particles. Discard the seeds and stem. Refrigerate the pepper until needed.

Julienned Vegetable Spring Rolls with Hot Curried Mustard Dipping Sauce

Spring rolls are a healthy, refreshing version of a deep-fried egg roll. If you are able to roll these spring rolls tightly, you can cut them into 1-inch slices. Otherwise, you can serve them whole or just slice them in half on the bias. The intense heat of the curried mustard sauce in this recipe is cut by the cool and refreshing spring rolls.

Preparation time: *30 minutes*

Yield: *4 spring rolls*

(continued)

$^1/_2$ cup finely julienned carrots

$^1/_2$ cup finely julienned leeks

$^1/_2$ cup finely julienned red bell pepper

$^1/_2$ cup shredded Napa cabbage

$^1/_2$ cup spinach, cut into a chiffonade

$^1/_2$ cup julienned roasted shiitake mushrooms

1 tablespoon lime juice

3 tablespoons julienned cilantro

2 tablespoons olive oil

3 tablespoons sesame oil

Salt and pepper

4 8-inch-round pieces rice paper

1 tablespoon sweet curry powder

$^1/_4$ cup Chinese mustard (a spicy brown mustard)

2 tablespoons sugar

2 tablespoons water

$^1/_4$ cup daikon sprouts

1 In a large bowl, toss together the carrots, leeks, red bell pepper, Napa cabbage, spinach, shiitake mushrooms, lime juice, and cilantro.

2 Drizzle the olive oil and sesame oil over the vegetables and season to taste with salt and pepper.

3 Soak the rice paper in cold water one piece at a time for 1$^1/_2$ minutes or until slightly soft. *Tip:* Soak the rice paper just before you use each sheet. Remove the rice paper from the water immediately; otherwise, it will begin to break apart.

4 Lay the rice paper flat and fill with a quarter of the vegetable mixture. Roll up tightly while folding in the sides of the rice paper until you have a tight, cigar-like shape. Repeat this process 3 more times with the remaining ingredients.

5 In a small bowl, whisk together the curry, mustard, sugar, and water.

6 Slice each spring roll in half on the bias and serve with the daikon sprouts and mustard sauce for dipping.

Parmesan and Eggplant Soup with Parmesan Crisps

Parmesan soup is not as heavy as it sounds. The soup's broth-like character, along with the textural elements from the eggplant and parmesan crisps, give this soup a refined complexity.

(continued)

Preparation time: *1 hour*

Cooking time: *1 hour*

Yield: *4 servings*

5 cups peeled and diced eggplant	*1 pound Parmesan cheese, chopped*
Salt and pepper	*³/₄ cup grated Parmesan*
1 cup diced Spanish onion	*4 tablespoons shaved Parmesan*
2 tablespoons butter	*4 tablespoons chives, cut into 1-inch-long pieces*
8 cups Chicken Stock (see Chapter 5)	

1 Toss the diced eggplant with 2 teaspoons of salt and let sit for 30 minutes at room temperature. Then gently rinse the eggplant with water and drain.

2 In a medium sauté pan, sweat the onion in the butter for 3 to 4 minutes or until the onion is translucent. Add the eggplant and continue to cook for 15 to 20 minutes or until the eggplant is tender. Set aside 1 cup of the cooked eggplant to use as a garnish.

3 In a large saucepan, bring the chicken stock to a simmer. Add the chopped Parmesan cheese and continue to simmer slowly for 45 minutes. Then strain the stock and discard the cheese.

4 Puree the cooked eggplant with the chicken stock and pass the mixture through a fine-mesh sieve into a large bowl, discarding the solids. Season the liquid to taste with salt and pepper.

5 To create the Parmesan crisps, sprinkle an even ¹/₈-inch layer of the grated Parmesan into the bottom of a large, nonstick sauté pan. Cook slowly over medium-low heat until the cheese melts and turns golden-brown.

6 Loosen the edges of the Parmesan from the pan by using a rubber spatula. Carefully slide the melted cheese from the pan onto a cutting board. Immediately cut the cheese into 6 irregularly shaped triangles. While the cheese triangles are still hot, lay them over a wine bottle or rolling pin to create a curve-shaped crisp. Let the crisps cool completely. Repeat the process again to create a total of 12 Parmesan crisps.

7 Ladle some of the hot soup into each of 4 bowls. Spoon some of the reserved eggplant into each bowl. Sprinkle with the shaved Parmesan flakes and long-cut chives. Place 3 of the Parmesan crisps in the center of each bowl of soup.

Herbs

Herbs can change an ordinary dish into something really special — the possibilities are truly endless. Here are a few ways I like to use herbs:

- ✔ Infuse them into stocks, sauces, or broths.
- ✔ Add them to vinaigrettes, doughs, and breads.
- ✔ *Crust* (or coat) meat, fish, or poultry with chopped herbs.
- ✔ Blend or infuse oils and vinegars with herbs, resulting in intense flavors.
- ✔ Infuse sweet herbs such as basil, rosemary, and tarragon into ice creams.

Herbs are inexpensive and easy to grow. If you plan early enough, you can start your herb garden with seeds, but for those of us who procrastinate, starter plants work just as well and are almost guaranteed to take. You can grow herbs in the window box of your high-rise in the city, on your back porch, or, if you have a backyard garden, you can section off an area for herbs. But wherever you grow your herbs, make sure that they're close to your kitchen door so that you don't forget to use them when you cook!

If you have the proverbial brown thumb, you can usually find fresh herbs in small packages at your supermarket or at farmers' markets. Use fresh herbs whenever possible, because the flavors are more delicate, crisp, and clean than those of dried herbs. Dried herbs are three to five times as strong as fresh ones, so use them sparingly.

You can store freshly picked herbs in the refrigerator wrapped in a wet paper towel. You can also use them for a table decoration by storing them in a small vase filled with water to keep them fresh, but keep them out of the sun or they'll wilt. Herbs should be chopped or snipped from the stems at the last moment so that they don't discolor; but, more important, after the leaves are cut, the volatile oils are released and the intense flavor begins to dissipate. Nothing has more flavor than an herb that is cut just seconds before being added to a plate.

If you have an abundance of herbs in your garden as the first frost approaches, snip them and tie them together in small bunches. Hang them with the tops downward in a warm, dry room without exposure to direct sunlight. After they are dry, they can be used for wreaths or for cooking. But remember that dried herbs begin to lose their flavor substantially after five or six months. Those that are more than a year old have no more flavor than the dust from your vacuum cleaner and should be thrown away.

You will most likely encounter the herbs in Table 7-1 (also see Figure 7-1) at some point, whether in your backyard, at your favorite restaurant, or at a farmers' market. I give you a few suggestions on how to use specific herbs, but nothing is written in stone, and there are no rights or wrongs. Experimenting with herb and food pairings is the best way to learn how to use them. Try to imagine how a food and an herb would taste together — if you have the herb on hand, give it a taste. After its flavor is on your palate, pairing the herb with other foods is much easier.

Figure 7-1:
Fresh
herbs are
essential to
gourmet
cooking.

Table 7-1	Herbs
Herb	**Description**
Basil	The flavor of basil is a cross between licorice and cloves. Several types exist, such as purple basil (also known as opal basil) and curly leaf basil. They have slightly different flavors, but they can be used interchangeably. You can use basil in tomato sauces, pesto, soups, salads, and infused oils.
Bay leaf	Also called *laurel leaf,* bay leaf comes from the evergreen bay laurel tree and has a pungent, piney flavor. You can use it in stocks or sauces that cook for an extended period of time. Be careful not to use too much at once, or your sauce may become bitter.
Chervil	This delicate-flavored herb is a member of the parsley family. The leaves are tiny and soft and have a slight anise flavor. You can use chervil in salads or as a garnish.
Chives	Related to the onion and leek, chives are long, slender, green stems with a hollow interior. They have a mild onion flavor. You can use them chopped as a garnish for many items, or infuse them into a vinaigrette or an oil.
Coriander	Found in both seed and leaf form. The leaves (also known as *cilantro*) have an extremely pungent flavor with a soapy after-taste. Coriander is often used in ethnic cuisine and can also be used in salads and curries.
Dill	Found in seed and leaf form, dill has a tangy flavor that dissipates during cooking, so you should add it at the last minute. It is often paired with smoked salmon, but it has numerous uses, such as in soups, vinaigrettes, and sauces and with all types of seafood.
Fennel	The feathery green tops of the fennel bulb have the flavor of fennel but a tad more delicate licorice flavor. You can use it with seafood, lamb, and sausage and in salads.
Lemon balm	The leaves have a lemon-scented, mint-like flavor and are often used to make tea. You can also use lemon balm in many dessert preparations.
Lemon verbena	The long, slender leaves of this potent herb have a strong lemon-like flavor. You can use lemon verbena to make tea or infuse it into ice creams or sorbets.
Lemongrass	Long, yellow-green stalks have a sour-lemon flavor and fragrance. Lemongrass is important in Thai cooking.
Marjoram	The tiny leaves have a mild oregano-like flavor. You can use marjoram anyplace you would use oregano.
Mint	The two most popular species are peppermint and spearmint. The leaves have a spicy-sweet menthol flavor. You can use mint in dessert preparations or with lamb in the form of a chutney.

(continued)

Table 7-1 *(continued)*

Herb	Description
Oregano	Sometimes called *wild marjoram*. Oregano has a sweeter, stronger, more pungent flavor than marjoram. You can use it in tomato sauces or with any meat, poultry, or seafood dishes. You can also use it to infuse flavor into oils and vinegars.
Parsley	Found in flat and curly leaf forms, parsley has a slightly peppery, fresh flavor. It is often used chopped as a garnish and can be used in salads and with various meats and seafoods.
Rosemary	This pungent herb has a piney flavor with hints of lemon. You can use rosemary with lamb, pork, veal, and beef or infuse it into sauces and stocks.
Sage	The leaves are somewhat bitter and have a musty-mint flavor and aroma. You can use sage with pork and most other meats, or you can fry the leaves and use them as a garnish.
Savory	Summer and winter varieties exist; both are related to the mint family. Savory's flavor is a cross between thyme and mint, with the summer variety being somewhat milder than the winter one. You can use it with most meats and in stuffings.
Tarragon	Tarragon has a distinctive anise flavor that can dominate other flavors. You can use it in salads or vinaigrettes or with seafood or delicate meats.
Thyme	These tiny gray-green leaves give off a pungent, minty, light-lemon aroma with a hint of clove. You can infuse thyme into sauces, stocks, vinaigrettes, and oils. You can also use it in marinating meat, fish, and poultry.

In the following recipes, I give you some ideas for using and combining various herbs. Feel free to add to or jazz up these dishes with other herbs.

Spicy Cumin-Infused Sweet Corn Soup with Cilantro

This sweet corn soup explodes with flavor and has a brilliant yellow color. You can even use it as a sauce for lobster or crab cakes.

Preparation time: *15 minutes*

Cooking time: *25 minutes*

Yield: *4 servings*

(continued)

6 fresh ears of sweet corn	*3 tablespoons butter*
1 cup chopped onion	*3 cups Vegetable Stock (see Chapter 5)*
1 teaspoon ground cumin	*Salt and pepper*
3 jalapeños, seeded and minced	*2 tablespoons chopped cilantro*

1 Sauté the corn, onion, cumin, and jalapeños with the butter in a large sauté pan for 20 to 25 minutes or until the kernels are cooked. Reserve 2 cups of the corn mixture for garnish.

2 Place the remaining corn mixture in a blender with the vegetable stock and puree until smooth.

3 Pass through a sieve, place in a medium saucepan, and warm over medium heat. Season with salt and pepper.

4 Spoon some of the reserved corn mixture into each bowl, and ladle the soup over the corn. Sprinkle with the chopped cilantro.

Herb-Crusted Warm Goat Cheese and Grilled Vegetable Salad

The warm goat cheese in this recipe melts into the vegetables as you cut into it. This dish makes a great luncheon salad.

Preparation time: *20 minutes, plus 30 minutes refrigeration*

Cooking time: *20 minutes*

Yield: *4 servings*

1 medium zucchini, sliced thinly on the diagonal	*2 tablespoons chopped chives*
	2 tablespoons chopped chervil
1 medium yellow squash, sliced thinly on the diagonal	*1 cup toasted bread crumbs*
1 small eggplant, with skin, sliced ¹/₄ inch thick	*1 egg yolk*
	2 tablespoons water
³/₄ cup olive oil	*1 tablespoon vegetable oil*
Salt and pepper	*3 tablespoons balsamic vinegar*
4 2-ounce pieces of goat cheese	*4 cups mesclun mix, cleaned*

(continued)

1 Rub the zucchini, yellow squash, and eggplant slices with ¹/₄ cup of the olive oil and season with salt and pepper. Grill over a medium flame, cool to room temperature, and set aside.

2 Form the goat cheese into 4 round discs that are about ¹/₂ inch thick.

3 In a small bowl, toss together the chopped herbs and bread crumbs. Whisk together the egg yolk and water in a separate bowl. Dip the goat cheese rounds in the egg yolk mixture and evenly cover with the bread crumb mixture. Pat firmly and refrigerate for 30 minutes.

4 Sauté the goat cheese rounds in a nonstick sauté pan with the vegetable oil for 2 to 3 minutes on each side or until golden-brown and crispy.

5 Whisk together the balsamic vinegar and the remaining ¹/₂ cup olive oil to make the vinaigrette. Season to taste with salt and pepper.

6 Toss the mesclun mix in a medium bowl with the vinaigrette just prior to use.

7 Arrange the mesclun mix and grilled vegetables in the center of each plate and top with the warm goat cheese rounds. Top with freshly ground pepper and serve immediately.

Herbed Roasted Olives

You can use herbed olives in the same ways you use calamata olives. Try them with pasta, on a salad, or just out of the bowl; they'll bring excitement to your palate. ***Tip:*** In this recipe, make sure that you use olives *with* pits — if you try to bake pitted olives, they'll end up looking like wizened little mummies.

Preparation time: *10 minutes*

Cooking time: *2 hours*

Yield: *4 cups olives*

4 cups assorted black and green Italian, French, and Greek olives, with pits

2 tablespoons chopped rosemary

2 tablespoons chopped thyme

2 tablespoons olive oil

1 Drain any liquid from the olives and toss them with the herbs and olive oil.

2 Place the olives in a shallow, ovenproof pan and roast in the oven at 250° for 2 hours or until the olives are slightly shriveled.

3 Remove the olives from the oven and refrigerate until needed.

Basil and Caramelized Red Onion Focaccia

Fresh baked focaccia stuffed with grilled vegetables and a slice of cheese makes a great sandwich. You can flavor focaccia with any type of herb; this bread is great when served either warm or at room temperature.

Specialty tools: *Parchment paper, spray bottle, mixer with dough hook*

Preparation time: *1 hour, plus 2 hours for dough to rise, 24 hours refrigeration, and 1$^1/_2$ hours to let dough warm after refrigeration*

Cooking time: *20 minutes*

Yield: *4 servings*

2 cups julienned red onion	$^1/_2$ teaspoon salt
$^1/_3$ cup olive oil	$^1/_2$ cup chopped basil
$^1/_2$ ounce active dry yeast	$^1/_4$ cup Basil Oil (see Chapter 5)
2$^1/_4$ to 2$^1/_2$ cups warm water	Cornmeal for dusting
6$^1/_2$ cups flour	Salt

1 In a medium sauté pan, cook the onion with 2 tablespoons of the olive oil over medium-high heat for 8 to 10 minutes or until golden-brown and caramelized. Cool the onion to room temperature.

2 Sprinkle the yeast into $^1/_2$ cup of the warm water and let sit for 3 minutes.

3 Whisk the remaining 2 cups of water with the remaining olive oil and set aside.

4 Combine the flour and salt in a large bowl and set aside.

5 Pour the water-oil mixture over the yeast mixture and blend. Add half the flour and stir with a rubber spatula to combine. Add the caramelized red onions and chopped basil.

6 Using a dough hook on an electric mixer, add the remaining flour and mix on low for 4 minutes or until the dough comes together and is one complete mass. (If the dough is dry, you can add a few more drops of water.) Continue to mix for about 20 minutes (to develop the gluten). If you don't have a dough hook, you can build up big Popeye forearms by kneading the dough by hand for 40 minutes.

7 Remove the dough from the mixing bowl and work it into a ball. Place the dough in an oiled bowl, brush the top of the dough with oil, and cover tightly with plastic wrap. Allow the dough to rise at room temperature until it doubles in size (about 1 hour).

8 Punch down the dough to deflate it and then let it rise until it again doubles in size (about 45 minutes to 1 hour).

(continued)

9 Punch down the dough again to deflate it. Divide the dough into 4 equal portions, shape each piece into a ball, and place each ball into an oiled 1-gallon resealable plastic bag. Refrigerate for 24 hours.

10 Remove the dough from the refrigerator 1½ hours before you plan to bake it. Place the dough on a lightly floured surface and dust with flour. Cover loosely with plastic wrap to prevent the dough from drying.

11 Line 2 baking sheets with parchment paper and dust with cornmeal. Fill a spray bottle with water and set aside.

12 Shape each ball into a rough square by pulling the dough with your fingers, stretching the dough until it is about 8 inches square. Score the dough 4 or 5 times with a razor blade (or very sharp knife) and brush the dough with the basil oil. Place 2 of the dough squares on each baking sheet and sprinkle with salt.

13 Bake the focaccia at 450° for 15 to 20 minutes or until lightly golden-brown. Open the oven 3 times during the first 9 minutes and use a spray bottle to quickly spray the oven with water to create steam.

14 As soon as you take the focaccia out of the oven, brush with some additional olive or basil oil.

Mushrooms

Mushrooms are wonderful earthy treats. They can be light and delicate or rich and meaty. They make wonderful broths; they can be grilled, sautéed, or roasted; and some can be eaten raw. (See Chapter 4 for information about various types of mushrooms.)

There are 38,000 different varieties of mushrooms — some are edible and some not. So unless you're a skilled mushroom hunter, you may be best off searching for wild mushrooms in the supermarket. If you must hunt for them, make sure that you know exactly what you're looking for, or it may be your last hunt!

Store mushrooms in the refrigerator covered with a damp paper towel to keep them moist. Do not store them in plastic bags, or they'll become slimy. Mushrooms are like sponges and should never be soaked or washed in water. To clean them, just brush them lightly with a soft brush, or wipe them with a damp cloth.

Small mushrooms taste the same as large ones. Both are equally mature.

Roasted Mushrooms

The recipes in this book use roasted mushrooms in many different ways, but the uses for mushrooms are limitless. You can sauté mushrooms to crisp them up and then toss them with vegetables or grains, add them to soups or ragouts, or puree them and use them to thicken and flavor sauces. So roast up a batch. They can keep in the refrigerator for several days and be ready to use in whatever you're cooking.

Preparation time: 3 minutes

Cooking time: 35 minutes

Yield: $1^1/_2$ cups

$2^1/_2$ *cups wild mushrooms (such as shiitake, cremini, portobello, or oyster), cleaned and stems removed*

2 sprigs thyme or rosemary

1 clove garlic

$^1/_2$ cup chopped onion

1 tablespoon olive oil

$^1/_3$ cup water

Salt and pepper

Place all the ingredients in an ovenproof pan, cover, and roast at 325° for 30 to 40 minutes or until tender. Cool in the liquid and refrigerate until needed.

Need an extra boost? Morel mushrooms contain a substance that's used in rocket fuel.

Mushroom Stock

Mushroom stock is ideal to have around. You can use it as a base for mushroom soup or reduce it and use it as a sauce to go with meat or vegetables. You can use it to roast mushrooms or as the liquid for cooking grains to give them a hearty mushroom flavor.

Preparation time: 2 minutes

Cooking time: 2 hours

Yield: About 1 quart

2 pounds button mushrooms, cleaned

3 cloves garlic

2 cups chopped onion

3 quarts cold water

(continued)

1 Place all the ingredients in a medium stockpot and simmer for 2 hours. Strain the broth through a fine-mesh sieve.

2 For a more concentrated flavor, return the liquid to the stockpot and continue to simmer for 30 to 60 minutes or until the desired flavor is achieved.

3 Cool and refrigerate or freeze until needed.

Wild Mushroom Ragout with Chicken-Chive Reduction

The richness of the chicken reduction enhances the hearty mushrooms in this dish. You can serve this ragout with some type of grain and a piece of sautéed chicken or beef for a hearty entree.

Preparation time: *5 minutes*

Cooking time: *1 hour*

Yield: *4 servings*

3 cups Chicken Stock (see Chapter 5)	*1 cup roasted oyster mushrooms*
4 tablespoons butter	*1 cup roasted portobello mushrooms, cut into small wedges*
3 tablespoons chopped chives	
Salt and pepper	*1 cup roasted cremini mushrooms, cut into quarters*
2 tablespoons chopped shallots	*4 tablespoons Madeira wine*
1 cup roasted shiitake mushrooms	

1 Place the chicken stock in a medium saucepan and simmer over medium heat for 40 to 50 minutes or until reduced to 1 cup.

2 Whisk 3 tablespoons of the butter and the chopped chives into the hot stock. Season with salt and pepper.

3 In a large sauté pan, cook the shallots in the remaining tablespoon of butter over medium heat for 3 to 4 minutes or until translucent but not brown. Add the mushrooms and sauté for 5 to 6 minutes or until hot.

4 Add the Madeira wine to deglaze the pan and continue cooking for 2 to 3 minutes or until all the liquid cooks away. Season with salt and pepper.

5 Arrange some of the mushrooms on each plate and spoon some of the chicken-chive reduction over the mushrooms.

Chapter 8

Vegetable Cuisine: Using Legumes, Grains, and Pasta

In This Chapter

▶ Cooking with legumes

▶ Creating dishes using grains and rice

▶ Preparing fresh pasta

Adding legumes, grains, and pasta to vegetable cuisine is a great way to turn vegetables into a more substantial and interesting meal. There are so many different and interesting types of grains, rices, and legumes available today in most grocery stores that it is easy to experiment with them and create new and exciting preparations. How about creamy risotto with slightly crunchy asparagus, or soft couscous tossed with some crunchy vegetables and served inside a sweet roasted onion? With the large number of vegetables, grains, rices, and legumes that are available, the possibilities are truly endless.

Legumes

Legumes (or *beans,* although gourmet chefs are usually too snobbish to use that simple term) are cholesterol-free and high in vitamins, minerals, and soluble fiber. For this reason, they have become a chic alternative to meat. Nothing is better than perfectly cooked legumes that melt in your mouth. The key to perfect legumes is to cook them slowly and, if your waistline can afford it, with lots of butter.

So *that's* what causes it!

Beans give you gas because as they dry, they store complex sugars called *oligosaccharides*. Normal digestive enzymes are unable to break down these chains of sugar, so they pass whole into the lower intestine, where bacteria eats the sugars and ferments them. This process is similar to the fermenting of other sugars, and a natural by-product is gas. Cooking beans with an equal portion of rice eliminates two-thirds of their flatulence production.

If you don't want all the butter, you can cook beans with water or chicken stock and a few whole garlic cloves. The garlic cloves slowly cook with the beans, creating a smooth, butter-like flavor. You can also add caramelized vegetables or herbs and infuse the flavors into the beans as they cook.

Soaking beans before cooking ensures even cooking. Several methods work well:

- **Overnight soak:** Put the beans in a bowl and cover by 2 inches with cold water. Let soak for at least 12 hours or overnight. Drain and cook.

- **Fast soak:** Place the beans in a saucepan and cover by 2 inches with cold water. Bring to a boil for 2 minutes, remove from the heat, cover, and let stand for 1 hour. Drain and cook.

- **Microwave soak:** Mix 2 cups of beans with 2 cups of water. Cover and microwave on high for 15 minutes; then let stand for 5 minutes. Add 2 more cups of cold water, cover, and let stand for 1 hour. Drain and cook.

A wide variety of beans are available; Table 8-1 describes some of the types you can find. Get creative and try a type you've never heard of!

Table 8-1	Various Types of Beans
Type	*Description*
Aduki/Adzuki beans	Small, dark red or black, very tender when cooked, sweet-strong flavor. Available fresh and dried.
Black-eyed peas	White beans with a black eye. Available fresh and dried.
Black turtle beans	Shiny, tender, and sweet-tasting.
Cannellini beans	Creamy white kidney beans that are slightly larger than navy beans.
Cranberry beans	Red to reddish brown beans with dark brown specks. Once cooked, they are plump and have a slight red color.

Type	Description
Fava beans	Available fresh or dried, green when fresh and brown when dried.
Flageolets	Pale green and a French classic; actually immature kidney beans.
Lima beans	Come in two sizes; are kidney-shaped and greenish white in color.
Navy beans	Small, white beans that are slightly flat in shape.
Red kidney beans	Sweet-tasting with a firm texture. Range from dark pink to maroon.
Soybeans	Range in color from yellow, green, and red to black. Can be eaten raw or cooked and are found dried and fresh. Used to make tofu, fermented to make pastes, and ground into flour.

When you cook beans, they absorb and take on the identities and flavors of the foods with which they are cooked. You can add spices or herbs at various stages of cooking to intensify flavors.

Try the following recipes to see how versatile and delicious beans can be.

Braised Legumes with Garlic and Thyme

Preparation time: *5 minutes, plus overnight soaking*

Cooking time: *2 hours*

Yield: *3 cups cooked beans (can serve 6 to 8)*

$^1/_2$ *cup dried black beans*

$^1/_2$ *cup dried cannellini beans*

$^1/_2$ *cup dried cranberry beans*

1 tablespoon vegetable oil

$^1/_2$ *cup chopped carrots*

$^1/_2$ *cup chopped celery*

1 cup chopped Spanish onion

3 cloves garlic

6 tablespoons butter

6 sprigs thyme

Salt and pepper

(continued)

1 Soak the beans in water overnight in separate containers; then drain.

2 Place 1 teaspoon of the vegetable oil and $^1/_3$ of the chopped carrots, celery, and onion in each of 3 small saucepans. Caramelize the vegetables over medium-high heat for 5 to 7 minutes or until golden-brown.

3 Add 1 type of bean and 1 clove of garlic to each saucepan and cover with water. Bring to a slow simmer, add 2 tablespoons of the butter to each saucepan, and continue to simmer for 45 minutes. (Add more water during cooking if necessary.)

4 Add 2 thyme sprigs to each saucepan and continue to simmer for 1 hour, or until the beans are extremely tender and melt in your mouth. Discard the thyme sprigs and toss the 3 separate types of beans together. Season with salt and pepper.

Some say that the phrase "spilling the beans" originated with the gypsies, whose fortune tellers used to predict the future from the way a handful of beans spilled out on a flat surface.

White Bean and Horseradish Spread with Sourdough Crostini

This slightly sharp spread can also be used in place of mayonnaise on a sandwich. Take a look at the color section of this book to see how this recipe should appear.

Preparation time: *5 minutes*

Cooking time: *2 hours*

Yield: *4 servings (8 crostini)*

1 cup white beans (such as navy beans or cannellini beans)

2 cloves garlic

$^1/_4$ cup chopped horseradish

2 tablespoons butter

Salt and pepper

3 tablespoons olive oil

8 thin slices of sourdough bread

2 tablespoons chopped chives

1 Place the white beans in a small saucepan with the garlic, horseradish, and butter and cover with water.

2 Simmer over low heat for $1^1/_2$ to 2 hours or until the beans are extremely tender and melt in your mouth. (Add more water during cooking if necessary.) Drain the beans and reserve the cooking liquid.

(continued)

3 Puree the beans with enough of the cooking liquid ($^1/_4$ to $^1/_2$ cup) to create a thick, spreadable paste. Season with salt and pepper.

4 Brush the sourdough bread with olive oil and place the bread on a half sheet pan. Toast the bread in the oven at 375° for 10 minutes or until golden-brown.

5 Put some of the white bean and horseradish spread on each slice of bread and sprinkle with the chopped chives. Serve warm or cold.

Several studies have found that beans help to fight cancer because they carry a high concentration of enzymes that counteract the development of cancer-causing compounds in the intestines. They are also thought to be beneficial in lowering blood cholesterol. The American Diabetic Association recommends a diet high in beans and other legumes because they help to stabilize blood glucose.

Braised French Green Lentils with Brussels Sprouts and Carrots

You can use the underused lentil almost anyplace that you would use beans. Dress them up or down, depending on what ingredients you choose to pair them with. In this recipe, I have you combine lentils with sweet caramelized carrots and slightly crunchy Brussels sprouts for interesting flavor and textural contrasts.

Preparation time: *10 minutes*

Cooking time: *50 minutes*

Yield: *6 to 8 servings*

$^1/_2$ cup diced onion

$^1/_2$ cup small diced carrots

2 tablespoons butter

$^1/_2$ cup French green lentils

2 sprigs thyme

$1^3/_4$ cups water

12 Brussels sprouts, steamed and quartered

Salt and pepper

1 In a small saucepan, sauté the onion and carrots in the butter for 2 to 3 minutes or until the onions are translucent. Add the lentils, thyme, and water. Simmer over low heat for 40 to 50 minutes or until tender.

2 Add the Brussels sprouts to the cooked lentils and season with salt and pepper. Serve while hot.

Grains

All grains are grasses. They all produce edible seeds or kernels with four basic features in common:

- The outer husk or *hull* is generally not edible and is usually removed.
- The *bran* is the layer that is richest in vitamins, minerals, and fiber.
- The *endosperm* is the starchy center, rich in carbohydrates.
- The *germ* is the embryo of the seed, containing enzymes, minerals, and vitamins.

Grains vary in cooking time and cooking-liquid-to-grain ratio, depending on the size of the grain and its density. You should always read the package for recommended cooking times and techniques. Table 8-2 lists common grains and describes their flavors and textures.

Table 8-2	Various Types of Grains
Type	**Description**
Amaranth	A tiny grain with a nutty, spicy flavor. Very high in protein.
Barley	Usually eaten *pearled* (polished with the hull removed). Has a chewy texture, very much like al dente pasta. Extremely nutritious.
Buckwheat	Available in flour and groat form. The flour can be used in pancakes and in baked goods. The *groats* are the hulled, crushed kernels. They come in coarse, medium, and fine grinds.
Bulgur	Cracked whole wheat with the hull removed. Very nutritious.
Couscous	A staple of Middle Eastern cuisine. The granular form of semolina. The most common form is very tiny. Israeli couscous is a much larger cut of the semolina and, when cooked, has a texture that is similar to pasta.
Grits	Coarsely ground corn. Come in a choice of grind: coarse, medium, or fine. Seldom found in fine dining but can be dressed up and elegantly presented. Have a porridge-like texture.
Kasha	Made from buckwheat groats. Not actually a grain, so people who are allergic to wheat usually can eat it.
Oats	Come in many forms. After being cleaned, toasted, hulled, and cleaned once more, oats are processed into oat groats, rolled oats, instant oats, steel-cut oats, oat flour, or oat bran.

Type	Description
Quinoa	Actually the fruit of an herb. Called the "supergrain" or "mother grain" because it comes closer than any other food to supplying all the nutrients needed to sustain life. Texture is crumbly and light with a slight crunch.
Rye	Has a strong, somewhat sour flavor and is high in protein.
Triticale	The first humanly engineered grain. A cross between rye and wheat, with a flavor that's stronger than wheat but milder than rye.

You can cook grains with water, or with vegetable, chicken, or beef stock, to create a more intense flavor. I also like to cook grains with different vegetables and herbs to create different flavors. The following two salad recipes combine grains with a variety of flavors to create two very different dishes.

Israeli (Middle Eastern) Couscous Salad with Artichokes and Lemon-Tarragon Vinaigrette

Israeli couscous has a similar flavor to the tiny version that most people are used to, but it has a larger grain and a chewier texture. It's starting to show up in grocery stores, but you may have to visit your local gourmet market or health food store to find it. Here, you use it in a refreshing cold salad that can be made a day ahead. See the color section of this book to find out how this recipe should appear.

Preparation time: *30 minutes, plus time for chilling*

Cooking time: *30 minutes*

Yield: *6 to 8 servings*

1¹/₂ cups raw Israeli couscous

3 cups water

Salt and pepper

9 tablespoons extra-virgin olive oil

1 medium red onion, sliced paper-thin

1 tablespoon balsamic vinegar

1 teaspoon cracked black pepper

¹/₄ cup lemon juice

3 tablespoons chopped tarragon

1 cup julienned red bell pepper

1 cup tiny yellow teardrop tomatoes (or red cherry tomatoes), cut in half

3 artichoke bottoms, cooked and cut into thin wedges (refer to Figure 4-14 for cleaning and trimming instructions)

1 cup small English cucumber, diced

1 cup snow pea sprouts

(continued)

1 Rinse the Israeli couscous in cold water through a sieve.

2 Simmer the water; then add the Israeli couscous and a pinch of salt. Simmer over medium heat for 12 to 15 minutes or until al dente, stirring occasionally. (Check the package directions for the exact cooking time, as products can vary.) Cover, remove from the heat, and let sit for 10 minutes. All the liquid should have been absorbed.

3 Place the couscous in a strainer and rinse under cold water for 3 minutes. (This helps to cool the couscous and removes the excess starch.) Drain and place in a large bowl. Toss with 3 tablespoons of the olive oil.

4 Place the sliced red onion on a half sheet pan and toss with 1 tablespoon of the olive oil, the balsamic vinegar, and the cracked black pepper.

5 Evenly spread out the onion and bake at 375° for 15 to 20 minutes or until all the balsamic vinegar has cooked into the onion. (The onions should be slightly dry and crunchy.)

6 To make the lemon-tarragon vinaigrette, place the lemon juice in a small bowl and slowly whisk in the remaining 5 tablespoons of olive oil. Season with salt and pepper and fold in the chopped tarragon.

7 Place the cooled Israeli couscous in a large bowl and toss with the red bell pepper, teardrop tomatoes, balsamic red onions, artichokes, English cucumber, and lemon-tarragon vinaigrette. Season with salt and pepper, sprinkle with the snow pea sprouts, and chill in the refrigerator until needed.

Cold Quinoa Salad with Curry, Portobello Mushrooms, and Carrots

You may have to do some hunting to track down quinoa (pronounced "KEEN-wah"). You probably won't find it at the grocery store, but many health food stores are starting to carry it on a regular basis. When you do find it, buy plenty. This healthy grain is great served warm or cold. Paired with the meaty portobello mushrooms in this dish, it's a meal in itself, but you can add a few grilled chicken breasts if you want a more substantial meal. See this recipe in the color section of this book.

Preparation time: *15 minutes, plus time for chilling*

Cooking time: *30 minutes*

Yield: *4 servings*

(continued)

1¹/₂ cups raw quinoa

3 cups water

¹/₂ tablespoon curry powder

Salt and pepper

2 tablespoons olive oil

2 large portobello mushrooms, roasted and chopped, roasting juices reserved (see Chapter 7)

2 cups green beans, cooked and cut diagonally into 1-inch pieces

1 cup blanched spinach, chopped

1 cup diced yellow beets, cooked

2 tablespoons chopped tarragon

1 cup chopped scallions

3 tablespoons lemon juice

1 tablespoon balsamic vinegar

1 Rinse the raw quinoa with cold water. Drain and place in a medium saucepan.

2 Add the water and curry powder and bring to a simmer. Continue to simmer over medium heat for 15 minutes or until most of the liquid has been absorbed. Turn off the heat, cover, and let stand for 10 minutes.

3 Remove the quinoa from the pan and let cool. Season with salt and pepper and toss with the olive oil.

4 In a large bowl, toss together all the ingredients and season with salt and pepper. Serve chilled.

Rice

Rice is a staple food for half the world's population. When consumed with beans, it forms a complete protein like that found in meat — great for vegetarians. Like grains, rice cooks by liquid-to-grain ratios and takes on the identity of the stock, herbs, or vegetables with which it is cooked. When cooking rice, always read the package for recommended cooking times and techniques.

For proper results, it's important to carefully measure dry rice and the liquid in which you cook it. Bring the rice to a boil and then turn down the heat to a slow simmer with the lid on to trap the steam. The best way to test for doneness is by tasting. If all the liquid has been absorbed but the rice is underdone, add more liquid. If the rice is done but all the liquid is not absorbed, drain the excess liquid. Ideally, you shouldn't have to do either if you follow the proper ratios.

White rice has such a low fiber content that it takes only one hour to digest, whereas most foods take at least two to four hours. (This may have something to do with the fact that you're always hungry an hour after you go out for Chinese food.)

All rice is brown to begin with. White rice goes through a complex transformation process that strips the kernel of its husk, bran, and germ to achieve pristine and polished whiteness. This leaves only the endosperm and very little in the way of nutritional fiber, so expanding your rice repertoire beyond basic white rice and exploring the brown and long-grain varieties is worth your while. Table 8-3 describes various types of rice.

Table 8-3	Various Types of Rice
Type	**Description**
Arborio	This short, shiny, smooth grain from Italy absorbs water slowly and is used for risotto.
Basmati	This fragrant, aromatic rice from India and Pakistan has long, tender grains and a nutty taste. It comes in brown and white varieties.
Brown	This unpolished grain has a dense, nutty flavor. It cooks more slowly than white rice but has more vitamins and fiber.
Converted	Converted rice is steamed and dried before the hull is removed, resulting in a fluffy rice that doesn't stick together.
Japonica	This rice blooms in warm weather and moist conditions. It's a short-grain rice that, depending on the crop, can have dark red to black grains. As it cooks, it softens and the kernels break apart.
Jasmine	This aromatic long-grain rice from the Far East cooks up very much like basmati. The grains separate from each other easily when cooked.
Long-grain	Long-grain rice is four to five times as long as it is wide. When cooked, the grains are light and fluffy, tending to stay separate.
Medium-grain	These plump but not round grains are moister and more tender than long grains when cooked.
Short-grain	These almost-round grains are softer than medium grains and tend to stick together.
Sticky rice (sushi rice)	A short-grain white rice that is rinsed before cooking. Once cooked, the rice grains stick together. Sticky rice is used mostly in sushi preparations.
Wild rice	Actually not rice at all, but a marsh grass. It has a nutty flavor and a firm texture.

To expand your rice repertoire beyond the basic white stuff, try one of the following recipes.

Wild Rice and Dried Cherry Pancakes with Pecan-Cherry Butter

You can top these tiny pancakes with apple chutney or a piece of meat and serve them as an appetizer, or you can serve them for breakfast with maple syrup.

Preparation time: *10 minutes*

Cooking time: *1 hour*

Yield: *6 servings, or 24 silver dollar pancakes*

1 cup wild rice	*2 teaspoons salt*
2¹/₄ cups water	*3 tablespoons sugar*
2 eggs, lightly beaten	*1 teaspoon baking soda*
2 cups buttermilk	*2 teaspoons baking powder*
1 tablespoon melted butter	*³/₄ cup chopped dried cherries*
2 cups flour	*³/₄ cup chopped pecans*

1 Place the wild rice in a small saucepan with the water. Simmer over medium heat for 40 minutes or until all the liquid has been absorbed and the rice is cooked. Set aside and let cool.

2 In a medium mixing bowl, whisk together the eggs, buttermilk, and melted butter.

3 In a separate bowl, sift together the flour, salt, sugar, baking soda, and baking powder. Whisk the flour mixture into the egg mixture. Add the cooked wild rice, the dried cherries, and the pecans and stir until fully incorporated.

4 Place a nonstick sauté pan or griddle over medium heat for 3 minutes to *condition* (heat) the pan. Drop 2 tablespoons of batter for each pancake onto the pan. Cook the pancakes for 2 minutes on each side or until golden-brown and cooked through. Remove from the pan and blot on paper towels. Serve while hot with the Pecan-Cherry Butter.

Pecan-Cherry Butter

This compound butter is wonderful with the pancakes because it perfectly mirrors the flavors. But don't stop there; try it on a muffin or fresh bread, and you'll never go back to plain butter again.

Preparation time: *2 minutes*

Yield: *³/₄ cup*

¹/₂ cup butter, softened	*2 tablespoons finely chopped dried cherries*
2 tablespoons ground pecans	

(continued)

Place all ingredients in a small bowl and mix together until thoroughly combined. Refrigerate until needed.

Caramelized Fennel Risotto with Asparagus and Pearl Onions

After you make risotto a few times, it doesn't seem as difficult. As long as you're patient and don't mind stirring gently for 45 minutes, this dish should turn out great. In this version, the crunchy fennel adds texture to the creamy rice. The color section of this book shows you how to plate this recipe.

Preparation time: *15 minutes*

Cooking time: *1 hour*

Yield: *4 servings*

2 cloves garlic, chopped

1/2 cup chopped onion

4 tablespoons butter

1 cup arborio rice

6 cups hot Vegetable or Chicken Stock (see Chapter 5)

Salt and pepper

1 1/2 cups julienned fennel

12 white pearl onions, peeled

12 asparagus spears, cut diagonally into 1-inch pieces

3 tablespoons chopped fennel tops

4 tablespoons shaved Parmesan cheese (optional)

1 In a medium saucepan over medium heat, sauté the garlic and onion with 2 tablespoons of the butter for 2 to 3 minutes or until translucent. Add the arborio rice and continue to cook for 2 minutes, stirring.

2 Slowly add 1/4 cup of the hot stock to the rice and stir until completely absorbed. Continue to add hot stock 1/4 cup at a time, stirring constantly and allowing the rice to completely absorb the liquid each time before adding more. Continue adding hot stock until the rice is cooked. (It should be creamy yet al dente.) Stir constantly with a smooth, gentle motion to avoid breaking the grains. Season the cooked risotto with salt and pepper.

3 While the risotto is cooking, sauté the fennel with 1 tablespoon of the butter in a hot sauté pan for 7 to 10 minutes or until caramelized. Season with salt and pepper.

4 Sauté the pearl onions with the remaining 1 tablespoon of butter in a hot sauté pan for 12 to 15 minutes or until golden-brown and tender. Cut into quarters and season with salt and pepper.

(continued)

5 Cook the asparagus in boiling salted water for 3 minutes or until tender. Drain and season with salt and pepper.

6 Fold all the cooked vegetables and chopped fennel tops into the risotto. Serve while hot. Sprinkle with the shaved Parmesan cheese if desired.

Pickled Vegetable Maki Rolls

After you master the art of rolling your own maki rolls, you can fill them with any of your favorites from the local sushi bar. You can replace the pickled vegetables in this recipe with strips of smoked salmon, raw tuna, or even crab. You can see this recipe in the color section of this book.

Specialty tools: *Bamboo maki roller*

Preparation time: *30 minutes, plus 2 hours refrigeration and 30 minutes standing*

Yield: *3 to 4 servings (10 to 12 pieces)*

4 4-inch-long carrot batons

4 4-inch-long mango batons

1 cup Pickling Juice (see following recipe)

1/2 teaspoon wasabi powder

1 1/2 teaspoons water

1 cup cooked maki rice (sushi/sticky rice)

1 1/2 tablespoons sugar

2 tablespoons rice wine vinegar

2 sheets Nori (dried, pressed seaweed)

6 long chives

4 4-inch-long red bell pepper batons

4 4-inch-long avocado batons

1 Place the carrots and mangoes in a small bowl, cover with the pickling juice, and refrigerate for 2 hours.

2 Place the wasabi powder and water in a small cup and stir until smooth.

3 Place the maki rice, sugar, and rice wine vinegar in a small bowl and stir gently until mixed.

4 Lay a sheet of Nori on a bamboo maki roller. Place 1/2 cup of the maki rice on top of the Nori. (***Tip:*** Moisten your hands with water before touching the maki rice to prevent the rice from sticking to your hands.) Spread the rice flat by using your hands, leaving a 2-inch border at the top of the Nori. (See Figure 8-1.)

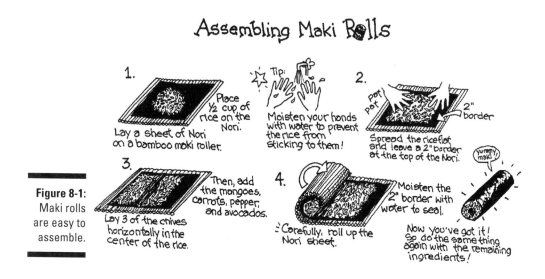

Figure 8-1:
Maki rolls are easy to assemble.

5 Spoon 1 teaspoon of the wasabi mixture on top of the rice. Lay 3 of the chives horizontally in the center of the rice.

6 Drain the pickling juice and lay 2 of the mango pieces end to end on top of the chives. Repeat the process with the carrot, red bell pepper, and avocado batons.

7 Using the maki roller, carefully roll up the Nori sheet, creating a firm, smooth maki roll. Moisten the 2-inch border of the Nori with water to create a seal. Set the maki roll aside and repeat this process with the remaining ingredients.

8 Let the maki rolls stand for 30 minutes at room temperature; then slice them into 1¹/₂-inch pieces on the diagonal.

Pickling Juice

Preparation time: *2 minutes*

Cooking time: *5 minutes*

Yield: *1 cup*

¹/₂ cup water

¹/₄ cup rice wine vinegar

¹/₄ cup sugar

1 tablespoon kosher salt

1 whole clove

1 teaspoon mustard seed

1 teaspoon black peppercorns

1 teaspoon chopped ginger

(continued)

1 Combine all the ingredients in a small saucepan and bring to a simmer, allowing the salt and sugar to dissolve.

2 Cool and use as desired. You can keep this pickling juice in the refrigerator for up to several weeks.

 The key to spicing up maki rolls and other sushi items is to add *wasabi,* an Asian root with a sharp, fiery flavor that resembles horseradish. Although you can often find wasabi in powered form, using wasabi paste in your sushi is easier. You can make your own wasabi paste by mixing four parts wasabi powder to one part water and kneading it with your fingers until mixed. Wasabi paste can be stored in the refrigerator indefinitely.

Pasta

Making your own pasta is fun, and it tastes so much better than dried pasta. You can flavor your fresh pasta with any type of herbs, spices, or vegetables, and then cut the pasta into shapes. (The sidebar "How to make ravioli and tortellini" explains how to create those shapes.) Fresh pasta cooks in 3 to 4 minutes, compared to dried pasta, which can take up to 12 minutes to reach the *al dente* (firm yet tender) stage.

Semolina Pasta

All you need to make this fresh pasta is a few pounds of semolina flour, some eggs, a rolling pin, and a small hand-crank pasta machine (if you don't want the workout from the crank machine, you can use an electric pasta maker). You can keep this pasta dough wrapped tightly in plastic wrap in the refrigerator for up to a week. This basic pasta can be accompanied by any type of sauce.

Specialty tools: *Pasta machine, electric mixer with dough hook*

Preparation time: *30 minutes, plus 1 hour refrigeration*

Cooking time: *4 minutes*

Yield: *6 to 8 servings (about 1¹/₂ pounds)*

4 cups extra-fine semolina flour   *6 eggs, lightly beaten*

(continued)

1 Place the semolina flour and eggs in a mixing bowl. Using a dough hook, blend on low for 3 minutes or until the dough comes together.

2 Form the dough into a ball and cover with plastic wrap. Refrigerate for a minimum of 1 hour before using.

3 Roll out the dough on a lightly floured surface with a rolling pin or through a pasta machine until $^1/_{16}$ inch thick. Cut into the desired shape (such as fettuccine or spaghetti). Refrigerate on a lightly floured, covered half sheet pan until needed. (After you roll out and cut the pasta, you should use it within a few days.)

4 Cook the pasta in boiling salted water for 3 to 4 minutes or until al dente. Serve with the desired sauce.

Variations: You can get creative with this basic pasta recipe by experimenting with the following variations:

- ✔ **Spinach Pasta:** Puree 1 cup of blanched spinach with the egg, use 4$^1/_2$ cups of flour, and proceed with the recipe.

- ✔ **Curry Pasta:** Add 3 tablespoons of curry powder to the eggs, use 4$^1/_2$ cups of flour, and proceed with the recipe.

- ✔ **Beet Pasta:** Add 1$^1/_2$ tablespoons of heavily reduced beet juice, use 4$^1/_2$ cups of flour, and proceed with the recipe.

Herb Pasta

Preparation time: *30 minutes*

Yield: *1$^1/_2$ pounds*

Semolina Pasta (see preceding recipe)

1$^1/_2$ cups picked tarragon, Italian parsley, or chervil leaves

1 On a floured surface, roll out the pasta using a pasta machine or by hand until $^1/_{16}$ inch thick.

2 Sprinkle the herbs sparsely along half the length of the pasta, fold over the remaining pasta, and gently press the sides together.

3 Run through the pasta machine until thin to seal in the herbs.

4 Cut into circles or squares for ravioli or tortellini.

How to make ravioli and tortellini

Making homemade ravioli and tortellini is fun and surprisingly easy. You can use any type of pasta and fill them with just about anything imaginable: a puree of roasted squash, finely chopped wild mushrooms, shredded chicken, beef, or lamb, tiny pieces of lobster meat, crab salad, duck confit, julienned vegetables, all types of cheeses — the list goes on and on. You can serve these little pastas with your favorite sauce or just toss them together with some olive oil, garlic, and fresh herbs for a simple but impressive meal.

Ravioli

1. Cut the pasta into 2-inch circles or squares.

2. Place 1 tablespoon of filling in the center of the pasta.

3. Brush the outside edge with an *egg wash* (a mix of a whole egg and 1 tablespoon of water), cover with another piece of pasta, and press the edges to seal.

4. Cook the ravioli in boiling salted water for 2 to 3 minutes or until al dente.

Tortellini

1. Cut the pasta into 3-inch squares or circles.

2. Place 1 tablespoon of filling in the center of the pasta.

3. Brush two of the sides with an egg wash and fold the pasta in half, corner to corner. Join the two ends of the long side of the triangle to form a tortellini, dab with a touch of egg wash, and gently press together to seal.

4. Cook the tortellini in boiling salted water for 2 to 3 minutes or until al dente.

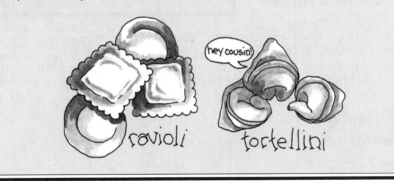

Roasted Garlic Sun-Dried Tomato Pesto

Pesto is a quick preparation that makes a great sauce for pasta or spread for bread. Pesto is traditionally made with basil, garlic, pine nuts, olive oil, and Parmesan cheese. In this recipe, I push the pesto into a more complex flavor combination by using sun-dried tomatoes and roasted garlic.

Preparation time: *25 minutes*

Yield: *1 cup*

1 cup sun-dried or Oven-Dried Tomatoes (see following recipe)

³/₄ cup olive oil

¹/₄ cup pine nuts, toasted for 15 minutes at 350°

¹/₄ cup Roasted Garlic Puree (see Chapter 9)

¹/₂ cup grated Parmesan cheese

Salt and pepper

Place all the ingredients in a food processor and puree until smooth. Refrigerate and use as desired.

Oven-Dried Tomatoes

Sun-dried tomatoes actually *are* dried in the sun, which results in a semi-dehydrated, intensely flavored tomato. However, sun drying can take several days, depending on the weather. So here I give you a recipe for oven-dried tomatoes, which produces a similarly flavored tomato. The low oven heat slowly dries the tomato slices, concentrating the flavor.

Preparation time: *15 minutes*

Cooking time: *4 hours*

Yield: *About 2 cups*

4 medium-sized ripe tomatoes

4 tablespoons olive oil

Salt and pepper

8 sprigs thyme

3 large sprigs rosemary

(continued)

1 Slice the tomatoes ¹/₆ inch thick. Lay the tomato slices flat on a wire rack on top of a half sheet pan.

2 Drizzle the tomatoes with the olive oil and season lightly with salt and pepper. Arrange the thyme and rosemary sprigs over the tomatoes.

3 Dry in the oven at 225° for 3 to 4 hours or until the tomatoes are dry to the touch.

4 Remove the tomatoes from the rack and store in an airtight container in the refrigerator for up to a week. Or cover them with olive oil and store refrigerated for up to several weeks.

Gorgonzola Tomato Sauce with Gnocchi

Tomato sauce is rich on its own, but sometimes you just have to indulge yourself and make it even richer. Adding Gorgonzola cheese does the trick; the richness of the tomato sauce is enhanced by this intensely flavored blue cheese. Spooning this sauce over the soft, melt-away *gnocchi* (pronounced "NYOH-key") makes for a wonderfully satisfying dish.

Preparation time: *20 minutes*

Cooking time: *1 hour and 10 minutes*

Yield: *4 servings*

1 cup julienned red onion	*1 cup Gorgonzola cheese, crumbled*
3 tablespoons olive oil	*Salt and pepper*
6 cups tomato concassé (see Chapter 3)	*Gnocchi (see following recipe)*
3 cloves garlic, sliced in half	*¹/₄ cup basil, cut into a fine chiffonade*
2 tablespoons balsamic vinegar	

1 In a medium saucepan over medium-high heat, cook the red onion in the olive oil for 7 to 10 minutes or until carmelized and golden-brown.

2 Add the chopped tomatoes, garlic, and balsamic vinegar. Lower the heat to medium-low and continue to cook, stirring occasionally, for 1 hour or until most of the liquid from the tomatoes has been cooked out.

3 Add ³/₄ cup of the Gorgonzola cheese and continue to cook for 3 minutes or until the cheese is incorporated. Season to taste with salt and pepper.

(continued)

4 Arrange some of the cooked gnocchi on each plate and spoon some of the tomato sauce over the gnocchi. Sprinkle with the basil and the remaining blue cheese. Top with freshly ground black pepper.

Gnocchi

These tiny Italian dumplings are great with pasta sauce or mushroom broth. You can serve them the same way you would most pastas. You should use gnocchi the same day you make them.

Preparation time: *15 minutes*

Cooking time: *5 minutes*

Yield: *4 to 6 servings (about 6 dozen gnocchi)*

2 large Idaho potatoes (about 1 pound), peeled, cooked, and riced	*1 to 1¹/₂ cups flour*
	Salt and pepper
2 egg yolks	*4 teaspoons butter*

1 Work the yolks into the potato and knead in enough flour so that the dough is not sticky. Season to taste with salt and pepper.

2 Divide the mixture into 4 sections. Roll each section into a long cigar shape about ¹/₂ inch in diameter.

3 Cut into ¹/₂-inch pieces and delicately pinch the pieces in the middle. Refrigerate on a lightly floured pan until ready to cook.

4 Poach the gnocchi in boiling salted water for about 2 to 3 minutes or until they float. Remove with a slotted spoon.

5 Place the gnocchi in a small bowl, toss with the butter, and season to taste with salt and pepper.

Chapter 9

125 Million Japanese Can't Be Wrong! Raw, Marinated, and Cooked Seafood

In This Chapter

▶ Buying and storing fresh seafood

▶ Preparing raw and marinated seafood

▶ Discovering cooking methods for seafood

*P*eople have been enjoying food from the sea since the beginning of time. Seafood has long been considered one of life's true pleasures. Unfortunately, most people grew up thinking of seafood as fish sticks, fried shrimp, and Friday night all-you-can-eat fish fries.

Well, it's time to expand your repertoire and discover how truly wonderful different types of seafood can be. Whether raw or lightly cooked, seafood has a beautifully smooth texture and richness. Seafood is very healthy and — more important — very easy to prepare. It's incredibly versatile and lends itself well to almost any type of preparation.

CHARLIE SAYS

I include many different types of seafood on the restaurant menu each night. I usually start out with a course (or even two courses) of raw or cold seafood. Then I move on to one or two hot seafood preparations, before ending with a meat course.

Buying Fresh Seafood

With the advent of overnight shipping, fresh seafood is more readily available today than ever before. Most supermarkets now carry may different types of fresh seafood, and specialty fish markets are springing up all over.

However, if you have trouble finding fresh seafood in your area, see Chapter 20 for information on Browne Trading Company. We purchase most of the seafood that we use in the restaurant from this company — they have great quality seafood and can ship directly to your home. (Also, check the "Scallops in cyberspace and wasabi on the Web" sidebar in Chapter 13 for more tips on locating hard-to-find gourmet foods.)

Whether you are buying fresh fish for raw or cooked preparations, you should always follow these steps when selecting a particular fish at the market:

1. **Smell the fish.** It should have a fresh, clean aroma. It should not smell fishy, have a strong odor, or smell like ammonia, which means that the flesh is starting to decay.

2. **Feel the skin.** It should feel slick and moist. If the scales are present, they should be firmly attached.

3. **Press the flesh.** It should feel firm and spring back when you release your finger. If a visible finger imprint remains, the fish is not fresh.

4. **Look at the eyes.** They should be bulging and crystal clear. (Follow this guideline for all fish except the walleye pike, whose eyes should appear milky.) As a fish ages, the eyes lose moisture and sink into the head. If the fish winks at you, it's *really* fresh.

5. **Look at the fins and tail.** They should be fresh, flexible, and full. They should not appear dry or brittle.

6. **Check the gills.** They should be moist and have a good red to maroon color with no traces of gray or brown.

7. **Check the belly.** There should be no sign of *belly burn,* which occurs when the guts are removed improperly (the stomach enzymes begin to eat the flesh, causing it to come away from the bones). The flesh should show no breaks or tears.

When shopping for live shellfish, check them for signs of movement. Lobster and crab should move when you touch them. The shells of clams, mussels, and oysters should be tightly closed; throw out any shells that are open and that do not close when you tap on them.

Always ask when the fish or shellfish came in, and don't buy anything that's more than two or three days old.

Storing Fresh Seafood

Ideally, you should purchase fresh seafood only on the day you plan to prepare it. But if your schedule doesn't allow for daily trips to the market, proper storage is the key to preserving freshness. After seafood begins to turn bad, you can get sick from it even if it's cooked.

Follow these steps to keep your seafood fresh and safe to eat:

1. **Rinse the fish with cold water.**

2. **Place the fish on a bed of crushed ice in a perforated container to allow for drainage.**

3. **Cover the fish with additional ice.**

4. **Place the perforated container inside another container to catch the melted ice. (See Figure 9-1.)**

5. **Store the fish in the refrigerator until you're ready to use it.** Remember to change the ice daily. Never leave fish sitting in a pool of water.

Figure 9-1:
Icing fish
keeps it
fresh.

The following list gives some additional tips for keeping your seafood fresh and delicious:

✔ Clams, mussels, and oysters should not be iced. Store these shellfish in the refrigerator and in the mesh bag in which you purchased them.

✔ Store fish fillets (and scallops that you purchase out of the shell) in plastic containers set on ice. Do not let this seafood come into direct contact with the ice, or the seafood will lose flavor and texture.

✔ Pack crabs, lobster, and other live shellfish in seaweed or damp paper (which they usually come wrapped in). Don't allow fresh water to come in contact with the shellfish — it will kill them.

Choosing Seafood That's Available Year-Round

Many types of seafood are now available year-round, thanks to advances in aquaculture. *Aquaculture,* or farm-raising fish, has made huge strides in the last decade. Many types of farm-raised fish are now of comparable quality to those found in the wild — aquaculturists have been able to closely mimic the conditions and foods of natural habitats.

In some cases, farm-raised fish are actually raised in huge nets in the wild, which allows the fish to feed on their natural diet. This method produces a farm-raised fish of even higher quality. Generally, the catfish, salmon, trout, snapper, lobster, prawns, and oysters that you buy at the store are farm-raised.

The following types of seafood are available year-round:

- ✔ **Bass** is a general term for numerous types of freshwater or saltwater fish. Bass are characterized by spiny fins and have firm, well-flavored flesh.

- ✔ **Calamari,** also known as *squid,* is available in a variety of sizes. Calamari has a mild and slightly sweet flavor. It ranges in size from 1 inch to the seldom-seen 80-foot squid. The ink is extracted from the ink sac and used to color pasta or flavor dishes. You should cook calamari quickly over high heat to avoid a chewy texture.

- ✔ **Catfish** gets its name from the long, whisker-like barbels that hang down around its mouth. The *channel catfish,* weighing from 1 to 10 pounds, is considered the best eating. The flesh is firm, low in fat, and mild in flavor.

- ✔ **Clams** come in many different sizes. Some of the more common types are the *littleneck, cherrystone,* and *chowder* clams.

- ✔ **Cod** has mild-flavored white meat that is lean and firm. (It's amazing that this mild-mannered fish can produce something as nasty as cod-liver oil.) Cod can weigh as little as 1½ pounds to as much as 100 pounds.

- ✔ **Crabs** are noted for their sweet and succulent meat. You can purchase either *freshwater* or *saltwater crabs* (saltwater crabs are more readily available). Some of the more common types of crab are *Dungeness crab, blue crab, king crab, snow crab,* and *stone crab.*

  Crabs are sold both fresh and precooked (with the meat removed from the shell). If you buy precooked crab meat, make sure that you pick through it carefully — small shell pieces may be buried in the sweet meat.

Clockwise, from top: Chipotle and Yellow Tomato Salsa; Caramelized Onion and Tomato Chutney; Apple-Fennel Relish; Hot and Spicy Zucchini, Napa Cabbage, and Mustard Relish; Tropical Fruit Salsa (all in Chapter 6).

Top: Tomato, Red Onion, and Roasted Yellow Bell Pepper Flat Bread with Fresh Mozzarella Cheese (Chapter 7); *Middle:* Caramelized Fennel Risotto with Asparagus and Pearl Onions; *Bottom:* Cold Quinoa Salad with Curry and Portobello Mushrooms (both in Chapter 8).

Top left: Caramelized Onion Tart with Sweet Curry Crust; Top right: Spicy Cumin-Infused Sweet Corn Soup with Cilantro; Bottom: Herb-Crusted Warm Goat Cheese and Grilled Vegetable Salad (all in Chapter 7).

Top left: Broiled Sweet
and Sour Halibut with
Bok Choy and Somen
Noodles; *Top right:*
Smoked Salmon
Beggar's Purses
with Crème
Fraîche;
Bottom:
Slow-Roasted
Cod with
Warm Tomato
Salad and
Roasted Garlic
Vinaigrette (all in
Chapter 9).

Top: Cumin-Crusted Sautéed Chicken Breast with Morel Mushrooms and Brown Butter-Hickory Nut Pan Sauce; *Bottom:* Grilled Thai Barbecue Squab Breasts with Soy-Bacon Braised Collard Greens (both in Chapter 10).

Top: Roasted Herb-Crusted Pork Loin with Roasted Butternut Squash and Port Sauce; *Bottom:* Cumin-Garlic Spice Rub Roasted Leg of Lamb with Potato-Parmesan Pavé (both in Chapter 11).

Top: Grilled Lamb Loin and Red Onion Salad with Artichoke Vinaigrette; Middle: Braised Veal Shank and Potato Tarts; Bottom: Sautéed Bacon-Wrapped Venison with Wild Mushroom Barley (all in Chapter 11).

Top left: Braised Pork and Cilantro Dumplings with Spicy Orange Sauce (Chapter 10); *Bottom left:* Vegetable Maki Rolls (Chapter 8); *Center:* Julienned Vegetable Spring Rolls with Hot Curried Mustard Dipping Sauce (Chapter 7).

Top right: Wok-Seared Scallops with Stir-Fried Vegetables and Sesame-Lime Vinaigrette (Chapter 9); *Bottom right:* Phad Thai with Ginger-Marinated Beef (Chapter 11).

Top: Smoked Salmon Rolls with Horseradish Potato Salad and Lemon-Horseradish Vinaigrette; *Bottom:* Smoked Salmon Terrine with Horseradish Potato Salad and Lemon-Horseradish Vinaigrette (both assemblies in Chapter 12).

Top: Roasted Garlic Soup with Chopped Tomato in a Bowl; *Bottom:* Whole Roasted Tomato Filled with Roasted Garlic Soup and Crispy Fried Leeks (both assemblies in Chapter 12).

Top left: Chilled Lemon Soufflé; *Top right:* Warm Bing Cherry Soup with Vanilla Yogurt Sorbet and Apple Chips; *Bottom:* Star Anise-Poached Pear Stuffed with Vanilla Mascarpone (all in Chapter 15).

Top left: Chocolate Profiteroles with Chocolate-Ginger Cream; *Top right:* Caramel-Chocolate Truffles; *Bottom:* Mini Chocolate-Hazelnut Torte (all in Chapter 16).

Seafood Fest menu:
Top left: *Sautéed Crab Cakes with Cilantro and Cumin Rémoulade (Chapter 9);*
Bottom left: *Sautéed Curry-Spiced Tuna with Crispy Polenta and Beef Stock Reduction (Chapter 9);*
Center: *Poached Lobster Wontons and Tomato-Saffron Broth (Chapter 9).*

Top right: Poppy Seed Crêpes with Warm Summer Berries and Cream (Chapter 15); Bottom right: Olive Oil-Poached Swordfish Salad with Spinach, Red Bliss Potatoes, and Calamata Olive Vinaigrette (Chapter 9).

Sunday Afternoon in the Park Picnic menu: Top: White Bean and Horseradish Spread with Sourdough Crostini (Chapter 8); Israeli Couscous Salad with Artichokes and Lemon-Tarragon Vinaigrette (Chapter 8); Grilled Jumbo Shrimp and Vidalia Onion Brochette (Chapter 9); Bottom: Blueberry and Mango Tart (Chapter 15).

- **Crayfish** are also know as *crawfish;* they resemble tiny lobsters. They range from 3 to 6 inches in length and weigh from 2 to 8 ounces. Crayfish turn bright red when you cook them.

- **Flounder** is often sold under its market name *sole.* It's generally quite delicate, with a tendency to flake readily.

- **Haddock** is young cod that weighs anywhere from 2 to 6 pounds. It has a firm texture and a mild flavor.

- **Lobster** has firm, succulent flesh. They can grow as large as 45 pounds, but because no one wants to wrestle a 45-pound lobster, they are usually available for purchase at between 1 and 2 pounds.

  Lobsters must be purchased live because when they die, bacteria spread quickly throughout the flesh, making the meat mealy and dangerous to consume.

- **Mussels** grow in clusters and attach themselves to rocks or other supports. Most mussels brought to the market are farm-raised. Some of the most common types are *green lip, Spanish,* and the *common* mussel. Mussels are available year-round; on the West Coast of the United States, however, mussel season is November through April.

  Mussels from the West Coast are unsafe to eat during the late spring and summer because of certain microscopic organisms that are present in the water during those months.

- **Prawns:** The term *prawn* is actually used pretty loosely. Jumbo shrimp are often referred to as prawns, but true prawns are more closely related to lobster than they are to shrimp. These succulent beauties (also referred to as *langoustines*) are tender and sweet, and grow to about 6 inches in length.

- **Salmon** are firm and moderately oily, with distinctively pink to light orange-colored flesh. The many different species of salmon can be farm-raised or caught in the wild.

- **Scallops** have a meaty texture and a sweet flavor. Three species of scallops are widely used: *sea scallops, bay scallops,* and *calico scallops.* Sea scallops, the most succulent of the three species, can be as large as 2 to 3 inches in diameter; the bay and calico varieties are substantially smaller. Bay scallops are considered superior in quality to the calico variety.

- **Shrimp** come in cold-water and warm-water varieties. A general rule is that the colder the water, the smaller and more succulent the shrimp — but, unfortunately, markets don't usually offer you a choice. Shrimp come in a wide range of colors, from brown to pink to gray to green. They also come in a wide range of sizes and are marketed by how many shrimp make up a pound.

- **Skate** is a kite-shaped fish that's also called a *ray.* Baby skate wings have a milder flavor and a more tender flesh. The fins, or wings, are the edible part of the skate, with delicious flesh that is firm, white, and sweet.

- **Snapper** is firm-textured and low in fat. About 250 species of this saltwater fish exist, with about 15 varieties found in the U.S. The most familiar species are *yellowtail snapper, red snapper,* and *gray snapper.*

- **Swordfish** has an extremely firm, meat-like texture and a mild flavor. This rather large fish can range in size from 200 to 600 pounds — some swordfish have even been caught weighing over 1,000 pounds.

- **Trout** are farm-raised in large quantities. *Rainbow trout* and *brown trout* are the most common species. Their flesh is firm-textured, with a medium-high fat content.

- **Tuna** has firm flesh that can range in color from pinkish beige to dark maroon. Tuna has a rich flavor and comes in many varieties, such as *bluefin, yellowfin,* and *big-eye.*

- **Turbot** is a diamond-shaped fish that is valued for its snowy white, moist, finely textured flesh.

- **Whitefish** is found in lakes and streams throughout North America. It is a member of the salmon family, with flesh that is mild-flavored, firm, and, of course, white.

Coconut-Crusted Prawns with Coconut Broth and Curry Oil

Coconut and curry are a natural flavor combination, especially when paired with succulent prawns. You can serve this recipe before the main course or as an entree for 2 people.

Preparation time: *30 minutes*

Cooking time: *30 minutes*

Yield: *4 servings*

4 cups coconut milk

2 cups chopped fresh coconut

¹/₄ cup coarsely chopped ginger

Salt and pepper

¹/₂ cup bread crumbs

¹/₂ cup shredded dried coconut

8 large prawns, cleaned and deveined, with tails left on

¹/₂ cup flour

1 egg yolk, whisked with 2 tablespoons water

Canola oil for frying

³/₄ cup chopped macadamia nuts, toasted

3 tablespoons cilantro, cut into a fine chiffonade

4 teaspoons Curry Oil (see Chapter 5)

(continued)

1 Prepare the coconut broth by placing the coconut milk, chopped coconut, and ginger in a medium saucepan. Simmer over medium heat for 15 minutes. Puree in a blender, pass through a fine-mesh sieve, and season to taste with salt and pepper.

2 In a small bowl, combine the bread crumbs and shredded coconut.

3 Season the prawns with salt and pepper and lightly dust with the flour, patting off any excess. Dip the prawns in the egg yolk mixture and completely coat in the bread crumb and coconut mixture.

4 Fry the prawns in hot canola oil until lightly golden-brown. Remove the prawns, blot on paper towels, and season with salt and pepper.

5 Ladle some of the coconut broth into each of 4 bowls and arrange 2 prawns in each bowl. Sprinkle with the macadamia nuts and cilantro and drizzle the curry oil around the broth.

Selecting Seasonal Seafood

The seafood items in this section are available at different times throughout the year. When these items are available varies based on different factors, such as when soft-shell crabs shed their shells or when smelts run. Some of them have a very short "season," so when you come across them, snap them up. This seafood is definitely worth trying:

- ✔ **Dover sole** is available in late fall, winter, and spring. The flesh has a fine, firm texture and a mild flavor. True Dover sole is imported to the U.S. from the coastal waters that range from Denmark to the Mediterranean Sea.

- ✔ **Halibut** is available in fall, winter, and spring. Halibut range in size from 50 to 100 pounds, but young halibut that weigh 2 to 10 pounds are considered the finest. Halibut meat is low in fat, white, firm, and mild-flavored.

- ✔ **Mackerel** is available from spring through early fall. The most common mackerel is the *king mackerel,* which has a firm, high-fat flesh with a pleasant, savory flavor. The least common mackerel is the *holy mackerel,* which is difficult to find, but if you can get your hands on one, you can be sure that there'll be enough to go around.

- ✔ **Mahimahi** is available from spring through early fall. It is a type of *dolphin fish* (and should not be confused with the *dolphin,* which is a marine mammal, so you can go ahead and enjoy it without worrying about Greenpeace getting on your case). It is a moderately fatty fish with firm, flavorful flesh. Mahimahi can range in weight from 3 to 45 pounds.

- **Monkfish** is available in late spring, summer, and mid-fall. Also known as *angler fish,* it is an extremely ugly fish. It is low in fat, firm-textured, and has a mild, sweet flavor that is often compared to lobster.

- **Oysters** are available from September to April. As the saying goes, "Only consume oysters during months with the letter *R.*" Oysters can be purchased shucked, but if possible, I recommend that you purchase them in their shells and shuck them at the last minute to preserve their fresh flavor. (See Figure 9-2 for instructions for shucking oysters.) Many species of oysters exist, and they are named for the area where they are harvested. Some common types are *Olympia, Pacific,* and *belon.*

- **Pike** is available from fall through early winter. These long-bodied fish have ferocious teeth and range from 4 to 10 pounds. *Walleye pike* is not really a pike, but a perch. Pike is known for its lean, firm, lowfat flesh.

- **Smelts** are available in the winter. These tiny 4- to 7-inch-long fish have delicate flesh that is rich, oily, and mild-flavored. The most common types of smelts are the *rainbow smelts.*

- **Soft-shell crabs** are available in late spring and early fall, when the blue crab casts off its shell in order to grow a larger one. The crab's skin takes several days to harden, and the crabs are harvested during this time. Soft-shell crabs are sautéed whole, and you can eat most parts of the crab.

- **Sturgeon** is available in summer and fall. Their average weight is 60 pounds, but they have been caught weighing as much as 3,000 pounds. Its flesh is rich, high in fat, and has a delicate flavor and a meatlike texture. Sturgeon *roe* (eggs) are the only true caviar.

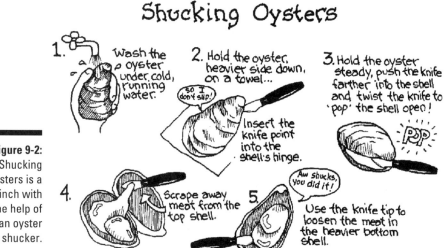

Figure 9-2:
Shucking oysters is a cinch with the help of an oyster shucker.

Enjoying Raw Seafood

Cooking your seafood is not always necessary — or even desirable. The Japanese have shown the world how delightful raw fish can be. The key to preparing raw seafood is to buy the best-quality product from a reputable supplier. Make sure to get *sashimi grade* fish, which is a term used to identify seafood that can be eaten raw. Don't be afraid to ask when the fish came in and when it was caught; any good fishmonger will be happy to share this information with you.

The following types of seafood can be consumed raw:

- Caviar
- Fluke
- Scallops
- Snapper
- Halibut
- Lobster
- Tuna
- Turbot
- Oysters
- Salmon

Pregnant women, children, and the elderly should not eat raw seafood. It can contain bacteria or parasites that, if eaten, can cause adults mild discomfort. But for children and elderly people, this bacteria can be deadly.

Adding a raw seafood dish to a menu is an easy way to add a special touch. It's considered by many to be among the most luxurious foods available. Any of the following recipes will instantly add that "Lifestyles of the Rich and Famous" feel to your next dinner party.

Caviar-Crusted Tuna Tartare with Avocado and Lemon-Herb Vinaigrette

This recipe is a wonderful start to a New Year's dinner; how luxurious you want your New Year to be can help determine how much caviar you use. The silky-smooth tuna melts in your mouth with the refreshing caviar, and the acidic vinaigrette perfectly cuts through the creamy avocado.

Specialty tools: *2-inch ring mold*

Preparation time: *15 minutes*

Yield: *4 servings*

10 ounces fresh raw tuna, finely diced

8 tablespoons olive oil

Salt and pepper

1 small ripe avocado, skin and pit removed

2 tablespoons lime juice

3 tablespoons lemon juice

1 tablespoon chopped chives

1 tablespoon chopped cilantro

1 tablespoon chopped shallots

1 to 2 ounces caviar

(continued)

1 Prepare the tuna tartare by tossing the tuna with 2 tablespoons of the olive oil. Season to taste with salt and pepper and refrigerate until needed.

2 To make the lemon-herb vinaigrette, whisk the remaining 6 tablespoons of olive oil together with the lemon juice. Fold in the chives and cilantro and season with salt and pepper.

3 Mash the avocado until smooth, add the lime juice and chopped shallots, and season with salt and pepper.

4 Place the ring mold in the center of a small plate. Place some of the avocado mixture in the bottom of the ring mold, layer with the tuna tartare, and top with as much caviar as desired. Remove the mold and repeat this process on three more plates. Spoon the lemon-herb vinaigrette around the plates.

Raw Oysters on the Half Shell with Champagne Mignonette

Nothing is more impressive (and gutsy) than ordering raw oysters on the half shell. People take turns "downing" these slimy delicacies and watch in awe as their turn approaches. Serving oysters with a Champagne mignonette is a classic and flavorful method of preparation.

Preparation time: *5 minutes*

Yield: *8 oysters*

8 fresh oysters, shucked and kept in their liquid, shells rinsed

¹/₄ cup Champagne

2 tablespoons Champagne vinegar

8 drops lemon juice

1 tablespoon minced shallots

Tabasco (optional)

1 Place 1 oyster on each of 8 half shells and refrigerate until needed.

2 To make the Champagne mignonette, mix together the Champagne, vinegar, lemon juice, and shallots in a small bowl. Pour some of the mignonette mixture over the oysters just prior to serving, and add a splash of Tabasco if desired.

Smoked Salmon Beggar's Purses with Crème Fraîche

Beggar's purses are crêpes with the edges gathered and tied up like a tiny purse (take a look at the color section of this book to see an example). Here, you add cold-smoked salmon that has been *cured,* but not cooked. Curing helps to preserve items without cooking them. You can purchase salt-cured or salt- and sugar-cured foods, depending on your tastes.

Smoked salmon wrapped in a crêpe is an impressive and simple flavor combination. These crêpes make a great pass-around appetizer — they're easy to pick up and pop into your mouth in one shot.

Specialty tools: *5-inch crêpe pan*

Preparation time: *15 minutes*

Cooking time: *15 minutes*

Yield: *8 servings*

1 cup milk	*Vegetable oil*
1 egg, lightly beaten	*1 cup chopped smoked salmon*
1 tablespoon butter, melted	*4 tablespoons chopped chives*
1 cup flour	*$^1/_2$ cup crème fraîche (see Chapter 3)*
1 tablespoon sugar	*3 tablespoons water*
$^1/_2$ teaspoon baking soda	*8 long chives, blanched*
1 teaspoon baking powder	

1 In a medium bowl, whisk together the milk, egg, and butter. Add the flour, sugar, baking soda, and baking powder and whisk until smooth.

2 Brush a hot crêpe pan lightly with vegetable oil. Pour the batter into the pan, a $1^1/_2$-ounce ladleful at a time, rolling the batter around to cover the entire pan. Cook over medium heat for 2 minutes or until the crêpe is lightly golden. Flip the crêpe and continue to cook for 1 minute or until golden-brown. Remove from the pan and repeat the process until you have at least 16 crêpes. Trim the crêpes into perfectly round circles.

3 Toss the smoked salmon with 2 tablespoons of the chopped chives.

4 Place 1 teaspoon of the crème fraîche in the center of each crêpe. Add 2 tablespoons of the smoked salmon mixture. Carefully bundle up the crêpe, creating a little purse. Tie closed with a chive. (See Figure 9-3.)

(continued)

5 Place the remaining creme fraiche, water, and chopped chives in a small bowl. Whisk together until smooth and season to taste with salt and pepper.

6 Spoon a touch of the cream mixture on a plate with 2 beggar's purses.

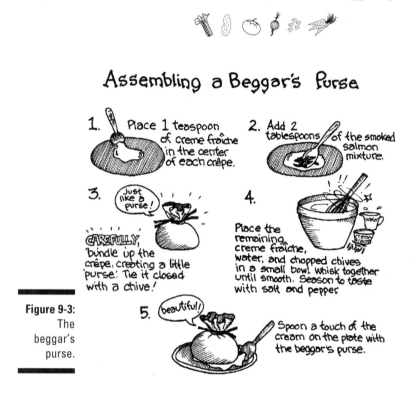

Figure 9-3:
The
beggar's
purse.

Using Seafood Marinades

Whether you serve your seafood raw or cooked, marinades add flavor to the fish and often help tenderize the meat. You can really use your imagination when making a marinade. By adding different herbs and spices to a base of olive oil and orange juice, for example, you can take your marinade to different corners of the world. Simple marinades are just as good as complex versions — it just depends on what flavor you're looking for.

You can control the strength of the flavor by adjusting the length of time that you marinate your seafood; marinate for as little as 30 minutes or as long as overnight, depending on how much flavor you want to impart.

Asian Ginger-Lemongrass Marinade

This marinade works well for grilled shrimp, scallops, tuna, or salmon, all of which absorb the marinade nicely.

Preparation time: *15 minutes*

Yield: *2 cups*

$^1/_2$ *cup orange juice*	$^1/_3$ *cup chopped lemongrass*
$^1/_4$ *cup soy sauce*	*1 jalapeño pepper, chopped*
3 tablespoons chopped ginger	$^1/_2$ *cup chopped cilantro*
2 tablespoons chopped garlic	$^1/_2$ *cup chopped scallions*
$^3/_4$ *cup olive oil*	*3 tablespoons lime juice*

1 Mix together all the ingredients in a medium bowl.

2 Pour the marinade over the raw seafood and marinate in the refrigerator for a minimum of 2 hours. Remove the seafood from the marinade and cook using the desired method. (See "Discovering Various Cooking Methods for Seafood," later in this chapter, for ideas.)

 Use plastic bags to marinate foods. You can turn the seafood easily for even marinating — and best of all: no clean-up.

Herb Marinade

This marinade works well with seafood or meat. You can use any combination of herbs, or just one type for a more specific flavor.

Preparation time: *10 minutes*

Yield: *2 cups*

1$^1/_4$ cups olive oil	$^1/_4$ *cup chopped parsley*
$^1/_4$ *cup chopped rosemary*	$^1/_2$ *cup chopped onion*
$^1/_4$ *cup chopped thyme*	*Pepper*

1 Mix together all the ingredients in a medium bowl.

2 Pour over the raw seafood and marinate in the refrigerator for a minimum of 2 hours. Remove the seafood from the marinade and cook using the desired method. (See "Discovering Various Cooking Methods for Seafood," later in this chapter, for ideas.)

Remember not to use an aluminum pan when using acidic marinades such as the following citrus marinade, or your food will pick up a metallic taste.

Citrus Marinade

Citrus flavors go well with any type of fish. For an interesting flavor variation, this particular recipe can also be used for chicken or pork.

Preparation time: *10 minutes*

Yield: *2¹/₂ cups*

1¹/₄ cup olive oil	*2 tablespoons lemon zest*
¹/₂ cup orange juice	*2 tablespoons lime zest*
2 tablespoons orange zest	*Pepper*

1 Mix together all the ingredients in a medium bowl.

2 Pour over the raw seafood and marinate in the refrigerator for a minimum of 2 hours. Remove the seafood from the marinade and cook using the desired method (see the following section for seafood cooking ideas).

Fruit juices are great in marinades, but stay clear of papaya in lengthy marinades; it breaks down the flesh of the fish, leaving it mealy and undesirable.

Discovering Various Cooking Methods for Seafood

Many people love to order seafood in a restaurant but don't like to cook it at home. Don't be afraid to try it; it's not that difficult, and the results are delicious. Just remember to cook the fish slightly less than the desired doneness — fish continues to cook even after you remove it from the heat source.

You can test for doneness by pressing on the flesh of the fish with your finger: If it feels firm, it's cooked; if it feels soft, it's underdone. Or just insert a knife into the fish, pull back the flesh a little, and take a look.

You can prepare seafood in a variety of different ways — each cooking method adds its own flavor and texture to the seafood. You can use the following descriptions to help you decide which cooking method is most appropriate for the seafood that you're preparing.

Grilling

Seafood is wonderful on the grill, but selecting foods that can stand up to the grates and the heat of the grill is important. Use seafood items like tuna, lobster, swordfish, and shrimp, which are sturdy and do not fall or flake apart. Marinating in a mixture of olive oil and spices (or other flavorings) helps to tenderize the fish and ensures that it will not stick to the grill (and also adds complexity to the flavor).

The wood that you use to grill seafood also adds subtle hints of flavor. You can add hickory, apple wood, cherry, oak, or mesquite chips to your grill to change the flavor of the seafood.

Grilled Jumbo Shrimp and Vidalia Onion Brochette

Whether they contain seafood, meat, or poultry, brochettes beg for marinades. Here, you give an Asian flair to the dish by using a marinade with ginger and lemongrass. These brochettes can be served over just about anything, from a lettuce salad to couscous or pasta (as shown in the color section of this book).

Specialty tools: *4 skewers*

Preparation time: *10 minutes, plus 2 hours marinating*

Cooking time: *10 minutes*

Yield: *4 servings*

16 jumbo shrimp, cleaned and deveined (see Figure 9-4 for deveining instructions)

2 medium Vidalia onions, cut into bite-sized wedges

2 cups Asian Ginger-Lemongrass Marinade (see recipe earlier in this chapter)

Salt and pepper

1 Alternate the shrimp and onion wedges on the skewers.

(continued)

2 Place the skewers in a large resealable bag and pour in the Asian ginger-lemongrass marinade. Marinate in the refrigerator for 2 hours.

3 Remove the brochettes from the marinade, season with salt and pepper, and grill over a medium flame for 4 to 5 minutes on each side or until cooked. (They turn pink when cooked.)

Cleaning and Deveining Shrimp

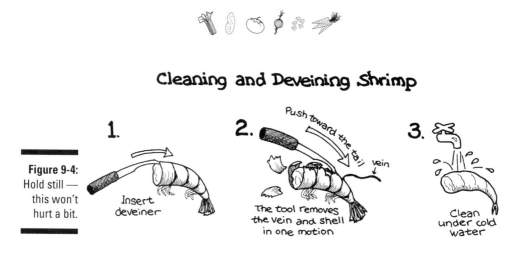

Figure 9-4: Hold still — this won't hurt a bit.

1. Insert deveiner

2. Push toward the tail — vein — The tool removes the vein and shell in one motion

3. Clean under cold water

Broiling

You can broil most types of seafood, even if they are fragile. Broiling fish on top of a bed of vegetables, such as chopped onions, celery, peppers, and fresh herbs, adds interesting flavors — and you can serve the vegetables right along with the fish. You can brush a glaze (like the one in the following recipe) onto the fish for a sweet, caramelized flavor.

Broiled Sweet and Sour Halibut with Bok Choy and Somen Noodles

In this recipe, the delicate flavor of the halibut stands up nicely to the sweet glaze, while the bok choy has a refreshing flavor element that keeps the glaze from being too sweet. This dish appears in the color section of this book.

Preparation time: *15 minutes*

Cooking time: *20 minutes*

Yield: *4 servings*

(continued)

¹/₄ cup sugar

¹/₄ cup rice wine vinegar

2 tablespoons soy sauce

1 jalapeño, seeded and finely chopped

2 cups bok choy, chopped

1 cup diced water chestnuts

¹/₄ cup sesame oil

Salt and pepper

4 5-ounce pieces of halibut

12 ounces somen noodles, cooked according to package directions just prior to use

2 tablespoons sesame seeds, toasted at 375° for 10 minutes

¹/₂ cup chopped scallions

¹/₄ cup basil, cut into a fine chiffonade

1 Simmer the sugar, vinegar, soy sauce, and jalapeño in a small saucepan over medium heat for 3 minutes. Cool and set aside.

2 In a medium pan, sauté the bok choy and water chestnuts with 1 tablespoon of the sesame oil for 3 to 4 minutes or until tender. Season with salt and pepper.

3 Season the halibut with salt and pepper and brush all over with the sugar-vinegar-jalapeño mixture. Place the halibut in the broiler for 4 to 5 minutes or until slightly underdone.

4 Toss the cooked somen noodles with the remaining sesame oil, sesame seeds, scallions, and basil.

5 Place some of the somen noodle mixture in the center of each plate. Arrange some of the bok choy mixture around the noodles and top with a piece of halibut.

Corn Meal-Crusted Catfish with Peanut-Scallion Sauce

The corn meal crust on the catfish adds flavor as well as texture to this dish, and the crunchy peanut sauce adds richness. This fish would be perfect served as the last appetizer in an Asian-oriented menu.

Preparation time: *10 minutes*

Cooking time: *10 minutes*

Yield: *4 servings*

(continued)

¹/₂ cup corn meal	2 teaspoons chopped garlic
3 tablespoons chopped cilantro	4 tablespoons butter
4 5-ounce catfish fillets, skin removed	¹/₄ cup white wine
Salt and pepper	2 tablespoons lemon juice
2 tablespoons canola oil	³/₄ cup chopped peanuts
2 tablespoons chopped shallots	1 cup chopped scallions

1 Place the corn meal and 2 tablespoons of the chopped cilantro in a small bowl. Season the catfish with salt and pepper and coat both sides with the corn meal mixture.

2 Sauté the catfish in a hot pan with the canola oil for 4 minutes on each side or until golden-brown.

3 To prepare the peanut-scallion sauce, cook the shallots and garlic with 1 tablespoon of the butter in a small saucepan over medium-high heat. Cook for 2 minutes or until golden-brown.

4 Add the white wine to deglaze the pan; then add the lemon juice and peanuts. Slowly whisk in the remaining butter, scallions, and cilantro. Season with salt and pepper.

5 Spoon some of the sauce over the catfish and serve while hot.

Sautéing

Sautéing is probably the most common method of cooking seafood. It's a quick and easy way to cook seafood while maintaining optimal flavor. For best results when you sauté, cook the side with the skin first (if it's left on).

Sautéed Curry-Spiced Tuna with Crispy Polenta and Beef Stock Reduction

The heat of the curry crust in this recipe is cooled by the flesh of the tuna and the richness of the polenta. This dish goes nicely with some wilted greens or sautéed asparagus. Flip to the color section of this book to see how this recipe turns out.

Preparation time: *15 minutes, plus 2 hours refrigeration*

Cooking time: *10 minutes*

Yield: *4 servings*

(continued)

2 tablespoons Roasted Garlic Puree (see following recipe)

2 cups cooked polenta, hot (follow the cooking instructions on the package)

Salt and pepper

1 tablespoon butter

2 teaspoons sweet curry powder

2 teaspoons hot curry powder

1 teaspoon cayenne

1 teaspoon paprika

2 10-ounce tuna loins

1 tablespoon vegetable oil

1 cup Beef Stock Reduction (see Chapter 5)

2 tablespoons chopped chervil

1 Fold the roasted garlic puree into the polenta and season with salt and pepper. Spread the cooked polenta onto a half sheet pan in a $^1/_2$-inch-thick layer. Refrigerate for 2 hours.

2 Cut the polenta into 4 3-inch round discs. Sauté the polenta with the butter in a hot, nonstick pan for 2 to 3 minutes on each side or until golden-brown and crispy. Blot on paper towels.

3 Toss together the curry powders, cayenne, and paprika in a small bowl.

4 Season the tuna with salt and pepper and then coat all sides evenly with the spice mixture. Sauté the tuna with the vegetable oil in a large, hot pan for 2 to 3 minutes on each side or until golden-brown (the middle should be medium-rare). Cut the tuna into thin slices and season with salt and pepper.

5 Warm the beef stock reduction in a small saucepan for 3 minutes or until hot.

6 Place a piece of polenta in the center of each plate and top with some of the tuna slices. Spoon the beef stock reduction around the plate and sprinkle with the chopped chervil.

Roasted Garlic Puree

Roasted garlic puree not only cries out to be spread on a piece of sourdough bread, but it also adds rich flavor to potatoes and polenta.

***Preparation time:** 5 minutes*

***Cooking time:** 1 hour and 40 minutes*

***Yield:** About $^3/_4$ cup*

4 garlic bulbs, tops cut off

3 cups milk

$^1/_2$ cup olive oil

Salt and pepper

1 Place the garlic in a small saucepan, cover with the milk, and simmer for 10 minutes.

(continued)

2 Drain the milk and then place the garlic bulbs bottom-side down in an ovenproof pan. Add the olive oil and cover the pan with a lid or foil. Bake at 350° for 1¹/₂ hours or until the garlic bulbs are soft.

3 Cool the garlic and oil, squeeze the soft garlic out of the skins, and place in a blender with the olive oil in which you baked the garlic. Puree the garlic and oil until smooth.

Sautéed Crab Cakes with Cilantro and Cumin Rémoulade

You can serve crispy crab cakes as an appetizer (as shown in the color section of this book), or you can add stir-fried vegetables and pureed potatoes and serve them as an entree. Spice them up to your liking with splashes of hot sauce and lemon juice.

Preparation time: *15 minutes*

Cooking time: *10 minutes*

Yield: *30 1-inch round crab cakes, or about 10 servings*

2 egg yolks	1 cup bread crumbs, toasted
1 tablespoon lemon juice	2 tablespoons chopped parsley
2 tablespoons chopped shallots	1 pound cooked crab meat, cleaned
1 cup plus 2 tablespoons vegetable oil	¹/₄ cup diced red bell pepper
3 tablespoons chopped cilantro	2 jalapeños, seeded and chopped
1 tablespoon toasted cumin seeds, ground	3 tablespoons chopped chives
1 teaspoon cayenne pepper	1 tablespoon lime juice
Salt and pepper	2 tablespoons cilantro, julienned

1 To make the rémoulade: Whisk together the egg yolks, lemon juice, and shallots in a medium bowl. Slowly whisk in 1 cup of the vegetable oil with a hand-held blender or a whisk until it forms a thick mayonnaise. Fold in the chopped cilantro, ground cumin, and cayenne pepper and season with salt and pepper. Keep refrigerated until ready to use because it contains raw egg.

2 Toss together the toasted bread crumbs and parsley in a small bowl and set aside.

3 Place the crab in a medium bowl. Fold in the red bell pepper, jalapeño, chives, and lime juice and season with salt and pepper. Fold in 3 tablespoons of the rémoulade and ¹/₄ cup of the bread crumbs.

(continued)

4 Divide the crab mixture into 30 equal portions. Form into round, 1-inch-thick patties. Coat the crab patties with the remaining bread crumbs. In a hot, nonstick sauté pan, cook the crab cakes in the remaining vegetable oil for 2 to 3 minutes on each side or until golden-brown and crispy.

5 Serve hot with a dollop of the rémoulade and sprinkle with the julienned cilantro.

SAFETY TIP

Be careful with those raw eggs! They can carry the salmonella bacteria. For an adult, salmonella poisoning can mean several days of nasty flu-like symptoms. But in children and elderly adults, salmonella poisoning can be fatal.

Wok-Seared Scallops with Stir-Fried Vegetables and Sesame-Lime Vinaigrette

Scallops are best if cooked quickly over high heat — and a wok is the perfect tool to do the job. The base of the wok becomes intensely hot in no time and sears the scallops golden-brown and crispy, leaving the inside moist and tender. (Check out the color section of this book to see this finished dish.)

Preparation time: *15 minutes*

Cooking time: *15 minutes*

Yield: *4 servings*

2 teaspoons minced garlic

1 tablespoon minced ginger

3 tablespoons canola oil

1 cup julienned snow peas

1/2 cup julienned yellow bell pepper

1/2 cup julienned leeks

1/2 cup julienned carrots

1/2 cup julienned red bell pepper

Salt and black pepper

8 large sea scallops

3 tablespoons lime juice

2 tablespoons chopped shallots

6 tablespoons sesame oil

4 tablespoons chives, cut into 1-inch-long pieces

1 In a hot wok (or large sauté pan), sweat the garlic and ginger in 2 tablespoons of canola oil for 30 seconds. Add the snow peas, yellow bell pepper, leeks, carrots, and red bell pepper and quickly stir-fry for 2 to 3 minutes or until tender. Season to taste with salt and pepper and remove from the wok.

(continued)

2 Season the scallops with salt and pepper and sear in the wok with the remaining 1 tablespoon canola oil for 1 to 2 minutes on each side or until just undercooked.

3 Place the lime juice and shallots in a small bowl and slowly whisk in the sesame oil. Season to taste with salt and pepper.

4 Arrange some of the stir-fried vegetables in the center of each plate. Place 2 scallops on top of the vegetables and spoon the lime-sesame vinaigrette over the scallops and around the plate. Sprinkle with the chives.

Cold and hot poaching

You can poach fish or shellfish in two ways: *Hot poaching* cooks the fish in a boiling liquid. Or you can *cold poach* the seafood by pouring a simmering liquid over the fish and allowing it to stand until the fish is cooked. Hot poaching works well with large pieces of fish or when the fish will be served hot. Cold poaching works well with small pieces of fish that don't take long to cook, or when the fish is being served cold or at room temperature.

Don't forget that the more flavorful the poaching liquid (such as a vinaigrette or a broth), the more flavorful the poached fish will be.

Cold-Poached Salmon with Herb Salad and Lemon-Thyme Vinaigrette

This cold-poached salmon melts in your mouth as you bite into it, while the vinaigrette cuts through the fat of the salmon, creating a perfect flavor combination. This salmon is best when served at room temperature.

Preparation time: *15 minutes*

Cooking time: *10 minutes*

Yield: *4 servings*

For the Salmon:

3 cups Fish Stock (see Chapter 5)

1 cup chopped onion

$^1/_2$ cup chopped carrots

$^1/_2$ cup chopped celery

1 tablespoon black peppercorns

$^1/_2$ lemon

5 fresh thyme sprigs

Salt

4 4-ounce pieces of salmon

(continued)

For the Herb Salad:

$^1/_4$ cup Italian parsley leaves

$^1/_4$ cup chervil leaves

2 tablespoons tarragon leaves

2 tablespoons cilantro leaves

2 tablespoons dill leaves

3 tablespoons tiny basil leaves

$^3/_4$ cup Lemon-Thyme Vinaigrette (see Chapter 5)

Salt and pepper

$^1/_2$ cup julienned daikon

1 Place the fish stock, onion, carrots, celery, peppercorns, lemon, and thyme in a medium saucepan. Simmer for 10 minutes and then season with salt.

2 Lay the salmon in an ovenproof pan and pour the hot fish stock over the salmon. Turn the salmon over after 4 minutes and allow to sit for 4 to 6 minutes or until medium-rare (where the inside is still deep pink and slightly raw-looking). Remove the salmon and set aside until ready to use.

3 Cool the liquid slightly (if it's still hot to the touch) and return the salmon to the cooking liquid until ready to serve. Do not refrigerate the salmon — the proteins will *coagulate,* or form solid white secretions on the skin that aren't very appetizing.

4 Prepare the herb salad by placing the parsley, chervil, tarragon, cilantro, dill, and basil in a medium bowl and tossing with 3 tablespoons of the vinaigrette. Season with salt and pepper.

5 Arrange some of the herb salad in the center of each plate. Place some of the julienned daikon on top of the herbs and top with a piece of salmon. Spoon some of the remaining vinaigrette over the salmon and season with salt and pepper.

Poached Lobster Wontons with Tomato-Saffron Broth

The lobster meat is wonderful in these wontons, but if you want more lobster meat, you can certainly slice some more and add it to the broth. The photo in the color section of this book shows how appealing this dish can be.

Preparation time: *15 minutes, plus overnight draining*

Cooking time: *10 minutes*

Yield: *4 servings*

(continued)

12 medium ripe tomatoes, chopped

Salt and pepper

2 cooked lobster tails

1 tablespoon chopped ginger

3 tablespoons chopped chives

$^1/_4$ teaspoon saffron

12 3 inch square, fresh wontons

1 egg yolk, mixed with 2 tablespoons water

2 cups fresh spinach, cleaned and blanched

$^1/_4$ cup chives, cut into 1-inch pieces on the diagonal

1 Puree the tomatoes with 1 teaspoon salt in a food processor. Tie up the pureed tomatoes in cheesecloth and allow the liquid to drip into a large bowl, as shown in Figure 9-5. (It's best to leave the pureed tomatoes in the refrigerator overnight to drain.) After the tomato water has drained, discard the tomato pulp.

2 Coarsely chop the lobster and season with salt and pepper. Toss with the ginger and chives and refrigerate until needed.

3 Place the tomato water and saffron in a medium saucepan. Simmer over medium heat for 4 to 5 minutes to infuse the saffron. Season with salt and pepper.

4 Lay the wonton skins flat and brush 2 adjoining edges with the egg yolk and water mixture. Place a heaping teaspoon of the lobster in the center of each wonton and fold it in half from one point to the other, creating a triangle. Firmly press the edges of each wonton together to close it.

5 Poach the wontons in boiling, salted water for 2 to 3 minutes or until al dente.

6 Place some of the spinach in the bottom of each bowl and top with 3 of the wontons. Pour some of the tomato-saffron broth over the wontons. Sprinkle with the chives and serve while hot.

Tying and Draining Tomatoes

Pureé the tomatoes with 1 teaspoon of salt in a food processor.

Tie up the pureed tomatoes in cheesecloth and allow the liquid to drain into a large bowl.

After the tomato water has drained, discard the tomato pulp!

Figure 9-5:
Tying and
draining
tomatoes.

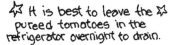

☆ It is best to leave the ☆ pureed tomatoes in the refrigerator overnight to drain.

Olive oil poaching

Poaching seafood in olive oil is a great way to slowly cook the fish. Cooking seafood in barely warm oil (you can test the temperature by actually putting you finger in the oil) keeps the proteins from coagulating. Olive oil poaching lessens the release of natural fat and oil from the fish, which helps to keep it moist. This slow cooking results in a succulent, perfectly cooked piece of fish — but not a lowfat one!

Olive Oil-Poached Swordfish Salad with Spinach, Red Bliss Potatoes, and Calamata Olive Vinaigrette

Shown in the color section of this book, this swordfish salad is my interpretation of a salad Niçoise. The calamata olive vinaigrette brings complexity to the swordfish. This dish makes a great cold lunch salad on the go.

Preparation time: 20 minutes

Cooking time: 12 minutes

Yield: 4 servings

4 5-ounce pieces of swordfish	*8 cups fresh baby spinach, cleaned*
Salt and pepper	*1 roasted red bell pepper, julienned (see Chapter 7)*
3 ¹/₄ cups olive oil	
¹/₂ cup pitted calamata olives	*2 cups haricots verts (thin green string beans), blanched*
¹/₄ cup balsamic vinegar	*8 small red bliss potatoes, boiled with the skin on and cut into quarters*
2 tablespoons chopped shallots	

1 Season the swordfish with salt and pepper. Place 3 cups of olive oil in a small saucepan and gently warm the oil over very low heat. (You should be able to hold your finger in the oil.)

2 Place the swordfish in the oil for 5 minutes, turn the fish, and continue to cook it for an additional 4 to 5 minutes (or until just firm and thoroughly cooked — it will bulge slightly). Remove the fish from the oil and keep it at room temperature.

3 To make the vinaigrette, coarsely chop the olives and place in a small bowl with the balsamic vinegar and shallots. Slowly whisk in the remaining ¹/₄ cup of olive oil and season with salt and pepper.

(continued)

4 In a large bowl, make the salad by tossing the spinach, roasted pepper, haricots verts, and potatoes. Add half of the calamata olive vinaigrette and season with salt and pepper.

5 Arrange some of the salad on each plate and top with a piece of the olive oil-poached swordfish. Sprinkle with pepper and spoon the remaining vinaigrette over the swordfish.

Steaming

Steaming keeps fish extremely moist and flaky. In fact, steaming is a great way to prepare many lowfat dishes — not just delicately flavored fish. You can even hand-craft your own steamer with a wire rack, a lid, and a sauté pan, as shown in Figure 9-6.

Hand-Crafted {Steamer} Setup

Figure 9-6:
Setting up your own steamer.

lid

saucepan

wire rack

water

Lemongrass Egg Drop Soup with Steamed Honey Glazed Halibut

Lemongrass is available in most Asian markets in fresh and dried forms. Fresh lemon balm leaves also have a great flavor if you have a hard time locating lemongrass.

Preparation time: *30 minutes*

Cooking time: *30 minutes*

Yield: *4 servings*

(continued)

8 cups Fish Stock (see Chapter 5)

³/₄ cup chopped lemongrass

1 cup lemon thyme

Salt and pepper

1 egg, lightly beaten

4 4-ounce pieces halibut

3 tablespoons honey

2 cups baby spinach, cleaned and blanched

1¹/₂ cups roasted oyster mushrooms

¹/₄ cup long-cut chives

1 Place the fish stock and lemongrass in a medium saucepan and simmer over medium heat for 15 minutes. Add the lemon thyme and continue to simmer for 3 more minutes. Strain and season to taste with salt and pepper.

2 Just prior to serving, simmer the stock, gently stir in the egg, and immediately remove from the heat.

3 Season the halibut with salt and pepper and then brush with some of the honey. Place in a steamer and steam the fish for 4 to 5 minutes or until it easily flakes apart. Remove the halibut from the steamer and brush with the remaining honey.

4 Arrange some of the spinach and mushrooms in each of 4 bowls. Place a piece of halibut in the center of each bowl and ladle the soup around the halibut. Sprinkle with the long-cut chives.

Roasting and slow-roasting

The only difference between roasting and slow-roasting is the temperature. Regular roasting takes place at about 350 to 400 degrees. Slow-roasting, on the other hand, takes place at temperatures as low as 175 to 250 degrees, and barely cooking a piece of fish can take as long as 20 to 30 minutes. When you slow-roast fish, the end result is a piece of seafood so moist that it melts in your mouth and falls apart when you touch it — which is why I generally prefer this method to roasting at a higher temperature.

Roasted Monkfish on the Bone with Mustard Spaetzle and Prosciutto

Monkfish is known as "poor man's lobster" because its flavor and texture are somewhat similar to lobster meat. In this recipe, I use intensely flavored prosciutto and mustard-flavored spaetzle to add complex flavors to the dish, while at the same time providing a chewy, textural contrast to the monkfish.

Preparation time: *20 minutes, plus 1 hour refrigeration*

Cooking time: *30 minutes*

Yield: *4 servings*

1 medium red onion, julienned

3 tablespoons butter

2 eggs, beaten

3 tablespoons stone-ground or coarse mustard

2 cups flour

1¹/₄ cups milk

Salt and pepper

2 baby monkfish tails (about 10 ounces each), on the bone, or 1 regular monkfish tail

2 tablespoons vegetable oil

¹/₂ cup julienned prosciutto

3 tablespoons chopped chives

1 In a medium sauté pan over medium-high heat, caramelize the red onion with 1 tablespoon of the butter for 7 to 9 minutes or until golden-brown.

2 Prepare the spaetzle by combining the egg, mustard, and flour in a mixing bowl. Add enough of the milk to make a somewhat stiff batter. Cover and refrigerate for 1 hour.

3 Using a pastry bag, spoon, or spaetzle maker, drop ¹/₂ teaspoonfuls of batter into simmering, lightly salted water. Cook for about 1 minute or until the spaetzle floats on the top of the water. Drain the spaetzle and set aside.

4 Just prior to use, sauté the spaetzle in a hot pan with the remaining 2 tablespoons of butter for 2 to 3 minutes or until golden-brown and crispy. Season with salt and pepper.

5 Season the monkfish with salt and pepper. Sear the fish in a hot pan with the vegetable oil for 2 to 3 minutes on each side or until golden-brown. Then place the fish in the oven at 375° and continue cooking for 6 to 8 minutes or until the center is no longer translucent. Remove the fish from the oven and cut the meat away from the bone. Slice into 2-inch pieces on the diagonal.

6 Toss the spaetzle with the prosciutto, caramelized red onion, and chives. Place some of the spaetzle mixture in the center of each plate and top with some of the monkfish pieces. Sprinkle with pepper.

Slow-Roasted Cod with Warm Tomato Salad and Roasted Garlic Vinaigrette

When they are slow-roasted, cod, salmon, bass, and halibut are so succulent and tender that you barely need to chew — but take your time and enjoy every luscious bite. Check out the color section to see this dish in all its glory.

Preparation time: _10 minutes_

Cooking time: _25 minutes_

Yield: _4 servings_

_$^1/_3$ cup Roasted Garlic Puree (see recipe earlier in this chapter)_

_$^1/_2$ cup olive oil_

1 tablespoon balsamic vinegar

Salt and pepper

6 red tomato wedges (about 1 large tomato), skin and seeds removed

6 yellow tomato wedges (about 1 large tomato), skin and seeds removed

4 5-ounce pieces of cod

1 cup fresh thyme

4 cups mesclun mix or baby lettuce, cleaned

2 tablespoons chopped chives

_1_ In a small bowl, whisk together the roasted garlic puree, $^1/_3$ cup of the olive oil, and the balsamic vinegar. Season to taste with salt and pepper.

_2_ Toss the tomato wedges with 3 tablespoons of the vinaigrette and lay them close together on a sheet pan.

_3_ Season the cod with salt and pepper and rub with a little of the olive oil. Place the cod on top of the tomato wedges. Cover the cod with the fresh thyme and roast at 225° for 20 to 25 minutes or until tender. Remove the thyme.

_4_ Place the mesclun mix or baby lettuce in a sauté pan with 2 tablespoons of the vinaigrette. Wilt the greens over medium heat for 1 minute; then season with salt and pepper.

_5_ Arrange some of the tomatoes and cod on each plate. Spoon the remaining vinaigrette over the cod. Place a small mound of the wilted greens on top of the cod and sprinkle with the chopped chives.

Chapter 10

Who Are You Calling Fowl?

Due to its relatively low levels of fat, cholesterol, and calories, poultry (or *fowl*) has enjoyed increasing popularity in recent years. In fact, the average American now eats over 70 pounds of poultry a year, and that number is rising.

CHARLIE SAYS

Chicken is by far the most widely consumed type of poultry. Its neutral flavor readily absorbs flavors from seasonings, marinades, and sauces, making it great for many different dishes. But don't stop with chicken. Because better methods of raising poultry have been developed, birds that at one time were reserved for special occasions are now readily available year-round. Squab, pheasant, and goose, for example, all have wonderful, distinct flavors that require very little "dressing up" to make a dinner party a real event.

How Poultry Is Raised

Poultry is raised in several different ways, each of which can affect the flavor of the bird:

✔ **Free-range** birds are allowed to forage for food outdoors. USDA regulations state that free-range coops must be open so that the birds can roam outside at will.

- ✔ **Mass-produced** poultry is raised commercially in massive numbers. These birds are raised in crowded but carefully supervised conditions, which bring the birds to market at exact sizes and weights.

- ✔ To earn the label **organic**, poultry must be fed chemical-free grain and be raised on land that has not been treated with chemical fertilizers or pesticides for at least three years.

Although purchasing poultry at the supermarket is convenient, it may not be the best choice — most supermarkets sell mass-produced poultry, which is raised and bred as quickly, cheaply, and efficiently as possible. For example, in 1960, it took ten weeks and 10 pounds of feed to produce a 4-pound broiler. By 1990, a mass-produced 4-pound bird could be produced in six weeks with only 8 pounds of feed. The result of these "advances" is a mass-produced bird with a much blander flavor than a naturally raised bird.

Free-range and organic poultry are equally good. Both are generally available at specialty markets and butcher shops, so finding a naturally raised bird may mean an extra stop while you're shopping. But after you try one of these flavorful birds, you'll never want to buy the mass-produced type again.

Storing and Handling Poultry

Uncooked poultry can contain bacteria that causes food-borne illnesses. It is extremely important that you handle poultry, and the tools that come in contact with it, properly in order to avoid illness. Follow these guidelines when working with poultry:

- ✔ Keep poultry refrigerated when it's not being used, and use it within two to three days of purchasing.

- ✔ Store raw poultry in clean, leak-proof containers, and do not place poultry above any cooked meats. If the poultry drips on the food below, it will contaminate that food.

- ✔ Thaw frozen poultry gradually in the refrigerator. Allow about 15 hours for a 3-pound bird. You can also thaw a frozen bird under cold running water in a sink with an open drain.

- ✔ Thoroughly clean and sanitize all tools with soap and bleach after using them on raw poultry.

- ✔ Wash your hands thoroughly with soap after handling raw poultry.

Which Came First: The Chicken or the Egg?

As I mentioned earlier, chicken is more popular than any other type of meat or poultry on the market. It is also very economical, although that was not always the case. When Herbert Hoover made his famous comment about "a chicken in every pot," only the affluent could afford that proverbial chicken. It wasn't until after World War II that the price of chicken started dropping.

Chickens are categorized by their age; generally, the younger the bird, the more tender it is. Each type of chicken is used for different purposes, as the following list explains:

- **Broiler-fryers** are chickens that are about seven weeks old and weigh from $2^1/_2$ to $4^1/_2$ pounds. Because these chickens have very little fat, they are best prepared by broiling or frying, as the name implies.

- **Roasting chickens** are usually hens that are eight or nine weeks old and weigh from 5 to 8 pounds. These chickens have enough fat to brown nicely as they roast.

- **Capons** are roosters that are about ten weeks old and weigh from 8 to 10 pounds. Capons have generous amounts of tender, white breast meat and are ideal for stuffing and roasting.

- **Poussins** are baby chickens that are five to six weeks old. They weigh about 2 pounds and are ideal for roasting or stuffing and serving whole.

Kosher chicken is simply a bird — free-range, organic, or mass-produced — that has been killed according to Jewish dietary laws, under the hand and supervision of a rabbi. These birds are usually available only at kosher butcher shops.

The skinny on white and dark meat

Why do some people prefer white meat over dark meat? Well, only your taste buds can answer that, but I thought this information was interesting, anyway.

Meat is muscle, and muscle that is active stores a lot of oxygen from the blood. This makes it darker than meat from muscles that are less frequently exercised. Because chickens rarely fly, their breast meat is quite pale, but their leg meat is dark because they walk around a lot. Dark meat is higher in calories and fat and often has a silkier texture than white meat does.

Chicken is a truly versatile food. You can use any technique to cook it, and almost any flavor can accompany it. Chicken is a great place to start experimenting with gourmet cooking because it's a "safe" food to most cooks: You're familiar with it, you know how to shop for it, and you can visualize how it will turn out using different cooking techniques. The following recipes are a perfect example of how ordinary ingredients can be combined for extraordinary results.

Ginger-Sesame Chicken with Hot and Sour Carrots

Serving this dish over Asian wide rice noodles or sticky rice would nicely complement the Asian influences in the ginger-sesame chicken.

Preparation time: *15 minutes, plus 1 hour refrigeration*

Cooking time: *20 minutes*

Yield: *4 servings*

3 tablespoons sesame oil	*¹/₄ cup sugar*
2 tablespoons olive oil	*¹/₄ cup rice wine vinegar*
3 tablespoons finely chopped ginger	*2 tablespoons Spicy Vinegar (see Chapter 5)*
1 tablespoon finely chopped garlic	
4 boneless chicken breasts, with skin	*3 cups carrots, cut into a batonette (see "Formal Knife Cuts" in Chapter 3)*
Salt and pepper	*4 teaspoons chopped cilantro*
1 tablespoon canola oil	

1 Combine the sesame oil, olive oil, ginger, and garlic in a medium bowl. Rub the mixture onto the chicken breasts and refrigerate for 1 hour.

2 Remove the chicken breasts from the refrigerator and season with salt and pepper. Sauté the chicken breasts in 1 tablespoon of canola oil, skin-side down first. Sauté for 5 to 6 minutes on each side or until golden-brown and cooked. (You may need to finish the chicken in the oven if the breast is especially thick.)

3 Place the sugar, rice wine vinegar, and spicy vinegar in a medium sauté pan. Simmer over medium heat for 2 to 3 minutes or until the sugar has dissolved. Add the carrots and continue to cook for 5 to 7 minutes or until the carrots are tender. Season with salt and pepper and toss with the chopped cilantro.

4 Slice the chicken on the diagonal just prior to serving. Spoon some of the carrots onto the center of each plate and top with the sliced chicken.

Crispy Curried Chicken Dumplings with Date Dipping Sauce

This recipe is a twist on the traditional *pot sticker.* The sweetness of the date dipping sauce helps to tone down the heat of the curry.

Preparation time: *30 minutes*

Cooking time: *20 to 25 minutes*

Yield: *24 dumplings*

3 cups Chicken Stock (see Chapter 5)

2 tablespoons curry powder

1 chicken breast, skin removed

¹/₄ cup golden raisins, chopped

¹/₂ cup chopped scallions

Salt and pepper

1 cup dried dates, pits removed

1 teaspoon rice wine vinegar

24 3-inch-round wontons (you may need to cut them out of square wontons if you can't find round ones)

1 egg yolk mixed with 2 tablespoons water

3 tablespoons butter

1 Place the chicken stock in a small saucepan with 1¹/₂ tablespoons curry powder and simmer over medium heat for 3 minutes. Add the chicken breast and poach for 10 minutes or until the chicken is cooked.

2 Remove the chicken (reserve 1 cup of the cooking liquid) and pull it apart into small pieces. Place this *pulled* chicken in a small bowl and toss with the chopped raisins, scallions, and the remaining ¹/₂ tablespoon curry powder. Season with salt and pepper.

3 Prepare the date sauce by placing the dried dates in a small saucepan with the reserved cooking liquid from the chicken. Simmer over medium heat for 3 minutes or until the dates are rehydrated. Puree the dates and vinegar in a blender and pass through a fine-mesh sieve. Season with salt and pepper.

4 Lay the wonton skins flat and brush half the edge with the egg yolk mixture. Place some of the chicken mixture in the center of the wontons and fold in half. Press firmly to create a seal around the edges of the dumpling.

5 Cook the dumplings in boiling salted water for 2 to 3 minutes or until tender.

6 Sauté the cooked dumplings in a hot pan with the butter for 2 to 3 minutes on each side, or until golden-brown and crispy.

7 Serve with the date sauce.

Cumin-Crusted Sautéed Chicken Breasts with Morel Mushrooms and Brown Butter-Hickory Nut Pan Sauce

The spongy morels in this dish soak up the aromatic cumin flavor. Adding butter and nuts to the combination gives it richness and helps to blend the flavors. If you have a hard time finding fresh morels, you can rehydrate dried ones. Or you can check the chart on wild mushrooms in Chapter 7 for mushrooms with a similar flavor.

Preparation time: *15 minutes*

Cooking time: *20 minutes*

Yield: *4 servings*

4 boneless chicken breasts, with skin

Salt and pepper

4 tablespoons cumin seeds, crushed

2 tablespoons olive oil

1 tablespoon chopped shallots

2¹/₂ cups roasted morel mushrooms (cut in half if large) (see Chapter 7)

3 tablespoons white wine

¹/₂ cup chopped hickory nuts

¹/₄ cup butter

2 tablespoons chopped tarragon

1 Season the chicken breasts with salt and pepper and sprinkle the tops with the cumin seeds. Sauté the chicken breast skin-side down in a hot pan with the olive oil; sauté on each side for 3 to 4 minutes or until cooked. Remove from the pan.

2 Sauté the shallots for 2 minutes in the same pan used for the chicken. Add the morel mushrooms and continue cooking until the morels are hot. Remove the mushrooms and season with salt and pepper.

3 To make the pan sauce, add the white wine to the pan and cook for 1 to 2 minutes or until the liquid is reduced by half. Add the nuts and cook for 2 minutes or until the nuts are toasted. Add the butter and cook over high heat for 4 minutes or until the butter has turned brown. Stir in the tarragon and season with salt and pepper.

4 Slice the chicken on the diagonal just prior to serving. Arrange some of the morel mushrooms on each plate and top with the sliced chicken. Spoon some of the pan sauce over the chicken.

Chicken Roulade with Prosciutto and Artichoke-Spinach Puree

The *roulade,* or roll, makes a beautiful presentation alongside some wilted greens. If you want a simpler preparation, you can leave the chicken breast whole, julienne the prosciutto, and serve it with the artichoke-spinach puree as a side dish.

Specialty tools: *Wooden mallet, cooking twine*

Preparation time: *30 minutes*

Cooking time: *30 minutes*

Yield: *4 servings*

2 cooked artichoke bottoms (refer to Figure 4-14 for instructions for cleaning an artichoke)

1 cup blanched spinach

Salt and pepper

2 teaspoons chopped garlic

2 tablespoons chopped shallots

2 tablespoons butter

2 large boneless chicken breasts, skin removed

6 thin slices prosciutto

1 Puree the artichokes and spinach together in a food processor and season with salt and pepper.

2 Sauté the garlic and shallots in the butter over medium heat for 2 minutes or until lightly golden. Add this mixture to the artichoke and spinach puree.

3 Lay the chicken breasts flat on a cutting board with the edges overlapping slightly, cover with plastic wrap, and pound with a mallet until they're about $1/4$ inch thick. Season both sides with salt and pepper.

4 Lay the prosciutto on top of the chicken and spread the artichoke-spinach puree on top of the prosciutto. Tightly roll up the chicken and tie together with string (just like you would with a roast), creating a roulade.

5 In a hot sauté pan containing the olive oil, sear the chicken for 2 minutes on all sides or until golden-brown. Then roast at 375° for 20 minutes or until cooked.

6 Remove the string and cut into 8 slices.

Poultry-cooking tips

You should truss all poultry before roasting it; the wings and thighs should be kept close to the body so that they don't overcook.

To tell whether a roasted bird is completely cooked, pierce the thigh with a fork. If the juices run clear, the bird is done. If the juices are slightly pink, the bird needs to cook longer.

Dark meat takes longer to cook than white meat. Cook whole birds until the temperature in the thigh reaches 180 degrees. Cook poultry breasts to a temperature of 170 degrees.

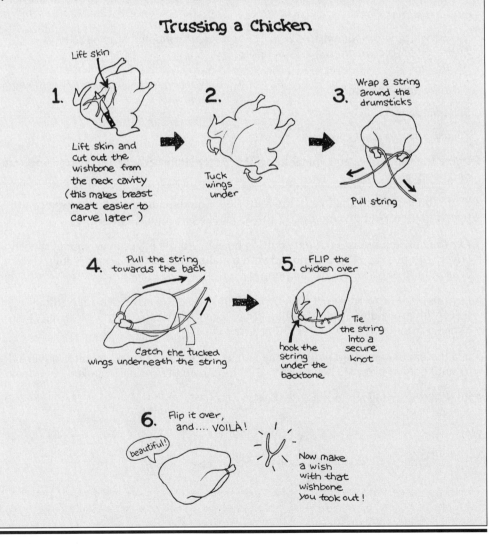

Trussing a Chicken

Discovering Different Types of Poultry

Although chicken is the most widely used type of poultry, don't forget about the other birds that are available. They may be a little more difficult to find, but they are well worth the effort.

Duck

Today's domestic ducks are descendants of either the mallard or the muscovy duck. Supermarkets and butcher shops usually sell them whole, as broiler/fryers, which are less than 8 weeks old, or as roasters, which are no older than 16 weeks. Ducks generally weigh between $3^1/_2$ and 5 pounds. They have dark, succulent flesh that, due to their high fat content, is best when roasted or cooked as a confit. Roasting allows the fat to cook off of the bird, leaving crispy skin and juicy meat. Confit takes advantage of the fat by slowly cooking the duck in its own fat until the meat becomes meltingly soft.

Duck Confit

Confit means to cook meat slowly, covered in its own fat or oil. The resulting flavors are intense, and the texture is extremely tender and moist.

Preparation time: *20 minutes, plus 1 day for curing the duck*

Cooking time: *4 hours and 35 minutes*

Yield: *4 servings*

1 5-pound fresh duck

6 tablespoons kosher salt

1 tablespoon sugar

1 tablespoon coarsely ground black pepper

1 tablespoon sliced garlic

2 teaspoons chopped ginger

$1^1/_2$ cups rendered duck or chicken fat

1 Cut the thighs and breasts from the duck (leaving the skin on) and set aside. Remove any skin and fat from the remaining body of the duck and discard the body.

2 Place the skin and fat in a large sauté pan. Over medium heat, slowly render the fat for 35 minutes or until the skin is crispy and all the fat has melted out. Discard the skin and strain the fat. Refrigerate the fat until needed.

3 Rub the duck pieces with the kosher salt, sugar, black pepper, garlic, and 2 teaspoons of ginger. Pack tightly in a small container and cover with plastic wrap. Refrigerate for 24 hours, turning over after 12 hours.

(continued)

4 Rinse the duck breasts and thighs and place in a heavy-bottomed pot. Cover with the duck fat (both the $1^1/_2$ cups listed above and the fat rendered from the duck in Step 1), cover, and bake at 225° for about 4 hours, or until the meat is quite soft and fork-tender. (You can make the duck confit ahead of time, leave it in the fat, and store it in the refrigerator for up to a week.)

5 Remove the duck from the fat. Pull the meat away from the bones, discarding the bones and skin.

Duck Confit Filo Wraps

The moist and tender duck confit is complemented in this recipe by crispy, flaky filo dough. These filo wraps can be cut into small pieces for appetizers, or in larger pieces as an entree.

Preparation time: *30 minutes*

Cooking time: *30 minutes*

Yield: *4 servings*

2 cups Duck Confit (see preceding recipe), pulled (or shredded)

3 tablespoons chopped cilantro

$^1/_2$ cup julienned roasted shiitake mushrooms (see Chapter 7)

$^1/_4$ cup julienned leeks

2 tablespoons lime juice

1 cup shredded Napa cabbage

1 tablespoon chopped ginger

Salt and pepper

8 sheets filo dough

$^1/_4$ cup melted butter

1 Place the duck meat in a medium bowl and toss with the cilantro, mushrooms, leeks, lime juice, Napa cabbage, and ginger. Season with salt and pepper.

2 Lay out a sheet of filo and brush lightly with the melted butter. Top with another piece of the filo and again brush with the melted butter. Continue this process until you have 4 layers of filo. Repeat with the remaining 4 sheets of filo.

3 Spoon half the duck confit mixture along the bottom third of each set of filo dough layers. Tightly roll up the filo sheets, tucking in the ends. Bake at 375° for 30 minutes or until golden-brown and crispy. Slice diagonally and serve while hot.

Tip: *See Chapter 14 for hints on working with thin, delicate filo dough.*

Goose

A goose can weigh from 5 to 18 pounds and is traditionally cooked for a holiday dinner. Geese are also prized for their livers, which are known as *foie gras.* Most geese marketed in the U.S. are frozen, but you can find fresh geese in specialty markets. (Finding a fresh goose is worth the trip.) Chefs usually roast geese whole, in much the same manner that they roast a turkey.

Cranberry-Ginger Glazed Roasted Goose with Sweet Potatoes

The skin on a goose craves to be cooked to a crisp (while the goose itself pleads for mercy). Basting a goose or coating it with a glaze is important to help keep the juices inside. This cranberry-ginger glaze adds a nice sweetness and a festive pink color to the goose.

Preparation time: *15 minutes*

Cooking time: *2¹/₂ hours*

Yield: *8 servings*

2 cups fresh cranberries	¹/₂ cup chopped carrots
3 tablespoons chopped ginger	¹/₂ cup chopped celery
¹/₂ cup sugar	6 tablespoons butter
1 tablespoon chopped lemon zest	2 sweet potatoes, peeled and cut into large dice
1 clove	
1 13-pound whole goose	2 tablespoons brown sugar
Salt and pepper	1 teaspoon ground nutmeg
1 cup chopped onion	1 tablespoon chopped tarragon

1 Place the cranberries, ginger, sugar, lemon zest, and clove in a small saucepan. Barely cover with water and simmer over medium heat for 7 to 10 minutes or until thick. Pass through a sieve, set the glazing mixture aside, and discard the solids.

2 Season the outside and inner cavity of the goose with salt and pepper. Place the goose on top of the onions, carrots, and celery in a deep roasting pan. (If you don't have a deep pan, you'll need to drain the fat during cooking.) Brush the outside of the goose with some of the cranberry-ginger glaze and roast at 375° for 2 to 2¹/₂ hours, or until golden-brown and crispy (or until your goose is cooked!). Brush the goose with the cranberry-ginger glaze every 15 minutes while it roasts.

(continued)

3 Sauté the diced sweet potatoes in 2 tablespoons of butter for 5 minutes over medium heat. Cover the sweet potatoes and bake at 375° for 10 minutes. Add the brown sugar and nutmeg and continue to bake for 10 more minutes or until the sweet potatoes are tender.

4 Remove the grease from the pan, leaving the meat juices. Whisk 4 tablespoons of butter into the meat juices, add the chopped tarragon, and season with salt and pepper.

5 Carve the goose and serve alongside the sweet potatoes and pan drippings.

Pheasant

Pheasant is a medium-sized game bird. Wild pheasants used to be more flavorful than the farm-raised variety, but in recent years, great strides have been made toward duplicating their natural growing conditions, resulting in more flavorful farm-raised birds. Pheasant farms are strictly governed by USDA regulations, which means that the chances of getting "a tough old bird" are virtually nil.

Pheasant and Lentil Soup

Pheasant can be roasted or sautéed, but here you roast it and then poach it to give the soup a more complex flavor. This way, you can snack on the poultry before it goes into the soup.

Preparation time: *15 minutes*

Cooking time: *2 hours*

Yield: *6 to 8 servings*

2 2-pound whole pheasants	*1 cup chopped portobello mushrooms*
Salt and pepper	*4 cups cooked lentils*
8 cups Chicken Stock (see Chapter 5)	*¹/₄ cup julienned basil*
1 cup chopped leeks	*¹/₂ cup chopped scallions*
1 cup diced carrots	

1 Season the outside and inner cavities of the pheasants with salt and pepper. Roast at 375° for 45 minutes.

(continued)

2 In a large stockpot, combine the chicken stock, leeks, carrots, mushrooms, and lentils. Bring to a simmer and add the whole pheasants. Continue to simmer for 30 minutes or until the meat falls off the bones.

3 Remove the pheasants from the stockpot. Discard the skin and bones and break the meat into small pieces. Return the meat to the soup and season with salt and pepper.

4 Garnish with the basil and chopped scallions.

Rock Cornish hen

Cornish hens weigh up to $2^{1}/_{2}$ pounds and are four to six weeks old. One hen is usually enough for one serving. Cornish hens are usually best roasted or broiled.

These beautiful hens make a statement when served whole. They can be stuffed with traditional stuffing, or with fruits and rice, as in the following recipe.

Whole Roasted Cornish Game Hens Stuffed with Wild Rice and Apricots

In this recipe, the nuttiness of the wild rice goes nicely with the slight gaminess of the hen and the sweetness of the apricots.

Specialty tools: *Cooking twine*

Preparation time: *15 minutes*

Cooking time: *40 minutes*

Yield: *4 servings*

4 small Cornish game hens	*2 tablespoons chopped chives*
Salt and pepper	*$^{1}/_{2}$ cup butter, melted*
4 cups cooked wild rice	*2 tablespoons chopped garlic*
$^{1}/_{4}$ cup diced dried apricots	*2 tablespoons chopped tarragon*
$^{1}/_{4}$ cup chopped pecans	

1 Season the outside and the inner cavities of the hens with salt and pepper.

2 In a medium bowl, toss together the wild rice, apricots, pecans, and chives. Stuff the hens with the wild rice mixture. Truss the hens with twine (see the earlier "Poultry-cooking tips" sidebar) and place on a rack in a roasting pan.

(continued)

3 In a small bowl, combine the melted butter, garlic, and tarragon and brush over the outside of the hens.

4 Roast the hens in the oven at 400° for 30 to 40 minutes, or until golden-brown and crispy and the juices from the thigh run clear. (Prick the thigh with a fork to check the juices.) Baste the hen with the butter mixture every 10 minutes while roasting. Remove the string before serving.

Squab

Squab is my favorite type of poultry. It's a four-week-old domesticated pigeon that has never flown and is therefore extremely tender. These birds usually weigh 1 pound or less and have a delicately flavored dark meat. You probably won't find squab at the supermarket, but it's available in many butcher shops, or you can ask them to order it for you. Squab is great grilled, sautéed, or treated like any prime cut of meat.

Grilled Thai Barbecue Squab Breasts with Soy-Bacon Braised Collard Greens

With the Thai and soy elements matched with the bacon and collard greens, this dish should be called "Yul Brynner Meets Jed Clampett"! The dark squab meat has a strong enough flavor to stand up to the heavy barbecue sauce and collard greens in this recipe. It is best served with the skin crisped and cooked barely medium-rare.

Preparation time: *15 minutes*

Cooking time: *20 minutes*

Yield: *4 servings*

4 squab breasts, with skin

Salt and pepper

$^1/_2$ cup Thai barbecue sauce (found in most specialty markets)

$^1/_2$ cup diced raw bacon

2 tablespoons chopped shallots

3 cups chopped collard greens

3 tablespoons red wine

$^1/_3$ cup soy sauce

$^1/_2$ cup water

2 tablespoons butter

(continued)

1 Season the squab breasts with salt and pepper and coat with the barbecue sauce. Grill over a medium flame for 3 minutes on each side. Slice on the diagonal just prior to serving.

2 Cook the bacon in a medium sauté pan until the fat is rendered, add the shallots, and cook for 1 minute or until golden-brown. Add the collard greens and red wine and continue to cook over medium heat for 3 minutes or until most of the wine is absorbed. Add the soy sauce and water. Continue to cook for 10 minutes or until the collard greens are tender.

3 Remove the collard greens from the pan, draining any liquid from the greens back into the pan. Whisk the butter into the pan and add additional soy sauce if desired.

4 Arrange some of the collard greens in the center of each plate and top with the sliced squab breast. Spoon the pan sauce over the squab and top with freshly ground black pepper.

Turkey

You probably couldn't imagine a Thanksgiving dinner without a turkey, but turkey is not just for Thanksgiving anymore. Turkey has had a tremendous surge in popularity in recent years because it's so low in fat. You can now regularly find it fresh or frozen in whole birds, breasts, drumsticks, or even ground.

Because of its low fat content, turkey meat can dry out very easily. You can do two things to avoid this problem: First, cook the turkey in a covered pan (or covered with foil) to create some steam; the added moisture helps to keep the meat juicy. You can remove the cover for the last quarter of the cooking time to allow the meat to brown.

Second, you can remove the turkey from the heat when it's still slightly underdone (or when its internal temperature reaches about 160 degrees) and allow it to rest on the countertop for 15 to 20 minutes. The bird continues to cook while it's resting, but it won't get overdone.

Boning poultry

Boning poultry is not difficult, but it can be time-consuming the first few times you do it. Just follow these simple instructions and you will be a pro in no time.

1. Cut the leg and thigh portions off the body.

2. Debone the legs and thighs by cutting along the back side of the leg and thigh until the bone is exposed. Using the tip of the knife, cut the meat away from the top of the bone. Slide the knife under the bone and loosen the meat. Pull the bones away from the meat and loosen the meat around the joint.

3. Cut the wings off the bird.

4. Make a cut along the breast bone and carefully cut down each side, staying as close to the ribs as possible.

5. You can then use the boned meat in any preparation and save the bones for making stock.

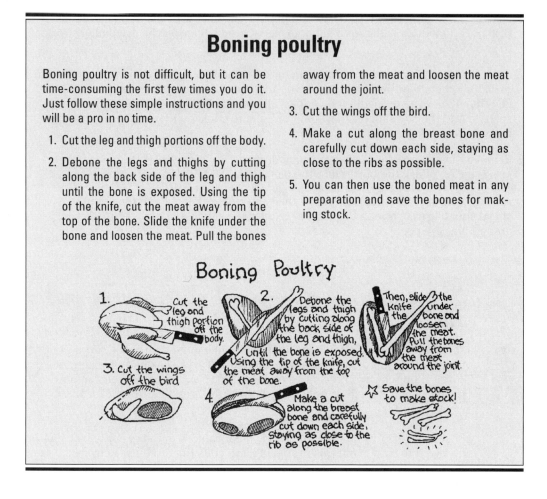

Boning Poultry

1. Cut the leg and thigh portion off the body.

2. Debone the legs and thigh by cutting along the back side of the leg and thigh, until the bone is exposed. Using the tip of the knife, cut the meat away from the top of the bone. Then, slide the knife under the bone and loosen the meat. Pull the bones away from the meat around the joint.

3. Cut the wings off the bird

4. Make a cut along the breast bone and carefully cut down each side, staying as close to the rib as possible.

Save the bones to make stock!

Sage and Garlic Roasted Turkey with Chestnut-Brioche Stuffing

Stuffing the skin of a turkey with herbs and spices not only adds flavor, but after the bird is cooked, a lovely pattern shows through the golden-brown skin. The buttery brioche makes an intensely rich stuffing that is enhanced by the pine nuts and the dried currants.

Preparation time: *20 minutes*

Cooking time: *3 hours*

Yield: *8 to 10 servings*

(continued)

1 10-pound turkey

Salt and pepper

12 whole sage leaves

8 cloves garlic, peeled and thinly sliced

$^1/_2$ cup olive oil

1 cup melted butter

3 cups chestnuts

$^1/_2$ cup chopped raw bacon

1 cup diced onion

6 cups diced brioche (see Chapter 14)

$^1/_2$ cup pine nuts, toasted for 10 minutes in a 350° oven

$^1/_2$ cup dried currants

1 cup diced celery

$^1/_2$ cup chopped chives

2 eggs, lightly beaten

$2^1/_2$ cups Chicken Stock (see Chapter 5)

1 cup heavy cream

1 Season the outside and inner cavity of the turkey with salt and pepper.

2 Starting at the edge of the large cavity, separate the skin from the meat. Using your hand, slide the sage leaves and garlic slices between the turkey skin and the meat, distributing evenly.

3 Rub the turkey with the olive oil and roast at 375° for $2^1/_2$ to 3 hours or until the internal temperature reaches 160°, basting occasionally with the melted butter. (You may need to cover it with foil toward the end of cooking to prevent overbrowning.) Let the turkey stand for 15 minutes before carving.

4 While turkey is roasting, cut slits in the shells of the chestnuts. Place them on a baking sheet and roast at 375° for 20 minutes or until the shells start to break away from the nuts. Remove the shells and chop up the nuts.

5 Render the bacon in a medium sauté pan for 5 minutes or until slightly crispy. Add the chopped onion and continue to cook for 3 to 4 minutes or until the onion is translucent.

6 Toss together the brioche, pine nuts, currants, celery, chives, and chestnuts in a large bowl. Add the bacon-onion mixture, eggs, chicken stock, and heavy cream and season with salt and pepper.

7 Place the stuffing in a large ovenproof pan and bake at 375° for $1^1/_2$ hours or until golden-brown and crispy. (The stuffing will be in the oven at the same time the turkey is roasting. Because the inside of the turkey never gets hot enough to kill bacteria, stuffing the stuffing inside the turkey is no longer recommended.)

Grilled Honey-Mustard Smoked Turkey Breast

Converting your grill into a smoker is easy: Just add some wet hickory chips to the coals. The aromas coming from your backyard will bring your neighbors out of their homes — which may be the perfect opportunity to get them to return that lawn mower or Garden Weasel that they keep borrowing. This Honey-Mustard Smoked Turkey Breast is intense with flavor and can be served cold on sandwiches or in salads.

Preparation time: *5 minutes*

Cooking time: *3 hours*

Yield: *8 to 12 servings*

1 8-pound boneless turkey breast	*1 cup honey*
Salt and pepper	*²/₃ cup Dijon mustard*
¹/₄ cup olive oil	*4 cups hickory wood chips, soaked in water*

1 Season the turkey breast with salt and pepper and rub with the olive oil.

2 In a small bowl, whisk together the honey and Dijon mustard. Brush the mixture over the turkey breast.

3 Grill the turkey over a medium-low flame with the lid on for 40 minutes, basting occasionally with the honey-mustard mixture.

4 Place some of the wet wood chips on top of the coals, creating a steady smoke, and cooling the heat of the coals to the point where you are able to hold your hand over them. Continue to cook slowly, basting occasionally, for 1¹/₂ to 2 more hours or until cooked, adding more wood chips as the smoke dies down.

5 Remove from the grill and serve hot or cold.

Chapter 11

What's Your Beef? Adding Meat to Your Repertoire

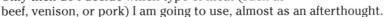
*N*ow it's time to get to the meat of the matter! Meat has long been the focal point of meals. But with all the health-related concerns about fat and cholesterol, portion sizes and the frequency with which people eat red meat is diminishing.

CHARLIE SAYS

To me, eating smaller portions of meat less frequently means that the meat you *do* eat needs to be better-tasting than ever. You don't have to spend an arm and a leg to get the finest cuts. Plenty of less-expensive cuts are wonderful if they are cooked properly. In fact, one of my favorite ways to cook meat is to slowly braise a shank or shoulder with some vegetables and herbs. The result is a wonderfully flavored, soft, succulent meat that almost falls off the bone.

Regardless of what type or cut of meat you're using, you most likely can substitute another type or cut. I often create dishes that include vegetables, grains, and an infused meat reduction. Only then do I decide which type of meat (such as beef, venison, or pork) I am going to use, almost as an afterthought.

Beef is the meat of choice for many people, but it has not always been as popular as it is today. In fact, when the American Civil War contributed to shortages of more-popular pork and chicken, people turned to beef as an attractive, less-expensive alternative. Today, beef is still as popular as ever.

But there's more to life than just beef, so it's time to open your mind and try some of the many other available types of meat. Finding great cuts of venison, lamb, veal, or pork is easy, and these meats have wonderfully unique flavors and textures. Oftentimes, you can use these meats interchangeably in recipes — the resulting flavors are quite diverse.

Meat Inspection and Quality Grades

By law, all meat must be inspected by U.S. Department of Agriculture (USDA) meat inspectors, ensuring that the meat is wholesome, safe to eat, and has accurate labeling. The inspectors check meat packing plants for proper sanitation, making sure that the meat is not contaminated or diseased in any way, and that it has no added chemicals (any added chemicals must be listed on the label).

Meat *grading,* on the other hand, is optional and is paid for by the meat packers (the cost is ultimately passed along to the consumer in the price of the meat). USDA graders assign quality grades according to a meat's palatability; they determine grades by evaluating the age of the animal, the amount of *marbling* (the mix of lean and fat), the texture of the meat, and the meat's color and appearance. Although grading is not required, most packers have their meat graded because it helps the consumer choose between higher- and lower-quality meat.

Although the USDA assigns eight different quality grades to meat, the following three grades for beef are the ones usually found in retail markets:

- ✔ **Prime grade:** Meat with the most evenly distributed marbling is assigned *Prime* grade — the highest quality, because the nice balance of fat with the lean meat results in a juicy, tender cut of meat. Prime grade meat is usually sold to restaurants but is also available in some specialty markets.

- ✔ **Choice grade:** *Choice* grade meat is the most widely available grade in retail markets.

- ✔ **Select grade:** *Select* grade meat has the least amount of marbling, and may not be as tender, juicy, or flavorful as Prime or Choice grades.

Prime or choice meats can be used interchangeably and are good for grilling, sautéing, or any time the meat is going to be cooked quickly. Select meats are best for braising, stewing, or other slow-cooking methods; they are also often used as ground meats.

The top grades for lamb and veal are *Prime, Choice,* and *Good. Grade A* is the top of the line for poultry, and pork is not graded at this time.

Selecting Fresh Meat

Selecting meat from a display case has long been a source of frustration for shoppers. With so many different cuts of meat to choose from, few people can be expected to know what to look for in each one. However, the following general guidelines (which apply to most meats) can simplify your shopping experience and help you select a fresh, quality cut of meat:

 ✔ Choose meats that have rich, red color, with no grayish or brown blotches. A darker color is typical of vacuum-packed meat because of the lack of oxygen. When exposed to oxygen, the meat returns to its natural color.

 ✔ Look for meat that is firm to the touch, rather than soft. Make sure that the package is cold and that the plastic wrap is free from holes or tears.

 ✔ Choose meats that do not have excessive *purge,* or juice in the package. Excessive juice may mean that the meat was left unrefrigerated or may have been frozen and then thawed.

 ✔ When you're shopping, select your meat just prior to going to the checkout counter. If it takes you longer than 30 minutes to get home, place the meat in a cooler to keep it cold.

Handling and Storing Meat

SAFETY TIP

As with fish and chicken, meat needs to be properly stored and handled. Handling meat improperly can result in food-borne illnesses, such as salmonella or E. coli. It's a good idea to set aside a separate cutting board for fish, meat, and poultry. But if you have only one cutting board, cleaning it with a solution of bleach and water between uses helps to eliminate cross-contamination.

Because fresh meat is so perishable, proper cooking and storage are important to minimize the health risks of food-borne illnesses. The following tips can help keep your meat fresh — and safe to eat:

 ✔ Store fresh meats in the refrigerator, loosely wrapped in plastic wrap. Store ground beef, on the other hand, wrapped *tightly* in plastic.

 ✔ Store frozen meats in the freezer, wrapped airtight in plastic wrap.

✔ Use fresh meat within three days of purchase.

✔ Never defrost meat at room temperature. Instead, place the meat in a small pan and thaw overnight in the refrigerator.

✔ Refrigerate leftover meat as soon as possible.

✔ You can keep frozen meat steaks in the freezer for 6 to 12 months.

✔ You can store ground meat in the freezer for 3 to 4 months.

✔ You can freeze leftover cooked meats for 2 to 3 months.

Is It Done Yet?

Most people are very particular about how they like their meat cooked, but many people aren't sure how to tell when it's done. Some people poke the meat, some use a meat thermometer, and some cut into the bottom side of the meat to peek (while nobody's looking). Other people just cook their meat until they are absolutely *positive* that it's done — and then wonder why it tastes like a piece of leather.

Using a meat thermometer is an easy and almost foolproof way to ensure that your meat is done just the way you like it. You can use one of two types of thermometers to check whether a large cut of meat is done:

✔ **Oven-safe thermometer:** Insert this thermometer into the piece of meat prior to cooking and leave it in during the cooking process. You generally use an oven-safe thermometer when roasting larger pieces of meat.

✔ **Instant-read thermometer:** When you think that the meat may be almost done, insert an instant-read thermometer into the meat for about 10 seconds to check the temperature. You can use this type of thermometer for any cut of meat.

Regardless of what type of thermometer you decide to use, roasts should be removed from the oven when the thermometer registers 5 to 10 degrees *below* the desired doneness and allowed to stand for at least 15 minutes. The temperature inside the roast continues to rise after you remove the meat from the oven.

Take a look at Table 11-1 to get an idea of the safe cooking temperatures for beef, lamb, veal, and pork.

Table 11-1		Stick a Fork in It — It's Done!
If You Like Your Meat Cooked Like This	*Cook Until the Internal Temperature Reaches*	*And the Meat Looks Like This*
Beef or Lamb		
Rare	130°	The center is bright red, and the meat turns pinkish toward the exterior portion.
Medium rare	135–140°	The center is very pink, and the meat is slightly brown toward the exterior portion.
Medium	145–150°	The center is light pink, and the outer portion is brown.
Well-done	160°	The meat is uniformly brown, inside and out.
Veal		
Medium	145–150°	For milk-fed veal, the center is light pink and the outer portion is white. For grass-fed veal, the center is richer pink and the outer portion is light pink.
Well-done	160°	For the milk-fed, the meat is uniformly white throughout. For the grass-fed, the meat is pinkish brown throughout.
Pork		
Medium	145–155°	The meat is white toward the outside and light pink in the center.
Well-done	160°	The meat is uniformly white throughout.

You should always cook ground meats to 155 degrees or until the center is no longer pink. Ground beef goes through more processing than other cuts of beef do, and has more chance of being exposed to dangerous bacteria.

How much should I buy?

Typically, 4 ounces of boneless, uncooked meat yields a 3-ounce cooked, trimmed serving. And 8 ounces of uncooked meat yields a 6-ounce serving. A 3-ounce, cooked, trimmed portion of meat is about the same size as a deck of cards. So you can choose meat to buy according to how many "decks of cards" you think each person will eat.

Choosing the Right Cut of Meat for the Right Cooking Method

Your choice of the best cooking technique for a piece of meat depends on the cut of meat that you buy — different cooking techniques benefit certain cuts more than others. (See Figure 11-1 for an illustration of the various cuts of beef.)

- ✔ Cuts that have a layer of fat on the outside, such as rolled roasts or crown roasts, are wonderful for roasting — the fat helps to keep the meat tender and juicy.

- ✔ Cuts labeled *steak, tenderloin,* or *chop* are best sautéed, broiled, or grilled. They have less fat and are naturally tender, so they don't need prolonged cooking.

- ✔ Tougher cuts of meat, such as brisket, back ribs, chuck roasts, and shanks, are best prepared by braising. Braising cooks the meat slowly for a long period of time, resulting in tender, juicy meat.

In general, the *loin* is the most tender piece of meat because it is the least exercised portion of the animal (and the most expensive because it is the smallest part of the animal, resulting in the smallest yield). The shoulder and the leg do have some tender cuts, but for the most part, shoulder meat is best prepared braised or stewed.

Figure 11-1:
Various cuts of beef and where they come from.

Beef

Beef is probably one of the most recognized types of meat. Most people are comfortable buying and cooking beef, and beef can take on many different flavors. It can be herb-crusted, marinated, or spice-rubbed. It's great for intensely flavored dishes because the beef will not overpower the other flavors.

Poached Beef with Braised Legumes, Oyster Mushrooms, and Beef Broth

Poaching a piece of beef may not sound ideal, but the end result is an extremely tender, moist, and intensely flavored piece of meat. You can serve poached beef hot or at room temperature in many different dishes. In this recipe, you serve the beef along with the poaching broth for an even more intense beef flavor.

Specialty tool: *Cooking twine*

Preparation time: *1 hour and 15 minutes*

Cooking time: *30 minutes*

Yield: *4 servings*

12 cups Beef Stock (see Chapter 5)	*2 teaspoons butter*
4 sprigs tarragon	*2 cups roasted oyster mushrooms (see Chapter 7)*
Salt and pepper	
4 4-ounce beef tenderloin medallions (small, round slices), tied with twine	*2 cups Braised Legumes (see Chapter 8)*
	4 teaspoons chopped tarragon
2 tablespoons chopped shallots	

1 Place the beef stock in a medium shallow pan. Simmer over medium heat for approximately 1 hour or until reduced to about 8 cups. Add the 4 sprigs of fresh tarragon and continue to cook for 15 minutes. Remove the tarragon and season the stock with salt and pepper.

2 Place the beef medallions in the reduced stock and poach for 7 minutes. Turn the beef medallions over and continue to poach for another 7 minutes or to the desired doneness.

3 Remove the beef medallions from the stock, discard the twine, and season the medallions with salt and pepper.

4 In a small sauté pan, sweat the shallots with the butter until they are translucent but not brown. Add the roasted oyster mushrooms and continue to sauté for 3 minutes or until hot.

(continued)

5 Place some of the braised legumes and oyster mushrooms in each bowl. Top with a piece of the poached beef and pour some of the cooking broth into each bowl. Sprinkle with the chopped tarragon and top with freshly ground black pepper.

Grilled Beef Teriyaki with Sesame Seeds and Spicy Soy Mustard

The key to great teriyaki is using a well-seasoned marinade. These finger foods make for easy appetizers at a cocktail party. The sugar in the marinade helps to caramelize the ingredients and gives the beef a subtle glaze. Teriyaki is almost always made with soy sauce and ginger. In this recipe, you add garlic and cilantro.

Specialty tools: *12 bamboo skewers, soaked in water*

Preparation time: *15 minutes, plus 2 hours refrigeration*

Cooking time: *5 minutes*

Yield: *12 pieces*

$^1/_2$ cup Dijon mustard

3 tablespoons soy sauce

2 jalapeño peppers, finely chopped

1 teaspoon cayenne pepper

2 tablespoons chopped ginger

2 tablespoons chopped garlic

2 tablespoons chopped cilantro

$^1/_2$ cup teriyaki sauce

1 tablespoon sugar

Salt and pepper

$^3/_4$ pound lean steak, cut into 12, 4-x-1-x-$^1/_4$-inch strips

2 tablespoons sesame seeds

1 In a small bowl, mix together the mustard, soy sauce, jalapeño, cayenne, 1 tablespoon of the ginger, 2 teaspoons of the garlic, and the cilantro.

2 In another small bowl, mix together the teriyaki sauce, sugar, the remaining 1 tablespoon of ginger, and 4 teaspoons of the garlic.

3 Season the steak with salt and pepper. Place a piece of steak on each skewer and brush generously with the teriyaki mixture. Place in a resealable bag and refrigerate for 2 hours.

4 Grill the teriyaki skewers over a medium flame for 2 minutes on each side or until cooked.

5 Spoon some of the spicy soy mustard on top of the skewers and sprinkle with sesame seeds. Serve while hot.

Which lamb is it?

With its tender texture and robust flavor, lamb is a perennial gourmet cook's delight. Vibrant flavors (like the cumin, garlic, and balsamic vinegar in the following recipes) can stand up to and complement lamb's full-bodied succulence. And recent breakthroughs in cloning could ensure a nearly inexhaustible supply of lamb for the world's kitchens (although I don't see what the big deal is about sheep cloning — like they don't look enough alike already).

Sheep slaughtered under the age of one year are labeled *lamb;* if they are slaughtered after that, they must be labeled *mutton.* Mutton has a tougher texture and stronger flavor and aroma that can put people off of lamb for life if they've never experienced spring lamb. Spring lamb and hot-house lamb are not fed grass or grain, but are given a diet of milk — after a lamb begins to eat grass, its flesh loses some of its delicacy.

Cumin-Garlic Spice Rub Roasted Leg of Lamb with Potato-Parmesan Pavé

Lamb and cumin are a natural combination. Lamb, by its nature, has a strong flavor, and it needs a strong spice like cumin to stand up to it. In this recipe, you use a leg of lamb — but this recipe works well with many other types of meat, such as beef or veal.

Preparation time: *40 minutes*

Cooking time: *2¹/₂ hours*

Yield: *4 servings*

3 large Idaho potatoes, peeled

1 cup heavy cream

1 tablespoon butter

1 cup grated Parmesan cheese

Salt and pepper

6 cloves garlic, peeled and chopped

8 tablespoons cumin seed

4 tablespoons chopped parsley

¹/₂ cup olive oil

2 tablespoons chopped thyme

³/₄ pound boneless, butterfly-cut leg of lamb

1 tablespoon vegetable oil

1 cup Beef Stock Reduction (see Chapter 5)

16 asparagus spears, blanched

1 To make the potato pavé (which you can do a day ahead), slice the potatoes lengthwise into thin slices and soak them in the cream until you're ready to use them, so they do not oxidize and turn color.

2 Line a 6-x-6-x-2-inch baking pan with foil and butter the foil.

(continued)

3 Remove the potato slices from the cream as you need them and layer them in the pan, sprinkling Parmesan cheese and freshly ground pepper on each layer. Continue layering until you use all the potatoes and cheese.

4 Cover with foil, place a similarly sized pan directly on top of the foil-covered potatoes, and weigh down the pan with a brick (the weight ensures a perfectly solid pavé without any holes or gaps). Bake at 375° for 1^1/$_2$ hours and cool with the brick on top of the potatoes (refrigerate if making ahead of time).

5 Puree the garlic, cumin, parsley, olive oil, and thyme in a blender to create the spice rub. Reserve 1 tablespoon of the rub.

6 Season the leg of lamb with salt and pepper and rub with the cumin-garlic spice mixture. Place the leg of lamb on a rack in a roasting pan. Roast the lamb at 375° for 1^1/$_2$ to 2 hours or until the lamb reaches an internal temperature of 125° or 130°. Remove from the oven and let rest for 15 minutes or until the temperature rises to 135° to 140° (see "Is It Done Yet?" earlier in this chapter). Reserve the pan drippings if you want to make a gravy.

7 When the potato pavé has cooled, remove it from the pan and cut it into 4 squares. Sauté the top and bottom of the pavé squares in the vegetable oil for 4 minutes on each side or until they are golden-brown and crispy.

8 Place the pavé squares in the oven at 350° for 15 minutes or until the center of the pavé is hot. You can test the pavé by inserting the tip of a knife into the center of it and then touching the tip of the knife to the inside of your wrist. If the pavé is hot, the knife tip will feel warm on your wrist.

9 Place the beef stock reduction in a small saucepan with the reserved tablespoon of the spice rub. Warm over medium heat for 3 minutes or until hot.

10 Cut the lamb into thin slices and season to taste with salt and pepper.

11 Place 4 blanched asparagus spears on each plate and top with some of the sliced lamb. Place a piece of the pavé next to the lamb and spoon the hot reduction sauce around the plate.

Grilled Lamb Loin and Balsamic Red Onion Salad with Artichoke Vinaigrette

If you have roasted lamb left over after the holidays, you can use it in this recipe. The artichoke vinaigrette helps to remoisten the meat.

Preparation time: *20 minutes*

(continued)

Cooking time: 30 minutes

Yield: 4 servings

2 tablespoons vegetable oil

12 ounces lamb loin

Salt and pepper

1 red onion, thinly sliced

$^1/_2$ cup olive oil

5 tablespoons balsamic vinegar

2 tablespoons chopped shallots

3 artichoke bottoms, cooked

$^1/_4$ cup chopped chives

4 cups tiny arugula leaves or baby lettuce (such as baby spinach, frisée, or mizuna)

1 tablespoon lime juice

1 avocado, diced

12 cherry tomatoes, quartered

1 Rub the vegetable oil on the lamb and season with salt and pepper. Grill the lamb over a medium flame for 5 to 7 minutes on each side or until it reaches the desired temperature. Cool the lamb and then slice thinly.

2 Toss the red onion slices with 1 tablespoon of the olive oil and 2 tablespoons of the balsamic vinegar, and season with salt and pepper. Place on a sheet pan and bake at 400°. Stir occasionally for 25 to 30 minutes or until all the balsamic vinegar has been absorbed and the onions are dry.

3 Place the remaining 3 tablespoons of balsamic vinegar and the shallots in a small bowl and slowly whisk in the remaining 7 tablespoons of olive oil.

4 Cut the artichokes into small wedges, add the vinaigrette, and season to taste with salt and pepper.

5 Toss the lamb with the chives and 4 tablespoons of the vinaigrette.

6 Toss the lettuce with 3 tablespoons of the vinaigrette and season with salt and pepper.

7 Pour the lime juice over the avocado and season to taste with salt and pepper.

8 Arrange some of the lettuce, avocado, and cherry tomatoes in the center of each plate. Top with some of the lamb slices and spoon the remaining vinaigrette around the plate.

Pork

Techniques for breeding and raising pork have changed over the years. The pork that is available in markets now is extremely lean and tender. In fact, pork today has 77 percent less fat and 53 percent fewer calories than it did 30 years ago — if the American public could do as well, Richard Simmons wouldn't make so much money on those "Sweatin' to the Oldies" videos. Between the improved quality of the meat and a great marketing program by the pork industry, more people than ever are eating "The Other White Meat."

Food scientists have discovered that *trichinae* (the parasitic worm that causes trichinosis) is killed at 137 degrees. So cooking pork to the hockey puck stage is no longer necessary; 150 to 160 degrees is more than safe and produces a more tender, juicy piece of meat.

Roasted Herb-Crusted Pork Loin with Roasted Butternut Squash and Port Sauce

Pork is traditionally paired with apples, but herbs, spices, and numerous vegetables complement pork as well. In this recipe, I pair the pork with a port sauce, allowing it to be served with a spicy red Zinfandel.

Preparation time: *15 minutes*

Cooking time: *45 minutes*

Yield: *4 servings*

1 small butternut squash, cut in half and seeds removed

Salt and pepper

1 cup water

8 tablespoons butter

1 1 1/2-pound pork loin, cleaned

3 tablespoons olive oil

1/4 cup chopped thyme

1/4 cup chopped rosemary

3/4 cup chopped parsley

3 tablespoons canola oil

1 cup port

1 Season the inside of the squash with salt and pepper and place each half in an ovenproof pan, cut-side down. Add the water and bake at 375° for 30 to 40 minutes or until tender. Remove the skin and cut the squash into small dice, toss with 2 tablespoons of the butter, and season to taste with salt and pepper.

2 Season the pork loin with salt and pepper, rub with the olive oil, and completely cover with the chopped thyme, rosemary, and 1/2 cup of the parsley. Place in a hot sauté pan with the canola oil and sear for 5 minutes on each side. Place the pan in the oven and roast at 375° for 15 to 20 minutes or until the internal temperature reaches 150°. Remove from oven and let rest for 10 minutes before slicing.

3 Place the port in a small saucepan and cook over medium heat for 15 minutes or until reduced to about 1/2 cup. Slowly whisk in the remaining 6 tablespoons of butter, fold in the remaining 1/4 cup of chopped parsley, and season to taste with salt and pepper.

(continued)

4 Place some of the butternut squash in the center of each plate and arrange a few slices of the pork roast on top. Spoon the port sauce over the pork and around the plate.

Braised Spare Ribs with Honey and Chipotle Peppers

You can use these tender spare ribs to make killer leftover pulled-pork sandwiches. But if you can't wait for them to cool to pull the meat, dig in and serve these ribs with potato wedges.

Preparation time: *15 minutes*

Cooking time: *2 hours and 15 minutes*

Yield: *6 to 8 servings*

1 cup chopped onions	*¹⁄₄ cup honey*
¹⁄₂ cup chopped celery	*3 chipotle peppers*
¹⁄₂ cup chopped carrots	*¹⁄₄ cup molasses*
2 tablespoons vegetable oil	*¹⁄₂ cup brown sugar*
20 baby back ribs (about 5 pounds)	*¹⁄₂ cup chopped cilantro*
Salt and pepper	*2 tablespoons white peppercorns*
¹⁄₂ cup chopped leeks	*8 cups Chicken Stock or Beef Stock (see Chapter 5)*
1 red bell pepper, chopped	

1 Place a large roasting pan over 2 stove burners and caramelize the onion, celery, and carrots with the oil.

2 Season the ribs with salt and pepper. Place on top of the caramelized vegetables and roast in the oven at 450° for 15 minutes.

3 Add the remaining ingredients and cover. Lower the temperature to 300° and continue to cook the ribs for 2 hours or until the meat falls off the bone. Remove the ribs from the braising liquid. *Tip:* You can strain and reduce the braising liquid to use for a great sauce.

Veal

The term *veal* generally refers to a young calf from 1 to 3 months old. *Milk-fed* veal comes from calves up to 12 weeks old, which have not been weaned from their mothers' milk. Technically, true veal calves are kept in pens and not allowed to graze on grains or grasses, which causes the flesh to darken.

You can also find a more politically correct form of veal called *farm-raised, grass-fed veal.* These calves are allowed to roam in the fields and graze the same way that cows do, so the meat looks almost like beef when it is raw. Its texture is more beeflike, and it has a stronger, more complex flavor. Farm-raised veal is available in some specialty markets.

Braised Veal Shank and Potato Tarts

Veal shank meat is delicious after it has been braised. You can use it in soups or mix it with pasta. The following recipe dresses up the veal shanks by preparing them in small, individual tarts.

Specialty tools: *4 3-x-¹/₂-inch tart molds*

Preparation time: *40 minutes*

Cooking time: *3 hours*

Yield: *4 tarts*

2 veal shanks (about 1¹/₂ pounds)	*3 sprigs thyme*
Salt and pepper	*2 tablespoons chopped cilantro*
3 tablespoons vegetable oil	*1 tablespoon lime juice*
1 cup chopped onions	*1 recipe Herb Tart Dough (see following recipe)*
¹/₂ cup chopped celery	
¹/₂ cup chopped carrots	*4 small yellow potatoes, baked and cut into ¹/₄-inch-thick slices*
2 cloves garlic	*1 egg yolk, mixed with 2 tablespoons water*
¹/₂ cup red wine	
3 cups water or Chicken Stock (see Chapter 5)	

1 Season the veal shanks with salt and pepper. In a hot, wide saucepan, sear the veal shanks in the vegetable oil for 3 minutes on each side or until golden-brown. Remove the shanks and add the onion, celery, carrots, and garlic. Caramelize the vegetables over medium-high heat for 5 minutes or until golden-brown.

(continued)

2 Add the red wine to deglaze the pan. Return the shanks to the pan and add the chicken stock and thyme.

3 Cover, bring to a simmer, and braise in the oven at 350° for 2 hours or until the meat falls off the bone.

4 Cool the veal shanks in the liquid. Remove the veal shanks from the liquid and strain the liquid. Place the strained liquid in a saucepan and reduce over medium heat for 20 to 30 minutes or until you have 1 cup. Pull the veal off the bones and place in a small bowl.

5 Add the cilantro and lime juice to the meat and season to taste with salt and pepper.

6 Line the tart molds with a piece of the herb tart dough, place some of the potato slices in the bottom of the tart mold, and top with $^1/_4$ of the veal. Top with a few more potato slices, cover with another piece of the dough, and crimp the edges closed.

7 Brush the tarts with the egg mixture and bake at 350° for 35 to 40 minutes or until the tarts are golden-brown. Remove the tarts from the rings and serve while hot.

Herb Tart Dough

Specialty tools: *Parchment paper*

Preparation time: *10 minutes, plus 1 hour refrigeration*

Yield: *About 1$^1/_4$ pounds dough*

1$^1/_2$ cups flour	*1 tablespoon chopped parsley*
1 teaspoon salt	*1 cup cold butter, chopped*
2 tablespoons chopped chives	*$^1/_3$ cup ice water*

1 Place the flour, salt, chives, parsley, and butter in a bowl. Using a fork or dough cutter, cut the butter into the flour until you have large, pea-sized chunks. Add the water and mix until just combined (the dough should contain visible pieces of butter).

2 Form the dough into a ball, wrap in plastic wrap, and place in the refrigerator for 1 hour before rolling out.

3 On a lightly floured surface, roll out the dough $^1/_8$ inch thick. Cut into 8 circles large enough to line your molds (such as 3-x-$^1/_2$-inch ring molds).

Sautéed Veal Chops with Eggplant, Zucchini, Yellow Squash, and Tomatoes

In this recipe, you use veal chops, but you certainly can use many other tender cuts of veal (such as the loin or the rib chop). You can spoon the ratatouille of vegetables on top of the chops like a sauce or serve it alongside the chops.

Preparation time: *30 minutes*

Cooking time: *30 minutes*

Yield: *4 servings*

1 cup diced onion	*1 tablespoon lemon juice*
4 tablespoons olive oil	*2 tablespoons chopped oregano*
2 cups diced eggplant	*Salt and pepper*
2 cups diced zucchini	*4 6-ounce veal loin chops*
2 cups diced yellow squash	*2 tablespoons vegetable oil*
2 cups diced red tomatoes	

1 To make the ratatouille, caramelize the onion with the olive oil in a large sauté pan. Add the eggplant, zucchini, and yellow squash and continue to cook for 15 minutes over medium heat.

2 Add the diced tomatoes, lemon juice, and oregano and season to taste with salt and pepper. Continue to cook for 10 minutes or until most of the liquid from the vegetables has been cooked out and the vegetables are tender.

3 Season both sides of the veal chops with salt and pepper and place in a very hot sauté pan with the vegetable oil. Sauté the chops for 4 to 5 minutes on each side or until cooked to desired doneness.

4 Spoon some of the ratatouille onto each plate and top with a veal chop.

Venison

The term *venison* is used for many different types of game animals, including deer, antelope, elk, reindeer, moose, and caribou. It's the easiest large game meat to find. Venison has a slightly gamey flavor that works well in many recipes in which you would use beef. If you can't find venison at your local butcher, check out Wild Game, Inc., in Chapter 20. This company is a great source for venison and many other game animals and birds, and they ship anywhere in the United States.

Grilled Venison Tenderloin Steaks with Braised Red Cabbage and Rosemary Potatoes

Grilling seems to be the natural preparation for venison, which is often hunted and then cooked over a campfire.

Preparation time: *15 minutes, plus 1 hour refrigeration*

Cooking time: *1 hour*

Yield: *4 servings*

4 5-ounce venison steaks, trimmed	*2 tablespoons butter*
1/2 cup olive oil	*4 cups shredded red cabbage*
Salt and pepper	*1 cup red wine*
3 large sprigs rosemary, stems removed	*1/2 cup water*
2 pounds small red bliss potatoes, quartered	

1 Rub the steaks with ¼ cup of the olive oil and season with pepper. Sprinkle half the rosemary leaves over the steaks and refrigerate for 1 hour.

2 Toss the potatoes with the remaining ¼ cup of olive oil and the other half of the rosemary, and season to taste with salt and pepper. Place the potatoes on a sheet pan and roast at 375° for 40 to 50 minutes or until golden-brown and tender.

3 Place the butter and red cabbage in a large sauté pan and cook for 5 minutes. Add the red wine and water, and continue to cook for 12 to 17 minutes over medium heat or until the cabbage is tender. Season to taste with salt and pepper.

4 Season the venison steaks with salt and grill over medium heat for 5 minutes on each side or until medium-rare or cooked to the desired temperature (generally the same temperature to which you would cook beef).

5 Serve the steaks alongside the cabbage and rosemary potatoes.

Sautéed Bacon-Wrapped Venison with Wild Mushroom Barley

The bacon in this recipe helps to give moisture and fat to the lean venison. You can cook the barley with a touch of bacon fat for a more-pronounced flavor.

Specialty tools: *Cooking twine*

Preparation time: *15 minutes*

Cooking time: *20 minutes*

Yield: *4 servings*

8 thick slices bacon	*2 tablespoons butter*
4 4-ounce venison tenderloin medallions (small, round loin pieces)	*2 cups roasted wild mushrooms, chopped (see Chapter 7)*
2 tablespoons olive oil	*3 tablespoons chopped chives*
Salt and pepper	*³/₄ cup Beef Stock Reduction (see Chapter 5)*
2 tablespoons vegetable oil	
4 cups cooked barley	

1 Wrap 2 slices of bacon around the outside of each venison medallion and tie with cooking twine. Rub the outside of the venison with the olive oil and season to taste with salt and pepper.

2 Sauté the venison in a hot pan with the vegetable oil for 5 to 7 minutes on each side or until the meat reaches the desired temperature. Remove the twine before serving.

3 Reheat the barley in a small saucepan if necessary. Fold the butter into the hot barley and add the wild mushrooms and chives. Season to taste with salt and pepper.

4 Heat the beef stock reduction in a small saucepan.

5 Spoon some of the barley onto each plate and top with the venison. Spoon the meat reduction around the barley.

Part III

Bumping It Up a Notch and Taking It to the Next Level

The 5th Wave   By Rich Tennant

@RICHTENNANT

"...because it's called architectural cuisine. That's why I'm garnishing the plates with Legos."

In this part . . .

After you get comfortable with the basics of gourmet cuisine, you may want to take things one step further. This part talks about *architectural* cuisine, explaining how you build layered, stacked, and molded dishes, such as terrines and napoleans, and how you create the nuts and bolts that you use to hold such dishes together, like tuiles and vegetable purees. This part also takes you on a tour of the more indulgent gourmet foods and shows you how you can incorporate them into your cooking if you're in the mood to splurge.

Chapter 12

Is Mies van der Rohe in the House? Architectural Cuisine Made Easy

• •

In This Chapter

▶ Getting innovative with crunchy structural things

▶ Gluing architectural cuisine together

▶ Adding height and texture with garnishes

▶ Creating layered and formed foods

• •

*J*ust as pioneering architect Mies van der Rohe created innovative building and furniture designs by juxtaposing various forms and textures, you can be an architect in the kitchen. By combining, stacking, and arranging the elements in a gourmet recipe, you can create exciting fare that's not only delicious but also "architecturally" impressive.

Presenting a gourmet dish (what a chef calls *plating a dish*) involves more than simply placing all the ingredients on a plate. Presentation is critical in gourmet cuisine. How you arrange the ingredients can make the difference between a good meal and an extraordinary dining experience. When you understand the basics of using ring molds, layering ingredients, and using tuiles, you can use these skills to create beautiful architectural dishes out of everyday foods.

Creating a Superstructure with Tuiles

Tuile is the French word for "tile," which is a perfect description of how these paper-thin, crisp wafers are often used. Tuiles are great for creating a *napoleon,* a dish that layers foods between these crispy wafers. You can use tuiles to add drama to a dish, or simply use them as a garnish. Not only do tuiles add structure to a recipe, but they also add texture and complexity to the dish. You can create tuiles in almost any size and shape — flat or curved or even molded into the shape of a cup.

Making perfectly shaped tuiles is easy with the aid of a *template.* You can buy templates (or stencils) of all shapes and sizes, but making one yourself by using a thin piece of cardboard or heavy plastic is just as easy. Simply cut the desired shape out of the cardboard or plastic, leaving at least a ¹/₄-inch border around the edge of the template. Tuiles are generally square, round, or triangular, but you can get creative with your template and make tuiles in almost any shape (see Figure 12-1).

Figure 12-1: Templates help you make perfectly shaped tuiles. Use a nonstick pan.

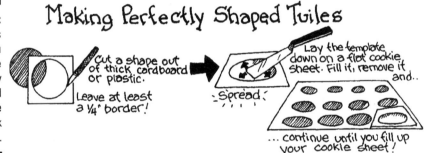

You can use the following tuile recipes interchangeably, but keep in mind the flavors of the dish that you're creating:

- ✔ The Basic Potato Tuiles and the Herbed Potato Tuiles are neutral in flavor and can add texture to almost any dish, from grilled beef and garlic mashed potatoes to sautéed salmon and parsnip puree.

- ✔ The Saffron Potato Tuiles and the Carrot Tuiles, on the other hand, have more-complex flavors. The saffron tuiles go great with any lobster dish, and the carrot tuiles work nicely in any dish that has a curry or strong spice influence. Just try to match the flavor of the tuiles to the food items you're preparing, and let your palate be your guide.

Basic Potato Tuiles

Specialty tools: *Template of desired size and shape*

Preparation time: *20 minutes*

Cooking time: *15 minutes*

Yield: *About 30 tuiles*

1 Idaho potato (about 10 ounces), baked, peeled, and chopped

2 tablespoons butter

4 egg whites

Salt and pepper

1 Place the warm potato in a mixing bowl with the butter and egg whites. Using an electric mixer, mix on medium speed for 3 to 4 minutes or until smooth. Pass the potato mixture through a fine-mesh sieve to remove any lumps. Season to taste with salt and pepper.

2 On a nonstick sheet pan, spread a very thin layer of the potato batter in the center of the template (or thinly spread the batter freehand). Remove the template. Repeat until you have the desired number of tuiles. (You can keep extra batter in the refrigerator for several days.)

3 Bake at 350° for 10 to 15 minutes or until the tuiles are golden-brown. Carefully remove the tuiles from the sheet pan and let cool. Store in an airtight container at room temperature.

Variations:

- **Herbed Potato Tuiles:** Add 3 tablespoons of chopped herbs (such as parsley, chervil, basil, or tarragon) to the batter and follow the method for Basic Potato Tuiles.

- **Saffron Potato Tuiles:** Place ¹/₂ teaspoon of crushed saffron in a small, dry pan over medium heat for 1 minute. Add 2 tablespoons of white wine and continue to cook for 1 minute or until most of the wine has been cooked out. Add the saffron mixture to the batter and follow the method for Basic Potato Tuiles.

If your tuiles lose their crunch, place them on a nonstick sheet pan and bake them at 250° for 3 minutes. Then reshape the tuiles as soon as they come out of the oven.

Herbed Tuile Baskets

This batter is good for making tuile baskets — the resulting tuiles are easier to shape than the potato tuiles. These tuile baskets are a great way to change the texture and look of ordinary foods. You can fill them with couscous, mashed potatoes, or even a small salad.

Specialty tools: *Template, small espresso cup*

Preparation time: *20 minutes*

Cooking time: *10 minutes*

Yield: *About 15 baskets*

1 egg, lightly beaten	*4 tablespoons butter, melted*
3 egg whites, lightly beaten	*3 tablespoons chopped chives*
³/₄ cup flour	*Salt and pepper*
5 tablespoons sugar	

1 Whisk together the egg and egg whites; then work the flour and sugar into the mixture.

2 Stir in the melted butter and chives and season to taste with salt and pepper.

3 On a nonstick sheet pan, spread a thin layer of the batter in the center of a 4-inch-round template (or thinly spread the batter freehand). Remove the template. Repeat until you have the desired number of tuiles. (You can keep extra batter in the refrigerator for several days.)

4 Place the sheet pan in the oven at 350° for 7 to 10 minutes or until the batter is golden-brown. Immediately remove the tuiles from the sheet pan (while they are still hot and pliable) and place around the outside of a small, upside-down espresso cup. Gently form the tuile into the shape of the cup, as shown in Figure 12-2. Let cool and then carefully remove.

5 Store the tuile baskets in an airtight container at room temperature.

Tuile Basket

Figure 12-2: Using an espresso cup to create a tuile basket.

Remove the tuiles from the pan immediately and drope over a cup or bowl while they are hot!

Carrot Tuiles

Carrot Tuiles are intensely flavored and sweet. Their crunch is even crisper than a raw carrot, and their bright orange color is a nice addition to almost any dish. In this recipe, you use a squeeze bottle rather than a template to create the tuiles — the carrot batter isn't very thick and would run right out of a template.

Specialty tools: *Squeeze bottle*

Preparation time: *10 minutes*

Cooking time: *1 hour*

Yield: *About 20 tuiles*

2 cups chopped carrots

1 cup water

Salt and pepper

1 Cook the carrots in boiling salted water for 10 to 15 minutes or until very soft. Remove from the liquid and puree in the blender with the water. Season to taste with salt and pepper.

2 Pass the carrot puree through a fine-mesh sieve; then place it in a squeeze bottle with a small tip.

3 Squeeze quarter-size amounts of the carrot puree onto a nonstick sheet pan, and spread the tuile batter into a thin circle about twice as large as a quarter. Bake at 275° for 30 to 45 minutes or until crispy.

4 Carefully remove from the sheet pan while hot and store in an airtight container at room temperature.

Gluing a Dish Together Using Vegetable Purees

When building an architectural dish with height, you need something to help hold everything in place. Of course, you can't use real glue — although a nice dollop of Elmer's might do the job of holding together a lobster napoleon, you don't want the whole dinner party to start whining, "Got milk?" However, you can use foods such as pulped avocado, pureed vegetables, or mashed potatoes to hold your towering gourmet dishes together and keep them from tumbling into your guests' laps. Pureed vegetables also add a nice flavor and textural component to the dish, while doubling as the glue that holds everything in place.

As with everything in gourmet cuisine, you need to understand the flavors of the foods you're working with *before* you can use these items interchangeably. For example, you wouldn't want to substitute cold pulped avocado for garlic mashed potatoes — besides the fact that one is hot and the other is cold, they have completely different flavors. But you *can* replace the garlic mashed potatoes with pureed parsnips, because both recipes are hot, and both have similar flavors. Just use a little common sense and look for flavors that are either similar or complementary to the dish you're making.

Garlic Mashed Potatoes

What could make mashed potatoes even better? Garlic, that's what! After trying these garlic potatoes, you may never eat regular mashed potatoes again. If you're a real garlic junkie, you can fold in some Roasted Garlic Puree (see Chapter 9). Just make sure that your date likes garlic as much as you do.

Preparation time: *1 hour*

Cooking time: *10 minutes*

Yield: *3 cups*

1 cup half-and-half

3 cloves garlic, minced

2¹/₂ cups peeled and chopped Idaho potatoes, boiled and riced

¹/₄ cup butter

Salt and pepper

1 Place the half-and-half and garlic in a small saucepan and simmer for 5 minutes over medium heat.

2 Place the warm riced potatoes in a mixing bowl and use an electric mixer to incorporate the butter and half-and-half. Season to taste with salt and pepper.

Pulped Avocado

This cool avocado is refreshing with lobster, crab, or grilled seafood. Use this recipe as the "glue" to hold together cold napoleons — if you use it in warm preparations, the avocado oxidizes and turns a disgusting green-brown color.

Preparation time: *15 minutes*

Yield: *1¹/₂ cups*

(continued)

3 ripe avocados, skin and pit removed

3 tablespoons chopped cilantro

2 tablespoons chopped shallots

Dash of Tabasco

2 tablespoons lime juice

Salt and pepper

1 Place the avocado, shallots, and lime juice in a small bowl and mash them together with a fork until the mixture is almost smooth.

2 Fold in the cilantro and season to taste with the Tabasco and salt and pepper. Keep covered in the refrigerator until needed.

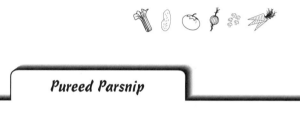

Pureed Parsnip

You can use this pureed parsnip dish as you would mashed potatoes if you desire a more complex, "adult" flavor (which means that your kids probably won't touch it).

Preparation time: *15 minutes*

Cooking time: *25 minutes*

Yield: *About 2 cups*

2 cups peeled and chopped parsnips

$^1/_2$ cup half-and-half

3 cups milk

Salt and pepper

1 tablespoon butter

1 Place the parsnips and milk in a medium saucepan and simmer over medium heat for 15 to 25 minutes or until the parsnips are extremely tender.

2 Remove the parsnips from the milk and puree the parsnips in the blender with the butter and half-and-half. Season to taste with salt and pepper and use while hot for better flavor.

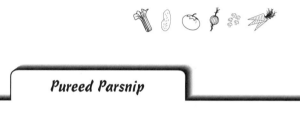

Pureed Sweet Potatoes

Who said that mashed potatoes had to be white, anyway? You can prepare this recipe with either sweet potatoes or yams. Pureed Sweet Potatoes are a nice addition to a pork or lamb dish, such as the Herb-Crusted Pork Loin in Chapter 11.

Preparation time: *10 minutes*

(continued)

Cooking time: *1 hour*

Yield: *About 2 cups*

1 large sweet potato (about 12 ounces), baked

¹/₃ cup milk

3 tablespoons butter

Salt and pepper

Puree the hot sweet potato, milk, and butter in a food processor for 2 to 3 minutes or until smooth. Season to taste with salt and pepper. Serve while hot.

Soft goat cheese, other spreadable cheeses, and cold flavored butters also work well as the "glue" in architectural dishes.

Adding Dimension with Crispy Garnishes

Tiny julienned beets, leeks, or parsnips are flavorful, while at the same time adding another dimension to a dish. Crisp julienned vegetables can be piled on top of a stack of food, while crispy strips can be placed upright around the food: Both methods add height and texture. You can make crispy garnishes ahead of time — they are quite simple to make. Use the garnishes in this section to top soups, salads, risotto, or meat and seafood items. These garnishes are an easy, fun way to add texture and to give your dishes a more dramatic presentation.

Crispy Fried Beets

These deep-red Crispy Fried Beets are a nice addition to any dish that uses beets. They also give an intense flavor and texture combination to a salad of mixed greens.

Preparation time: *20 minutes*

Cooking time: *10 minutes*

Yield: *2 cups*

2 cups very finely julienned red beets

Canola oil for frying

Salt and pepper

Fry the julienned beets in the canola oil for 2 to 3 minutes or until crispy. (Cook them in batches.) Remove from the oil, blot on paper towels, and season to taste with salt and pepper.

(continued)

Variations:

> ✔ **Fried Parsnip Strips:** Using a peeler, peel long, straight strips of 2 parsnips. Fry them in the canola oil as directed.
>
> ✔ **Crispy Fried Leeks:** Fry 2 cups of finely julienned leeks (in batches) in the canola oil for 1 to 2 minutes (or until golden-brown and crispy); then proceed with the recipe.

Oven-Dried Carrot Strips

Skinny Alert: These Oven-Dried Carrot Strips are a nice light twist on the fried parsnip strips or other fried garnishes; you still get all the flavor and crunch — without the fat. For a little flavor variation, try these carrots in place of the parsnip strips in the Barley "Risotto" recipe (later in this chapter).

Preparation time: *20 minutes*

Cooking time: *30 minutes*

Yield: *About 20 strips*

2 large carrots, peeled   *Salt*

1 Using a hand peeler, peel strips the length of the carrot.

2 Lay the strips flat on a nonstick sheet pan and sprinkle lightly with salt.

3 Dry in the oven at 250° for 20 to 30 minutes or until lightly golden and dry to the touch. The carrots may curl up a bit. Store in an airtight container at room temperature until needed.

Constructing Layered and Formed Foods

When you understand the basic components that go into creating architectural cuisine, you're ready to put it all together and build your own dishes. Just be sure to layer your napoleons evenly — otherwise, you may experience a landslide on your way to the table.

Terrines (see Chapter 3 for more information about these molded foods) are another interesting way to display ingredients in a precise, architectural manner. A terrine may take some extra time to prepare, but when your guests arrive, all you need to do is slice and serve!

Potato, Portobello Mushroom, Caramelized Onion, and Goat Cheese Terrine

You can serve this terrine cold or hot, depending on where in the meal you decide to serve it. In this recipe, goat cheese acts as the glue that holds all the ingredients together, though any spreadable cheese can do the trick. I recommend wrapping the terrine, which gives it a more finished look. In this recipe, you use a wrap made with pieces of spinach, which you lay flat and then wrap around the terrine.

Specialty tools: *Terrine mold, 8 x 1¹/₂ x 2¹/₄ inches*

Preparation time: *1 hour, plus 2 hours refrigeration*

Cooking time: *45 minutes*

Yield: *8 to 12 servings*

2 Idaho potatoes, peeled and cut into long, ¹/₄-inch-thick slices

4 tablespoons olive oil

Salt and pepper

3 large portobello mushrooms, roasted and stems removed (see Chapter 7)

1 large Spanish onion, julienned

5 ounces goat cheese

3 cups spinach leaves, stems removed

3 tablespoons heavy cream

4 teaspoons aged balsamic vinegar

8 teaspoons Herb Oil (see Chapter 5)

¹/₄ cup chervil leaves

1 Brush the potato slices with 3 tablespoons of the olive oil and season with salt and pepper. Lay the potato slices flat on a nonstick sheet pan and bake at 375° for 20 to 30 minutes or until cooked. Remove from the oven and trim the potato slices to fit the width of the terrine mold.

2 Cut the portobello mushrooms to fit the width of the terrine mold, and then carefully slice the mushrooms in half horizontally, creating thinner slices of mushroom.

3 In a large sauté pan over high heat, caramelize the onion with the remaining 1 tablespoon of olive oil for 7 to 10 minutes or until golden-brown. Cool the onion to room temperature and season to taste with salt and pepper.

4 Line the terrine mold with plastic wrap, allowing some to hang over the sides.

5 Place a layer of the potato in the bottom of the terrine mold. Spread on a very thin layer of the goat cheese and top with a thin layer of the caramelized onions. Place a layer of the mushrooms on top of the onions and spread with another very thin layer of the goat cheese (reserve 1 ounce of the goat cheese). Repeat this process until you have 4 layers of potato and 3 layers of the onions and mushrooms. Chill the terrine for at least 2 hours before serving.

(continued)

6 To make the wrap, blanch the spinach in boiling salted water, shock in ice water, and blot on paper towels. (See Figure 12-3 for an illustration of Steps 6 through 9.)

7 Lay the spinach leaves flat on a piece of plastic wrap, creating a single layer that's large enough to cover the entire terrine.

8 Carefully remove the terrine from the mold and remove the plastic wrap. Invert the terrine onto one of the wider edges of the spinach, wrap the spinach around the terrine, and then wrap the whole terrine tightly with plastic wrap. (You can refrigerate the terrine for up to 3 days, or until needed.)

9 Slice the terrine into $^1/_3$-inch slices and season each slice with salt and pepper.

10 Place the remaining 1-ounce piece of goat cheese in a small bowl. Whisk together with the cream until smooth. Season to taste with salt and pepper.

11 Place a slice of the terrine in the center of each plate. Spoon the goat cheese and cream, balsamic vinegar, and herb oil around the terrine. Sprinkle with the chervil leaves.

Alternative Assembly

1 Place some of the spinach in the center of each plate and top with some of the potato slices.

2 Spread a layer of goat cheese on the potatoes and top with some of the caramelized onions and mushrooms.

3 Spoon the goat cheese cream, balsamic vinegar, and herb oil on top of the mushrooms and around the plate.

Figure 12-3: Wrapping a terrine involves a lot of steps, but the results are spectacular!

How to Wrap a Terrine

1. Cook spinach in boiling water for 30 seconds.

2. Brrr! Shock in a bowl of ice water!

3. drip dry. Hang the leaves over the side of a bowl so the water drips off....

4. blot blot Lay the leaves out flat on plastic wrap and blot dry with paper towels. don't forget to remove the plastic!

5. Unmold the terrine onto the leaves and fold the first side over the terrine.

6. Continue to roll until all 4 sides are covered.

7. Slice the terrine with the plastic still on.

Smoked Salmon Terrine with Horseradish Potato Salad and Lemon-Horseradish Vinaigrette

In this recipe (shown in the color section of this book), the sharp horseradish and the tart lemon in the vinaigrette cut through the richness of the smoked salmon, while allowing its flavors to shine through. In the potato salad, the potatoes and horseradish are a natural flavor combination. But if the horseradish is too hot for you, try adding a little grated parsnip or turnip in place of some of the horseradish.

Specialty tools: *Terrine mold, 8 x 1^1/$_2$ x 2^1/$_4$ inches*

Preparation time: *1 hour, plus 3 hours refrigeration*

Cooking time: *30 minutes*

Yield: *8 to 12 servings*

1^1/$_2$ pounds smoked salmon, thinly sliced

^{1}/$_4$ cup butter, room temperature

1 shallot, finely minced

1 tablespoon plus 1^1/$_2$ teaspoons lemon juice

1 tablespoon lemon zest, finely chopped

1^1/$_2$ cups peeled and small diced red bliss potatoes, cooked

2 tablespoons finely diced red bell pepper

2 tablespoons chopped chives

2 tablespoons grated fresh horseradish

1 tablespoon finely chopped red onion

Lemon-Horseradish Vinaigrette (see following recipe)

Salt and pepper

1 Cut the salmon to fit the width of the terrine mold.

2 In a small bowl, combine the butter, shallot, 1 tablespoon of lemon juice, and lemon zest. Mix until smooth.

3 Line the terrine mold with plastic wrap. Place a layer of smoked salmon on the bottom of the mold and spread it with a very thin layer with lemon butter. Continue to layer the salmon and butter until you use all the salmon. Cover the terrine with the plastic wrap and refrigerate for 2 hours.

4 In a small bowl, prepare the potato salad by combining the diced potatoes, red bell pepper, chives, horseradish, 1^1/$_2$ teaspoons lemon juice, and red onion. Gently toss together with ^{1}/$_2$ cup of the lemon-horseradish vinaigrette and season to taste with salt and pepper. Refrigerate for at least 1 hour before serving.

5 Slice the terrine into ^{1}/$_4$-inch slices. Place 2 pieces overlapping each other in the center of each plate. Place heaping teaspoons of the horseradish potato salad at 4 separate points around the plate. Spoon the remaining lemon-horseradish vinaigrette over the terrine and around the plate; then top with freshly ground pepper.

(continued)

Alternative Assembly

1 Lay 2 slices of smoked salmon flat, slightly overlapping each other.

2 Spread a very thin layer of the lemon butter over the salmon slices.

3 Spoon 2 teaspoons of the horseradish potato salad on top of the salmon and tightly roll up, creating a cigarlike roll. Repeat the process with the remaining salmon and potato salad.

4 Place a few smoked salmon rolls on each plate, spoon some of the lemon-horseradish vinaigrette around the plate, and top with freshly ground pepper. You can see this alternative presentation in the color section of this book.

Lemon-Horseradish Vinaigrette

Preparation time: *10 minutes*

Yield: *³/₄ cup*

3 tablespoons lemon juice	*¹/₂ cup olive oil*
1¹/₂ tablespoons freshly grated horseradish	*1 tablespoon chopped chives*
1 tablespoon minced shallot	*Salt and pepper*

Place the lemon juice, horseradish, and shallots in a small bowl. Slowly whisk in the olive oil. Fold in the chopped chives and season to taste with salt and pepper.

Barley "Risotto" with Caramelized Root Vegetables, Sliced Beef Tenderloin, and Fried Parsnip Strips

The process of making risotto (traditionally made with arborio rice) entails patience and constant attention. In this recipe, I use the technique for making risotto, but replace the arborio rice with barley. The result is a creamy, perfectly cooked, al dente barley "risotto." (See Chapter 8 for a recipe for true risotto.)

Specialty tools: *3-inch ring mold*

Preparation time: *20 minutes, plus 2 hours marinating*

Cooking time: *1 hour*

Yield: *4 servings*

(continued)

20 ounces beef tenderloin, outer membranes removed

Herb Marinade (see Chapter 9)

$^1/_2$ cup chopped onion

2 cloves garlic, minced

4 tablespoons butter

1 cup pearl barley, uncooked

$4^1/_2$ cups Chicken Stock (see Chapter 5)

Salt and pepper

$^1/_4$ cup small diced rutabaga

$^1/_4$ cup small diced celery root

$^1/_4$ cup small diced turnip

$^1/_4$ cup small diced parsnip

3 tablespoons chopped herbs (such as parsley, chives, or chervil)

$^1/_2$ cup Beef Stock Reduction (see Chapter 5)

Fried Parsnip Strips (see recipe earlier in this chapter)

1 Marinate the beef tenderloin in the herb marinade in the refrigerator for at least 2 hours.

2 In a large saucepan, sweat the onions and garlic with 2 tablespoons of butter over medium heat for 3 minutes or until translucent. Add the barley and continue to cook for 2 more minutes.

3 Add the chicken stock slowly, $^1/_2$ cup at a time, stirring constantly. Add more chicken stock only after most of the liquid has been absorbed. Continue adding the chicken stock for 30 to 45 minutes or until the barley is cooked al dente. (You may not need to add all the liquid.) Season to taste with salt and pepper.

4 In a large sauté pan, caramelize the diced root vegetables with the remaining 2 tablespoons of butter over medium-high heat for 8 to 12 minutes or until golden-brown and tender. Add the vegetables to the barley and fold in the chopped herbs.

5 Season the beef tenderloin with salt and pepper and grill over a moderate flame for 6 minutes on each side or until it reaches the desired doneness. Let the tenderloin rest for 10 minutes before slicing.

6 Slice the tenderloin into thin slices and season to taste with salt and pepper.

7 Warm the beef stock reduction in a small saucepan just prior to serving.

8 Place a 3-inch ring mold in the center of each plate. Fill with the barley and remove the mold. Arrange the beef tenderloin slices in a pinwheel on top of the barley. Place a few of the fried parsnip strips on top of the beef and spoon the beef stock reduction around the plate.

Alternative Assembly

Spoon some of the barley in the center of each plate and place some of the sliced tenderloin on top of the barley. Spoon the beef stock reduction around the plate and sprinkle with the fried parsnip strips.

Whole Roasted Tomato Filled with Roasted Garlic Soup and Crispy Fried Leeks

Using a whole tomato as the serving vehicle for a hot or cold soup is a fun way to present the soup. As you eat the soup, you can cut into the tomato as well. In this recipe, the fried leeks add just the right amount of texture and zip to the garlic soup. Take a look at the color section to see how appetizing this recipe can be.

Preparation time: *30 minutes*

Cooking time: *20 minutes*

Yield: *4 servings*

4 large red tomatoes

Roasted Garlic Puree (see Chapter 9)

4 cups Chicken Stock (see Chapter 5)

Crispy Fried Leeks (see recipe earlier in this chapter)

Salt and pepper

1 Score the top of the tomatoes with a knife (creating an X), but do not core the tomatoes.

2 Place the tomatoes in boiling salted water and cook for 2 minutes. Remove and immediately shock the tomatoes in ice water. Carefully remove the skin, cut off the tops of the tomatoes, and hollow out the tomatoes. *Tip:* Be careful not to make any holes in the sides or bottom of the tomatoes, or your soup will leak out. Discard the tops and the inner tomato pulp.

3 Puree the roasted garlic with the chicken stock and place in a medium saucepan. Warm over medium heat for 10 minutes or until hot, and season to taste with salt and pepper.

4 Place the tomatoes on a sheet pan and roast at 350° for 10 minutes or until just hot.

5 Place a tomato in the center of a shallow bowl or soup plate. Fill the tomato with the roasted garlic soup and sprinkle with the crispy fried leeks. (You should serve the tomato in a bowl so that you can eat it along with the soup.)

Alternative Assembly

Dice the tomatoes and place them in the bowl. Pour the hot soup over the tomatoes and sprinkle with the crispy fried leeks. This alternative presentation also appears in the color section of this book.

New Potatoes and Tiny Lettuces with Red Bell Pepper and Pine Nut Vinaigrette

In this recipe, the ring of crispy potato holds the tiny lettuces in a tight, freeform, upright arrangement. This display has height, and the pinwheel of potatoes adds preciseness. The potato ring that holds the lettuces breaks apart as you consume the dish, adding a nice textural element.

Specialty tools: *2-inch ring mold, cooking string*

Preparation time: *1 hour*

Cooking time: *1 hour*

Yield: *4 servings*

1 Idaho potato, peeled	*2 ^{1}/$_4$ cups tiny lettuces*
2 tablespoons butter, melted	*^{1}/$_4$ cup pine nuts, roasted*
2 tablespoons fresh bread crumbs	*1 red bell pepper, roasted, cleaned, and cut into a fine julienne*
2 tablespoons chopped chives, parsley, or other fresh herbs	*^{1}/$_2$ cup Red Bell Pepper and Pine Nut Vinaigrette (see following recipe)*
Salt and pepper	*4 teaspoons pine nuts*
2 shallots, thinly sliced	*^{1}/$_4$ cup Anchovy Puree (see recipe later in this chapter)*
4 tablespoons balsamic vinegar	*4 teaspoons chopped chervil*
6 red new potatoes, thinly sliced	
2 tablespoons olive oil	

1 Slice the Idaho potato lengthwise into paper-thin slices; then cut the slices into 1^1/$_2$-inch-wide strips.

2 Lightly butter both sides of the potato and sprinkle one side with the bread crumbs, chopped herbs, and salt and pepper.

3 Wrap the potato slices around the outside of a 2-inch ring mold (with the bread crumb side against the mold). You may have to overlap more than one potato slice in order to surround the mold. Then tie a piece of string around the potato slices to hold them in place. Bake at 350° for 10 to 12 minutes or until golden-brown. When slightly cool, cut away the string, remove from the molds, and cool completely.

4 Place the shallots and 8 teaspoons of the balsamic vinegar in a small sauté pan. Cook for 3 to 5 minutes or until the shallots have absorbed all the balsamic vinegar.

(continued)

5 Form the new potato slices into four pinwheels that are slightly larger than the potato ring by overlapping the potato slices and arranging them in a circle. Place the potato pinwheels on a nonstick sheet pan and coat lightly with the olive oil. Season with salt and pepper and bake at 375° for 20 to 25 minutes or until lightly golden-brown.

6 Place the greens in a mixing bowl with the roasted pine nuts, roasted pepper, and 3 tablespoons of the red bell pepper and pine nut vinaigrette. Gently toss together and season to taste with salt and pepper. Use immediately.

7 Place a potato pinwheel in the center of each plate and place a potato ring on top. Fill the potato ring with the mixed greens.

8 Place some of the balsamic shallots and the pine nuts around the plate. Spoon some of the warm red bell pepper and pine nut vinaigrette, anchovy puree, and the remaining 4 teaspoons of balsamic vinegar around each plate. Sprinkle with the chervil.

Alternative Assembly

1 Omit the potato ring.

2 Place a new potato pinwheel in the center of each plate and arrange some of the greens on top of the potatoes.

3 Place some of the balsamic shallots and the pine nuts around the plate. Spoon some of the warm red bell pepper and pine nut vinaigrette, anchovy puree, and the remaining 4 teaspoons balsamic vinegar around each plate. Sprinkle with the chervil.

4 If you still want the crunch of the crispy potato ring, you can quickly fry some thin potato slices and toss them with the greens.

Red Bell Pepper and Pine Nut Vinaigrette

Preparation time: *15 minutes*

Yield: *About 1 cup*

2 cloves garlic, minced	$^{1}/_{4}$ cup balsamic vinegar
$^{1}/_{2}$ cup olive oil	$^{1}/_{4}$ cup pine nuts, roasted
1 red bell pepper, coarsely chopped	Salt and pepper

1 Sweat the garlic in a medium sauté pan with 1 tablespoon of the olive oil. Add the red bell pepper and continue to cook for 3 to 4 minutes or until tender.

2 Add the balsamic vinegar and cook for 2 minutes. Place in a blender with the pine nuts and the remaining olive oil and puree until smooth. Strain through a fine-mesh sieve and season to taste with salt and pepper. Warm in a small saucepan just prior to use.

(continued)

Anchovy Puree

Preparation time: 10 minutes

Yield: About $^1/_3$ cup

5 anchovy fillets

4 tablespoons water

Salt and pepper

Place the anchovies and water in a blender. Puree until smooth and season with salt and pepper. If the puree is too thick, adjust the consistency with a few teaspoons of water. Cover tightly and store in the refrigerator until needed.

Lobster and Pulped Avocado Napoleon with Saffron Potato Tuiles and Herb Vinaigrette

In this recipe, the Lobster Napoleon is presented with Saffron Potato Tuiles (see recipe earlier in this chapter). Lobster and saffron complement each other's extravagance, but you can use crab in place of the lobster if you want. This dish should be served immediately after it is assembled to ensure that the tuiles stay crisp and are not wilted by the moist lobster and avocado.

Preparation time: 30 minutes

Cooking time: 20 minutes

Yield: 4 servings

2 tablespoons rice wine vinegar

2 tablespoons lemon juice

9 tablespoons olive oil

2 tablespoons chopped herbs (such as chives, parsley, or chervil)

Salt and pepper

1 cup finely julienned jicama

12 ounces lobster tail, cooked and sliced into 12 medallions

1 cup Pulped Avocado (see recipe earlier in this chapter)

16 Saffron Potato Tuiles (see recipe earlier in this chapter)

$^1/_2$ cup thinly sliced mango, cut into small pieces

1 Place the rice wine vinegar and 1 tablespoon of the lemon juice in a small bowl. Slowly whisk in the olive oil. Fold in the chopped herbs and season to taste with salt and pepper.

2 Place the finely julienned jicama in a small bowl, toss with the remaining 1 tablespoon of lemon juice, and season to taste with salt and pepper.

(continued)

3 Place the lobster medallions in a small bowl, toss with $^1/_2$ cup of the vinaigrette from Step 1, and season to taste with salt and pepper.

4 Place a teaspoon of the pulped avocado in the center of each plate. Top with a saffron tuile, a lobster medallion, some of the jicama and mango, and another teaspoon of pulped avocado. Top with another tuile and repeat the process until you have three layers of lobster. Top with a final tuile and spoon the remaining vinaigrette around the plate.

Alternative Assembly

Spoon the pulped avocado in the center of each plate. Arrange the mango on top of the avocado. Place the jicama on top of the mango and layer the lobster medallions over the jicama. Spoon the remaining vinaigrette around the plate.

Herbed Tuile Basket with Portobello Mushrooms, Rabbit Loin, and Garlic Mashed Potatoes

This beautiful herbed tuile basket showcases the delicate and tiny rabbit loin (which you can ask your butcher to order for you). The garlic mashed potatoes add structure to the dish while supplying just the right amount of zip. This dish also works well with chicken (instead of rabbit) and parsnip puree (in place of the mashed potatoes), if you prefer.

Preparation time: *1 hour*

Cooking time: *30 minutes*

Yield: *4 servings*

4 medium rabbit loins, membranes removed

2 tablespoons olive oil

Salt and pepper

12 white pearl onions, peeled and halved

2 tablespoons butter

1 cup small diced carrots

6 teaspoons chopped tarragon

2 portobello mushrooms, roasted and thinly sliced (see Chapter 7)

$^1/_2$ cup Beef Stock Reduction (see Chapter 5)

2 cups Garlic Mashed Potatoes (see recipe earlier in this chapter)

4 Herbed Tuile Baskets (see recipe earlier in this chapter)

16 thin green beans, cooked and cut in half

(continued)

1 Rub the rabbit loins with olive oil and season with salt and pepper. Gently grill the rabbit loins over moderate heat for 3 to 4 minutes on each side or until cooked through. Remove from the grill and let rest for 2 minutes before slicing.

2 In a medium sauté pan, caramelize the pearl onions with 4 teaspoons of the butter over medium-high heat for 8 to 12 minutes or until golden-brown. Season to taste with salt and pepper.

3 In a medium pan, sauté the carrots with the remaining butter for 5 to 7 minutes or until cooked and slightly golden-brown. Season to taste with salt and pepper, and then toss with 2 teaspoons of the tarragon.

4 Toss the warm roasted portobello mushroom slices with the remaining 4 teaspoons of tarragon and season to taste with salt and pepper.

5 Slice the rabbit loin into long pieces on the diagonal and season to taste with salt and pepper.

6 Spoon $1/4$ cup of the garlic mashed potatoes in the center of each plate. Place a tuile basket on top of the mashed potatoes and press it firmly into place. (See Figure 12-4.) Spoon the remaining garlic mashed potatoes into the bottom of the tuile cups. Fan the rabbit slices around inside the cup toward the front.

7 Warm the beef stock reduction in a small saucepan just prior to use. Arrange some of the portobello mushroom slices and green beans behind the rabbit. Arrange the pearl onions and diced carrots around the plate and spoon the hot beef stock reduction around the carrots.

Alternative Assembly

Omit the herbed tuile baskets. Spoon the garlic mashed potatoes in the center of each plate. Arrange the mushroom slices, green beans, pearl onions, and rabbit slices on top of the potatoes. Spoon the diced carrots and beef stock reduction around the plate.

Figure 12-4: Assembling the Herbed Tuile Basket with Portobello Mushrooms & Rabbit Loin.

1. Spoon about 1/4 of a cup of the potatoes into the center of each plate...

2. ..Place the tuile cup on top and press firmly into place.

3. Spoon the remaining potatoes into the bottom of the cups.

4. Fan the rabbit slices inside the cup towards the front.

5. Arrange some of the mushroom slices and green beans behind the rabbit.

6. Arrange the pearl onions and diced carrots around the plate and spoon the hot beef stock around the carrots.

Chapter 13

So You're Loaded and Have Great Taste in Food: Edible Indulgences

*E*veryone has his or her own idea of what constitutes a luxury food. Some people consider prime rib, a $20 bottle of wine, or even a pint of specialty ice cream a luxury, whereas to others, only caviar or truffles truly fit the bill. "Luxury" is certainly a category that is defined by the individual palate and pocketbook.

For this chapter, I've used my own definition of the crème de la crème of foodstuffs: gourmet foods that are difficult to come by because they have very short seasons or very small growing regions, and foods that are labor-intensive to grow or harvest. In either case, I can guarantee you that gourmet food stores won't be giving these items away.

Luxury items may be expensive, but they can add so much to a meal. Even if you can't afford to indulge in these treats every day, don't be afraid to try them on special occasions; they can change an ordinary meal into something that you'll remember for years to come. With all luxury items, the simpler the preparation the better; you certainly don't want to overpower their exquisite flavors.

Tiny White Asparagus

White asparagus is as common in Europe as the green variety is in the United States. But the tiny variety is a rare find. White asparagus grows underground, covered with a dirt and sand combination, with no exposure to sunlight. If the tips of the asparagus break through the dirt and sand during the daylight hours, they immediately begin to turn purple and then green once exposed to sunlight. The value of this asparagus decreases dramatically once the chlorophyll reacts with the sunlight. Farmers who grow tiny white asparagus monitor it very closely and often have workers patrol the plants at night, making sure that no cracks are appearing in the soil (evidence that the asparagus tips are about to break through).

This growing process yields an asparagus with a smoother skin and a white color. Tiny white asparagus is a little more tender than regular asparagus and has a slight bitterness that works well for cleansing sweet flavors from your palate.

Tiny white asparagus, if you can find it, can go for as much as $36 a pound in specialty markets. Asparagus with thicker white stalks cost considerably less per pound. Check out the "Diver Scallops" section in this chapter for a delicious recipe that includes white asparagus and diver scallops.

Aged Balsamic Vinegar

True balsamic vinegar comes from the producer Reggio Emilia in Modena, Italy. Balsamic vinegar is made from the finest grapes, such as Trebbiano, Lambrusco, and Spergols. The juice is fermented, cooked over an open flame, cooled, and decanted. The vinegar is then aged in a series of wooden casks, starting with chestnut and oak, and then chestnut, cherry, juniper, and mulberry casks, in that order.

As it ages, balsamic vinegar picks up flavors from the different types of wood. It also changes in consistency due to evaporation. The result is a syrupy, smooth vinegar that is sweet enough to serve with ice cream. After the aging process is complete, trained professionals taste the vinegar and then give it the appropriate grading label. The gold label is the most prized, followed by the silver and red labels.

The labels of some aged balsamic vinegars may not display one of these three color-coded labels, but rather the number of years the bottle was aged, such as 7, 10, 12, or 27 years. As the age of the vinegar increases, the quality and price increase as well. An 8-ounce bottle of gold-label balsamic vinegar can cost over $100! You can find aged balsamic vinegar at gourmet stores or in gourmet catalogs (see Chapter 20 for information about the Dean & Deluca catalog).

Caviar

Caviar is one of the world's premier luxury foodstuffs — the word alone implies wealth, good taste, and indulgent living. True caviar can cost anywhere from $19 to $60 per ounce, depending on the grade, the type, and the producer. The finest caviar available in the world today comes from three different types of sturgeon found in the Caspian Sea: the beluga, osetra, and sevruga sturgeons.

Only true sturgeons eggs (or *roe*) may be legally labeled with the simple title *caviar.* The labels for all other types of caviar must also identify the source of the eggs, such as *whitefish caviar* or *lumpfish caviar.*

If your budget (or your brain) can't handle spending $100 for a couple ounces of beluga, try *salmon roe, flying fish roe,* or *black lumpfish caviar.* They aren't beluga, but neither are their prices. I wouldn't use them for a traditional caviar service (where the caviar is the focal point), but you could add ¹/₂ teaspoon or so to a Smoked Salmon Beggar's Purse (see Chapter 9 for the recipe). These less-expensive options can give a beggar's purse the saltiness and *pop* that makes caviar famous.

Selecting the finest caviar

Some people judge caviar by its color, and others judge it by the size of the eggs. But the only true test is placing the caviar in your mouth and tasting the tiny eggs popping and bursting with flavor. Unfortunately, before you can judge caviar, you have to buy some and experience it yourself. But you can use some of the following basic label information to determine what type of caviar you are buying.

At up to 3,000 pounds, the *beluga* is the largest species of sturgeon; accordingly, belugas also have the largest eggs. *Osetra* eggs are slightly smaller, and the *sevruga* eggs are smaller yet (in fact, sevruga is the smallest commercially produced caviar). Beluga caviar receives a numerical designation that represents the color of the eggs. They range from 0 for the darkest eggs, to 000 for the lightest eggs.

People generally seem to think that the larger, darker eggs are the best, but color and size don't guarantee good taste. All things considered, the finest beluga and the finest osetra are equally good, with the sevruga coming in at a close second.

Caviar should have a light, oily scent and should never smell fishy. If it is even slightly spoiled, your nose will know. Look for caviar that has the word *malossol* on the label, which means *lightly salted.* If the label doesn't say *pasteurized,* you can presume that it's fresh. It is best to serve fresh caviar within one to two weeks of purchase. Unopened, vacuum-packed caviar keeps for approximately four months. But after it's opened, go ahead and indulge yourself, because opened caviar doesn't last more than a week.

Salt is the only ingredient used to turn sturgeon roe into caviar. The entire process takes less than 15 minutes, but don't try it at home! The expertise behind the process can take a lifetime to acquire. A person called a *salt blender* must first determine the type and amount of salt to be added and then mix the salt and eggs with his or her hands to avoid breaking the delicate eggs.

When serving caviar, it's important to keep the caviar from coming into contact with silver, which alters the flavor of the caviar. Spoons for serving caviar are made of wood, bone, tortoise, mother of pearl, or horn.

Traditional Caviar Service

Traditional caviar service is a family-style presentation for this elaborate luxury item. A caviar service allows each person to hand-select the accompaniments (such as shallots or capers) that they want to have with the tiny fish eggs. Caviar is usually served on small triangles of toast (called *toast points* by gourmets) because they provide a neutral-flavored base that doesn't cover up the flavor of the caviar.

Preparation time: *30 minutes*

Yield: *4 servings*

4 thin slices of bread, toasted and crust removed	*1 tablespoon chopped chives*
	2 tablespoons capers
2 hard-cooked eggs	*¹/₄ cup crème fraîche*
2 to 4 ounces caviar (or as much as you can afford)	*1 tablespoon cold butter*
¹/₄ cup finely chopped shallots	

1 Cut each piece of toast into 4 triangles.

2 Separate the egg whites from the yolks. Using the back of a spoon, press the hard-cooked egg yolks through a fine sieve and set aside. Repeat the process with the egg whites and set aside in a separate bowl.

3 Place the caviar in the center of a large plate. Arrange the remaining ingredients around the edge of the plate and serve. People can create their own caviar toast points by selecting a combination of the ingredients.

Diver Scallops

Trained scuba divers go to great lengths (and depths of up to 100 feet) to acquire these large, beautiful sea scallops. The divers hand-select the scallops, carefully place them in a net bag, and bring these prizes to the surface. The scallops are then shipped live in their shells to a few select markets.

You can order diver scallops from Browne Trading Company (see Chapter 20 for more information). You should expect to pay anywhere from $5 to $10 apiece for these wonderfully rich-flavored scallops, but one per person would certainly suffice.

The bright pink, orange, or green roe that surrounds the scallop has many uses as well. You can add it to a custard or flan, make a great earthy-flavored mayonnaise, or even use the roe to make beautifully colored pasta.

The following recipe brings diver scallops together with the aged balsamic vinegar and the white asparagus from preceding sections. If you can't get your hands on some of these tasty ingredients, try the following substitutions:

- ✔ For the diver scallops, try substituting large sea scallops.
- ✔ For the tiny white asparagus, try using large white asparagus or thin green asparagus.

Sautéed Diver Scallops with Tiny White Asparagus, Wilted Greens, and Aged Balsamic Vinegar

The buttery and tender scallops explode with flavor alongside the barely bitter white asparagus and sweet balsamic vinegar. My mouth waters just thinking about this dish.

Preparation time: 10 minutes

Cooking time: 10 minutes

Yield: 4 servings

4 large diver scallops

Salt and pepper

1 tablespoon vegetable oil

4 cups baby lettuces (such as spinach, frisée, or romaine)

1 tablespoon olive oil

6 teaspoons aged balsamic vinegar (such as 10- or 20-year-old)

2 cups tiny white asparagus, trimmed and blanched

(continued)

1 Season the scallops with salt and pepper. Sauté in a hot pan with the vegetable oil for 2 minutes on each side or until golden-brown and just cooked.

2 Place the baby lettuces in a medium sauté pan with the olive oil and 2 teaspoons of the balsamic vinegar. Cook over medium-low heat for 1 to 2 minutes or until the lettuce is barely wilted. Season to taste with salt and pepper.

3 Arrange some of the wilted lettuce in the center of each plate. Place a scallop on top and arrange the cooked white asparagus over the scallop. Spoon the remaining aged balsamic vinegar around the plate and top with freshly ground black pepper.

Foie Gras

Foie gras (pronounced "FWAH grah") is goose or duck liver that comes from birds that have been specially bred to produce huge, fatty livers. Foie gras is usually served sautéed, roasted, or smoked. It has a wonderful, rich flavor that goes very well with apples, berries, pears, rhubarb, candied ginger, or figs. Foie gras also works well when paired with other rich foods, such as scallops, lobster, or squab. For the ultimate treat, serve your foie gras dish with a Sauternes or a sweet, aged Pinot Gris.

Foie gras is often sold in gourmet shops, but if you can't locate it, call Wild Game, Inc. (see Chapter 20). They usually carry two types of foie gras: Hudson Valley and Sonoma, which are equally good. Foie gras can cost anywhere from $30 to $45 a pound, but this is another situation where a little goes a long way. Two or three ounces of this rich treat should be plenty for all but the most avid (or gluttonous) foie gras fans.

Seared Foie Gras with Preserved Ginger and Roasted Figs over Toasted Brioche

The brioche in this recipe is the perfect vessel to soak up the luscious juices that seep from the cooked foie gras. The sweet, roasted figs complement its savory richness, while cutting through the luscious intensity of the foie gras. The ginger has a sharpness that adds another dimension to the dish.

Preparation time: *15 minutes*

Cooking time: *15 minutes*

Yield: *4 servings*

(continued)

4 2-ounce pieces of foie gras, veins removed

Salt and pepper

4 ripe black mission figs

4 3-inch-square pieces Brioche (see Chapter 14), toasted

4 teaspoons Preserved Ginger (see Chapter 14)

1 Season the foie gras with salt and pepper. Place in a very hot sauté pan and sear over high heat for 2 to 3 minutes on each side or until golden-brown and medium-rare.

2 Remove the foie gras from the sauté pan, reserving 4 teaspoons of the rendered fat.

3 Cut the figs lengthwise into 4 slices, and lay them shingled in an ovenproof pan, brush with the reserved foie gras fat, and bake at 400° for 10 minutes.

4 Lay a piece of brioche in the center of each plate and top with 1 teaspoon of preserved ginger. Place a piece of foie gras on top of the ginger and arrange the fig slices on top of the foie gras.

Fraises des Bois

These tiny wild strawberries are found in France and in various parts of the United States. They are intensely sweet and full of flavor, with an aroma so strong that you can almost taste the berry when you get a whiff of it. Fraises des bois (pronounced "FREZ day BWAH") are extremely perishable and can spoil with the slightest temperature change. These wild berries must be closely monitored and picked early in the morning on a cool day, which reduces the risk of spoilage.

Fraises des bois come in white and red varieties, with the tiny stems usually attached. Because they are so perishable, grow wild within a specific season, and must be packed with extreme care, their price per half-pint can be rather high (around $5).

If you can't locate these beautiful berries, substitute perfectly ripe chandler strawberries and cut them into small wedges.

Warm Summer Berry Compote with Vanilla Bean Ice Cream and Aged Balsamic Vinegar

This recipe is a sophisticated version of berries and cream (which means "don't waste it on your kids"). When these berries are in the height of their season, they are irresistible. The sweet and slightly acidic balsamic vinegar in this recipe is wonderful when spooned over the ice cream, allowing the flavors to come alive.

(continued)

Preparation time: 15 minutes

Cooking time: 5 minutes

Yield: 4 servings

1 cup fraises des bois	4 teaspoons basil, julienned
$^1/_2$ cup fresh raspberries	Vanilla Bean Ice Cream (see Chapter 14 for a basic ice cream recipe)
$^1/_2$ cup fresh blueberries	
2 tablespoons Simple Syrup (see Chapter 14)	4 teaspoons aged balsamic vinegar (at least 12 years old)

1 Place the berries in a medium saucepan with the simple syrup and cook over medium heat for 3 to 4 minutes or until hot. Add the basil and stir.

2 Place a scoop of ice cream in the center of each of 4 bowls, spoon the warm berries on top, and drizzle with the balsamic vinegar.

Kobe Beef

This exclusive grade of beef comes from cattle raised in Kobe (pronounced "KOH-bee"), Japan. These cattle are massaged with saki and graze on a rare diet that includes large amounts of beer. The farmers even play classical music to relax the animals. All this pampering results in beef that is extraordinarily tender and richly flavored.

All this special treatment also makes Kobe beef outrageously expensive and rarely available in the United States. The meat melts in your mouth like butter and is beautifully marbled, but you can expect to pay over $100 per pound for this delicacy (when you can find it). (I know you're probably not going to run out to buy Kobe beef tomorrow, but this tidbit is great to share with friends to show your expansive food knowledge.)

Because Kobe beef is so hard to come by, you can also make the following recipe with regular beef or venison tenderloin.

Grilled Kobe Beef with Salsify, Portobello Mushrooms, and Braised Cranberry Beans

The extremely tender texture of the Kobe beef is echoed by the portobello mushrooms and braised beans in this recipe. The salsify (see the "Salsify" section later in this chapter) provides the flavor that ties this dish together by adding an earthy sweetness and a crisp tenderness.

(continued)

Preparation time: *30 minutes, plus 2 hours refrigeration*

Cooking time: *45 minutes*

Yield: *4 servings*

1 pound Kobe beef	*Salt and pepper*
4 tablespoons olive oil	*1 tablespoon butter*
1 sprig rosemary, stem removed	*2 tablespoons chopped chives*
4 stalks salsify	*¹/₂ cup Beef Stock Reduction (see Chapter 5)*
3 cups milk	
¹/₂ lemon, cut in half	*1¹/₂ cups braised cranberry beans (see Chapter 8)*
2 medium portobello mushrooms, cleaned and stem removed	

1 Rub the Kobe beef with 2 tablespoons of the olive oil and the rosemary and refrigerate for 2 hours.

2 Peel the salsify and cut it into 2-inch-long pieces on the diagonal. Place in a medium saucepan, cover with the milk, and add the lemon. Simmer over medium-low heat for 30 to 40 minutes or until the salsify is tender. Remove from the milk and cut each piece in half lengthwise.

3 Rub the portobello mushrooms with the remaining 2 tablespoons of olive oil and season with salt and pepper.

4 Season the Kobe beef with salt and pepper. Place the beef and portobello mushrooms on the grill over medium heat.

5 Grill the mushrooms for 4 minutes on each side or until tender. Slice into thin strips and season to taste with salt and pepper.

6 Grill the Kobe beef for 5 to 7 minutes on each side or until medium-rare (or the desired doneness). Let rest for 5 minutes and cut into thin slices. Again, season to taste with salt and pepper.

7 Sauté the salsify pieces in a medium pan with the butter for 2 minutes or until slightly golden-brown. Season to taste with salt and pepper and toss with the chopped chives.

8 Warm the beef stock reduction in a small saucepan. Reheat the braised cranberry beans, if necessary.

9 Arrange some of the beans, mushrooms, salsify, and beef in the center of each plate. Spoon some of the beef stock reduction around the plate and top with freshly ground black pepper.

Saffron

Saffron is the yellow-orange stigmas from a small purple crocus. Each flower provides only three stigmas, and it takes over 14,000 dried stigmas to make a single ounce of saffron. The stigmas must be carefully hand-picked and then dried. This extremely labor-intensive process makes saffron the most expensive spice — luckily, most recipes call for only a few strands.

Saffron is an essential ingredient in many dishes, especially in cuisine like paella and bouillabaisse. This spice is used not only for its flavor but also for its color; in fact, years ago, saffron was even used to dye cloth. Saffron is available in most gourmet shops in powdered and thread forms.

I prefer to use saffron threads — the powdered form loses its flavor too quickly, and unscrupulous manufacturers can easily cut it with artificial saffron powder. To extract the optimal flavor, you should store saffron threads in an airtight glass container and then warm and crush the threads just before using them.

Saffron Risotto with Porcini Mushrooms

The thirsty risotto immediately soaks up the juices released from the porcini mushrooms (see the upcoming "Porcini Mushrooms" section). The saffron in this recipe not only colors the risotto a vibrant yellow, but the resulting flavor is so pungent and aromatic that it's not easy to forget the power of these tiny saffron threads.

Preparation time: *15 minutes*

Cooking time: *45 minutes*

Yield: *4 servings*

8 ounces porcini mushrooms, cleaned

2 sprigs thyme

1 tablespoon olive oil

$1/2$ cup chopped onion

2 teaspoons chopped garlic

2 tablespoons butter

$1^1/2$ cups arborio rice

1 teaspoon saffron threads

4 to $4^1/2$ cups hot Chicken Stock (see Chapter 5)

Salt and pepper

2 tablespoons chopped chives

1 tablespoon chopped chervil or parsley

1 Place the mushrooms, thyme, and olive oil in an ovenproof baking dish. Cover and roast at 375° for 20 to 30 minutes or until the mushrooms are tender. Chop the mushrooms into small wedges and set aside.

(continued)

2 In a medium saucepan over medium heat, sweat the onion and garlic in the butter for 3 minutes or until translucent. Add the arborio rice and saffron threads and continue to cook for 2 minutes.

3 Slowly add ¼ cup of the hot chicken stock to the rice and stir until completely absorbed. Continue to add the hot stock ¼ cup at a time, stirring constantly with a smooth, gentle motion to avoid breaking the grains. Allow the rice to completely absorb the liquid each time before adding more. Continue adding hot stock until the rice is cooked. (It should be creamy, yet al dente.)

4 Season the risotto with salt and pepper. Fold in the mushrooms, chives, and chervil.

Salsify

Salsify grows mostly in Belgium and throughout Europe, but it can also be found growing wild throughout the United States. Salsify is a root vegetable that embodies the flavors of parsnip, celery root, potato, apple, and artichoke (if you can imagine that). You can find salsify in some organic health food stores that sell produce.

You can find two different types of salsify, or *oyster plant:* white and black (the color refers only to the skin). I prefer black salsify because it has a more pronounced flavor, a longer root, and is more evenly shaped. White salsify looks like an irregularly shaped parsnip and is covered with tiny rootlets.

White and black salsify do not resemble each other when unpeeled, but their uses and preparations are similar. Both types need to be peeled either before or after cooking. If you peel salsify before cooking, it is essential to cover it with milk (or water with lemon juice) to keep it from turning brown. When cooking salsify, watch it carefully — it can change from tender to mushy in a matter of minutes.

Porcini Mushrooms

These delicious, earthy mushrooms (also known as *cepes* — pronounced "seps") have a pale brown cap and stem. They range in size from 1 ounce up to a pound; their caps range from 1 to 10 inches in diameter. Porcinis (pronounced "por-CHEE-nees") have a smooth, meaty texture and a pungent flavor. Both the cap and the stem are edible.

When they are brought to market, these mushrooms are sliced in half so that their inner cavity can be inspected. Make sure that the cavity is free of worms, which are commonly found inside these large mushrooms. Porcinis are hard to come by in the United States, but you can find them in some specialty markets. Select those porcini mushrooms with firm caps and pale undersides.

Fresh porcinis have a superior taste and texture. But when you can't find them fresh, you can use dried porcinis, which are more widely available. Select porcinis that have a tan to pale-brown color; avoid mushrooms that are crumbly. For best results, soften dried porcinis in hot water or mushroom stock for about 20 minutes before using them. The dried variety is cheaper than fresh porcinis, at about $8 for a 2-ounce package.

Scallops in cyberspace and wasabi on the Web

If you're not located in a big city, it may be tough to find specialty gourmet foodstuffs such as foie gras or diver scallops. However, if you have a computer and access to the Internet, you can easily get your hands on hundreds of foods that may not be available at your corner grocery.

Fire up your Web browser and go to your favorite search engine. Search for the food item you need for your recipe, or simply search for "gourmet foods." If you're not yet Web-savvy, but would like to be, pick up a copy of *World Wide Web Searching For Dummies,* 2nd Edition, by Brad Hill (published by IDG Books Worldwide, Inc.).

Your Web search is likely to yield some great sites where you can order gourmet food items, such as the following:

✔ **Abadac: The Gourmet French Shop:** Check out this *très Euro* Web site at www.abadac.com. Among the specialty foods you can order are duck and goose foie gras, confit, and truffles. Although the prices at this French Web site are listed in francs, the U.S. dollar equivalent is also shown.

✔ **The Gourmet's Source:** Can't find aged balsamic vinegar at the Piggly Wiggly? Try this Web site at www.gourmetsource.com. You can order everything from Nori and wasabi powder (used in the Vegetable Maki Rolls recipe in Chapter 8) to coconut milk (used to make Coconut Broth in Chapter 9) to capers to serve with your caviar. You can even order saffron and dried porcini mushrooms to spice up the risotto recipe in this chapter.

✔ **All-Internet Shopping Directory:** The gourmet foods page at this Web site (www.all-internet.com/gourmet.html) has links to dozens of food sites where you can order smoked meats, Alaskan seafood, and gourmet herbs and spices.

Truffles

To me, truffles are the ultimate luxury food. These little beauties have a strong, pungent, earthy aroma and a flavor that is highly prized in gourmet circles. This rare find can be hunted only by female pigs and dogs that have been trained to carefully sniff out the truffle scent. This intense fungus grows 3 to 12 inches underground near the roots of trees, usually oak trees. Pigs have keener noses, but dogs are less inclined to gobble up the prize.

A truffle is a round and irregularly shaped fungus with a thick, rough, wrinkled skin that varies in color from almost pure black to beige. The most desirable truffle is the *black truffle* of Perigord, France. In season, Perigord black truffles cost about $300 a pound; out of season, they can go as high as $600 a pound.

The most expensive of all truffles is the *white truffle* from Italy's Piedmont region. Depending on their availability and the time of year, these truffles can cost from $600 to $1,200 a pound. White truffles are seldom cooked; they are generally just grated or sliced finely over pasta or risotto. The best fresh truffles are available from December to February.

Some varieties are also available during the summer months from May through September. Although they have a less-intense flavor and aroma, at $100 a pound, these out-of-season truffles are certainly a less-expensive alternative.

Canned truffles are available in most gourmet shops and catalogs. These truffles have a less-intense flavor and a softer texture because they are cooked during the canning process. They are fine to use during the off-season, but during truffle season, by all means, get fresh. If you can't find truffles locally, call Tartuferia (see Chapter 20) — they'll ship them directly to your home.

You should wear gloves when handling truffles because the oils from your hands can cause the truffles to spoil. Underripe truffles can be reburied and then later reharvested.

When choosing truffles, select ones that are firm, with no signs of bruises. Use them as soon as possible after purchasing them. If you need to keep the truffles for a short time, store them covered in arborio rice or next to raw eggs, tightly sealed and refrigerated. Truffles have a strong perfumey aroma that permeates whatever they're stored with, even eggshells. After all those truffles are gone, you can cook the eggs or the rice and relive the experience.

Red Bliss Potatoes Stuffed with Black Truffles and Caramelized Onions

You can serve these truffles and tiny potatoes as a canapé at a fancy cocktail party. Potatoes and truffles are a classic combination — and the sweet caramelized onions melt away in your mouth as the truffle aroma permeates the potatoes.

Preparation time: *30 minutes*

Cooking time: *20 minutes*

Yield: *4 to 6 servings*

12 small red bliss potatoes, baked	*2 tablespoons olive oil*
2 tablespoons crème fraîche	*¹/₄ cup finely diced black truffles*
Salt and pepper	*2 tablespoons chopped chives*
2 cups julienned yellow onions	*12 chervil leaves*

1 Cut the tops off the potatoes; then hollow out each potato with a melon baller.

2 Pass the potato pulp through a ricer, fold in the crème fraîche, and season to taste with salt and pepper.

3 In a medium sauté pan, caramelize the onions with the olive oil for 15 to 20 minutes or until golden-brown. Add the truffles and chives and continue to cook for 2 minutes. Season to taste with salt and pepper.

4 Fill the potato shells halfway with the potato pulp mixture and top with some of the onion-truffle mixture. Reheat the potatoes in the oven, if necessary, and garnish with the chervil leaves.

Part IV
Ooh, You Sweet Thing!

The 5th Wave   By Rich Tennant

"Why don't we forget about trying to flambé the dessert and just eat around the matches?"

In this part . . .

As we all know, dessert is often the course that makes a meal memorable. This part shows you how to prepare the basic building blocks of desserts, like doughs and custards. It also explains how to make luscious fruit desserts and — how could I forget? — chocolate concoctions that can satisfy even the most sophisticated chocoholics.

Chapter 14

Have Your Cake and Eat It, Too: Basic Dessert Techniques and Starter Recipes

*I*n most cases, varying a recipe's ingredients, amounts, or flavorings can make a dish your own unique creation; in fact, improvising in a recipe is encouraged. But improvisation should be sharply curtailed when you create desserts, where following the recipe to the letter is often essential.

With a touch of common sense, you may be able to substitute spices, herbs, or different types of fruits in your dessert recipes. Don't go too far, however, or you could be in for a disappointment. Most desserts have very specific ratios that allow them to turn out successfully. Desserts also involve very specific techniques that may seem laborious, but which exist for good reason. Deviating from the instructions in a dessert recipe can result in everything from flat cakes and curdled custards — to shoe-leather pie crusts and fallen soufflés.

This chapter shows you the basics and the foundations of creating gourmet desserts. When you see how easy and delicious your own pie dough, ice cream, or caramel sauce can be, you may never want to buy their store-bought counterparts again.

Preparing Basic Pastry Doughs and Sponge Cakes

The basic doughs and cakes in this section are the building blocks for many other desserts. Pie wouldn't be pie without the crust, and you'd be hard-pressed to make bread pudding without the bread. These recipes are all necessary ingredients to other desserts. The good news is that you can prepare all these building blocks ahead of time and then use them to assemble your main desserts later.

Brioche and pastry doughs

Mastering the art of making your own pie and bread doughs is rather simple and easy to do. You no longer need to purchase premade or prebaked frozen pie shells. You can prepare cream cheese dough and pâte brisée in large batches and keep them in the freezer so that you always have some available.

TIP

The nuts and bolts of the perfect pie crust

When prebaking a pie crust, you need to weigh the dough down. In gourmet shops, you can purchase tiny metal weights designed specifically for weighing down pie crusts (so they don't bubble up during baking). But you can also use a cup or two of bolts, washers, screws — or plain-old beans — to weigh down your crust.

Simply cover the crust with parchment paper or aluminum foil, spread out the weights, and then prebake according to the recipe. Make sure that you remove all the hardware before adding the pie filling, unless you don't mind paying your guest's dental reconstruction bills.

Cream Cheese Dough

Cream cheese dough is a quick recipe for an extremely flaky and rich dough. You can use it in place of pie dough or instead of puff pastry (it's a pretty close second to puff pastry, if you're in a pinch). After you master this recipe, you may want to play around and substitute the cream cheese with other cheeses such as blue cheese, goat cheese, or mascarpone. You will have marvelous results. Try this cream cheese dough with the Open-Faced Strawberry and Peach Pie in Chapter 15.

Preparation time: *15 minutes, plus 1 hour refrigeration*

Yield: *1^1/$_2$ pounds*

1 cup butter	*1^1/$_2$ cups flour*
8 ounces cream cheese	

1 Cream the butter, cream cheese, and flour together in an electric mixer until incorporated. Form the dough into a ball, cover with plastic wrap, and refrigerate for at least 1 hour before using.

2 On a lightly floured surface, roll out the dough into the desired thickness.

Pâte Brisée

Pâte brisée is a widely used dough for tarts and pies. This sweet, buttery, and flaky dough browns nicely and melts in your mouth. Pâte brisée freezes well, so you can always have some on hand, and it thaws rather quickly on the countertop. The Mango and Blueberry Tart in Chapter 15 uses pâte brisée to create wonderfully flaky, individual tarts.

Preparation time: *15 minutes, plus 30 minutes refrigeration*

Yield: *About 1 pound*

1^1/$_4$ cups flour	*^{2}/$_3$ cup cold butter, cubed*
2 tablespoons sugar	*1 egg yolk*
^{3}/$_4$ teaspoon salt	*3 tablespoons ice water*

1 Place the flour, sugar, salt, and butter in a mixing bowl. Using an electric mixer, mix on low until all the ingredients are combined, but the butter remains in pea-sized chunks.

2 Add the egg yolk and water all at one time. Mix on low until the dough just begins to come together.

(continued)

3 Remove the dough from the mixer and work into a ball on a floured surface. Wrap the dough in plastic wrap and refrigerate for at least 30 minutes before using.

4 On a lightly floured surface, roll out the dough into the desired thickness.

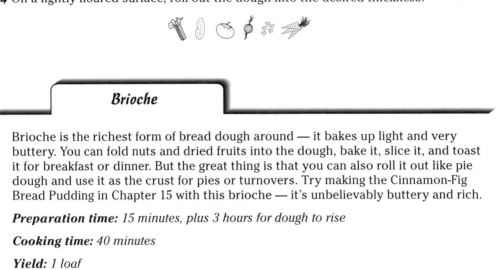

Brioche

Brioche is the richest form of bread dough around — it bakes up light and very buttery. You can fold nuts and dried fruits into the dough, bake it, slice it, and toast it for breakfast or dinner. But the great thing is that you can also roll it out like pie dough and use it as the crust for pies or turnovers. Try making the Cinnamon-Fig Bread Pudding in Chapter 15 with this brioche — it's unbelievably buttery and rich.

Preparation time: *15 minutes, plus 3 hours for dough to rise*

Cooking time: *40 minutes*

Yield: *1 loaf*

1¹/₂ teaspoons active dry yeast

2 tablespoons warm water

2 tablespoons sugar

3 eggs

1 ¹/₂ teaspoons salt

2 cups flour

1 cup butter, softened

1 Butter and flour a 4-x-9-inch loaf pan.

2 Place the yeast in the water with 1 tablespoon of the sugar and let sit for 3 minutes to activate (or *proof*) the yeast.

3 In a large bowl, whisk together the eggs, the remaining sugar, and the salt. Add the yeast mixture, and then stir in the flour. Using your hands, work the butter into the dough until it is fully incorporated.

4 Place the dough in an oiled bowl and cover with plastic wrap. Let rise in a warm place for about 2 hours or until the dough has doubled in size.

5 Punch down the dough with your fist to deflate it and then place into the prepared bread pan. Cover and let sit in a warm place for 1 hour.

6 Bake at 375° for 35 to 45 minutes or until golden-brown. Remove from the oven and from the pan. Allow the brioche to cool completely on a wire rack.

Filo dough

Extremely thin sheets of pastry dough, filo (also spelled phyllo) is similar to strudel dough. Filo is as thin as tissue paper — it is so delicate that, if not handled gently and with extreme care, it falls apart in your hands.

The trick to working with filo is to carefully unroll the dough and lay it flat. Cover the filo with a barely damp cloth to prevent it from drying out as you work with it. Filo dough comes fresh and frozen, and can usually be found in the freezer section of your grocery store. If you can, get your hands on the fresh variety because it is much easier to work with. Both fresh and frozen filo dough keep well in the refrigerator when stored in a tightly sealed bag.

The paper-thin filo sheets are usually brushed with butter (and sometimes sprinkled with sugar or nuts) and then stacked to give them more strength. The filo can then be cut into squares with a dollop of fruit in the center and then gathered into little beggar's purses (as in the nearby Honey and Maple Syrup Braised Pears recipe).

You can cut filo into squares or triangles, bake it, and use it to layer custards and fruits; or you can just spread some cooked fruit on one edge and roll it up for a quick strudel. No matter how you prepare it, this crispy, flaky dough is sure to get rave reviews.

Crispy Filo Squares

Crispy filo squares are perfect to use in layered desserts. You can layer filo squares with ice cream or custard and then some fruit for a beautiful presentation (such as in the following recipe for Sautéed Peach Napoleon). These sweet, crispy squares add a buttery richness to anything you serve with them.

Specialty tools: *Parchment paper, paint brush*

Preparation time: *7 minutes*

Cooking time: *15 minutes*

Yield: *16 2-inch squares*

6 sheets filo dough	*Approximately 3 tablespoons sugar*
3 tablespoons melted butter	

1 Lay 1 sheet of filo flat on a work surface. Use a paint brush to coat the filo with the melted butter (see the following sidebar, "Giving your desserts the brush-off"). Then sprinkle lightly with the sugar. Lay another sheet on top and repeat with the melted butter and sugar. Top with 1 more piece of filo and set aside.

2 Repeat this process to complete another set of 3 layers.

(continued)

3 Cut each filo sheet into 8 2-inch squares, for a total of 16 squares. Place a piece of parchment paper on a sheet pan. Lay the filo squares on the parchment paper and cover with another piece of parchment and another sheet pan.

4 Bake at 350° for 10 to 12 minutes or until golden-brown.

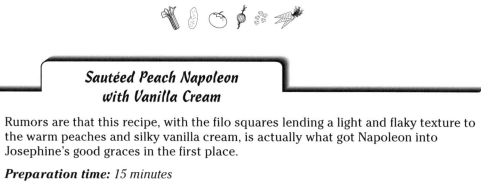

Sautéed Peach Napoleon with Vanilla Cream

Rumors are that this recipe, with the filo squares lending a light and flaky texture to the warm peaches and silky vanilla cream, is actually what got Napoleon into Josephine's good graces in the first place.

Preparation time: *15 minutes*

Cooking time: *7 minutes*

Yield: *4 servings*

¹/₂ cup Simple Syrup (see recipe later in this chapter)

1 vanilla bean, cut in half and pulp scraped from skin

2 peaches, peeled and thinly sliced

1 cup heavy cream

2 tablespoons sugar

16 Crispy Filo Squares (see preceding recipe)

1 Place the simple syrup and half of the vanilla bean pulp into a sauté pan. Add the peach slices and cook over medium heat for 5 minutes or until the peaches are warm.

2 Whip the heavy cream in an electric mixer with the sugar and remaining vanilla bean pulp for 3 minutes or until medium peaks form.

3 Place a filo square in the center of each plate, top with a spoonful of whipped cream and some of the warm peaches. Repeat this process until you have 4 layers of filo and 3 layers of peaches and cream. Spoon any of the remaining cooking juices from the peaches around the plate.

Honey and Maple Syrup Braised Pears and Pecan Filo Beggar's Purses

These little filo beggar's purses are an easy individual dessert that is full of flavor and texture. The braised pears are so sweet and tender that they practically melt in your mouth while the flaky filo dough adds a nice crunch.

(continued)

Preparation time: *15 minutes*

Cooking time: *25 minutes*

Yield: *4 servings*

2 cups diced Bartlett pears, peeled	*2 tablespoons sugar*
2 tablespoons honey	*6 sheets filo dough*
¹/₄ cup maple syrup	*3 tablespoons melted butter*
3 tablespoons finely ground pecans	*2 teaspoons Preserved Ginger (see recipe later in this chapter), chopped*

1 Place the pears, honey, and maple syrup in a medium sauté pan. Cook over medium heat for 15 minutes or until the pears are tender. Remove the pears and reserve the cooking liquid (which you use as your sauce).

2 Mix together the ground pecans and sugar in a small bowl.

3 Lay 1 sheet of filo flat on a work surface. Brush with the melted butter and sprinkle lightly with the sugar-pecan mixture. Lay another piece of filo on top and repeat with the melted butter and sugar mixture. Top with 1 more piece of filo and set aside.

4 Repeat this process to complete another set of 3 layers.

5 Cut each filo piece into 2 5-inch squares. Spoon some of the cooked pears in the center of each square. Sprinkle with some of the preserved ginger.

6 Carefully bunch up the filo by pulling all the corners up to a point. Gather tightly together and pinch closed at the top, creating a sack.

7 Place on a sheet pan and bake at 350° for 10 minutes or until golden-brown and crispy.

8 Place a filo beggar's purse on each plate and spoon around some of the cooking liquid.

Giving your desserts the brush-off

It's good to have a variety of paint brushes handy in the kitchen, ranging in size from the thinnest possible to about 1 inch wide. You can find diverse uses for paint brushes, such as brushing butter onto filo, applying glazes or *egg washes* (a mix of egg and water) to tarts, painting designs on wedding cakes, or moistening the edges of dough or pasta to seal them.

Génoise

Gourmet cooks say *génoise,* but don't be intimidated — it's just sponge cake. Sponge cake is made from three basic ingredients that you probably already have in your kitchen: eggs, sugar, and flour (some sponge cakes contain butter, too).

Sponge cake is a basic element of many gourmet desserts — it is airy, sweet, and has numerous uses. You can flavor sponge cakes with cocoa powder, ground nuts, citrus, or spices. At the restaurant, we usually make génoise in thin layers in half sheet pans. Then we glaze them (or layer them with fresh fruits and cream), and then cut them into small bite-sized treats.

Basic Sponge Cake

This sponge cake recipe contains no baking powder or baking soda (which is sometimes used to give sponge cake its characteristic volume and light texture). Instead, this recipe uses the whipped eggs to act as a leavening agent, taking the place of baking soda or baking powder.

Specialty tools: *Parchment paper*

Preparation time: *20 minutes*

Cooking time: *20 minutes*

Yield: *8-inch round cake or 11-x-17-inch sheet cake*

6 large eggs	*2¼ cups sifted flour*
3 teaspoons vanilla extract	*9 tablespoons melted butter*
1¾ cups sugar	

1 Line the bottom of your pan with parchment paper.

2 Place the eggs, vanilla, and sugar in a mixing bowl. Place the bowl over a saucepan of simmering water, and whip the mixture continuously until the sugar dissolves. Remove from the heat and whip at high speed with an electric mixer until the mixture has cooled and is light and fluffy (it should triple in volume).

3 Fold the flour into the whipped eggs in 2 additions, using your hand or a rubber spatula.

4 Fold in the melted butter and pour the batter into the prepared pan.

5 Immediately bake at 350° for 15 to 20 minutes or until the cake springs back when gently pressed. Remove the cake from the pan after it cools.

Hazelnut-Chocolate Sponge Cake

This sponge cake is so good that you can simply cover it with a chocolate glaze and serve it with some chocolate sauce. But you can also use it in any recipe that calls for basic sponge cake.

Specialty tools: *Parchment paper*

Preparation time: *20 minutes*

Cooking time: *50 minutes*

Yield: *2 9-inch cakes*

14 eggs

1¹/₂ cups sugar

1 teaspoon vanilla extract

1 teaspoon salt

1¹/₂ cups sifted flour

1¹/₄ cups hazelnuts, toasted in the oven for 10 minutes at 350° and then ground

3 ounces semisweet chocolate, melted and then cooled to room temperature

4 ounces melted butter

1 Line the bottom of the pans with parchment paper, butter, and dust with flour.

2 Combine the eggs, sugar, vanilla, and salt in a mixing bowl. Place the bowl over a saucepan of simmering water and whip continuously until all the sugar dissolves. Remove from heat and whip at high speed until the mixture cools and has a light and fluffy consistency (again, the mixture should triple in volume).

3 Sift the flour into a small bowl and add the hazelnuts.

4 In 2 additions, fold the flour mixture into the whipped eggs, using your hand or a rubber spatula. Fold in the chocolate and melted butter.

5 Pour into the prepared pans and bake immediately at 350° for 35 to 45 minutes or until the cake springs back when gently pressed.

Creating Custards and Ice Creams

Custards and curds are perfect fillings for pies and tarts, or for layering with fruit and crispy filo dough. Custards can be temperamental, though: so follow these recipes closely.

However, you *can* easily adjust the flavor of curds to complement the fruit you are using. And with ice cream, the sky's the limit — you can flavor ice creams with herbs, fruits, spices, nuts, praline, or even cookie dough or brownies. You can serve ice cream with cakes, pies, or sauces. And even on a plain old cone, ice cream is hard to beat.

Citrus curds

Here's another gourmet term for you: *curd.* It sounds intimidating (and chunky), but it's neither — it's just pudding. Citrus curds are made from the juice of lemons, limes, or oranges, which is then mixed with a combination of egg yolks and sugar. Citrus curd is cooked over a double boiler and then chilled. You can spread the finished curd in the bottom of a prebaked tart shell and then top it with fresh fruit.

Lemon Curd

You can easily change the flavor of this lemon curd by substituting any other type of citrus juice for the lemon juice. Choose which flavor to substitute by matching up the citrus to the fruits you're serving it with.

Preparation time: *10 minutes*

Cooking time: *25 minutes*

Yield: *2 cups*

1 cup lemon juice

3 egg yolks

³/₄ cup sugar

1 Place the lemon juice, egg yolks, and sugar in a medium bowl and whisk together until smooth.

2 Place the bowl over a pot of simmering water and continue to whisk for 25 minutes. Cool over an ice bath and refrigerate until needed.

Custards

Custards are a combination of eggs, cream, and other flavorings. These basic dessert recipes are baked very slowly at low temperatures, usually in a water bath to evenly distribute the heat and to prevent the eggs from curdling. Though all custards have the same basic properties, they can be quite diverse in their final presentations. Custards can range anywhere from bread pudding to pumpkin pie, ice cream, flan, or crème caramel.

Vanilla Crème Brûlée

This basic recipe can be infused with almost any type of spice, herb, or zest by simply adding the herbs or spices while you heat the cream (make sure that you strain the cream before adding the egg mixture). This smooth, creamy custard has a wonderful, thin, glasslike layer of caramelized sugar. When your spoon breaks through the caramelized surface and meets the creamy custard, the combination explodes with contrasting flavors and textures. *Tip:* You can bake the crème brûlées earlier in the day and caramelize the sugar when you are ready to serve them.

Specialty tools: *6 crème brûlée molds*

Preparation time: *10 minutes*

Cooking time: *45 minutes*

Yield: *6 crème brûlées*

2 egg yolks

2 eggs

5 tablespoons sugar

1¹/₂ cups heavy cream

¹/₂ cup milk

1 vanilla bean, sliced open lengthwise and scraped, with pulp reserved

Sugar for dusting

1 In a medium bowl, whisk together the egg yolks, eggs, and sugar until smooth.

2 Place the heavy cream, milk, and vanilla bean pulp in a small saucepan. Bring to a boil over medium heat.

3 Slowly pour the hot cream mixture into the egg mixture, whisking constantly to *temper* the eggs (bring the eggs up to temperature without scrambling the eggs). Strain through a fine-mesh sieve. Cool over an ice bath.

4 Pour the custard mixture into 6 crème brûlée molds. Bake at 300° in a baking pan with ¹/₂ inch of water for approximately 35 to 45 minutes or until the custard jiggles slightly when shaken.

5 Cool in the refrigerator. Sprinkle an even, heavy dusting of sugar over the top of the custard. Using a small hand-held blow torch, slowly caramelize the sugar by moving the torch around the top of the custard (as shown in Figure 14-1) until the sugar melts and turns golden-brown. You can also caramelize the sugar in the broiler — just be sure to turn the custard a few times so that no hot spots develop.

FYI: Crème brûlée molds are round, shallow ceramic dishes that are about four or five inches across and about one inch deep. These molds are great for baking and serving custard in individual servings. The large surface area also allows for a nice representation of the caramelized sugar.

Figure 14-1:
The versatile blow torch gives a crème brûlée a thin, glasslike crust.

Chocolate-Espresso Custard

This creamy, mocha-flavored custard is a fun twist on traditional crème brûlée. You can also bake this chocolate-espresso custard in a sheet pan with short sides. You can then freeze the custard and cut it into triangles or squares. Remove the shapes with a small spatula and layer them with tuiles to create a napoleon.

Specialty tools: *4 crème brûlée molds*

Preparation time: *10 minutes*

Cooking time: *25 minutes*

Yield: *4 servings*

2 egg yolks	*1 tablespoon finely ground dark coffee*
2 eggs	*4 ounces dark chocolate, chopped*
5 tablespoons sugar	*2 tablespoons cocoa powder*
1¹/₂ cups heavy cream	*Sugar for dusting*
¹/₂ cup milk	

1 In a medium bowl, whisk together the egg yolks, eggs, and sugar until smooth.

2 Place the heavy cream, milk, and coffee in a small saucepan and bring to a boil over medium heat for 1 minute.

3 Slowly pour the cream mixture over the egg mixture to temper the eggs, while whisking constantly. Add the chopped chocolate and cocoa powder and whisk smooth (the heat of the cream melts the chocolate). Strain through a fine-mesh sieve, and then cool over an ice bath.

(continued)

4 Pour the custard mixture into 4 crème brûlée molds, place in a baking pan with
¹/₂ inch of water, and bake at 300° for approximately 25 to 30 minutes or until the
custard jiggles slightly when shaken.

5 Cool in the refrigerator. Sprinkle with an even yet heavy dusting of sugar and
caramelize the sugar with a blow torch or in the broiler.

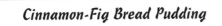

Cinnamon-Fig Bread Pudding

In this recipe, you take basic bread pudding to the next level by adding a little rum,
figs, and chopped pecans. You can easily change the flavors of this pudding by
adding different fruits, nuts, spices, or even chocolate pieces. This cinnamon-fig
bread pudding makes a great dessert paired with some anglaise sauce or ice cream
(both recipes that you can find in this chapter). You can bake this dessert in individual molds for a more refined presentation.

Preparation time: *1 hour*

Cooking time: *1 hour*

Yield: *8 to 10 servings*

1¹/₂ cups heavy cream

2 cinnamon sticks

4 eggs

3 tablespoons dark rum

¹/₂ cup sugar

*6 cups diced, day-old bread (such as
brioche, French, or sourdough)*

1¹/₂ cups dried figs, chopped

³/₄ cup chopped pecans

(continued)

FYI

Blow-torching your custard

Blow torches are not just for welding metal
anymore. A small hand-held blow torch is actually quite essential in many dessert preparations, especially in crème brûlée. You just
sprinkle the top of the crème brûlée with some
sugar and run the blow torch over it with a
circular motion for about 30 seconds or until
the sugar turns golden-brown.

The torch makes it easy to control the temperature and direction of the flame. If you don't
own one, it really is worth the investment. Besides, after you finish caramelizing the crème
brûlée, you can crawl under the sink and fix
that leaky drain pipe. You can purchase a
kitchen blow torch at William-Sonoma (see
Chapter 20).

1 Place the cream and cinnamon sticks in a small saucepan and slowly simmer over medium-low heat for 5 minutes. Cool over an ice bath and remove the cinnamon sticks.

2 Place the eggs, rum, sugar, and cream in a large bowl and whisk together until smooth. Add the bread, figs, and nuts. Toss together and let sit for 20 minutes or until most of the liquid is absorbed into the bread.

3 Fill a small loaf pan (approximately 3 x 8 inches) with the bread mixture, pressing down so it is tightly packed. Bake at 375° for 1 hour or until golden-brown and crispy on top.

4 Cut into slices and serve hot.

Homemade ice cream

Making your own ice cream at home is a wonderful treat — and a perennial summertime favorite. You can make any kind you want and as much as you can handle. Whether you have a electric ice cream machine or a hand-crank machine, the quality of the finished product is similar.

You can flavor ice cream with just about anything you want, such as raspberry, coffee, basil, or even black truffles, if you really want to go over the edge. When making flavored ice creams, you need to remember a few basic techniques for the different types:

- ✔ When making spice-flavored ice cream, whisk the ground spice into the cream mixture as it's coming to a simmer, proceed with the recipe, and then spin in an ice cream machine.

- ✔ When making fruit ice creams, such as raspberry, mango, peach, and so on, puree the fruit before incorporating it into the ice cream. If the fruit is fibrous or has seeds, you should strain it through a sieve before incorporating it into the ice cream base.

- ✔ When making herb-flavored ice creams, add the herbs when you are heating the cream mixture, but before you add the egg yolks. You can puree the herbs with the ice cream base for more concentrated flavor, or you can remove them for a lighter herb flavor.

- ✔ When making ice creams flavored with a syrup or liquor, simply incorporate the liquid into the cold ice cream base.

- ✔ When making ice creams flavored with chopped nuts, diced fruit, or brittle, all you need to do is fold in the item just before you finish spinning the ice cream.

No matter what flavor of ice cream you're making, a good ice cream *base* is the key to a smooth and creamy finished product.

Ice Cream Base

Ice cream base is like a blank canvas waiting for paint. You can take it in any direction that you choose. If you prefer traditional flavors, you can add vanilla or peach. If you're feeling a little adventurous, try adding cinnamon-basil or pear-rosemary, for example.

Specialty tools: *Electric or hand-crank ice cream machine*

Preparation time: *10 minutes, plus 2 hours freezing*

Cooking time: *15 minutes*

Yield: *1 quart*

$1^1/_2$ cups heavy cream	6 egg yolks
$^3/_4$ cup milk	$^3/_4$ cup plus 2 tablespoons sugar
$^3/_4$ cup half-and-half	

1 Combine the heavy cream, milk, and half-and-half in a medium saucepan and bring to a boil over medium heat.

2 Whisk the yolks and sugar together in a medium bowl. Temper the egg yolks by slowly adding the hot cream while whisking constantly. Return the egg yolk and cream mixture to the saucepan.

3 Cook over medium-low heat for 2 minutes, stirring constantly. Strain through a fine-mesh sieve.

4 Immediately cool over an ice bath and then freeze in an ice cream machine.

Variation: *Puree $1^1/_2$ cups chopped peaches (skin removed) with the ice cream base and pass through a fine-mesh sieve. Spin in an ice cream machine and then fold in $^1/_2$ cup diced peaches (skin removed).*

R-E-S-P-E-C-T ... That's what eggs mean to me

Eggs may be fragile and unassuming, but they do deserve a little respect. Eggs (like poultry, meat, and seafood) are certainly safe when handled properly. Because undercooked eggs can potentially carry bacteria like salmonella, follow these guidelines when handling and using eggs in your dessert recipes:

✔ Use refrigerated grade AA or A eggs that have clean, uncracked shells.

✔ Always keep eggs refrigerated until you're ready to use them.

✔ Wash your hands, your kitchen tools, and work areas with hot, soapy water before and after you handle eggs.

✔ Cook eggs to at least 140 degrees to kill any bacteria that may be present.

✔ Don't serve foods containing raw eggs to pregnant women, kids, elderly folks, or to people with lowered immune systems.

Sorbets

Sorbets are usually made from a combination of fruit purees and simple syrup (see recipe later in this section). Sometimes, light corn syrup or glucose is added to a sorbet to create a smoother texture. Sorbets are generally fat-free unless they are made with yogurt or other ingredients that contain traces of fat.

Sorbets add a refreshing, primary element to any dessert recipe; sorbets can also work as a dessert all on their own. Some restaurants serve sorbet as an *entremezzo* before the main course — the fruit acid in the sorbet helps to cleanse and refresh the palate.

The trick to making perfect sorbet is getting the proper balance of sweetness. One almost-foolproof way to test the balance is to taste the sorbet and use your palate as a guide. But if you don't trust your palate, use a raw egg. Place the egg in your sorbet base:

✔ If the egg floats (with a portion the diameter of a quarter breaking through the surface), you have the perfect sugar balance.

✔ If the egg sinks, add more simple syrup to the sorbet base.

✔ If the egg floats too high, add more water.

If your sorbet comes out icy, you can melt it down and add 1/4 cup of light corn syrup or glucose. Then spin the sorbet again in the ice cream machine and enjoy!

Mango Sorbet

Thin mango slices, barely warmed in vanilla syrup, are a nice addition to this mango sorbet. This recipe makes a refreshing, light dessert.

Specialty tools: *Electric or hand-crank ice cream machine*

Preparation time: *15 minutes, plus 2 hours freezing time*

Yield: *1 quart*

3 cups chopped mango

2 cups Simple Syrup (see following recipe)

1 Puree the mango and the simple syrup together until smooth. Strain through a fine-mesh sieve.

2 Spin in an ice cream machine until frozen and keep covered in the freezer until needed.

Variations:

  ✔ **Bing Cherry Sorbet:** Puree 4 cups of pitted cherries and reduce the amount of simple syrup to 1¹/₂ cups.

  ✔ **Vanilla Yogurt Sorbet:** Use 2¹/₂ cups lowfat yogurt instead of the fruit. Reduce the amount of simple syrup to 1¹/₂ cups and add 2 tablespoons of lime juice and 1 teaspoon of vanilla bean pulp.

Simple Syrup

Simple syrup is usually made from equal parts granulated sugar and water. It is used as a sweetening agent in sorbets, as a moistener when brushed on sponge cake, or as a glaze when brushed over fruits. You can even flavor it with spices, fruits, or herbs and use it as a sauce.

Preparation time: *1 minute*

Cooking time: *7 minutes*

Yield: *2 cups*

1 cup water

1 cup sugar

Place the water and sugar in a small saucepan and bring to a simmer over medium heat. Stir occasionally until all the sugar dissolves. Cool and refrigerate until needed.

Doing Up Dessert Sauces

Most dessert preparations need a sauce to complete the dish. Dessert sauces can either introduce a new flavor to a dish, or they can repeat a flavor theme that is already present in the dessert (as does the Blood Orange Chocolate Sauce with Chocolate Crêpes and Blood Orange Fillets in Chapter 16). Dessert sauces are easy to make and can be used with numerous desserts. They can also be made ahead of time and reheated just before use, if necessary.

Anglaise Sauce

Anglaise sauce is a basic dessert sauce that you can use on a variety of levels in dessert preparations. It's a sweet, creamy sauce, which is usually infused with other flavors. Vanilla, brandy, cinnamon, nutmeg, tea, nuts, or herbs are all used often. Anglaise sauce works well as an accompaniment to sponge cakes, bread puddings, soufflés, chocolate desserts, and most other dessert preparations. This sauce is normally used chilled and keeps for a couple days in the refrigerator.

Preparation time: *15 minutes*

Cooking time: *10 minutes*

Yield: *1¹/₄ cups*

2 egg yolks   *1 cup heavy cream*

4 teaspoons sugar

1 In a medium bowl, whisk together the egg yolks and sugar until smooth.

2 Place the heavy cream in a small saucepan and bring to a boil.

3 Slowly whisk the cream into the yolk mixture. Return the mixture to the saucepan and cook over medium heat, stirring, for 2 minutes or until the sauce coats the back of a spoon. (Do not boil the mixture or the eggs will curdle.)

4 Strain through a fine-mesh sieve and cool over an ice bath.

I'll take the power drill, the hacksaw, and that *lovely* little mousse mold

You may wonder what good a trip to the hardware store will do you when you are making desserts, but you'll be surprised at what you can find there. Investing in all-new, professional pastry equipment can be expensive — but a trip to the hardware store can yield some economical alternatives that work just as well.

Discover how you can use these everyday items from the hardware store the next time you create a new dessert. *Tip:* You may already own some of the following items, but make sure to thoroughly clean and sanitize them before using them for your dessert preparations:

✔ **Single-edged razor blades:** These tools can be dangerous, but they're good to have around. You can use razor blades to shave chocolate, slit bread dough before baking it, or to score the tops of tarts. *Tip:* You may want to invest in a *box knife* — the razor retracts into the handle for safe storage and gives you more to hold on to while you use it.

✔ **Thin wire:** You can use strong, thin pieces of wire to cut cheesecake, semifirm desserts, or cheeses into perfect slices.

✔ **PVC pipe:** Not just for plumbing anymore; these pipes come in many widths and can be cut to any depth you want. You can use sections of PVC pipe as a ring mold for rice pudding, mousses, or anything frozen. You can even use PVC pipe in the oven at low temperature (325 degrees or less), and you can run it through the dishwasher. A couple feet of PVC costs only a few bucks.

✔ **Wide blade scraper:** This tool works wonderfully for shaving chocolate into long pieces. You can also use a blade scraper to smooth frosting onto the sides of a cake.

✔ **Hair dryer:** A hair dryer can be useful to loosen chilled desserts from their molds (without worrying about getting water in the food, as you might if you dip a mold into warm water). Just blow hot air from the hair dryer around the sides of the mold for a few seconds to loosen the dessert.

✔ **Clear, heavy-duty plastic:** You can use large sheets of clear, smooth, pliable plastic to mold tempered chocolate (which picks up the smooth shine of the plastic). As the chocolate begins to set, you can wrap the plastic around a cake, let the chocolate set completely, and then peel the plastic back, leaving a tempered chocolate coating on the cake. If you take care of the plastic, you can reuse it many times.

You make caramel sauces by melting and caramelizing granulated sugar, and then adding cream and butter, vinegar, or apple juice for different flavors and textures. Remember that adding some type of liquid to caramel sauce recipes is essential — otherwise, your caramel hardens when cooled and turns as solid as glass.

Caramel Sauce

Caramel sauce is simple to make and has so many variations. A perfectly made caramel sauce begs to be licked off the spoon — but be careful, the sauce can be very hot! Caramel sauces go great with chocolate preparations, but try using them on fruit desserts, as well. For example, the Sour Caramel Sauce would be wonderful with the Peach Napoleon (found earlier in this chapter).

Preparation time: *10 minutes*

Cooking time: *15 minutes*

Yield: *1$^{1}/_{2}$ cups*

1 cup sugar   *2 tablespoons butter*

$^{1}/_{2}$ cup heavy cream

1 In a medium nonstick sauté pan, cook the sugar over medium-low heat until melted and golden-brown. Add the heavy cream and butter. The mixture may *seize up* (harden for a short time), but continue cooking and it will melt down again.

2 Stir the mixture until it is smooth and fully incorporated. Use while hot. Cover the caramel and store for up to a week in the refrigerator; reheat when needed.

Variations:

✔ **Sour Caramel Sauce:** Substitute 1 cup rice wine vinegar for the cream and butter.

✔ **Basil Caramel Sauce:** Substitute 1 cup apple juice and $^{1}/_{4}$ cup chopped basil for the cream.

Chipping In with Garnishes and Textural Treats

Like many savory foods, desserts benefit from varying textural elements. You can introduce texture to your dessert recipes by adding items such as crunchy nuts, crispy thin tuiles, or fruit chips. When you create a dessert like a smooth custard, try to incorporate a praline crust or a thin filo wafer. Also, folding some chopped candied zest into the custard results in a more complex flavor and gives that extra touch of texture to the custard.

Candied Lemon Zest

Candying *zest* not only helps to preserve the skin of the fruit, but also removes the bitterness from the zest (the colored, outer skin of citrus fruits). After you candy the zest of oranges, grapefruit, lemons, limes, or any other citrus fruit, you can use it as a garnish, a textural element, and an intense flavoring agent, all at the same time.

Preparation time: *10 minutes*

Cooking time: *45 minutes*

Yield: *¹/₄ cup*

¹/₄ cup julienned lemon zest

1 cup Simple Syrup (see recipe earlier in this chapter)

1 Blanch the zest in boiling salted water for 2 minutes. Repeat this process 2 more times with fresh boiling water. (Doing so helps to remove the bitterness from the zest. If using grapefruit, repeat the process at least 4 times.)

2 Place the simple syrup and blanched lemon zest in a small saucepan and simmer over low heat for 45 minutes. Let the zest cool in the syrup. Refrigerate until needed.

Preserved Ginger

This recipe uses julienned ginger poached in simple syrup. You can serve preserved ginger with peaches or pears, paired with chocolate, or folded into whipped cream. Although I frequently use this recipe in desserts, preserved ginger has many other savory uses, such as being paired with foie gras or tossed in a salad with fresh figs.

Preparation time: *10 minutes*

Cooking time: *45 minutes*

Yield: *¹/₄ cup*

6 tablespoons julienned ginger

1¹/₂ cups Simple Syrup (see recipe earlier in this chapter)

1 Place the ginger and ¹/₂ cup of the simple syrup in a small saucepan. Simmer over medium-low heat for 15 minutes. Strain off the syrup, add a fresh ¹/₂ cup of simple syrup to the ginger, and simmer again for 15 minutes. Repeat this process once more.

2 Cool the ginger in the final batch of simple syrup. Refrigerate in the syrup until needed.

Dried fruit chips

Forget those infomercials; who needs one of those big and clunky food dehydrating machines? All you really need are your oven and a nonstick sheet pan for an economical, easy, and healthy way to create dried fruit slices. They add great texture, design, and height to desserts — plus, you can make them ahead of time and keep them in an airtight container for a few weeks. Try adding these fruit chips to the fruit soups in Chapter 15.

Oven-Dried Strawberry Chips

You can also use this simple recipe to create banana, apple, pineapple, mango, or kiwi chips. I like to add a dried fruit chip to the top of sorbets or ice creams for a nice textural contrast, but they also make a great, healthy snack all by themselves.

Preparation time: 2 minutes

Cooking time: 45 minutes

Yield: About 40 pieces

6 nicely shaped fresh strawberries, stems removed

1 Slice the strawberries paper-thin. Lay them flat, not touching each other, on a nonstick sheet pan.

2 Bake at 225° for 30 to 45 minutes or until dry to the touch. Remove from the sheet pan while still warm. (Doing so results in unbroken chips.) As they cool, they become crispy. Store in an airtight container at room temperature until needed.

Variations:

- **Oven-Dried Apple Chips:** The baking time may be slightly shorter.
- **Oven-Dried Pineapple Chips:** The baking time may be slightly longer.

Praline

Praline is so easy to make. You only need two ingredients: sugar and nuts. You can fold praline into ice cream, cakes, or mousses. Try using praline as a garnish or a topping on your desserts — it adds great crunch and nutty flavor. You can use any type of nut to make pralines, but almonds and pecans are the traditional preferences. You can break praline into any size piece you want, but often it is finely ground, almost to the form of a powder.

Pistachio Praline

In this recipe, I use pistachios to make praline. You can experiment — substitute different types of nuts (like hazelnuts or macadamia nuts) for a different flavor variation in this recipe.

Preparation time: *10 minutes*

Cooking time: *15 minutes*

Yield: *About 2 cups*

$1^1/_2$ *cups sugar* $^3/_4$ *cup pistachios, toasted*

1 Place the sugar in a medium nonstick sauté pan. Slowly caramelize over medium-low heat until golden-brown.

2 Add the nuts to the caramelized sugar and stir until incorporated. Immediately pour the hot praline onto a greased surface (such as a nonstick sheet pan or marble). Cool and break into the desired size.

Tuiles

Tuiles add a great structural and textural component to a dessert. You can use them between layers of stacked fruit, custard, or ice cream. Or try rolling them up while they are still warm and using them as a garnish on ice cream or other desserts. They can even be shaped into baskets to hold other ingredients (see Chapter 12 for more about tuiles that you can use in your savory recipes, and for information about using templates).

Basic Tuile Batter

You can create tuiles in just about any shape or size, and then flavor them with herbs, spices, fruit purees, nuts . . . the list could go on forever. Try modifying this basic tuile batter recipe by adding just a touch of any of these flavorings.

Preparation time: *10 minutes*

Cooking time: *15 minutes*

Yield: *About 1 cup batter (or about 20 tuiles)*

$^1/_4$ *cup sugar*   *3 egg whites*

5 tablespoons flour   *5 tablespoons butter, melted and then cooled to room temperature*

(continued)

1 Combine the sugar and flour in a mixing bowl. Stir in the egg whites and melted butter and mix until smooth.

2 Lightly oil the back side of a 12-x-16-inch sheet pan. Spread a thin, even layer of the tuile batter on the back side of the sheet pan, covering the whole area. (Or you can use templates in the same manner as you do when preparing the savory tuiles in Chapter 12.)

3 Bake at 300° for 8 to 12 minutes or until golden-brown.

4 Quickly remove from the oven. Using a pizza cutter, a mold, or a knife, cut the tuile into the desired shape. (If the tuiles begin to crack or break, put the tray back in the oven for 2 minutes — cutting tuiles when they're hot is easiest.) Mold the tuiles over a rolling pin, a bowl, or a cup if you want tuiles with a curved shape.

5 Store in an airtight container at room temperature until needed.

Lace Tuiles

This tuile batter separates slightly when baked, leaving small holes in the finished tuiles that gives the impression of lace. You can use lace tuiles the same way as basic tuiles — but they look so pretty, you may want to just place them on the edge of a dessert plate where they can show off.

Preparation time: *10 minutes*

Cooking time: *15 minutes*

Yield: *About 1 cup batter (or about 15 tuiles)*

$^1/_2$ cup butter, softened	*1 tablespoon brandy*
$^3/_4$ cup sugar	*$^1/_3$ cup flour*
1 tablespoon honey	*Pinch of salt*

1 Place the butter and sugar in a small bowl and combine with a fork. Add the honey, brandy, flour, and salt and stir until smooth.

2 Place 15 rounded teaspoons of batter on a nonstick sheet pan about 3 inches apart Bake at 350° for 10 minutes or until golden-brown and lacy. Remove the tuiles from the pan when slightly cool.

Chapter 15

How Sweet It Is: Fruit Desserts and Individual Pastries

I hope you saved room for dessert — many people think that it's the best part of the meal! The person who first came up with the *dessert progression* (multiple courses of desserts) was a genius, in my opinion, and probably had a good-sized sweet tooth (as I do). Dessert progressions usually begin with a sorbet course, followed by a more substantial fruit dessert, and end with a chocolate dessert (see Chapter 16).

The dessert progression is part of the reason that so many gourmet desserts are made in small tart and ring molds. These individual pastries not only impress your guests but are also just as easy to make as their full-sized parents. Keep in mind that, with their smaller size, the cooking times for individual pastries are substantially shorter.

Unless you're lucky enough to live in sunny California or Chile, where you can find a plethora of wonderful fruits and berries year-round, you need to keep in mind the time of year that you use certain recipes. For example, if you have a recipe for a warm berry compote but it's the middle of winter and berries aren't available, try substituting some diced poached pears and citrus segments for the berries and proceed with the recipe.

Basically, if you use your head and some "seasonal" common sense with your dessert preparations, you'll have no problem creating great desserts in any season. See Chapter 4 to find out when various fruits are at their best and to gather ideas on what fruits you can substitute in your dessert recipes when your first choice isn't available.

Starting with Sorbets

Sorbets are a great way to start a dessert progression because they're light, refreshing, and not too sweet. They cleanse the richness of the entree from your palate and prepare you to move on to sweeter desserts. Sorbet recipes are easy to make, but if you're in a pinch, you can buy one of many different flavors available at the supermarket.

Warm Bing Cherry Soup with Vanilla Yogurt Sorbet and Apple Chips

A warm fruit soup with an ice cold sorbet is a wonderful temperature contrast and a great way to start a dessert progression. You can make this soup with any type of cherry; you can even substitute plums for an interesting flavor variation.

Preparation time: *10 minutes*

Cooking time: *20 minutes*

Yield: *6 servings*

4 cups Bing cherries, pitted	*Vanilla Yogurt Sorbet (see Chapter 14)*
1 1/2 cups water	*12 Oven-Dried Apple Chips (see Chapter 14)*
1/3 cup sugar	

1 Place the cherries, water, and sugar in a medium saucepan. Simmer over medium heat for 20 minutes.

2 Pass the cherries through a fine-mesh sieve and discard the skins and pulp.

3 Place two small scoops of the sorbet in the center of each bowl. Place an apple chip in each scoop of sorbet and ladle the warm soup around the bowl. Serve immediately.

Grandma's cherry-pitting trick

One of my favorite memories from my childhood is of picking cherries with my grandparents. We would drive up to Sturgeon Bay, Wisconsin, and pick buckets full of the dark, juicy fruit. Then we'd sit around my grandmother's kitchen table and pit the cherries while she made preserves and pies. Grandma wasn't big on fancy tools, so she gave us each a paper clip. She showed us how to insert the paper clip at the stem end of the cherry, alongside the pit, and pop it out. This way, we could remove the pits while the cherry stayed whole.

Chilled Melon Soup with Lemon-Ginger Sorbet

This melon soup is so refreshing that I'm tempted to drink it as cold fruit juice. You can use a ripe honeydew or watermelon in place of the cantaloupe in this recipe. Regardless of what type of melon you select, this soup is a perfect light dessert to follow a summer meal of grilled fish or shrimp and a cold grain salad.

Specialty tools: *Cheesecloth, ice cream machine*

Preparation time: *15 minutes, plus 2 hours refrigeration and overnight draining*

Yield: *4 servings*

For the sorbet:

3 cups Simple Syrup (see Chapter 14)

¹/₄ cup chopped ginger

³/₄ cup lemon juice

3 tablespoons corn syrup

For the soup and garnish:

2 very ripe cantaloupes, pared, seeded, and chopped

1 cup diced cantaloupe

4 teaspoons Preserved Ginger (see Chapter 14)

1 To prepare the sorbet, place the simple syrup and chopped ginger in a medium saucepan. Simmer for 15 minutes over medium-low heat. Cool over an ice bath and strain through a fine-mesh sieve once cool.

2 Add the lemon juice and corn syrup to the mixture and spin in an ice cream machine. Place the sorbet in the freezer for at least 2 hours before using.

3 To create the melon soup, puree the chopped cantaloupe in a food processor or blender until smooth.

(continued)

4 Line a fine-mesh sieve with cheesecloth and place in a tall container. Pour the pureed cantaloupe into the cheesecloth-lined sieve and let drain in the refrigerator overnight. Discard the pulp and keep the melon soup refrigerated until needed.

5 Spoon some of the diced cantaloupe into the bottom of each bowl. Place a medium-sized scoop of the lemon-ginger sorbet on top of the cantaloupe and ladle the chilled melon soup around the bowl. Arrange some of the preserved ginger over the sorbet.

Creating Tasty Tarts

The little tarts in this section work perfectly as the second course in a dessert progression. They are sweeter than sorbets, but still light enough to leave you wanting more. You *could* prepare any of these tarts in an 8-inch tart pan — but I think it's more elegant (and more fun) to prepare and serve them individually.

Blueberry and Mango Tarts

You can make fruit tarts with just about any fruit. They can be served hot or cold, depending on how you prepare them. Fruit tarts are easy to make, yet they are impressive to guests, especially when you prepare them in individual servings, as in this recipe.

Specialty tools: *6 4-inch tart ring molds*

Preparation time: *10 minutes*

Cooking time: *20 minutes*

Yield: *6 servings*

Cream Cheese Dough (see Chapter 14)	*2 cups blueberries*
1¹/₂ cups Lemon Curd (see Chapter 14)	*Powered sugar for dusting*
1¹/₂ cups small diced mango	

1 Line the tart rings with the cream cheese dough and prebake the tarts in the oven at 325° for 15 minutes or until golden-brown. Cool and remove from the molds.

2 Spoon the lemon curd into the bottom of each tart shell. Arrange some of the mango and blueberries on top of the lemon curd. Keep refrigerated until ready to serve and dust with powered sugar just prior to serving.

(continued)

Tip: *These tarts are best if eaten the day you make them. You can wrap extra pie dough in plastic wrap and keep it in the freezer for several weeks.*

Dried Cranberry, Apricot, and Currant Crumble Tarts with Pistachio Praline

These dried fruit tarts are a great dessert during the winter months, when fresh, ripe fruits aren't readily available. You can make them a day ahead of time and serve them at room temperature, or you can warm the tarts slightly in the oven just before serving.

Specialty tools: *6 4-inch tart ring molds*

Preparation time: *10 minutes*

Cooking time: *20 minutes*

Yield: *6 servings*

5 tablespoons cold butter, chopped

5 tablespoons brown sugar

1 cup flour

1¹/₂ teaspoons ground cinnamon

¹/₃ cup dried cranberries

¹/₃ cup dried apricots, diced

¹/₃ cup dried black currants

Pâte Brisée (see Chapter 14)

¹/₂ cup Pistachio Praline, chopped (see Chapter 14)

1 To make the filling, place the butter, brown sugar, flour, and cinnamon in a medium bowl and mash together with a fork until incorporated.

2 Add the cranberries, apricots, and currants and toss together.

3 Line each of the tart rings with the pâte brisée dough and sprinkle the inside with the pistachio praline. Gently press some of the praline into the dough.

4 Spoon some of the filling into each tart. Bake on a sheet pan at 350° for 20 minutes or until golden-brown. Cool slightly and remove from the molds.

Honey-Macadamia Nut Tart

Macadamia nuts burst with a light, buttery crunch and are wonderful when paired with honey. In this recipe, you can substitute Brazil nuts, whole almonds, or even peanuts if desired. I give instructions for preparing this recipe in a large tart mold to show you the difference in procedure and cooking times. But you can just as easily make this recipe in individual tart rings — just remember to adjust the cooking time to 20 minutes if you make individual tarts.

Specialty tools: *8-inch tart ring mold, parchment paper*

Preparation time: *20 minutes*

Cooking time: *35 minutes*

Yield: *6 servings*

Pâte Brisée (see Chapter 14)

¹/₂ cup honey

3 egg yolks

1 cup heavy cream

2 cups macadamia nuts, coarsely chopped

1 Line the tart ring with the pâte brisée.

2 In a small bowl, whisk together the honey, egg yolks, and heavy cream until smooth.

3 Place the tart ring on a parchment paper-lined sheet pan. Arrange the macadamia nuts in an even layer in the tart ring and pour the honey mixture over the nuts. Bake at 350° for 40 minutes or until golden-brown. Cool slightly and remove from the mold.

Preparing Poached Fruit and Pudding Desserts

Poaching is a great way to get the most flavor out of slightly underripe fruits. I like to add herbs or spices to the poaching liquid to add different flavors.

You can store poached fruit in its poaching liquid for up to a week in the refrigerator, which results in an even more intensely flavored fruit. You can serve poached fruit hot, warm, or cold. They can be stuffed, sliced or diced, or used in a light green salad. Or try serving poached fruit with soft cheeses, glazed with chocolate, or even covered with praline.

Sautéing is another way to intensify the flavor of fruits. This method brings out the flavor of the fruit, and the juices that are released during cooking make a wonderful syrup. Sautéed fruit is great to use as a topping on puddings or cakes, or for stuffing crêpes. But my favorite way to use sautéed fruit is over ice cream.

Star Anise Poached Pears Stuffed with Vanilla Mascarpone

In this recipe, you poach the fruit with star anise (see Chapter 4) to give it a slight licorice flavor and then stuff it with *mascarpone* cheese for a creamy textural contrast. Mascarpone is an Italian cheese that is a little softer and sweeter than cream cheese. Its wonderful texture and sweetness lend themselves well to many different dessert preparations.

Preparation time: *10 minutes*

Cooking time: *1 hour and 10 minutes*

Yield: *8 servings*

2 whole pieces of star anise	*1 cup mascarpone cheese*
4 cups Simple Syrup (see Chapter 14)	*2 tablespoons sugar*
¹/₄ cup dark rum	*¹/₄ teaspoon vanilla bean pulp (scraped from the inside of the bean)*
4 Bosc pears, peeled	

1 Place the star anise, simple syrup, dark rum, and pears in a large saucepan.

2 Bring to a simmer and cook over medium heat for 20 to 30 minutes or until the pears are tender. Remove the pears from the liquid, chill the pears in the refrigerator, and continue to simmer the liquid for 30 to 40 minutes or until it is golden-brown and has a syrup-like consistency. Keep the liquid warm.

3 Slice the pears in half lengthwise. Using a melon baller (or a small spoon), remove the seeds and hollow out some of each pear half, creating a section for the filling. (You can snack on the pieces of the pear that you remove.)

4 In a small bowl, whisk together the mascarpone, sugar, and vanilla bean pulp until smooth. Fill the hollowed-out section of each pear half with the mascarpone mixture. Refrigerate until ready to serve.

5 Place a pear half on each plate and spoon the reduced cooking liquid around the pear.

Rice Pudding with Sautéed Figs

Rice pudding is soothing when cold and comforting when hot. You can make it with just about any type of rice you have in your cabinet: basmati, wild rice, arborio, jasmine, sticky rice, or even plain white rice.

Specialty tools: *2-inch-round ring mold*

Preparation time: *10 minutes*

Cooking time: *30 minutes*

Yield: *6 servings*

³/₄ cup rice	*¹/₂ cup sugar*
1¹/₂ cups milk	*1¹/₂ cups Anglaise Sauce (see Chapter 14)*
¹/₂ cup water	*1 cup diced figs*
1 vanilla bean, sliced open lengthwise and scraped, with bean and pulp reserved	*6 ripe figs, sliced*
	6 Lace Tuiles (see Chapter 14)

1 Place the rice in a small saucepan with the milk, water, vanilla bean, vanilla bean pulp, and sugar. Simmer over low heat for 25 to 35 minutes or until the rice is cooked. Cool the rice to room temperature and remove the vanilla bean.

2 Fold the anglaise sauce and diced figs into the rice.

3 Gently warm the fig slices by sautéing them quickly in a medium nonstick sauté pan with a splash of water for 2 minutes.

4 Place a lace tuile in the center of each plate. Place a 2-inch-round ring mold on top of the tuile and fill with the rice pudding. Remove the ring mold and arrange the fig slices in a pinwheel shape on top of the rice pudding.

Fashioning Fluffy Soufflés

Soufflés are known for their light, airy qualities. However, they tend to be unstable and require minimal changes in temperature and movement to keep them from collapsing, so you don't want to make a soufflé if you live by the train tracks or if you have teenagers who play really loud music.

After a soufflé comes out of the hot oven and into your room-temperature kitchen, it begins to fall because of the temperature change, so it is essential to have all your guests sitting at the table, waiting to be served. If the thought of a fallen soufflé makes you nervous, try making a frozen soufflé. They are light and airy, but they aren't temperamental like the hot versions.

Warm Pineapple Soufflé with Caramelized Pineapple Slices

The only tips I can give you for keeping a soufflé from falling are to avoid loud noises and temperature changes while the soufflé is baking. Unfortunately, no tricks, tips, or solutions exist for fixing a fallen soufflé. The only guarantee is that no matter how many times you have made a perfect soufflé, you can still have one fall. If fact, there should be a corollary to Murphy's Law that states "the chance of a soufflé falling is directly proportional to the importance of the dinner party." So brace yourself and remember that it's only dessert.

Specialty tools: *8-cup gratin dish*

Preparation time: *10 minutes*

Cooking time: *35 minutes*

Yield: *6 servings*

3 cups chopped pineapple	*1 cup pineapple, cut into thin slices*
³/₄ cup sugar	*³/₄ cup Sour Caramel Sauce (see Chapter 14)*
6 large egg whites	
Pinch of salt	*Powered sugar for dusting*

1 Puree the chopped pineapple in a food processor or blender. Place in a medium saucepan with the sugar. Bring to a simmer and cook for 15 minutes, stirring occasionally. Cool to room temperature.

2 Whip the egg whites with the salt until they hold a soft peak. Fold in the cooled pineapple puree. Pour the batter into a buttered and sugared 8-cup shallow gratin dish. Bake at 400° for 7 minutes, and then lower the temperature to 350° and cook for another 8 or 10 minutes or until the soufflé is well-risen and slightly golden-brown. (You should serve the soufflé as soon as you remove it from the oven.)

3 While the soufflé is baking, place the pineapple slices in a medium sauté pan with the caramel sauce. Sauté the slices over medium heat for 3 minutes on each side.

4 Spoon some of the pineapple slices and caramel sauce in the center of each plate. Spoon some of the soufflé over the pineapple slices, dust with powered sugar, and serve immediately.

Chilled and frozen soufflés (such as the one in the following recipe) are a piece of cake compared to baked soufflés. They require minimal patience, and your kids can stomp around as much as they want. Even when the soufflés are set, you can't mess them up. A cold soufflé is a fresh and light dessert that's especially refreshing in the summer.

Chilled Lemon Soufflé

Not all soufflés live in imminent danger of implosion. This light, chilled soufflé is a perfect addition to a desert progression, but most important — it never falls.

Preparation time: *30 minutes, plus 3 hours refrigeration*

Cooking time: *10 minutes*

Yield: *6 servings*

6 lemons	*1 teaspoon unflavored gelatin*
3 eggs, separated	*¹/₃ cup water*
³/₄ cup sugar	*¹/₂ cup heavy cream*
¹/₂ cup lemon juice	*2 tablespoons Candied Lemon Zest (see Chapter 14)*
3 tablespoons grated lemon zest	

1 Cut the top and a small portion of the bottom from each lemon (just enough to allow it to stand up). Carefully hollow out each lemon, removing all the pulp and the inner lining. (You may be able to squeeze enough juice out of the pulp to use in Step 2.)

2 In a large bowl, beat the egg yolks with ¹/₂ cup of the sugar, the lemon juice, and the grated lemon zest until blended. Place the bowl over a pot of simmering water and whip for about 5 minutes or until the mixture is thick and creamy. Remove from the heat.

3 Sprinkle the gelatin over ¹/₃ cup water in a small saucepan and warm over very low heat, stirring until melted. Stir into the hot lemon mixture and continue to beat until cool.

4 In a large bowl, beat the egg whites until soft peaks form. Add the remaining ¹/₄ cup sugar and continue beating until stiff and glossy.

5 Beat the heavy cream until stiff peaks form.

6 Place the lemon-egg yolk mixture over a bowl of ice water and stir until it begins to thicken and set. Gently fold in the whipped cream, followed by the egg whites.

7 Place a ring mold on top of the opening in the lemon. Cut a piece of aluminum foil 1 inch wide and long enough to go around the ring mold. Spoon some of the soufflé mixture into the lemon and carefully remove the ring mold, leaving the foil in place. Repeat this process with the remaining lemons. Smooth the tops with a spatula and refrigerate for at least 3 hours or until set. (See Figure 15-1 for assembling instructions.)

8 When you're ready to serve the soufflé, carefully remove the foil from the lemons and garnish with a few strands of the candied lemon zest.

Assembling the Chilled Lemon Soufflé

1. Place a ring mold on top of the opening in the lemon.

2. Cut a piece of foil 1" wide, long enough to go around the ring mold.

3. Spoon some of the soufflé mixture into the lemon and CAREFULLY remove the ring mold, while leaving the foil in place.

4. Smooth the tops with a spatula... ...and refrigerate for at least 3 hours (or until set).

brrr!!

Figure 15-1:
Putting together the Chilled Lemon Soufflé.

Putting New Twists on Old Favorites

Making gourmet desserts doesn't mean that you have to throw away the recipes for your old favorites (like cakes, pies, and puddings). As you can see in this section, you can make great desserts that start with most basic recipes.

Take a look at your tried-and-true dessert repertoire and think about what you can do to dress up each recipe to make it a little more interesting — and more *gourmet*. Try some of the following suggestions to turn an ordinary dessert recipe into something extraordinary:

- Prepare the dessert in individual servings.

- Add an herb or spice to give the dessert a new flavor.

- Substitute other fruits (or fruit combinations) for a more interesting flavor.

- Add a fruit puree or sauce to the dessert plate.

- Serve the dessert with a sorbet or ice cream that complements the flavors of the dessert.

- Add textural contrast with tuiles.

This may sound overwhelming, but it really isn't that difficult. For example, you can start with a basic cake such as gingerbread, add some sautéed apples, and top it with a loose whipping cream flavored with rum or cinnamon to create a wonderful, tasty, and beautiful dessert. So start looking at those old recipes with an eye toward taking them to the next level.

Plum Upside-Down Spice Cake with Cinnamon Ice Cream

I usually make this upside-down cake in a 9-inch cake pan, but it also works nicely in individual cake pans. You can substitute peaches for the plums in the cake. If you really like caramel sauce, make a little extra and spoon some around the plate with the ice cream.

Specialty tools: *Ice cream machine*

Preparation time: *15 minutes*

Cooking time: *50 minutes*

Yield: *12 servings*

For the Cake:

1 cup brown sugar

3 eggs, at room temperature

2 tablespoons ground cinnamon

$^1/_2$ teaspoon ground cloves

1 teaspoon ground cardamom

$^1/_2$ teaspoon salt

$^1/_2$ teaspoon baking soda

1 tablespoon baking powder

$1^1/_2$ cups flour

1 teaspoon chopped ginger

$^3/_4$ cup melted butter

$^3/_4$ cup half-and-half, at room temperature

12 $^1/_4$-inch-thick round plum slices

$^1/_2$ cup Caramel Sauce (see Chapter 14)

For the Cinnamon Ice Cream:

1 tablespoon ground cinnamon

1 quart Ice Cream Base (see Chapter 14)

1 Butter and flour the inside of a 9-inch-round cake pan.

2 In a small bowl, whip the brown sugar and eggs to a foamy consistency.

3 Sift together the cinnamon, cloves, cardamom, salt, baking soda, baking powder, and flour. Add the chopped ginger and the brown sugar and egg mixture; stir until smooth.

4 Combine the melted butter and half-and-half; add to the egg mixture.

5 Arrange the plum slices in the bottom of the prepared cake pan and pour the caramel sauce over the plums. Pour the batter into the pan and bake at 350° for 45 to 50 minutes or until the cake springs back when touched.

6 To make the ice cream, whisk the cinnamon into the cream in Step 1 of the Ice Cream Base recipe in Chapter 14, and continue with the recipe as listed. *Tip:* You can prepare the ice cream a day ahead if desired.

(continued)

7 Remove the spice cake from the pan while it is still hot and cut it into 12 slices. Serve with the cinnamon ice cream.

Open-Faced Basil-Studded Strawberry and Peach Pie

I love open-faced pie. If you have the time, you can also add a lattice top. In this recipe, the basil adds an interesting flavor — the sweet basil complements the sweetness of the peaches and strawberries, adding complexity at the same time. You can even make a basil syrup or a basil anglaise sauce to go along with this pie.

Preparation time: *30 minutes, plus 1 hour refrigeration*

Cooking time: *1 hour*

Yield: *8 to 10 servings*

Pâte Brisée (see Chapter 14)	*1 tablespoon chopped ginger*
3 cups strawberries, halved	*¹/₄ cup julienned fresh basil*
2 ripe peaches, peeled and sliced into ¹/₄-inch wedges	*³/₄ cup sugar*
	¹/₄ cup flour
1 tablespoon lemon juice	*2 teaspoons grated lemon zest*

1 Line a 12-inch pie pan with the pâte brisée and refrigerate for 1 hour.

2 In a large bowl, combine the strawberry halves, peach slices, lemon juice, ginger, and basil. Sprinkle the sugar, flour, and lemon zest over the top and gently toss together. (Drain any excess juices that collect.)

3 Spoon the filling into the chilled pâte brisée. Bake at 350° for 40 to 60 minutes or until the crust is golden-brown and the filling is cooked. Cool to room temperature before serving.

Poppy Seed Crêpes with Warm Summer Berries and Cream

Crêpes can be made ahead of time and then refrigerated, but you need to reheat them before use. You can make these crêpes with vanilla bean pulp or with spices such as cinnamon or nutmeg.

Specialty tools: *6-inch crêpe pan*

Preparation time: *10 minutes*

Cooking time: *10 minutes*

Yield: *6 servings*

¹/₂ cup water	*¹/₂ cup raspberries*
¹/₂ cup milk	*¹/₂ cup blueberries*
¹/₂ cup flour	*¹/₂ cup huckleberries*
Pinch of salt	*¹/₂ cup sliced strawberries*
1 egg	*4 tablespoons julienned lemon balm*
2 teaspoons poppy seeds	*¹/₂ cup heavy cream*
2 teaspoons melted butter	*1 tablespoon sugar*

1 In a medium bowl, combine ¹/₄ cup of the water and the milk. Whisk in the flour and salt until smooth. Add the egg, poppy seeds, and butter; whisk until fully incorporated.

2 Lightly oil a small crêpe pan. Heat the pan over medium heat for 30 seconds. Ladle approximately 1 ounce of the batter into the center of the pan, just enough to barely cover the bottom of the pan. Quickly roll the pan from side to side, completely covering the bottom of the pan with a thin layer of the batter.

3 Cook the crêpe for 1 minute or until the batter begins to dry. Flip the crêpe over and cook for another 15 seconds. Remove the crêpe from the pan and repeat with the remaining batter until you have 6 crêpes.

4 Place the berries and remaining ¹/₄ cup water in a medium sauté pan and cook over medium heat for 3 to 4 minutes or until warm. Toss with 3 tablespoons of the lemon balm.

5 Place the heavy cream and sugar in a medium bowl and whisk until soft peaks form.

6 Fill each crêpe with the warm berries and fold into quarters. Place a spoonful of the whipped cream over the crêpes and sprinkle with the remaining lemon balm.

Chapter 16

The Grand Finale: Chocoholics Unanimous!

Chocolate can send you flying; it can brighten your mood; and it can satisfy powerful cravings — all while tasting incredible. It's not uncommon for people to eat chocolate for lunch, to sneak bites while no one's looking, or to hide chocolate bars under their bed. Once you have your first taste of chocolate, the addiction begins.

Most serious chocoholics desire chocolate not only in bar form (which is very handy in a pinch) but also in interesting dessert preparations. Rich chocolate tortes, truffles, ganaches, and sauces are a good start. The recipes in this chapter are both intense with chocolate, and elegant and complex in their flavors and presentations.

Chocolate is traditionally served at the end of a dessert progression, and with good reason. The flavors and textures of chocolate desserts are usually very rich, and anything that's served afterward seems to pale in comparison.

A little chocolate history

The word *chocolate* comes from the Aztec language, meaning "bitter water." The Aztecs pounded cocoa and blended it with spices and water to create a drink. The Spanish later began adding sugar to the drink, making it less bitter and more closely resembling our version of hot chocolate. Montezuma, the conqueror of many parts of Central America, made a bitter chocolate drink, or *nectar* as he referred to it, which he drank by the goblet to bring him luck and strength — and to enhance his sexual experiences.

It was said that after you drank the chocolate beverage, you could travel all day without fatigue and without taking any other nourishment. An aphrodisiac of kings *and* an unlimited energy source? Hershey's should get their marketing people hot on *that* concept!

Discovering Different Types of Chocolate

The world loves chocolate, and Americans are no exception — in fact, U.S. consumers purchase the largest share of the world's chocolate production: 2.5 billion pounds a year! Children usually prefer the sweet milk chocolate varieties. However, as your palate matures, you begin to appreciate the more elegant and complex flavors of the semisweet and bittersweet chocolate varieties.

White chocolate

Because it contains no chocolate liquor, *white chocolate* isn't technically chocolate, according to that font of gourmet-cooking wisdom, the U.S. government. *Chocolate liquor* is not something you drink; it's a paste that's made from the pulverized roasted cocoa bean and consists of cocoa butter and cocoa solids. White chocolate contains cocoa butter but not cocoa solids.

Beware of so-called white chocolate that is inexpensive; chances are that it is not made with cocoa butter but with less-expensive vegetable fat. Because of the cocoa butter, the best white chocolates are ivory or cream colored, but never pure white.

Migraine sufferers who cannot consume chocolate may want to give white chocolate a try. Often, people whose migraines are triggered by dark and milk chocolate have more success with white chocolate.

Milk chocolate

Milk chocolate actually contains milk in a dry or concentrated form. It also contains chocolate liquor, cocoa butter, and sugar. Milk chocolate does not keep as well as dark chocolates, such as bittersweet and semisweet chocolate, so buy it in smaller amounts.

Bittersweet and semisweet chocolate

Bittersweet chocolate (which must contain at least 35 percent chocolate liquor) and *semisweet chocolate* (which must contain at least 15 to 35 percent chocolate liquor) are most frequently used in baking. You can use these chocolates interchangeably without significantly altering the outcome of your recipe.

Never substitute milk chocolate or white chocolate for bittersweet or semisweet chocolate without altering the other ingredients of the recipe — these chocolates are much sweeter and will alter the flavor and end result of the dish.

Cocoa

Cocoa powder is the pasty chocolate liquor with a portion of the cocoa butter pressed out. The remaining portion is then finely ground into a powder that contains 10 to 24 percent cocoa butter and no sugar. Two types of cocoa powder are available, and you can use them interchangeably, according to your tastes:

- ✔ **Natural or nonalkalized:** Nonalkalized cocoa is lighter in color and slightly more bitter than the alkalized version.
- ✔ **Dutch-processed cocoa:** *Dutched,* or alkalized, cocoa is less acidic and has a richer, more appealing color.

Cocoa is often used in flourless chocolate cakes, in chocolate custards, and to garnish truffles and tortes.

Choosing Chocolate

Numerous brands of chocolate are available to the consumer, and they come from all parts of the world. Each brand of chocolate has a different taste and texture because of several factors: the quality of the cocoa beans, the cocoa butter content, and the various methods that are used to process the chocolate.

I recommend Valrhona, Hawaiian Vintage Chocolate, Callebaut, Lindt, or Ghirardelli for cooking, or just for eating. These fine chocolates may seem a bit pricey, but you'll find that they're well worth the expense when you taste the finished product.

Storing Chocolate

You should store chocolate tightly wrapped in a cool, dry place — like the pantry. If you store chocolate in a warm place, such as a cabinet above the stove, the chocolate tends to *bloom:* The cocoa butter rises to the surface and covers the outside of the chocolate with white streaks or blotches. The flavor and texture of the chocolate are altered slightly, but you can still use it.

 You can store bitter or semisweet chocolate for years. Milk chocolate and white chocolate, however, should be stored for only about eight or nine months — they contain milk solids, which tend to get stale.

Melting Chocolate

Melted chocolate can be used for dipping fruits or truffles or for making glazes, icings, ganaches, cakes, or even brownies. The best way to melt chocolate is in a bowl over a pot of barely simmering water; chocolate melts smoothest and fastest over low heat. Break the chocolate into small bits before melting it, and remove it from the heat before it melts completely. Chocolate continues to melt when you take it off the heat, and you can always rewarm it if necessary.

 Never cover chocolate while it is melting — doing so can create condensation. (See the following section to find out how to avoid moisture when melting chocolate.)

You can also use a microwave to melt chocolate successfully, but don't melt it at full power. To melt 6 ounces of chocolate in the microwave, I recommend the following times and power levels:

- **Dark chocolate:** $2^1/_2$ minutes at 50 percent power
- **Milk or white chocolate:** 3 to $3^1/_2$ minutes at 30 percent power

Keeping Chocolate from Seizing

How did you turn your chocolate from a shiny, smooth fluid into a dull, thick paste that resembles wet cement? Most likely, one of the following three situations occurred:

- ✔ **Your chocolate burned.** Briefly place your finger in the seized chocolate. If it's very hot or too hot to touch, it's probably burned. Sorry, but it will taste awful and be grainy, so throw it away and start over.

- ✔ **A touch of moisture found its way into your chocolate.** Small amounts of moisture or liquid increase the viscosity of the chocolate to a degree that it stops being fluid and cannot be remelted. The good news is that seized chocolate can be used in recipes that call for the chocolate to be melted with cream or butter, such as in brownies or cakes. To avoid seizing chocolate, make sure that your bowl, knife, cutting board, and everything else that comes in contact with your chocolate is completely dry. Even a wet spoon used to stir the chocolate can cause it to seize.

- ✔ **You added cold liquid to warm chocolate.** If you add melted chocolate to cold whipped cream, you get a bowl full of cream streaked with hard, gritty chocolate flecks. You can avoid this problem by cooling your melted chocolate to room temperature before folding it into your cream, or you can melt the chocolate with a small amount of cream to help loosen its consistency.

Creating the Building Blocks of Chocolate Desserts

The recipes in this section are some of the pieces that you use to make various chocolate desserts. They can all be made ahead of time and stored in the refrigerator so that they're available when you need them. This makes it faster and easier for you to put together more intricate desserts.

Bittersweet Chocolate Ganache

Bittersweet Chocolate Ganache is great to have on hand. You can quickly melt it down and use it as a chocolate sauce, or make it into truffles by scooping it into balls and dusting them with cocoa powder.

Preparation time: *3 minutes, plus 3 hours refrigeration*

Cooking time: *5 minutes*

Yield: *About 3 cups*

12 ounces bittersweet chocolate, chopped   *$1^3/_4$ cups heavy cream*

3 tablespoons butter

1 Place the chocolate and butter in a medium bowl.

2 Place the heavy cream in a small saucepan and bring to a boil over medium heat.

3 Pour the boiling cream over the chocolate and butter and let sit for 3 minutes. Whisk together until smooth.

4 Pour into a container and refrigerate for 3 hours or until firm.

White Chocolate Ganache

White Chocolate Ganache can be rolled into tiny balls for truffles, or cut into shapes and coated with chocolate and nuts for individual candies. You can add some chopped praline to create praline truffles, or you can warm up this ganache and use it as a sauce.

Preparation time: *10 minutes, plus 1 hour refrigeration*

Cooking time: *15 minutes*

Yield: *20 truffles*

6 ounces white chocolate, chopped   *$^3/_4$ cup heavy cream*

$1^1/_2$ tablespoons butter

1 Place the white chocolate and butter in a small bowl.

2 Bring the heavy cream to a boil over medium heat and then pour over the chocolate and butter. Let sit for 3 minutes and then whisk until smooth.

3 Refrigerate for 1 hour or until firm.

Bittersweet Chocolate Glaze

This bittersweet chocolate glaze is a quick icing for a rich torte — all you need to do is pour it over the torte and let it drip down the sides.

Preparation time: *3 minutes*

Cooking time: *3 minutes*

Yield: *Enough to cover an 8-inch torte*

6 ounces bittersweet chocolate, chopped   *1 tablespoon light corn syrup*

¹/₂ cup butter, chopped

1 Place all the ingredients in a small bowl over a water bath (see Chapter 3) and slowly melt over low heat, stirring frequently.

2 Remove the bowl from the water bath and stir the mixture until smooth. Pour over a torte or other desired item while warm.

Blood Orange Chocolate Sauce

Oranges and chocolate are a traditional pairing; the orange flavor adds complexity to regular chocolate sauce. If you can't find blood oranges, regular sweet oranges work just as well. This sauce is the perfect accompaniment to the Chocolate Crêpes with Blood Orange Fillets recipe later in this chapter.

Preparation time: *2 minutes*

Cooking time: *2 minutes*

Yield: *1 cup*

¹/₂ cup heavy cream   *³/₄ cup blood orange juice*

2 ounces bittersweet chocolate, chopped

1 Place the heavy cream in a small saucepan, bring to a boil, and then remove from the heat. Add the chocolate and whisk until smooth.

2 Add the blood orange juice and whisk until smooth. Use while warm.

Caramel Chocolate Truffles

In this recipe, you take caramel chocolate ganache and make it into truffles. *Truffles* are semifirm balls of ganache that are coated with tempered chocolate. They can be made several days in advance and kept in a cool place. They are best, though, at room temperature, when the ganache is slightly soft and luscious. You can use the procedures for coating truffles in this recipe with any type of ganache and any type of chocolate coating. Take a look at these truffles in the color section of this book.

Specialty tools: *Parchment paper*

Preparation time: *10 minutes, plus 3 hours refrigeration*

Cooking time: *10 minutes*

Yield: *20 truffles*

¹/₂ *cup sugar*	*6 ounces bittersweet chocolate, chopped*
2 tablespoons butter	*8 ounces tempered milk chocolate (see the sidebar "Tempering chocolate" for more information)*
³/₄ *cup heavy cream*	

1 To make the ganache: Place the sugar in a sauté pan and melt over medium heat until golden-brown. Add the butter and cream and continue to cook for 2 to 3 minutes or until fully incorporated.

2 Place the chopped bittersweet chocolate in a medium bowl and pour the hot cream mixture over the chocolate. Let sit for 3 minutes and then whisk until smooth.

3 Refrigerate for 3 hours or until firm.

4 Scoop the ganache into small balls with a Parisian scoop or melon baller. Form them smooth and perfectly round with the palms of your hands.

5 Dip your fingers into the tempered milk chocolate and lightly cover the truffles with the tempered chocolate. Place the truffles on a parchment-lined half sheet pan and allow the chocolate to set.

Note: You can keep truffles in the refrigerator for several days, but set them out at room temperature for 30 minutes before serving.

TIP

Tempering chocolate

To temper or not to temper, that is the question. *Tempering* is a process that involves heating and cooling chocolate, resulting in a harder, glossier finish. You don't need to temper chocolate for use in cakes, tortes, butter creams, and ganaches, but tempering is essential when coating candies and truffles or when using the chocolate for decorative purposes.

At room temperature, tempered chocolate dries rapidly to a hard and shiny consistency and breaks with a snap. You can line plastic molds or flexible metal molds with a coating of tempered chocolate to create a chocolate shell for pudding or mousse; after it sets, the chocolate pops out easily. Chocolate that has been melted but not tempered, on the other hand, sets slowly to a soft, dull, streaky texture at room temperature, and it sticks to the inside of a mold. A piece of tempered chocolate keeps at room temperature for a month without losing its luster.

Tempering chocolate takes practice and a little patience. The process involves three steps: slowly heating, cooling, and then re-heating the chocolate. If you follow these steps, your results should be perfect.

1. **Chop the chocolate into small pieces.**

2. **Place the chocolate in a small bowl and then place the bowl in a pot of barely simmering water. Heat dark chocolate to a temperature of 115°; heat milk chocolate or white chocolate to a temperature of 110°.**

   Use a candy thermometer to gauge the temperature of the chocolate.

3. **Remove from the heat. While stirring continually, cool the chocolate to 80°.**

   You can speed up the cooling process by adding a medium chunk of unmelted chocolate to the mixture. (If the piece doesn't melt completely, you can remove it.)

4. **Reheat the chocolate over a water bath to 84° to 86° for dark chocolate, to 82° to 84° for milk chocolate, and 80° to 82° for white chocolate.**

   Now the chocolate is tempered and ready to use.

To make sure that your chocolate is tempered, spread a small amount on a piece of marble or on the side of a chef's knife. If the chocolate is properly tempered, it should set up in minutes and chip off easily with your fingernail.

Chocolate Sauce

Chocolate sauce is easy to make — and you can make this sauce with any type of chocolate. It keeps nicely in the refrigerator and goes with just about anything sweet.

Preparation time: *2 minutes*

Cooking time: *2 minutes*

Yield: *2 cups*

1¹/₄ cups heavy cream

4¹/₂ ounces bittersweet chocolate, chopped

Place the heavy cream in a small saucepan and bring to a boil. Add the chocolate and whisk until smooth. Use while hot.

Chocolate Tart Dough

You can use chocolate tart dough interchangeably with regular tart dough (if the flavor of chocolate complements the main recipe). This dough is not as flaky as regular pie dough, but it has a wonderful flavor and texture.

Preparation time: *7 minutes, plus 1 hour refrigeration*

Baking time: *12 to 14 minutes*

Yield: *Enough for a 9¹/₂-inch fluted tart shell*

6 tablespoons butter

Dash of salt

¹/₂ cup sugar

¹/₃ cup sifted unsweetened cocoa powder

³/₄ teaspoon vanilla extract

³/₄ cup flour

1 Using an electric mixer, cream together the butter, sugar, vanilla, and salt until smooth.

2 Add the cocoa powder and mix until smooth. Add the flour and mix until incorporated.

3 Work the dough into a ball and then cover with plastic wrap. Refrigerate for 1 hour.

4 Roll out the dough on a lightly floured surface until it's ¹/₈ inch thick. Line the inside of a tart or pie pan, discarding any excess dough that hangs over the sides of the pan.

5 Prick the dough all over with a fork. Bake at 375° for 12 to 14 minutes or until the tart is set around the edges. Cool on a rack and use as desired.

Milk Chocolate Ice Cream

This ice cream rules! I often find myself looking at an empty container wondering where it all went. For a more intense flavor, you can use bittersweet chocolate in place of the milk chocolate.

Specialty tools: *Ice cream machine*

Preparation time: *15 minutes, plus 2 hours freezing*

Cooking time: *15 minutes*

Yield: *1 quart*

³/₄ cup heavy cream	*6 egg yolks*
¹/₂ cup half-and-half	*¹/₃ cup sugar*
¹/₂ cup milk	*8 ounces milk chocolate*

1 Place the cream, half-and-half, and milk in a small saucepan and bring to a simmer.

2 Place the egg yolks and sugar in a medium bowl and whisk until combined. Slowly whisk in the hot cream mixture. Add the milk chocolate and whisk until all the chocolate has melted and the mixture is smooth. Pass through a fine-mesh sieve.

3 Cool over an ice water bath (see Chapter 3 for information about water baths) and spin in an ice cream machine. Store in the freezer until needed.

Sweet Honey Chocolate Glaze

The sweetness of the honey in this glaze subtly shines through the bittersweet chocolate, creating a rich flavor that borders on perfect sweetness. You can experiment with all types of honey, such as white honey, vanilla honey, or chestnut honey.

Preparation time: *10 minutes*

Cooking time: *10 minutes*

Yield: *1 cup*

6 ounces bittersweet chocolate, chopped	*2 tablespoons honey*
6 tablespoons butter, chopped	

(continued)

1 Place all the ingredients in a small bowl. Place over a simmering water bath and slowly melt over low heat, stirring frequently.

2 Remove from the water bath and stir until smooth. Pour over a torte or other item while warm.

Chocolate Overkill: How to Get Yours

The chocolaty desserts in this section are a rich, satisfying end to a dessert progression. You make most of them ahead of time, so you can just sit back and enjoy (which is a good thing, because by now you're probably too tired to cook anything anyway!). They are all delicious, and they're guaranteed to take care of any level of chocolate craving.

Bittersweet Chocolate Truffle and Pecan Praline Tart

This recipe is the perfect solution for all those chocoholics who think that bite-sized truffles are just the beginning. This tart is so intense and velvety smooth that you'll be lucky to have any leftovers.

Preparation time: *10 minutes, plus 1¹/₂ hours refrigeration*

Yield: *10 to 12 servings*

1 cup Pecan Praline, ground
(see Chapter 14)

1 Chocolate Tart Dough shell, baked
(see recipe earlier in this chapter)

Bittersweet Chocolate Ganache, warm
(see recipe earlier in this chapter)

Cocoa powder for dusting

1 Sprinkle the pecan praline in the bottom of the prebaked tart shell.

2 Pour the bittersweet chocolate ganache into the tart shell and refrigerate for 1¹/₂ hours or until firm.

3 Dust lightly with cocoa powder and cut into 10 to 12 slices.

Chocolate Almond Torte

You *must* present this torte whole to your guests before slicing it. The shiny, seamless glaze with the toasted almonds makes for a stunning presentation.

Specialty tools: *9-inch springform pan, parchment paper*

Preparation time: *20 minutes*

Cooking time: *40 minutes*

Yield: *10 to 12 servings*

6¹/₂ ounces bittersweet chocolate, chopped

³/₄ cup butter, cubed

2 tablespoons brandy

4 large eggs, separated

³/₄ cup sugar

²/₃ cup ground almonds

¹/₄ cup flour

Bittersweet Chocolate Glaze (see recipe earlier in this chapter)

¹/₂ cup sliced almonds, toasted

1 Combine the bittersweet chocolate and butter in a small bowl. Place over a barely simmering water bath and stir occasionally until melted and smooth. Stir in the brandy and set aside.

2 With an electric mixer on medium-high, whip the egg yolks with ¹/₂ cup of the sugar until pale and thick. Fold in the warm chocolate mixture, ground almonds, and flour.

3 Whip the egg whites at medium speed until soft peaks form. Gradually add the remaining ¹/₄ cup of sugar and beat at high speed until stiff peaks form.

4 Fold the egg whites into the chocolate mixture in 3 additions. Place in a parchment-lined 9-inch springform (or cake) pan. Bake at 375° for 35 to 40 minutes or until a toothpick inserted into the center of the cake shows moist crumbs.

5 Cool the torte completely on a wire rack. (Don't worry; the middle of the torte will fall slightly.) Remove from the pan and peel away the parchment paper. Using a long knife, cut off the rounded top of the cake so that it is completely flat, and remove the crunchy top layer.

6 Return the torte to the wire rack with the bottom side up. Place a sheet of wax paper under the wire rack. Pour the bittersweet chocolate glaze over the torte, starting in the center and working your way out to the edge of the cake in a swirl, letting the glaze fall down the sides of the torte. Don't spread it or you'll cause streaks.

7 Let sit for 10 minutes and then carefully apply the sliced almonds to the sides of the torte. Store at room temperature, uncovered, until ready to serve.

Chocolate Crêpes with Blood Orange Fillets and Blood Orange Chocolate Sauce

Delicate chocolate crêpes filled with pieces of fruit make a light and satisfying dessert. A dollop of whipped cream or a scoop of ice cream is a nice addition to the crêpes.

Specialty tools: *Crêpe pan*

Preparation time: *20 minutes*

Cooking time: *15 minutes*

Yield: *4 servings*

¹/₂ cup plus 2 tablespoons flour

1 tablespoon cocoa powder

1¹/₂ tablespoons sugar

1 teaspoon salt

2 eggs

1 egg yolk

3 tablespoons melted butter

³/₄ cup warm milk

3 blood oranges, broken into sections and membranes removed, with juices reserved

1 cup Blood Orange Chocolate Sauce (see recipe earlier in this chapter)

1 Combine the flour, cocoa powder, sugar, and salt.

2 Place the eggs and egg yolk in a small bowl and whisk together. Add the flour mixture and stir.

3 Add the melted butter and milk and mix until smooth.

4 Heat a 6-inch crêpe pan or small sauté pan over a medium flame for 1 minute. Brush the bottom of the pan lightly with oil or butter. Ladle 2 or 3 tablespoons of batter into the hot pan and quickly tilt the pan to evenly distribute the batter, completely covering the surface.

5 Cook for 2 minutes or until the crêpe appears dry and begins to turn golden-brown. Flip the crêpe and continue cooking on the other side for 30 seconds. Remove from the pan. Repeat this step until you have 12 crêpes.

6 Warm the blood orange fillets in a small saucepan.

7 Warm the blood orange chocolate sauce just prior to use, if necessary.

8 Place a few blood orange segments in the center of each crêpe. Fold the crêpe in half and in half again, creating a triangle.

9 Place three crêpe triangles in the center of each plate. Spoon the blood orange chocolate sauce around the crêpes.

Mini Chocolate Hazelnut Tortes

These mini tortes are an elegant and rich dessert. You can replace the ground hazelnuts in this recipe with hazelnut praline for a crunchier texture, or you can sprinkle the praline onto the sides of the tortes. Turn to the color section of this book for an example of this mouth-watering torte.

Specialty tools: *2-inch ring cutter, parchment paper*

Preparation time: *20 minutes*

Baking time: *35 minutes*

Yield: *8 servings*

6 ounces bittersweet chocolate, chopped

³/₄ cup butter

4 large eggs, separated

³/₄ cup sugar

¹/₂ cup ground toasted hazelnuts

³/₄ cup flour

Sweet Honey Chocolate Glaze (see recipe earlier in this chapter)

Candied Hazelnuts (see following recipe)

1 Line the bottom of a 9-inch cake pan with parchment paper.

2 Combine the chocolate and butter in a small bowl. Melt over a barely simmering water bath, stirring frequently until melted.

3 Whip the egg yolks with ¹/₂ cup of the sugar until pale and thick. Fold in the warm chocolate mixture, toasted hazelnuts, and flour; then set aside.

4 Whip the egg whites until soft peaks form. Add the remaining ¹/₄ cup of sugar and con-tinue to whip until firm peaks form. Fold this into the chocolate mixture in 3 additions.

5 Pour the batter into the prepared cake pan. Bake at 375° for 30 to 35 minutes or until a toothpick inserted into the center shows moist crumbs. Cool on a wire rack and then remove from the pan. Using the ring cutter, cut the torte into 8 individual round cakes (or you can leave it whole and then cut it at the table).

6 Place a piece of parchment paper on a work surface and set a wire rack over the paper. Place the 8 individual tortes on the wire rack and pour the sweet honey-chocolate glaze over the tortes. Do not spread the glaze, but allow it to drip down the sides of the tortes. Let sit for 10 minutes.

7 Place one candied hazelnut in the center of each torte. Serve at room temperature.

(continued)

Candied Hazelnuts

Candied nuts are a great way to jazz up any dessert; they even double as a great snack. You can use this recipe for any type of nut. If you like, make these candied nuts a few days ahead and store them layered with parchment paper in an airtight container.

Specialty tools: *8 bamboo skewers*

Preparation time: *10 minutes*

Cooking time: *10 minutes*

Yield: *8 pieces*

8 whole hazelnuts, peeled   *$^1/_2$ cup sugar*

1 Place a hazelnut on the pointed end of each skewer.

2 Place the sugar in a saucepan and melt over medium-low heat for 15 minutes or until liquid and golden-brown.

3 Dip each hazelnut individually into the melted sugar. Place the skewers in a tall glass with the nut end up, making sure that the nuts don't touch each other. Carefully remove the nuts from the skewers after the sugar hardens.

Profiteroles with Chocolate-Ginger Cream

Delicate *profiteroles,* or cream puffs, beg to be filled with cream — and even more so with chocolate cream (like the ones shown in the color section of this book). If the chocolate-ginger cream is too sweet for your taste, try filling the profiteroles with vanilla or espresso cream. These pastries are great for a dessert reception.

Specialty tools: *Pastry bag, parchment paper*

Preparation time: *20 minutes*

Cooking time: *30 minutes*

Yield: *20 profiteroles*

$^1/_2$ cup butter   *4 eggs*

1 cup water   *Chocolate-Ginger Cream (see following recipe)*

Dash of salt

$^1/_2$ cup flour   *Cocoa powder for dusting*

$1^1/_2$ tablespoons cocoa powder

(continued)

1 In a small saucepan, combine the butter, water, and salt and bring to a boil.

2 In a small bowl, combine the flour and cocoa. Add the flour mixture to the saucepan, stir until combined, and cook for 1 minute. Remove from the heat and transfer to a medium bowl.

3 Crack an egg into the hot dough. Beat vigorously with a wooden spoon until the egg is completely incorporated and the paste is no longer slippery. Repeat this process with the remaining eggs.

4 Spoon the batter into a pastry bag fitted with a $^1/_2$-inch plain tip. Pipe 1-inch mounds 2 inches apart on a parchment-lined half sheet pan.

5 Bake at 400° for 10 minutes. Reduce the oven temperature to 350° and bake for another 15 to 20 minutes or until puffy and hollow. Cool completely on a wire rack. (You can make these profiteroles ahead of time and freeze them.)

6 Place the chocolate-ginger cream in a pastry bag. Make a slit in each profiterole about $^1/3$ of the way down from the top. Squeeze (or *pipe*) the chocolate-ginger cream into each profiterole. Dust with cocoa powder.

Tip: If you don't have a pastry bag, you can fill a sealable bag with the pastry dough or cream and snip off one corner of the bag.

Chocolate-Ginger Cream

Preparation time: *10 minutes*

2 ounces bittersweet chocolate, chopped

1 cup heavy cream

3 tablespoons Preserved Ginger (see Chapter 14)

1 Melt the chocolate with $^1/_4$ cup of the heavy cream and then cool to room temperature.

2 Whip the remaining cream until barely stiff peaks form. Fold in the melted chocolate and chopped preserved ginger.

White Chocolate Frozen Soufflé with Warm Bing Cherries

This light, cool, sweet, and refreshing frozen soufflé is practically foolproof to make and delicious to eat. The warm cherries melt into the rich white chocolate, almost creating a sauce of their own.

Specialty tools: *6 2¹/₂-inch ring molds, parchment paper*

Preparation time: *5 minutes, plus 2 hours freezing*

Cooking time: *10 minutes*

Yield: *6 servings*

8 ounces white chocolate, chopped

1¹/₂ cups heavy cream

2 cups Bing cherries, pitted and quartered

1 Melt the chopped chocolate and ¹/₂ cup of the heavy cream slowly over a double boiler; then cool to room temperature.

2 Place the remaining heavy cream in an electric mixer bowl and whip until stiff peaks form. Fold the melted chocolate into the whipped cream.

3 Place the ring molds on a parchment-lined half sheet pan. Fill to the top with the white chocolate and whipped cream mixture. Using a knife, scrape off the excess so that the mixture is level with the top of the mold. Freeze for 2 hours or until solid.

4 Remove the molds from the freezer. Warm the sides of the molds with a hair dryer or a hot wet towel and then carefully remove the molds.

5 Place the cherries in a small saucepan. Warm over medium heat with a splash of water for 2 to 3 minutes or until hot.

6 Spoon some of the cherries in the center of each plate. Place a frozen soufflé on top of the cherries.

White Chocolate Liquid Center Chocolate Cake with Milk Chocolate Ice Cream

This dessert takes chocolate to a whole new level. Moist, flourless, bittersweet chocolate cake surrounds a center of warm white chocolate ganache that oozes out onto the plate when you cut it. As if that's not enough, a scoop of milk chocolate ice cream adds even more richness.

Specialty tools: *6 1¹/₂-inches-high x 2¹/₂-inches-wide ring molds, parchment paper*

Preparation time: *30 minutes*

Baking time: *30 minutes*

Yield: *6 servings*

9 tablespoons sugar	*3 eggs*
¹/₃ cup water	*6 ounces White Chocolate Ganache (see recipe earlier in this chapter)*
3 ounces bittersweet chocolate, chopped	
¹/₂ cup plus 1 tablespoon cocoa	*Milk Chocolate Ice Cream (see recipe earlier in this chapter)*
9 tablespoons butter, softened	

1 In a small saucepan, bring 5 tablespoons of the sugar and the water to a boil. Remove from the heat. Stir in the bittersweet chocolate and cocoa. Add the butter and stir until completely combined.

2 In a large bowl, use an electric mixer to whip the eggs and 4 remaining tablespoons of sugar to a ribbon (see Chapter 3) or until it has tripled in volume.

3 Fold in the chocolate mixture in 3 additions.

4 Butter the ring molds and place them on a parchment-lined half sheet pan. Fill the molds halfway with the batter. Place a 1-ounce scoop of the white chocolate ganache in the center of the mold and cover with the remaining batter.

5 Bake at 350° for 20 to 25 minutes or until just firm to the touch. Cool briefly before removing the molds.

6 Place a cake on each plate while hot and top with a scoop of ice cream.

Part V
The Home Stretch: Taking It to Your Dinner Table

The 5th Wave   By Rich Tennant

"OK Cookie - your venison in lingdonberry sauce is good, as are your eggplant soufflé and the risotto with foie gras. But whoever taught you how to make a croquembouche should be shot!"

In this part . . .

You may feel confident that you can prepare individual gourmet dishes, but you may need help in combining those dishes to create interesting and appealing menus. This part is here to help. Not only does it show you how to put together a menu for almost any occasion, from a romantic dinner to a summer picnic in the park, but it also tells you which wines to serve with each course.

Chapter 17

From Champagne to Cappuccino: Creating a Complete Meal

*H*ere's the part you've been waiting for: bringing together all your gourmet cooking skills to create a meal that delights and impresses your friends and family. If you're feeling adventurous, use the guidelines in the following section and design your own menu. If you're still a little nervous about this prospect, I've included 13 different menus for you to try. Each menu is made up of recipes found in earlier chapters; simply look in the index to locate them. After each menu, I've listed the things that you can do ahead of time to help in your planning. Remember, proper planning is the key to putting it all together with style.

For each course in the following menus, I've listed several wine recommendations. (You can also see Chapter 18 for more information about pairing wine and food; or read *Wine For Dummies,* also published by IDG Books Worldwide, Inc., for more information about wine in general.) If you can't find some of the wines, you can substitute similar ones — just tell the clerk at your wine store what type of wine you're looking for. But remember that, for many gourmets, the name on the label means everything. To be sure that the wines you serve are as impressive as the food, stay with better-known fine-wine producers and leave the experimenting for a dinner with close friends.

Planning Ahead for a Gourmet Dinner

Planning the perfect gourmet menu can send even the most experienced host over the edge long before the guests arrive. But careful planning can make the difference between a flawless meal and an unmitigated disaster.

Planning a multicourse gourmet menu involves more than just cooking the food, too. To make the whole menu really come together, you need to do the following:

✓ **Creatively match flavors, colors, and textures.** The foods you use in the various courses must complement or give a counterpoint to each other. For example, you wouldn't want to serve a creamy soup followed by pureed vegetables unless the vegetables were accompanied by some type of textural contrast.

✓ **Coordinate cooking times and temperatures.** Make sure that you have enough burners on your stove to have everything ready at the right time. Make sure that you have enough room in your oven, and remember to check the cooking temperatures of things that need to be in the oven at the same time. You can't cook one thing at 400 degrees and another at 250 degrees at the same time!

✓ **Make sure that you have enough cookware, dishes, glassware, and silverware.** Imagine preparing a beautiful soup for a party of eight and realizing at the last moment that you have only seven soup bowls.

The good news is that designing successful dinner party menus gets easier with experience. In the meantime, the following sections give some guidelines to help you get started.

Planning your attack

Before you select specific dishes, you need to strategize:

✓ **Choose your menu a week in advance** so that you have time to get organized — and to make changes to the menu if certain recipe ingredients are not available.

✓ **Try to determine your guests' likes, dislikes, and food allergies.** Make sure to find out whether any vegetarians are on the guest list.

✓ **Don't kill yourself by planning a six- or seven-course meal for ten guests** — unless you expect your guests to help you cook. But if you have several helpers at your disposal, then by all means, give it a shot. Going all out on a meal can be fun!

✓ **Keep the season in mind.** Shorter, lighter menus work well in the summer and spring, whereas heavier foods work better in autumn and winter.

Planning your menu

Deciding on a menu isn't as simple as flipping open a cookbook and picking out a bunch of recipes that sound good. Think about these things as you select the dishes you're going to serve:

✔ **Don't follow strongly flavored courses with very delicate courses.** Garlic is great, and many people love it; but don't serve a roasted garlic spread as an early course, followed by delicate scallops. Your guests will be unable to taste the wonderful flavors of the scallops if they are preceded by spoonfuls of garlic.

✔ **Unless you're planning an "around-the-world" menu, try not to confuse your guests with too many ethnic flavors in the same meal.** There's a difference between *fusion* cuisine and just plain *confusing* cuisine!

✔ **Arrange the menu to first present lighter dishes and then move on to heavier dishes.** Generally, you should begin with cold dishes and serve hot dishes later in the meal. Begin, too, with dishes that lean toward white wines; as the courses become meatier, switch to red wines.

✔ **Avoid having too many dishes that have last-minute preparations.** You don't want to spend the entire evening in the kitchen!

✔ **Stay true to the season's produce.** For example, don't try to locate fresh asparagus, ripe tomatoes, and spring peas in the dead of winter, and don't prepare a root vegetable stew in the middle of summer. Be smart and use the produce available in your market as an inspiration to plan your menu.

✔ **Try not to repeat foodstuffs in the same meal.** For example, if you serve cold poached salmon with asparagus as a first course, you don't want to serve asparagus risotto as an entree.

If you choose to highlight a certain food as a theme in your menu, however, make it apparent throughout the meal. For example, a menu that has potatoes as a central theme should have potatoes present in every course.

✔ **Don't forget dessert, because your guests won't!** Many beautiful desserts can be made a day ahead (or earlier the same day). Chocolate tortes taste even better the next day, ice creams and sorbets can be made ahead of time, and tarts can be prebaked and rewarmed.

Approaching the menu you have selected

After you choose which dishes to serve, you need to plan your time so that you use it efficiently and you get everything ready on time. Make sure that you do the following:

✔ **After you determine a menu, make copies of all the recipes.** Having them all spread out in front of you makes it easier to do your planning without having to keep searching through the book, and it keeps your cookbooks clean.

✔ **Make a comprehensive shopping list.** Include not only the items you need, but notes to yourself as well — for example, 1 cup parsley for parsley oil. Listing what the ingredient is used for can be helpful in deciding whether you can make a substitution if that ingredient isn't available.

✔ **Recheck your shopping list.** I know that you were very careful putting the list together, but check it anyway. Nothing is more frustrating than having three things going on the stove and realizing that you're missing a key ingredient.

✔ **Decide on the china, silver, and glassware that you want to use for each course.** If you plan to reuse any items, it's best to have at least one course between uses to allow time for washing.

✔ **Make sure that you have adequate oven and burner space** — be aware of the preparation times, cooking times, and temperatures required for each recipe. You can't have two things in the oven at the same time that require different cooking temperatures.

✔ **Try to complete most of your preparation ahead of time so that you can spend more time with your guests.** Store the ingredients in separate resealable bags, but make sure that you label everything. (I learned this the hard way. I thought I had two containers of beef consommé, so I mixed them together. Unfortunately, one of them was fry oil — it wasn't pretty.)

Save your menu and notes from each dinner party — they come in handy when planning future dinners.

Menus for Every Occasion

If the thought of planning a gourmet dinner menu from scratch makes you break out in hives, the following menus can help you get started. You can also use these menus to guide you in creating your own unique gourmet dinner menus. Feel free to substitute courses wherever you want; just remember the guidelines listed in the preceding section. Have fun, and bon appétit!

The "Impressing the Boss" dinner

Your boss is coming over for dinner, and you've heard that she's quite a gourmet. Don't hyperventilate; with a few impressive presentations and a little extra effort, you're a shoo-in for that promotion!

Smoked Salmon Beggar's Purse with Crème Fraîche
Non-vintage brut Champagne, such as Bollinger, Krug, or Veuve Clicquot

* * *

Slow-Roasted Cod with Warm Tomato Salad and
Roasted Garlic Vinaigrette
Rich, buttery Chardonnay by Talbott, Au Bon Climat, or
Mount Eden Vineyards

* * *

Barley "Risotto" with Caramelized Root Vegetables, Sliced Beef Tenderloin,
and Fried Parsnip Strips
Any Bordeaux from 1988, 1989, or 1990

* * *

Chilled Lemon Soufflé
Sweet, sparkling wine, such as Moscato d'Asti

* * *

Bittersweet Chocolate Truffle and Pecan Praline Tart
Late-bottled vintage Port from Grahams, Taylor, or Warres

Planning notes:

7 days ahead:	Make the beef stock reduction and freeze it.
3 days ahead:	Roast the garlic.
	Cook the barley.
1 day ahead:	Make the crêpes; then wrap tightly in plastic wrap with waxed paper between the crêpes.
	Make the lemon soufflés.
	Make the chocolate truffle and praline tart.
That morning:	Cut up the smoked salmon.
	Make the fried parsnip strips and store them in an airtight container.
	Clean and dice the root vegetables for the barley "risotto."
	Clean the pearl onions, tomatoes, and lettuce for the cod.
	Marinate the beef.
	Make the roasted garlic vinaigrette.

The "Getting Yourself Out of the Doghouse" dinner

You really messed up this time, and saying "I'm sorry" just isn't working. Nothing heals the heart better than a good meal prepared with a little tender loving care. If this menu doesn't work, give begging a try.

Smoked Salmon Terrine with Horseradish Potato Salad and Lemon-Horseradish Vinaigrette

Champagne with romantic appeal, like Perrier-Jouet Fleur de Champagne, Louis Roederer Cristal, or Dom Perignon

* * *

Parmesan and Eggplant Soup with Parmesan Crisps

* * *

Sautéed Bacon-Wrapped Venison with Wild Mushroom Barley

Big, smoky red wine, such as Ridge Zinfandel from the Geyserville, Sonoma, or Paso Robles vineyards or Gallo Sonoma

* * *

Chocolate Crêpes with Blood Oranges and Blood Orange-Chocolate Sauce

Rich, orangey Sauternes, such as Muscat de Beaume de Venise from Domaine de Coyeux or Paul Jaboulet Ainé

Planning notes:

7 days ahead:	Make the meat reduction and freeze it.
3 days ahead:	Make the parmesan strips and store them in an airtight container.
	Make the orange-chocolate sauce.
2 days ahead:	Cook the potatoes.
	Make the parmesan and eggplant soup.
	Cook the barley.
	Roast the mushrooms.
1 day ahead:	Make the crêpes; then wrap them tightly in plastic wrap with wax paper between the crêpes.
	Make the smoked salmon terrine.
That morning:	Make the horseradish potato salad.
	Make the lemon-horseradish vinaigrette.
	Wrap the venison with bacon.

The "Aphrodisiac" dinner

The libido-enhancing qualities of certain foods have never been scientifically proven, but many people are still willing to test the theorem. Oysters, Champagne, lobster, saffron, caviar, garlic, parmesan, mango, honey, and chocolate all have been purported to be aphrodisiacs. But just in case, an extra glass of Champagne can never hurt.

Raw Oysters on the Half Shell with Champagne Mignonette

Grand Cru Chablis with no oak, such as Drouhin or Moreau

* * *

Lobster and Pulped Avocado Napoleon with Saffron Tuiles and Herb Vinaigrette Sprinkled with Caviar

Crisp, oaky Chardonnay, such as Lewis Cellars Reserve, Kistler, Sonoma-Cutrer, or Gallo Estate Chardonnay

* * *

Cumin-Garlic Spice Rub Roasted Leg of Lamb with Potato-Parmesan Pavé

Spicy, intense Côte-Rôtie from Guigal, Chapoutier, Gentaz-Dervieux, or Jasmin

* * *

Mango Sorbet

Creamy demi-sec, such as Veuve Clicquot White Label

* * *

Mini Chocolate-Hazelnut Tortes

10- to 20-year-old tawny Port from Barros, Graham's, or Yalumba

---

Planning notes:

2 days ahead:	Make the mango sorbet.
1 day ahead:	Make the potato pavé.
	Make the saffron tuiles and store them in an airtight container.
	Make the chocolate-hazelnut tortes.

That morning:	Make the Champagne mignonette.
	Make the vinaigrette (Step 1) for the lobster napoleon.
	Cook the lobster tails and cut into medallions.
	Julienne the jicama and toss it with lemon juice for the lobster napoleon.
	Slice the mango.

The "Sunday Afternoon in the Park Picnic" menu

You probably have at least one picnic basket stored in the back of a closet — and it's probably as good as new! Dig it out; pack it up with these light, summery dishes; and head to the park or to your favorite secret spot. I don't think that you'll want to lug along the whole wine cellar on your picnic, so I've only listed two wine selections for this menu. If getting to your favorite spot involves a backpack and rock-climbing gear, you can easily skip the rosé.

White Bean and Horseradish Spread with Sourdough Crostini
Blended wine, like Caymus Conundrum

* * *

Israeli Couscous Salad with Artichokes and Lemon-Tarragon Vinaigrette

* * *

Grilled Jumbo Shrimp and Vidalia Onion Brochette
Refreshing, young rosé, such as Bruno Clair's Marsannay Rosé

* * *

Assorted Cheeses

* * *

Blueberry and Mango Tart

Planning notes:

3 days ahead:	Make the white bean horseradish spread.
	Cook the Israeli couscous.
2 days ahead:	Make the sourdough crostini.
	Cook the artichokes.
	Make the lemon curd.

1 day ahead:	Make the lemon-tarragon vinaigrette.
	Make the tart shells.
	Make the Asian marinade.
That morning:	Assemble the tarts.
	Put together the brochettes.
	Put together the Israeli couscous salad.

The "Meeting the In-Laws" dinner

Meeting your in-laws is always an intimidating proposition, but you can't avoid it forever. Make the best of it by impressing them with a great meal.

Coconut-Crusted Prawns with Coconut Broth and Curry Oil
Rich Condrieu from Guigal, Vernay, or Cuilleron

* * *

Grilled Beef Teriyaki with Sesame Seeds and Spicy Soy Mustard
American Syrah, such as Columbia, Qupé, or Swanson

* * *

Roasted Monkfish on the Bone with Mustard Spaetzle and Prosciutto
Italian Barbera from Aldo Conterno or Angelo Gaja

* * *

Chocolate Almond Torte
10- to 20-year-old tawny Port from Graham's or Barros

Planning notes:

7 days ahead:	Make the curry oil.
3 days ahead:	Make the spicy soy mustard.
2 days ahead:	Make the coconut broth.
1 day ahead:	Make the spaetzle, boil it, and toss it with a little olive oil to keep it from sticking.
	Make the chocolate almond torte.
That morning:	Put together the beef teriyaki skewers.
	Julienne the prosciutto.

The "Sure Thing" dinner

This is as close as you can get to a foolproof menu. These dishes are all fairly easy to make, and, more important, they're hard to ruin. After making this menu once, you'll find yourself reverting to it over and over.

Braised Pork and Cilantro Dumplings with Spicy Orange Sauce

Crisp, dry, fruity Muscat, such as Meyer-Fonné, Domaine Zind Humbrecht, or Hugel

* * *

New Potatoes with Tiny Lettuces and Red Bell Pepper and Pine Nut Vinaigrette

Toasty Chardonnay from Sonoma-Cutrer Russian River Ranches

* * *

Cumin-Crusted Sautéed Chicken Breast with Morel Mushrooms and Brown Butter Hickory Nut Pan Sauce

Rhone-style wine, such as Le Cigare Volant from Bonny Doon Vineyards

* * *

Vanilla Crème Brûlée

Sauternes-style wine, such as Delice du Semillon from Joseph Phelps

Planning notes:

2 days ahead:	Braise the pork.
	Make the spicy orange sauce.
	Roast the morels.
1 day ahead:	Make the bell pepper vinaigrette.
	Make the potato rings and store them in an airtight container.
That morning:	Assemble the dumplings and poach them.
	Make the anchovy puree for the new potatoes.
	Make the crème brûlée (but caramelize the sugar just prior to serving).
	Cook the potatoes.

The "What Do You Mean One of Them Is a Vegetarian?" dinner

Cooking for a vegetarian can be challenging if you're a meat-and-potatoes person, but vegetable cuisine can also be very exciting. More and more often, cooks are designing menus around vegetables and adding fish or meat only as an afterthought. If you serve the following menu, you'll delight the vegetarian, and the rest of your guests will never even miss the meat. For an avid meat-eater, you can always add a piece of grilled beef, lamb, or chicken to the top of the risotto.

Caramelized Onion Tart with Sweet Curry Crust

Toasty, creamy Champagne, such as Mumm Cramant Grand Cru

* * *

Herb-Crusted Warm Goat Cheese and Grilled Vegetable Salad

*Minerally wine with some acid, such as Sancerre from Cotat,
Lucien Crochet, or Lucien Thomas*

* * *

Asparagus Risotto with Caramelized Fennel and Pearl Onions

*Richer-style Chassagne-Montrachet from Etienne Sauzet, Colin-Deleger,
or Joseph Drouhin*

* * *

Assorted Cheeses

* * *

Open-Faced Basil-Studded Strawberry and Peach Pie

Mildly sweet dessert wine, such as Black Muscat by Elysium

Planning notes:

7 days ahead:	Make the stock for the risotto and freeze it.
3 days ahead:	Mix the curry dough.
	Mix the pie dough.
2 days ahead:	Partially cook the risotto.
	Cook the pearl onions.
1 day ahead:	Make the onion tart.
	Crust the goat cheese (but do not cook it).

That morning:	Make the pie.
	Cut up the cheeses.
	Slice the vegetables to be grilled.
	Clean the mesclun mix.
	Make the vinaigrette.
	Cook the fennel and asparagus.

The "So You Just Inherited Some Extra Cash" dinner

This isn't an everyday menu, but it's a meal that you'll never forget. If you can't find — or afford — all these items at once, try substituting one of these courses in another menu for a luxurious touch.

Caviar-Crusted Tuna Tartare with Avocado and Lemon-Herb Vinaigrette

Luxurious Champagne, such as Veuve Clicquot "La Grand Dame"

* * *

Sautéed Diver Scallop with Tiny White Asparagus, Wilted Greens, and Aged Balsamic Vinegar

Chevalier-Montrachet from Domaine Leflaive, Michel Niellon, or Ramonet

* * *

Seared Foie Gras with Preserved Ginger and Roasted Figs over Toasted Brioche

Complex Sauternes from Chateau d'Yquem

* * *

Grilled Kobe Beef with Salsify, Portobello Mushrooms, and Braised Cranberry Beans with Shaved Truffles

Earthy, complex northern Rhône, such as Hermitage "La Chapelle" by Paul Jaboulet Ainé

* * *

White Chocolate Liquid Center Chocolate Cake with Milk Chocolate Ice Cream

Vintage Port by Grahams, Taylor, or Warres from 1963, 1977, or 1985

Planning notes:

7 days ahead:	Make the brioche and freeze it.
	Make the beef stock reduction and freeze it.
3 days ahead:	Make the preserved ginger.
	Make the ganache for the cake.
2 days ahead:	Braise the cranberry beans.
1 day ahead:	Assemble the cakes (but do not bake them).
	Make the ice cream.
That morning:	Toast the brioche.
	Make the lemon-herb vinaigrette.
	Clean the lettuce for the scallops.
	Blanch the asparagus.
	Clean the foie gras.
	Cook the salsify and cut it in half.

The "Help Me Eat Healthy" dinner

Eating healthy doesn't necessarily mean eating bland and flavorless food. For example, by steaming your fish, you not only eliminate the cooking fat but also guarantee a moist and juicy piece of fish. Remember, if you start with fresh, flavorful foods and cook them with minimal amounts of oil or butter, the results can be delicious *and* low in fat.

Pickled Vegetable Maki Rolls

Champagne, such as Veuve Clicquot Yellow Label Brut, or saki by Momakawa Gold and Hakusan

* * *

Lemongrass Egg Drop Soup with Honey-Glazed Halibut

Alsace Riesling from Domaine Zind Humbrecht, such as Brand, Hengst, or Rangen de Thann

* * *

Warm Bing Cherry Soup with Vanilla Yogurt Sorbet and Apple Chips

Rich, acidic, late-harvest Riesling from Chateau St. Michelle or Blackwood Canyon

---

Planning notes:

3 days ahead:	Make the stock for the soup.
2 days ahead:	Make the Bing cherry soup.
	Make the sorbet.
	Make the apple chips and store them in an airtight container.
1 day ahead:	Pickle the vegetables for the maki rolls.
That morning:	Assemble the maki rolls.
	Clean the spinach.

The "Even Your Teenagers Will Like It" dinner

Life with teenagers is hard enough without having to struggle over dinner, and ordering pizza for a dinner party just doesn't cut it. Instead, try introducing your kids to these interesting twists on "teenager food." And if you serve the sparkling cider with the meal, you won't be able to keep them away from the table!

Tomato, Red Onion, and Roasted Yellow Bell Pepper Flat Bread with Fresh Mozzarella

Chardonnay, such as Cakebread, Chalone, Sonoma-Cutrer, or Logan

* * *

Spicy Cumin-Infused Sweet Corn Soup with Cilantro

* * *

Grilled Venison Tenderloin Steaks with Braised Red Cabbage and Rosemary Potatoes

Smoky, rich red Zinfandel by Ridge, Kenwood, or Deloach

* * *

Plum Upside-Down Spice Cake with Cinnamon Ice Cream

Nonalcoholic sparkling cider from Calvados, or a sweet red wine like Bonny Doon Framboise

Planning Notes:

2 days ahead:	Roast the peppers.
	Make the flat bread crust and store it in an airtight container.
	Make the ice cream.

1 day ahead:	Make the corn soup.
	Braise the red cabbage.
That morning:	Make the spice cake.

The "Seafood Fest" dinner

You don't have to catch your own fish to enjoy the simple pleasures of a seafood meal. This menu will make you feel as if you are dining outdoors on the Cape, breathing in the salty breeze. After a full day on the water or walking along the coast, going home to a refreshing seafood dinner is the perfect end to a memorable summer day.

Sautéed Crab Cakes with Cilantro and Cumin Rémoulade

Delicate Pouilly-Fumé from Serge Daganeau or Didier Daganeau

* * *

Poached Lobster Wontons with Tomato-Saffron Broth

Aromatic, nutty, and complex Chateauneuf-du-Pape blanc, such as Chateau la Nerthe, Domaine de Vieux Telegraph, or Chateau de Beaucastel

* * *

Olive Oil-Poached Swordfish Salad with Spinach, Red Bliss Potatoes, and Calamata Olive Vinaigrette

Spicy, smoky California Sangiovese from Swanson, Silverado, or Shafer Vineyards

* * *

Sautéed Curry-Spiced Tuna with Crispy Polenta and Beef Stock Reduction

Light, fruity, sweet wine, such as Huet Vouvray Moelleux

* * *

Poppy Seed Crêpes with Warm Summer Berries and Cream

Light dessert wine, such as Muscat Beaumes des Venise from Paul Jaboulet

---

Planning notes:

| 7 days ahead: | Make the beef stock reduction and freeze it. |
| 3 days ahead: | Make the roasted garlic puree. |

2 days ahead:	Make the tomato-saffron broth.
	Cook the potatoes and refrigerate them.
	Roast the red bell pepper.
1 day ahead:	Make the rémoulade.
That morning:	Make the crêpes; then wrap in plastic with waxed paper between the crêpes.
	Assemble the crab cakes (but do not cook them).
	Assemble the wontons.
	Make the vinaigrette for the swordfish.
	Cook the polenta and add the roasted garlic.
	Clean the spinach.
	Blanch the wax beans.
	Put together the polenta mixture and refrigerate it.
	Clean all the berries.
	Make the olive vinaigrette.

The "Cook Dinner One Day Ahead So That You Can Enjoy the Party" dinner

Nothing's worse than slaving away in the kitchen while your guests are laughing and enjoying themselves in the next room. The key to solving this problem is to be organized and prepare as much of your menu as possible the day before (or earlier the same day), without having the food suffer.

Potato, Portobello Mushroom, Caramelized Onion, and Goat Cheese Terrine

Full-bodied Puligny-Montrachet from Domaine Leflaive, such as Les Pucelles, Les Combettes, or Les Champ Gains

* * *

Whole Roasted Tomato with Roasted Garlic Soup and Crispy Fried Leeks

* * *

Chicken Roulade with Prosciutto and Artichoke Spinach Puree with Garlic Mashed Potatoes

Rich, acidic Italian Barbera from Angelo Gaja or Aldo Conterno

* * *

Star Anise-Poached Pear Stuffed with Vanilla Marscapone

Sweet, complex Hungarian Tokaji, such as Szt. Tamas, Birslama's, Nyulaszo, or Essencia

* * *

Caramel Chocolate Truffles

Planning notes:

3 days ahead:	Poach the pears.
	Make the truffles.
2 days ahead:	Roast the tomatoes.
	Make the garlic soup.
	Make the crispy leeks and store them in an airtight container.
	Cook the artichokes.
1 day ahead:	Make the potato terrine.
	Peel the roasted tomatoes.
	Stuff the pears.
	Assemble the roulade.
That morning:	Peel and chop the potatoes.

The "Saving Room for Dessert" dinner

If you have a sweet tooth like mine, you know all about looking at the dessert menu before you order your meal. So what could be better than a meal with four desserts? Possibly only a meal with five desserts!

Cold-Poached Salmon with Herb Salad and Lemon-Thyme Vinaigrette

Sauvignon Blanc with herb flavors, such as Duckhorn, Philip Togni, or Spottswoode

* * *

Grilled Lamb Loin and Red Onion Salad with Artichoke Vinaigrette

Intense, earthy Barolo from Giacomo Conterno or Angelo Gaja

* * *

Chilled Melon Soup with Lemon-Ginger Sorbet

Sweet sparkling wine, such as Moscato d'Asti by Saracco

* * *

Warm Pineapple Soufflé with Caramelized Pineapple Slices
Sweet, fragrant late-harvest Riesling from Chateau St. Michelle

* * *

Honey and Maple Syrup-Braised Pears and Pecan Filo Beggar's Purses
Sweet, fruity Hungarian Tokaji, such as Szt. Tamas, Birslama's, Nyulaszo, or Essencia

* * *

Profiteroles with Chocolate-Ginger Cream
Vintage Port, such as Grahams, Warres, or Taylor, from 1963, 1977, or 1985

Planning notes:

7 days ahead:	Make the fish stock and freeze it.
3 days ahead:	Make the preserved ginger.
2 days ahead:	Make the artichoke vinaigrette.
	Make the lemon-thyme vinaigrette.
	Make the sorbet.
	Make the melon soup.
	Braise the pears.
That morning:	Make the profiterole batter.
	Blanch the beans.
	Make the chocolate-ginger cream.
	Bake the profiteroles.
	Chop the onion, carrot, and celery for the poaching liquid.
	Clean the herbs.
	Clean the lettuce.
	Cook the pureed and sliced pineapple.
	Put together the filo beggar's purses (but do not bake them).

The Cheese Course

They say that the English have 250 political parties and three cheeses. The French, on the other hand, have three political parties and 250 cheeses. With that many cheeses to show off, it's no wonder that the French developed the tradition of serving cheese before dessert. That tradition has remained the standard even in American gourmet cuisine.

Cheese courses are generally served with a selection of four to eight bite-sized pieces of cheese on each plate, along with some apple or pear slices and few small pieces of toasted brioche, sourdough bread, French bread, or fruit and nut breads.

If you have a comprehensive book about cheese and a photographic memory, you can go to the market armed with all the information you need. For the rest of us, selecting a good combination of cheeses involves a few basic guidelines and personal tastes. You want to have a mix of softer and harder cheeses that include light and full-flavored varieties. And if that mix includes some color variations, better yet. Go to the market, look over the cheeses, and taste the types that interest you; any reputable market will be happy to give you a small piece to try. After you decide what types to buy, make sure to get only what you can eat within a week, when the cheese is at its best.

Cheese goes very well with red wine, so if you have designed a menu with only one red wine course, you may want to follow it with a cheese course to allow your guests to enjoy the rest of their wine.

Literally hundreds of different kinds of cheese exist. Table 17-1 lists some of the types you may not be familiar with to help guide you the next time you get overwhelmed at the deli case.

Table 17-1	Soft, Semi-Soft, and Hard Cheeses
Name	*Characteristics*
Soft and Semi-Soft Cheeses	
Abbaye de la Coudre	Strong, penetrating smell with a smooth elastic texture
Brillat-Savarin	Buttery texture, smells of light mold and cream, tastes slightly sour
Bel Paese	Mild, buttery taste
Blue de Bresse	Soft and creamy, blue veins, milder than most blues
Boursault	Cream-enriched, very smooth and mild
Brie	Creamy and buttery
Bucheron	Soft and creamy with a tang
Camembert	Creamy and somewhat tangy
Crottin de Chavignol	Has a rancid smell when dried or a fermentation smell when in tubs, and a sharp taste
Explorateur	Triple cream, mild and creamy flavor

(continued)

Table 17-1 *(continued)*

Name	Characteristics
Feta	Crumbly, tangy, salty
Gorgonzola	Semi-pungent blue
Havarti	Cream-enriched, buttery, often contains caraway seeds
Liederkranz	Smooth, highly flavored, and strongly aromatic
Limburger	Very strong taste and aroma
Montrachet	Creamy and mild
Muenster	Mild and pungent
Point-L'Eveque	Savory with a pronounced tang
Port-Salut	Smooth and buttery
Roquefort	Semi-soft, blue-veined, with a sharp flavor
Valencay	Light goat smell, slightly tart
Hard Cheeses	
Appenzeller	Firm with a fruity taste
Caerphilly	Firm, flaky, slightly salty
Cheshire	Firm like cheddar if white or orange, piquant if blue-veined
Edam	Known for its red casing; mild when young, sharper later
Emmentaler	Mild with a nutty flavor
Fontina	Nutty with a strong aroma
Gruyère	Firm with widely dispersed holes and a nutty flavor
Jarlsberg	Firm and buttery, with a slight tang
Provolone	Usually smoked, firm, mild when new, piquant when aged
Romano	Pale yellow, very firm, sharp and tangy
Stilton	Crumbly blue

Part VI
The Part of Tens

The 5th Wave   By Rich Tennant

"Do I like arugula? I _love_ arugula!! Some of the best beaches in the world are there."

In this part . . .

*I*f you're looking for inspiration, or you're just taking a break in the middle of a recipe, you can come to this part. These quick chapters give you information about classic food and wine pairings, gourmet restaurants around the globe, sources of gourmet tools and foods, and handy food and wine reference books.

Chapter 18

Ten Classic Food and Wine Pairings

*P*airing gourmet foods with *just* the right wine can be one of the most exciting parts of planning a meal, but it can also be the most confusing part. Generally, pairing food with a wine that complements it is a trial-and-error process that involves your own personal tastes.

The old school of thought about white wine with fish and red wine with meat is understandable, but not entirely correct. When pairing food and wine, the preparation of the food is as important as the food itself. For example, tuna served as sushi would go perfectly with a Champagne or a Riesling, because these light wines have enough acidity to cut through the oiliness of the tuna but are not so rich as to hide its delicate flavors. But if the tuna is grilled, you would want to serve it with a Pinot Noir, because grilling adds richness and texture to the tuna that is well matched, yet not overpowered, by a lighter-style red wine.

I know that this seems confusing; unfortunately, though, there are no easy answers in food and wine pairing. If you're looking for some relatively simple rules to start with, try the following matches:

- Oily foods with crisp wines that have high acidity

- Meaty-fat foods with wines that have tannins

- Salty foods with high-alcohol or effervescent wines

- Fruit with wines that have oak flavors

Trying the classic food and wine combinations in this chapter can help you develop a taste for which wines best complement different types of foods and preparations.

Sauternes and foie gras

Sauternes and foie gras is probably the most classic wine and food pairing that exists. By that, I mean that if you ask wine professionals what to pair with foie gras, their immediate answer will be Sauternes.

Foie gras is almost always served with a fruit element. The fruit element of the foie gras complements the sweet, rich flavor of the Sauternes, while the acidity of the wine cuts through the fat in the foie gras. Even though both foie gras and Sauternes have rich flavors, they complement each other rather than masking each other's delicate flavors.

Sauvignon Blanc and smoked salmon

Sauvignon Blanc and smoked salmon is another traditional food and wine pairing. Smoked salmon is very delicate — and the herbal characteristics and fresh acidity of the Sauvignon Blanc really complement that delicateness.

Sancerre, which is made from Sauvignon Blanc, also plays well against smoked salmon because of the mineral flavors, or "earthiness," in the Sancerre.

Port and blue cheese

Port and blue cheese create another great marriage of wine and food. Many blue cheeses are very pungent, so you need a rich wine to cut through the richness of the cheese. Port is the perfect wine for the job — port is *fortified,* meaning that alcohol is added to stop the fermentation process. This leaves the wine with sweetness and a higher-than-normal alcohol content. The higher alcohol content perfectly offsets the saltiness of the cheese, and the sweet berry flavors of the port enhance the sweetness of the cream in the blue cheese.

Champagne and oysters

Champagne and oysters are another great food and wine combination. Similar to salmon, oysters go well with wines that have a dry, minerally, or earthy characteristic to them. The mineral flavors in the wine are perfectly matched by the "sea" flavor of the oysters. Because most *brut,* or dry, Champagnes are crisp and light (which enhances the mineral flavors of the wine), Champagne complements oysters nicely. The bubbles in the Champagne also have a cleansing quality that can reduce the aftertaste of some oysters.

Chardonnay and lobster

When selecting a wine to accompany a particular dish, think about what other flavors would complement the main dish. For example, lobster is traditionally served with drawn butter, which adds great flavor without masking the delicate richness of the lobster. Chardonnay has always been a great accompaniment to lobster for the same reason — the Chardonnay grape is well-known for its "buttery" characteristic. The buttery Chardonnay complements the lobster, but is not so overwhelming as to hide the incredible flavor of fresh lobster.

Côte-Rôtie and lamb

Lamb and Northern Rhône wines, specifically Côte-Rôtie, have always been a perfect pair. Côte-Rôtie is known for its richness and aromatic intensity. This wine offers a spicy, berry-fruit characteristic that enhances certain gamey qualities in the lamb. If you're grilling the lamb, better yet: Côte-Rôties are known for a smoky characteristic that matches the smokiness of wood-grilled meat.

Burgundy and game birds

Game birds and Burgundy are another great combination. Game birds, particularly squab and quail, are a common food staple in the Burgundy region of eastern France — and the wineries seem to inherently produce wines that go well with the foods eaten in the areas around the winery. Quail is closer to white meat, so a white Burgundy works well with most recipes that include quail. The earthy characteristics of a Chassagne or Puligny Montrachet enhance the gaminess of the quail. A rosé from Burgundy is a good match for quail as well.

Squab, on the other hand, has a delicate red meat, making red Burgundy or Pinot Noir the perfect counterpart to this game bird. These oaky wines embody an almost-candied berry characteristic. These two flavors are a marvelous pairing with the lightly gamey meat of the squab because the berry flavor complements the meat, while the oak and light tannins cut through the fat.

Chilled vodka and caviar

The ethnic origins of a food often can help you choose the best wine to complement the dish. For example, some of the best caviar in the world comes from Russia, which is not known for its wine — but *is* known for its vodka.

Caviar can be difficult to pair with any wine other than Champagne. Caviar is quite salty, and alcohol cleanses the salt from your palate. Although the cleansing effervescence of a Champagne works well to cleanse your palate, few wines have a high enough alcohol content (or the effervescence) to do so. Chilled vodka, on the other hand, goes perfectly with caviar. By chilling the vodka, you reduce the alcohol flavor and also enhance the mineral characteristics of the vodka.

You probably don't want to do a vodka progression with your meal, but instead of beginning the meal with a martini, try a good, chilled vodka, such as Stolichnaya Cristal, Ketel One, or Belvedere, with a bit of caviar. You'll feel like you're on *Lifestyles of the Rich and Famous.*

Sancerre and goat cheese

Sancerre and other Sauvignon Blanc-based Loire Valley wines, such as Pouilly-Fumé, are the perfect partner to goat cheese. The Loire Valley is famous for its different types of goat cheese, one of which is Crottin de Chavignol. Chavignol is a village within the region of Sancerre, and winemakers there make their wines to go with the cheese. The racy acidity and mineral, or earthy, qualities of Sancerre wines make these wines perfect for the delicate and slightly powdery characteristics of most *chèvre* (goat) cheeses.

Cabernet Sauvignon and beef

Cabernet Sauvignon and beef are another great combination. Most Cabernets have a black currant or cassis flavor that complements the flavor of beef, while the tannins in the wine help to cut through the fat in the beef. This combination works even better if the meat is grilled — the toasty characteristics of the oak flavor in the wine perfectly complement the grilled flavor of the meat.

Chapter 19

Ten Dining Cities and Their Recommended Gourmet Restaurants

*E*ven though you're well on your way to becoming a gourmet chef yourself, it's always a good idea to check out the competition. Here's a list of my favorite restaurants around the world.

Boston, Massachusetts

Biba

Reading the whimsical menu is always a treat in this Boston dining institution. High energy, a striking modern decor, and a well-dressed crowd give this place a sophisticated feel. Breads from the Tandoori oven are outstanding. Biba also has a small and interesting bar menu.

Cuisine: Eclectic American
Chef/Owner: Lydia Shire
272 Boylston St.
Boston, MA 02116
617-426-7878

L'Espalier

Set in a beautiful townhouse, this is Boston's most refined dining spot. Exotic ingredients, polished service, and a fine wine list complete the package. The chef's degustation menu is the way to go.

Cuisine: Contemporary French
Chef/Owner: Frank McClelland
30 Gloucester St.
Boston, MA 02115
617-262-3023

Olives

Food lovers from all over have been packing chef Todd English's open-kitchen restaurant every night since it opened in 1989. They come for the fantastic homemade pastas, the wood-grilled meats, and a long list of ever-changing daily specials that sound so good that it's almost impossible to decide what to order. Get there early, as they don't take reservations for parties of fewer than six. Also, save room for the Chocolate Falling Cake or one of the other outstanding desserts.

Cuisine: Mediterranean Country-Style
Chef/Owner: Todd English
10 City Square
Charlestown, MA 02129
617-242-1999

Chicago, Illinois

Of course, your first choice in Chicago should be Charlie Trotter's (located at 816 W. Armitage, Chicago, IL 60614; telephone 773-248-6228), but the following restaurants are a wonderful representation of dining in the city.

Arun

The simple surroundings and the artwork (created by Arun himself) do not prepare you for the amazing gustatory experience you'll have here. The beautiful dishes that the chef creates by using the freshest possible ingredients will dazzle you. For a real treat, put yourself in Arun's hands and let him create a tasting menu for you; I guarantee that you'll experience flavors you've never had before.

Cuisine: Upscale Thai
Chef/Owner: Arun Sampanthavivat
4156 N. Kedzie Ave.
Chicago, IL 60618
773-539-1909

Le Français

Roland Liccioni's food is beautifully presented in a very gracious setting, somewhat like a French country manor. Le Français has astute service and an excellent wine list. Make sure that you try some of their excellent chocolate truffles.

Cuisine: Contemporary French
Chef/Owner: Roland and Mary Beth Liccioni
269 S. Milwaukee Ave.
Wheeling, IL 60090
847-541-7470

Gordon

This contemporary setting features a live jazz trio and dancing on Saturday nights, and a pianist performs on other days. You can order à la carte from the eclectic American menu, or you can try the daily tasting menu prepared by the chef.

Cuisine: Contemporary American
Owner: Gordon Sinclair
500 N. Clark St.
Chicago, IL 60610
312-467-9780

London, England

Aubergine

This is probably the finest French restaurant in London. Aubergine has superb service in a light, airy setting that's filled with natural light that shines through its numerous skylights. Chef Gordon Ramsay creates an amazing tasting menu for lunch and dinner. Make sure to try the marvelous array of French cheeses that are available at the end of the meal.

Cuisine: French
Chef: Gordon Ramsay
11 Park Walk
London SW10 0AJ
0171-352-3449

Le Manoir aux Quat' Laisons

This beautiful manor in the Oxfordshire countryside features elegant lounges and rooms that are filled with antique furniture. The chef, Raymond Blanc, is a master at drawing out the essence of the purest products and creating exciting dishes.

Cuisine: Eclectic French
Chef: Raymond Blanc
Church Road
Great Milton, Oxford OX44 7PD
0184-427-8881

Zafferano

This intimate restaurant is located in a storefront in Sloane Square, just blocks from Harrods and Harvey Nicks. Zafferano has a great wine list that features many different types of Italian wines. You order by the number of courses you want to have; but no matter how many courses you choose, make sure that you try the Wind-Dried Tuna Salad and the Black Truffle Risotto.

Cuisine: Contemporary Northern Italian
Chef: Giorgio Locacelli
15 Lowndes St.
London SW1X 9EY
0171-235-5800

Los Angeles, California

Campanile

Mark Peel and his wife, Nancy Silverton, transformed Charlie Chaplin's former office building into one of the most popular spots in Los Angeles. An open kitchen and an enclosed courtyard provide the backdrop for excellent wood-grilled items, as well as great pastas and vegetable dishes. Wine plays a big role here, with a small but very interesting list. Nancy is one of the country's premier pastry chefs, so check out the breads and desserts, too. When I'm in town, I never miss the great breakfasts.

Cuisine: Californian
Chefs/Owners: Mark Peel and Nancy Silverton
624 S. La Brea Ave.
Los Angeles, CA 90036
213-938-1447

Matsuhisa

I love chef Nobu's creativity and always look forward to having him and his amazing staff create a menu for me. Although this is where it all started and where Nobu spends much of his time, he also has restaurants in New York and London, with more on the way. The restaurant is crowded and noisy, and reservations are difficult to get, but the food makes it worth all the trouble. Super-fresh sushi, plus innovative Japanese dishes with hard-to-find items flown in from the Far East, make dining here an exciting adventure.

Cuisine: Japanese gourmet seafood and sushi
Chef/Owner: Nobu Matsuhisa
129 N. La Cienega Blvd.
Beverly Hills, CA 90211
310-659-9639

Patina

A simple and elegant space provides the stage for the sophisticated food and wine lovers who have made this one of the premier tables in town. Chef Joachim Splichal is well-known for his creative potato dishes — one of my favorites is the Santa Barbara Shrimp with Mashed Potatoes and Black Truffles. Here, too, you can find LA's most dedicated wine program, with a great sommelier and a serious wine list.

Cuisine: French-Californian
Chef/Owner: Joachim Splichal
5955 Melrose Ave.
Los Angeles, CA 90038
213-467-1108

Melbourne, Australia

Blake's

This modern and very busy bistro is the perfect place to sit and watch the world go by. It's situated right along the Yarra River on the ground level of Southgate Complex. Blake's has a nice wine list with a major emphasis on high-quality Australian wines. I like the way that they suggest a wine by the glass for every dish on the menu.

Cuisine: Australian Bistro
Southgate Complex
Ground Level
South Melbourne
03-9699-4100

Flower Drum

Owner Gilbert Lau is certainly one of the world's most gracious hosts, and his restaurant provides one of the greatest dining experiences in Australia. Exotic foods are always available, as well as more-familiar Chinese dishes. Try the daily specials; they're great. This is a very large restaurant, but getting a table is always difficult — make sure to book your reservations early.

Cuisine: Cantonese
Owner: Gilbert Lau
17 Market La.
Melbourne
03-9662-3655

The Pavillion

Located right on the beach, this open and airy spot was once a bathing pavilion. Owners Gail and Kevin Donovan have created a beautiful modern space that opens up to the water. They serve a menu that focuses on fresh seafood of the highest caliber. In good weather, the place to be is on the outdoor patio, just steps from the sand.

Owners: Gail and Kevin Donovan
Cuisine: French/Fusion
40 Jacka Boulevard
St. Kilda Beach
03-9534-8221

New Orleans, Louisiana

Bayona

Located in a serene area of the French Quarter, this beautiful room, set in a renovated 19th-century cottage, abounds with fresh flowers and exudes a sense of tranquillity. This is the perfect spot to enjoy a leisurely lunch or dinner of chef Susan Spicer's creative Creole-inspired American fare. Try the Duck Breast in Red Pepper Jelly, which is phenomenal. In good weather, ask for a table on the small but lovely outdoor patio.

Cuisine: Contemporary American
Chef/Owner: Susan Spicer
430 Rue Dauphine
New Orleans, LA 70112
504-525-4455

Commander's Palace

If you look up *hospitality* in the dictionary, you should see a picture of the Brennan family, who have been operating a restaurant in this Garden District mansion since 1880. Here, you can experience what New Orleans is all about: great food, great service, and great people. All the classic New Orleans dishes are served here, as well as more contemporary dishes, and they have a superb wine list. Don't miss the Sunday Jazz Brunch, a New Orleans tradition. Leave room for the cheesecake, too; the chef learned the recipe from his grandmother, and it's amazing.

Cuisine: Haute Creole
Chef: Jamie Shannon
1403 Washington Ave.
New Orleans, LA 70130
504-899-8231

Emeril's

If you're into food, a visit to New Orleans is not complete without a stop here. Chef Emeril Lagasse bumps Creole cooking up a notch, which is why this large, high-energy, modern space is always packed. The menu is huge and combines dishes that change daily with many dishes that have become Emeril classics. Try the Double Cut Grilled Pork Chop with Tamarind Glazed Roasted Sweet Potatoes or the Grilled Andoulli Sausage with homemade Worcestershire sauce, for example. You'll also find that Emeril's has one of the most serious wine lists in the U.S., with a master sommelier on staff as well. If you can't decide what to have, order the tasting menu composed daily by the chef.

Cuisine: New New Orleans
Chef/Owner: Emeril Lagasse
800 Tchoupitoulas
New Orleans, LA 70130
504-528-9393

New York, New York

Aquavit

Set in a beautiful townhouse, Aquavit has a lovely bar on the main level, where you can enjoy light fare, and a bright, beautifully appointed dining room downstairs. The chef's extensive training in Europe helps him add interesting twists and turns to the traditional Scandinavian dishes that you may have thought you'd find here. Everything is wonderful, with fresh, vibrant flavors abounding. They also have a large selection of flavored Aquavits that are fun to try.

Cuisine: Innovative Scandinavian
Chef: Marcus Samuelsson
13 W. 54th St.
New York, NY 10019
212-307-7311

Lespinasse

One of the United States' most regal, elegant, and romantic rooms, this palace of gold provides the backdrop for some of the country's most innovative and exciting food. This is fine dining at its highest level. Chef Kunz brings flavors from around the world to his ever-changing creative menu. If available, request the Oxtail with Black Truffles — a great dish that's amazing for its simplicity and great flavors. However, a chef's tasting menu is also in order here, because everything is superb. Tables are well spaced, a true luxury in a major city where space is always at a premium.

Cuisine: French with Asian influences
Chef: Gray Kunz
St. Regis Hotel
2 E. 55th St.
New York, NY 10022
212-339-6719

Restaurant Daniel

Daniel Boulud is at the top of his game. On the top rung of restaurants in the U.S., this restaurant is on par with the greatest restaurants in Europe (and it's a lot closer to home!). Everything is excellent, including the stellar wine list. This is another place where a tasting menu is in order, and where truffles and foie gras rule. But make sure to save room for the fantastic desserts, too.

Cuisine: French
Chef/Owner: Daniel Boulud
20 E. 76th St.
New York, NY 10021
212-288-0033

Paris, France and surrounding areas

Alain Ducasse

Truly one of the great restaurants — and chefs — of the world. Chef Alain Ducasse has an extraordinary grip of ultra-modern cuisine. His restaurant is set in a luxurious townhouse in the heart of Paris.

Cuisine: Modern French
Chef/Owner: Alain Ducasse
59, Avenue Raymond Poincare
75016 Paris
01-47-27-12-27

Arpège

I had my first meal here in 1993, and have been drawn back many times. Chef Alain Passard's menu relies on updated classics that are perfectly executed, as well as some highly original dishes. I'll never forget the delicious Caramelized Tomato with Pan Caramel Sauce and Vanilla Ice Cream that he served us for dessert. They also have a well-chosen wine list with pricing that is more reasonable than at many of the other Michelin three-star restaurants.

Cuisine: Modern French
Chef/Owner: Alain Passard
84, rue de Varenne
75007 Paris
01-47-05-09-06

Auberge de l'Éridan

This is one of the ultimate destinations in the world for any lover of food and wine. Located about 45 minutes from Geneva, Switzerland, the restaurant has one of the most picturesque settings I've seen: It sits on the edge of Lake Annecy with the French Alps towering behind. The chef, Marc Veyrat, is one of France's most innovative chefs, creating luscious dishes from local foods. I strongly recommend staying in one of the 11 rooms or suites to complete the experience. The restaurant and hotel are very costly, but it doesn't get much better than this.

Cuisine: Modern French
Chef: Marc Veyrat
13 Vieille Route des Pensières
74290 Veyrier-du-Lac
04-50-60-24-00

Les Loges de l'Aubergade

Chef Michel Trama welcomes you to experience his simple and unexpected creations. He has his own vintage wine called *Buzet,* which is definitely worth trying. After dinner, you can relax and enjoy Havana cigars and old armagnacs.

Cuisine: Modern French
Chef: Michel Trama
52, rue Royale
47270 Puymirol
04-53-95-31-46

Le Moulin de Mougins

Chef Roger Vergé creates cuisine with passion. Seven rooms and suites are available to prolong your stay at his wonderful restaurant, which he owns with his wife, Denise.

Cuisine: Classic French
Chef: Roger Vergé
424, Chemin du Moulin
Quartier Notre-Dame-de-Vie
06250 Mougins
04-93-75-78-24

Pierre Gagnaire

Gagnaire did not miss a beat in his move from Saint-Étienne (outside Lyon) to Paris. Though I miss the grandeur of his former restaurant, I love the fact that such a major talent is now located in a much more accessible place. No question, Gagnaire is one of the world's most innovative and creative chefs. Every meal here is an adventure. This small restaurant (it has just 44 seats) is a culinary treasure that is a must for any adventuresome gourmet.

Cuisine: Modern French
Chef/Owner: Pierre Gagnaire
6, rue Balzac
75008 Paris
01-44-35-18-25

San Francisco Bay area, California

Aqua

I think that Aqua is one of San Francisco's most beautiful rooms, especially during lunch, when the daylight fills the room. Soft colors, great lighting, and fresh flowers create a wonderful atmosphere that is perfect for chef Michael Mina's always-changing menu. The emphasis here is on seafood of the highest quality and freshness. Great service, a well-chosen wine list, and superb desserts make this one of my favorite San Francisco stops.

Cuisine: Californian
Chef: Michael Mina
252 California St.
San Francisco, CA 94111
415-956-9662

Chez Panisse

Chef/owner Alice Waters writes the daily *prix fixe* (fixed price) menu for the dining room. At the beginning of the week, the menu has fewer courses and a lower price; toward Friday and Saturday, several courses are added, and the price goes up as well. There's a cafe on premise, too, if you don't care for the *prix fixe* menu of the dining room. Chef Waters is known for her love of organic vegetables and simply flavored dishes.

Cuisine: Californian
Chef/Owner: Alice Waters
1517 Shattuck Ave.
Berkeley, CA 94709
510-548-5525

The French Laundry

Thomas Keller's tranquil restaurant in Napa Valley is a treasure. Set in a house that was once a laundry, the restaurant serves up some of the finest cuisine on the entire West Coast. Top that with the fact that the setting alone is worth the trip, and this place becomes hard to beat. The only problem with this restaurant is getting a table — make sure to reserve one early.

Cuisine: American and French
Chef/Owner: Thomas Keller
6640 Washington St.
Yontville, CA 94599
707-944-2380

Rubicon

The food is excellent, but the wine rules in this great spot in San Francisco's financial district. Master sommelier Larry Stone, one of the world's greatest wine professionals, is worth the trip; his knowledge of wine will astound you. He has put together a list with a lot of hard-to-find California wines, as well as offerings from Europe and beyond.

Cuisine: French-Californian
Owners: Robin Williams, Francis Ford Coppola, Drew Nieporent, and
    John Gaul
558 Sacramento St.
San Francisco, CA 94111
415-434-4100

Stars

With its high ceilings, long bar, and open kitchen, this is one of the greatest grand cafe/bistro restaurants in the world. The chef, Jeremiah Tower, is one of the founding fathers of California cuisine. The straightforward Californian-American menu and well-chosen wine list draws a mixed crowd of locals and tourists. Try to sit at the small food bar, where you can catch all the action.

Cuisine: Contemporary American
Chef/Owner: Jeremiah Tower
150 Redwood Alley
San Francisco, CA 94102
415-861-7827

Terra

The dining rooms in this white-tablecloth restaurant have exposed brick walls and hardwood floors. The simple elegance of the dining rooms has a California cellar ambiance that is comfortable yet charming at the same time, and the service is friendly. I recommend the sweetbreads as a main course.

Cuisine: Southern French and Northern Italian
Chef/Owner: Hiro Sone
1345 Railroad Ave.
St. Helena, CA 94574
707-963-8931

Sydney, Australia

Kables

Located in one of Sidney's top hotels, you'll find Kables to be one of the city's temples of grand cuisine. The chef is one of the most dedicated and hard-working in the city, and it shows. With its impressive wine list, this restaurant is a must for wine lovers.

Cuisine: Australian
Chef: Serge Dansereau
Regent of Sydney
199 George St.
The Rocks
Sydney
02-9238-0000

Rockpool

This is possibly Sydney's most popular restaurant, and for good reason. Chef/owner Neil Perry serves an eclectic menu that concentrates on using fresh local ingredients but draws on flavors from around the world. The great use of color also exudes a very cool and happening atmosphere. No wonder Rockpool is packed nightly with Sydney's "power" crowd.

Cuisine: Contemporary Mediterranean/Thai
Chef: Neil Perry
107 George St.
The Rocks
Sydney
02-9252-1888

Tetsuya's

Located about 15 minutes from downtown, Tetsuya's is not easy to find. From the outside, you may ask yourself, "Am I in the right place?" — but, believe me, you're in the right place. Consider yourself lucky if you have a table in the restaurant that serves what may be the most exciting and creative food in Australia. Chef Tetsuya operates his tiny kitchen with a dedicated staff that seems to be able to read his mind and anticipate his every unpredictable move. This reservation is tough to get, so book it as far in advance as possible.

Cuisine: Fusion
Chef/Owner: Tetsuya Wakuda
729 Darling St.
Rozelle
02-9555-1017

Chapter 20

Ten Charlie-Endorsed Vendors

. . . .

In This Chapter

▶ Finding hard-to-get gourmet foods

▶ Ordering gourmet food over the World Wide Web

. . . .

Although I've tried to use easy-to-find ingredients for the recipes in this book, you may want to try a recipe that calls for something that your neighborhood grocery store doesn't carry. The vendors that I list in this chapter supply a variety of gourmet foods and products, which you can order by phone or even through the Internet. These vendors are especially helpful for people who live in small towns and rural areas and may not have access to specialty-food markets.

American Spoon Foods

American Spoon Foods offers an assortment of over 100 high-quality preserves, dried fruits, fruit butters, condiments, sauces, and vinaigrettes. They have everything from kumquat-orange butter and pineapple passion fruit butter to blueberry blossom honey and dried Michigan morel mushrooms. You can give them a separate ship-to address and gift card information to send food products as gifts, too. They have retail shops in Michigan and Maryland, and their products are also available in some retail outlets. To get more information or to order a catalog, call 800-222-5886. You can also order a catalog or products through their Web site at www.spoon.com.

Browne Trading Company

I order most of the seafood for the restaurant from Browne Trading Company in Portland, Maine. They have every type of fish and shellfish you can imagine (and a few you can't imagine). Browne is a great source for diver scallops, caviar, tuna, salmon, lobster, crabmeat, hamachi, and just about any other fish found on eastern shores. They even carry Charlie Trotter's Citrus Cured Smoked Salmon! (I had to get that plug in somewhere.) Browne's products are very fresh; in fact, fish brought to the docks today is in my restaurant tomorrow. You can order by calling 207-766-2402 or 800-944-7848.

Charlie Trotter's

Here's one more plug for my products. Since my first cookbook was published, I've gotten hundreds of phone calls from people wondering where to get some of the different pieces of equipment that I use in the recipes. Most of the equipment that I use is available only in institutional sizes, so I decided to have a few good-quality pieces made that would be more appropriate for home cooks. It all started with terrine molds (which are used in Chapter 12), but I recently added fish spatulas, ring molds, cutters, and pallet knives to the list. These items are used throughout this book. For information about ordering these products, call 773-248-8949.

Dean & Deluca

Dean & Deluca started out as a neighborhood grocery store in the SoHo area of New York City. About 15 years ago, they started a small mail-order business that has been parlayed into *the* premier gourmet cooking catalog. Dean & Deluca carries everything from truffles, caviar, sauces, and herbs to utensils, dishes, and cookware. You can order their catalog by calling 800-221-7714, or you can shop online at www.dean-deluca.com.

Diamond Organics

Diamond Organics ships all types of organically grown produce anywhere in the U.S. They have year-round access to a large selection of herbs, vegetables, fruits, and many different types of lettuce.

Diamond Organics caters strictly to home cooks, and they have no minimum order. Try one of their sampler packs (they have several to choose from) to see the range of great products they have to offer. To get a catalog or to place an order, call 888-674-2642. They have a cool Web site at www.diamondorganics.com, too. You can't order products through the site, but it gives descriptions of different produce and the sampler packs.

Maytag Dairy Farms

This dairy was started by one of the heirs of the Maytag washing machine company. Maytag makes all different types of cheese, but they are particularly well known for their wonderful blue cheese. It is of a similar quality to the imported Roquefort or Stilton at a fraction of the cost — and better yet, it's American-made. Maytag's cheeses are available in many supermarkets, but if you can't find them in your store, you can order from Maytag Dairy Farms directly by calling 800-247-2458.

Napa Valley Kitchens

Napa Valley Kitchens produces a wide range of flavored vinegars, oils, vinaigrettes, and mustards under the label Consorzio that were developed in consultation with chef/owner Michael Chiarello of Tra Vigne restaurant in Napa Valley. These high-quality products are available in most supermarkets; you can order them by calling 800-288-1089. You can also visit their Web site at www.consorzio.com to view product and pricing information.

Tartuferia

Tartuferia is a great source for truffle products. They carry both white and black truffles, fresh and canned. They also have truffle oils, butters, juices, and sauces. In addition to truffles, Tartuferia carries a line of different porcini mushroom products, including dried, pureed, and oil. Call 201-902-0881 to place an order or to get current pricing. (Fresh truffles vary in price from $100 per pound for summer truffles up to $1,200 per pound for white truffles, depending on the harvest.)

Wild Game, Inc.

As the name implies, this company carries all kinds of wild game, including squab, quail, pheasant, venison, and rabbit. But they also carry fresh herbs, wild mushrooms, caviar, truffles, foie gras, and all manner of gourmet products. Their small retail outlet in Chicago is open only in November and December, but you can order their products by mail year-round. To order a catalog or products, call 773-278-1661.

Williams-Sonoma

Williams-Sonoma is chock-full of interesting kitchen gadgets, cookware, dishes, linens, and even some specialty food items. They have good-quality products that cater to the home gourmet. You can find their stores all over the United States, or you can call 800-541-2233 to get a catalog or place an order.

Chapter 21

Ten Food and Wine Books to Stock in Your Library

In This Chapter

▶ Discovering great food reference books

*N*o gourmet kitchen is complete without at least a few — or in my case, a few hundred — cookbooks. Whether you're new to cooking or have been cooking for years, you can always learn something new. Even if you never cook a single dish out of a book, the book can still help to keep your cooking fresh by putting new ideas in front of you. What you learn can be something as small as a spice used in a way you hadn't thought of before, or as large as a revolution in your whole cooking philosophy.

When you get a new cookbook, *read* it; don't just look at the pictures. Read the introduction or opening chapter, review any information the book gives on different foods, and look through the notes that are included with the recipes. These sections are usually loaded with good technical information and, at the same time, they show the author's personal cooking style. This is where you can get your best ideas.

Hundreds of great cookbooks are available in stores today, but because my editor wouldn't let me list them all, this chapter lists ten of my very favorites.

Chez Panisse Menu Cookbook, by Alice Waters

(Random House, 1982)

Chef/owner Alice Waters of Chez Panisse in Berkeley, California, has compiled 120 of the best meals served at Chez Panisse and describes them in this book. The menus range from simple picnics to elaborate dinner parties.

The Cooking of South-West France, by Paula Wolfert

(The Dial Press, 1983)

Paula Wolfert's book is a collection of both traditional and new recipes from France's magnificent rustic cuisine. Traditional recipes are prepared in a lighter style. This book is a personal collection of Paula's favorite South-West regional specialties, which have been modified for the home chef.

Emeril's New New Orleans Cooking, by Emeril Lagasse

(William Morrow and Company, 1993)

Chef Emeril Lagasse shares his secrets for preparing Creole delights. His book comes alive with New Orleans flair. Lagasse includes over 200 recipes that are true to the flavors of classic Creole, with influences from his New England and Portuguese culinary heritage.

The Food Lover's Companion, by Sharon Tyler Herbst

(Barron's Educational Series, Inc., 1990, 1996)

This compact-sized book is packed with explanations and descriptions of just about any vegetable, fruit, meat, or seafood product that you can think of. The author includes descriptions of various cooking techniques, as well as menu and wine terms.

James Beard's American Cookery, by James Beard

(Little, Brown and Company, 1972)

The melting pot of American cooking is influenced by many ethnic cuisines, which we are melding to develop a cuisine of our own. James Beard has created a book that is a sampling of that American cuisine, which inevitably reflects his own American palate.

Mastering the Art of French Cooking, Volumes 1 and 2, by Julia Child, Louisette Bertholle, and Simone Beck

(Alfred A. Knopf, 1961)

Julia Child has documented the way traditional French cuisine was prepared years ago — none of the finer details have been lost through the years. Her step-by-step explanations guide you along the way to the successful preparation of many traditional favorites.

Norman's New World Cuisine, by Norman Van Aken

(Random House, 1997)

The premier American new world cuisine chef celebrates our ethnic diversity with over 225 recipes in this cookbook. (*New world cuisine* uses Italian and French cooking techniques, with food flavors from the Caribbean and Central America, with the slightest influence of Asian flavors; it is often referred to as *fusion cuisine*.) Norman Van Aken is the chef and owner of Norman's in Coral Gables, Florida.

An Omelette and a Glass of Wine, by Elizabeth David

(Elizabeth Sifton Books, Viking, 1985)

Elizabeth David's prose in *An Omelette and a Glass of Wine* is like enjoying an entertaining evening with the writer herself. She describes how her love and taste for good food were aroused, and how she has pursued her passion in the many places she's lived.

The Oxford Companion to Wine, by Jancis Robinson

(Oxford University Press, 1994)

The depth and breadth of knowledge in this lengthy wine companion will enlighten and inform novices and connoisseurs of wine. *The Oxford Companion to Wine* has 3,000 entries with brief and more extensive essays on the nuances of wine. This book is the ultimate wine reference.

Uncommon Fruits and Vegetables, by Elizabeth Schneider

(Perennial Library, Harper & Row, Publishers 1986, 1989)

Because vegetables and fruits are so important to my cooking, I consider this book an invaluable resource — it offers a wealth of knowledge. Elizabeth Schneider's *Uncommon Fruits and Vegetables* is a must-have reference guide to exotic fruits and vegetables. This book guides you through the history, selection, uses, and preparation of some wildly interesting produce.

Index

(continued)